"Papists" and Prejudice:
Popular Anti-Catholicism and Anglo-Irish
Conflict in the North East of England, 1845-70

By

Jonathan Bush

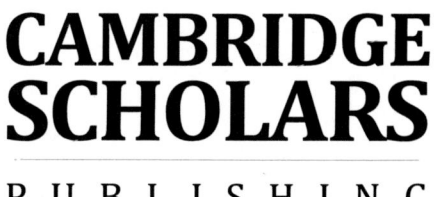

**CAMBRIDGE
SCHOLARS**

P U B L I S H I N G

"Papists" and Prejudice:
Popular Anti-Catholicism and Anglo-Irish Conflict in the North East of England, 1845-70,
by Jonathan Bush

This book first published 2013

Cambridge Scholars Publishing

12 Back Chapman Street, Newcastle upon Tyne, NE6 2XX, UK

British Library Cataloguing in Publication Data
A catalogue record for this book is available from the British Library

ISBN (10): 1-4438-4672-4, ISBN (13): 978-1-4438-4672-1

"Papists" and Prejudice

TABLE OF CONTENTS

ACKNOWLEDGEMENTS

This book would not have been written without the assistance of a number of people. Aside from the support and encouragement of my family, I am particularly grateful to Professor Donald MacRaild for inspiring me to research this area in the first place and also Dr. Sheridan Gilley for his support, advice, and encyclopaedic knowledge of nineteenth century Catholic history. I would also like to thank the staff of the public libraries, university libraries, and archives in the North East, particularly Newcastle Central Library and Durham University Special Collections. My thesis (and ultimately this book) would probably not have seen the light of day if I had not received a very generous (and unexpected) one-year studentship from Durham University to allow me the luxury of working full-time for a year on my research. Mr. Alastair Fraser also deserves a special mention for proof-reading my script and pointing out some glaring inaccuracies.

CONVENTIONS

County Durham refers to the pre-1973 boundaries of the old county of Durham and is used throughout to avoid confusion with the city of Durham. The county at this time stretched from the south of the Tyne to the northern banks of the Tees (including Stockton and Hartlepool). Tyneside incorporates those settlements on the banks of the Tyne (including Tynemouth, North Shields, Wallsend and Newcastle).

The word "Evangelical(s)" (upper case) refers exclusively to the distinctive body of Low-Church Anglicans of that name. The word "evangelical(s)" (lower case) refers either to the general culture itself or evangelicals of all persuasion. However, capitalisation of organisation names, such as the Evangelical Alliance, is retained.

The word 'popular anti-Catholicism' in the title, and its usage throughout the text, refers to a culture shared by all classes (including both lay and clerical), rather than a specific class grouping (such as the working class) or a specific religious denomination.

ABBREVIATIONS

TWAS   Tyne and Wear Archives Service

DCRO   Durham County Record Office

DULSP   Durham University Library Special Collections

RCHNDA   Roman Catholic Hexham and Newcastle Diocesan Archives

INTRODUCTION

Until comparatively recently, anti-Catholic feeling was considered to be a central tenet of English national identity.[1] Developing out of an atmosphere of bitter religious divisions in the sixteenth century, anti-Catholicism (broadly defined as fear of, and hostility towards, the Catholic Church and its adherents) reached its zenith as a cultural force in the seventeenth and eighteenth centuries.[2] Even as the era of the Gordon Riots gave way to a more enlightened age symbolised by the passing of the Roman Catholic Relief Acts of 1778, 1781 and 1829, old prejudices continued to resurface.[3] Indeed, Mary Hickman has suggested that anti-Catholicism "remained the sentiment which most clearly defined the nation" well after 1829.[4] The principal reasons for its continued longevity during the Victorian period are well-known. These included the infusing of strands of evangelical thought with anti-Catholicism; the growing influence of Tractarianism and, later, Ritualism, within the Church of England; the rise of nonconformity with an evangelical anti-Catholic worldview; and the visible resurgence of the Roman Catholic religion greatly influenced by ultramontane priests and large numbers of Irish

---

[1] John Wolffe has dated the centrality of anti-Catholicism to British national identity until as recently as Pope John Paul II's visit to Britain in 1982. See John Wolffe, 'Change and Continuity in British Anti-Catholicism, 1829-1982', *Catholicism in Britain and France since 1789*, ed. by Nicholas Atkin and Frank Tallett (London: The Hambledon Press, 1996), p. 68.

[2] For the relationship between anti-Catholicism and national identity in the post-Reformation period, see C.Z. Wiener, 'The Beleaguered Isle: A Study of Elizabethan and Early Jacobean Anti-Catholicism', *Past and Present*, 51 (1971), pp. 27-62; David Loades, 'The Origins of English Protestant Nationalism', *Studies in Church History*, 18 (1982), pp. 297-307; R. Clifton, 'The Popular Fear of Catholics during the English Revolution', *Past and Present*, 52 (1971), pp. 168-87; and J.H. Hexter, 'The Protestant Revival and the Catholic Question in England 1778-1829', *Journal of Modern History*, 8 (1936), pp. 297-319.

[3] Wolffe, 'Change and Continuity', p. 68.

[4] Mary J. Hickman, *Religion, Class and Identity: The State, the Catholic Church and the Education of the Irish in Britain* (Ashgate: Aldershot, 1995), p. 43.

immigrants.[5] Whatever the reasons for its prevalence, Victorian anti-Catholicism was more than simply a theological standpoint against the Church of Rome. Its many different and often disparate strands, whether political, social, economic or cultural, helped to define national identity not only in England but also in the rest of the British Isles and the Anglophone world generally.[6]

It is perhaps only from a regional, rather than national or even transnational, perspective where it is possible to observe the way in which anti-Catholicism influenced, and was influenced by, specific cultural contexts. The purpose of this book, therefore, is to examine anti-Catholicism in a relatively neglected but potentially fruitful regional area (the North East of England) during a specifically heightened period of

---

[5] For a broader discussion of nineteenth century Protestant evangelical activity, see David W. Bebbington, *Evangelicalism in Modern Britain: A History from the 1730s to the 1980s* (London: Unwin Hyman, 1989); and D. Englander, 'The Word and the World: Evangelicalism in the Victorian City', *Religion in Victorian Britain,* ed. by Parsons, G., II (Manchester: Manchester University Press, 1988), pp. 14-38. For the role of Tractarianism within the Church of England, see Sheridan Gilley, 'The Church of England in the Nineteenth Century' *A History of Religion in Britain*, pp. 298-303. For the growth of the Catholic community see E.R. Norman, *The English Catholic Church in the Nineteenth Century* (Clarendon Press: Oxford, 1984); and for the role of Irish immigrants in religious violence: D.M. MacRaild, *Irish Migrants in Modern Britain, 1750-1922* (Basingstoke: Macmillan, 1999).

[6] For anti-Catholic studies in other areas of the British Isles, see Steve Bruce, *No Pope of Rome: Militant Protestantism in Modern Scotland* (Edinburgh: Mainstream, 1985); P. O'Leary, 'When was Anti-Catholicism? The Case of Nineteenth- and Twentieth-Century Wales', *Journal of Ecclesiastical History*, 56.2 (2005), pp. 308-25. For other Anglophone countries, see Ray Allan Billington, *The Protestant Crusade 1800-1860: A Study of the Origins of American Nativism* (Quadrangle: Chicago, 1964); J.R. Miller, 'Anti-Catholic Thought in Victorian Canada', *Canadian Historical Review*, 66 (1985), pp. 474-94; Patrick O'Farrell, *The Catholic Church and Community in Australia: A History* (Kensington, New South Wales, Australia: New South Wales University Press, 1992). For transnational comparisons, see John Wolffe, 'Anti-Catholicism and Evangelical Identity in Britain and the United States, 1830-1860', *Evangelicalism: Comparative Studies of Popular Protestantism in North America, the British Isles, and Beyond, 1700-1990*, ed. by Mark A. Noll, David W. Bebbington, George A. Rawlyk (New York: Oxford University Press, 1994), pp. 179-97; J. Wolffe, 'A Transatlantic Perspective: Protestantism and National Identities in Mid-Nineteenth-Century Britain and the United States', *Protestantism and National Identity: Britain and Ireland, c. 1650-c. 1850*, ed. by Tony Claydon and Ian McBride (Cambridge: Cambridge University Press, 1998), pp. 291-309.

anti-Catholic tension (1845-1870).[7] The little research carried out on this subject in this region suggests that this area was largely immune from the all-encompassing anti-Catholicism evident in other areas of the country. This theory was first posited by Roger Cooter in 1973 for a dissertation on the subject of Irish immigration in Newcastle and County Durham which has recently been published, unchanged, in book form.[8] Cooter's research is based around a theory that, for a variety of political, economic, social and cultural reasons, anti-Irishness and anti-Catholicism were "notable by their absence" in the North East. A combination of a dominant Liberal and Dissenter culture, a well-established and strong Catholic community, a favourable economic situation and the North East's isolation from events in London, ensured that "anti-Catholicism was confined to a very small minority of devoted upholders of the Establishment".[9] His findings are crucial for those who wish to posit the theory of a North East "exceptionalism", one in which the region's identity is based upon isolation from certain cultural trends evident elsewhere in the country, most notably a uniquely welcoming attitude towards "outsiders". The question of this identity has become a hotly contested issue but Cooter's theories on the absence of a local anti-Catholic culture, even after nearly 40 years of historical scholarship, largely remain, if not unquestioned, then certainly broadly accepted.[10]

There are, however, several problems with Cooter's hypothesis which this book seeks to address. Firstly, it is well known that many areas in the North East of England were strongholds of Nonconformity and the North East generally was the very "citadel of Liberalism". [11] However, these generalisations hide disparities between different areas with the relative importance of various religious groups differing from setting to setting.

---

[7] Limitations of space have prevented this book from including the rest of Northumberland within its area of study. These years (1845-70) are widely accepted by historians as the most fruitful for a study of anti-Catholicism owing to a variety of political and cultural reasons which will be addressed in this book.

[8] R.J. Cooter, 'The Irish in County Durham and Newcastle, 1840-1880' (unpublished MA thesis, University of Durham, 1973); Roger Cooter, *When Paddy Met Geordie: The Irish in County Durham and Northumberland, 1840-80* (Sunderland: University of Sunderland Press, 2005).

[9] Cooter, *Paddy*, p. 102.

[10] For a recent discussion on the question of a coherent North East 'identity', see *Regional Identities in North East England, 1300-2000*, ed. by Adrian Green and A.J. Pollard (Woodbridge: Boydell Press, 2007).

[11] T.J. Nossiter, *Influence, Opinion and Political Idioms in Reformed England: Case Studies from the* North East, *1832-74* (Hassocks, Sussex: Harvester Press, 1975), p. 21.

Durham was an Anglican and (almost by definition) Conservative stronghold, Presbyterianism was influential in South Shields, Darlington was effectively run by a Quaker elite, and in Newcastle, "it was the Quakers, Baptists, and Independents who mattered" politically.[12] The situation outside the major towns was different still where, in many (although not all) of the Durham pit villages, Primitive Methodism appealed to the predominantly working class population.[13] Anti-Catholicism was also far from the exclusive domain of Conservative and Anglican interests. Liberals and Dissenters, particularly the Baptists, Methodists and Congregationalists that dominated most of the North East, could be as anti-Catholic as their Anglican and Tory adversaries if the issue suited them.[14] Dissenting support for these campaigns was often not directly anti-Catholic but their reasons for doing could be coloured by anti-Catholic arguments. Furthermore, interdenominational co-operation between Dissenters and Anglican Evangelicals was a common occurrence in the North East, particularly when confronting the Papal threat.[15]

Secondly, while there was certainly a long-established tradition of Catholicism in the North East[16], Catholic communities did not, in themselves, dampen the anti-Catholic mood. There can be no doubt that these communities experienced an unprecedented expansion during the mid-nineteenth century. Indeed, the total Catholic population in Newcastle and County Durham increased from 23,250 in 1847 to 86,397 in 1874.[17] The number of places of worship also expanded significantly, funded

---

[12] B.I. Coleman, *The Church of England in the Mid-Nineteenth Century: A Social Geography* (London: Historical Association, 1978); Anne Orde, *Religion, Business and Society in North East England: The Pease Family of Darlington in the 19th Century* (Stamford: Shannon Tyas, 2000); Jeff Smith, 'The Making of a Diocese, 1851-1882', *Newcastle upon Tyne: A Modern History*, ed. by Robert Colls and Bill Lancaster (Chichester: Phillimore, 2001), p. 93.

[13] For a discussion on the role of Primitive Methodism which draws heavily on sources from County Durham, see Robert Colls, *The collier's rant: song and culture in the industrial village* (London: Croom Helm, 1977).

[14] For the role of Dissenters in anti-Catholicism, see Paz, *Popular Anti-Catholicism*, chapter 6.

[15] For a study of evangelical co-operation in the North East, see A.F. Munden, 'The Origin of Evangelical Anglicanism in Newcastle-upon-Tyne', *Archaeologia Aeliana*, Fifth Series, Vol XI (1983), pp. 301-7.

[16] For a general introduction to the Catholic Church in the North East that combines many local parish histories see Michael Morris and Leo Gooch, *Down Your Aisles: The Diocese of Hexham and Newcastle* (Hartlepool: Northern Cross, 2000).

[17] Cooter, *Paddy*, p. 49.

primarily by voluntary subscriptions from the laity.[18] This increase in Catholic numbers had initially overwhelmed the clergy. At Gateshead, the only priest available ministered, with one derelict warehouse, to 3,000 Catholics in 1851.[19] Between 1846 and 1876, however, there was a 76% increase in church buildings in the same area, with 56 churches, chapels and missions established by the latter date.[20] These communities, large and growing in confidence, could just as easily act as a catalyst for religious controversy rather than moderate anti-Catholic feeling.[21] This was certainly true historically. The continuation of the Catholic faith by gentry families during the recusant period had, in turn, generated a long and parallel tradition of anti-Catholicism which included frenzied attacks on Mass houses during the 1745 Jacobite Rising; a large, very active, and nationally renowned Newcastle Protestant Association agitating during the passing of the Catholic Relief Act of 1788; and a pamphlet war during the debates on the Catholic Relief Bill in the 1820s involving some of the country's leading anti-Catholic zealots that was unparalleled anywhere else in the country.[22]

The increase in Catholic numbers and places of worship in the North East was "almost wholly attributable to the Irish" as English Catholics accounted for less than 5% of the Catholic population in the region.[23] Indeed, there is no doubt that the region proved to be an attractive destination for Irish immigrants during this period. The Irish were generally attracted to the burgeoning industries of the region, which

---

[18] Morris and Gooch, *Down Your Aisles*, p. 12.

[19] K.S. Inglis, *Churches and the Working Classes in Victorian England* (Toronto: University of Toronto Press, 1963), p. 125.

[20] Cooter, *Paddy*, p. 50.

[21] Paz, *Popular Anti-Catholicism*, chapter 3.

[22] For local anti-Catholicism in the eighteenth and early-nineteenth centuries, see C. Haydon, *Anti-Catholicism in Eighteenth Century England, c. 1714-80* (Manchester: Manchester University Press, 1993), pp. 155-56, 208, 211; L.P. Crangle, 'The Roman Catholic Community in Sunderland from the 16th Century', *Antiquities of Sunderland*, 24 (1969), p. 66; Leo Gooch, 'Lingard v. Barrington, et al: Ecclesiastical Politics in Durham 1805-29', *Durham University Journal*, 85.1 (1993), p. 7; C.L. Scott, 'A Comparative Re-examination of Anglo-Irish Relations in Nineteenth Century Liverpool, Manchester and Newcastle-upon-Tyne' (unpublished doctoral thesis, University of Durham, 1998), p. 96. Leo Gooch has noted that 33 anti-Catholic petitions were sent from the North East between 1820 and 1829: Leo Gooch, 'From Jacobite to Radical: the Catholics of North East England, 1688-1850' (unpublished doctoral thesis, University of Durham, 1989), p. 262.

[23] Cooter, *Paddy*, pp. 45.

included, among others, shipbuilding on Tyneside, coal mining in the Durham pit villages and the ironstone industries of the Cleveland Hills.[24] The total number of Irish-born in County Durham and Newcastle rose from 8,264 in 1841 to 44,419 in 1871. Most of the major districts in the region experienced a huge influx of immigrants during this period with the large Catholic communities in a number of the smaller towns and villages such as Crook, Jarrow and Blackhill, almost wholly attributable to Irish immigrants.[25] In the larger towns, such as Newcastle and Sunderland, Irish immigrants joined the already long-established Catholic communities. Nevertheless, the reception of these immigrant communities by the English and Protestant host population has been a matter of some debate among historians and, in particular, the long-held assertion that English-Irish relations in North East England were relatively harmonious has been criticised in recent years. This is particularly evident in the work of Frank Neal, whose pioneering research on English-Irish violence in the North East region can be viewed as a direct response to Cooter (and has been hugely influential in setting down preliminary markers for this study).[26]

Finally, although there were definite similarities in the religious, political, and ethnic composition of many areas of the North East, it would be dangerous to make generalisations about a "regional culture" as a

---

[24] For a detailed breakdown of the occupations undertaken by the Irish in this region, see Neal, F., 'Irish Settlement in the North East and North-West of England in the Mid-Nineteenth Century', *The Irish in Victorian Britain: The Local Dimension*, ed. by Roger Swift and Sheridan Gilley (Dublin: Four Courts Press, 1999), pp. 86-7. For a local town-based survey of the Irish in Gateshead which also makes use of census records, see F. Neal, 'A Statistical Profile of the Irish Community in Gateshead – The Evidence of the 1851 Census', *Immigrants and Minorities*, 27.1 (2009), pp. 50-81.

[25] J.M. Tweedy, *Popish Elvet: The History of St. Cuthbert's, Durham: Part II* (Durham: [St. Cuthbert's Church], 1984), pp. 4-5.

[26] Studies of the Irish in North East England have tended to fall within two camps. Those who agree with Cooter's findings, such as S. Doherty, *English and Irish Catholics in Northumberland, 1745-1860* (unpublished doctoral thesis, Queen's University, Belfast, 1987); MacRaild, *Faith, Fraternity and Fighting*; and Joan Allen, '"High Days and Holy Days"; St. Patrick's Day in the North East of England, c.1850-1900', *Faith of our Fathers: Popular Culture and Belief in Post Reformation England, Ireland and Wales*, ed. by Joan Allen and Richard C. Allen (Newcastle, 2009), and those studies which, to varying degrees have questioned this harmonious relationship: Frank Neal, *English-Irish Conflict in the North East of England* (Salford: University of Salford Press, 1992); D.M. Jackson, '"Garibaldi or the Pope!": Newcastle's Irish Riot, 1866', *North East History*, 35 (2001), pp. 49-76.

whole. Indeed, the assumption that the "North East" is a monolithic area representing a unique and coherent identity is open to question. In commenting on the elusiveness of regional identity, Green and Pollard have argued that:

> "Finding regional identity in the past, in any region in England, is problematic. The region is elusive and it is protean. Whichever way we choose to look at it, it is unlikely to be all inclusive, all embracing or continuous. We have multiple social identities and look different ways, deal with different agencies and move in different directions according to the different aspects of our lives".[27]

This is particularly the case in the North East where, Purdue has argued, the region has been "endowed with a somewhat spurious and certainly unhistorical, precision, character and unity".[28] As will be shown in this book, different forms of anti-Catholicism, which were often the result of local peculiarities, existed in different areas even *within* Tyneside and in County Durham so a regional anti-Catholic culture cannot be viewed as either coherent or consistent. Furthermore, the North East generally may have felt isolated from events in London but it did not necessarily follow that it was immune from the anti-Catholic strands of thought evident elsewhere, nor was it slow in responding to national anti-Catholic political campaigns.

Clearly, therefore, the cultural conditions necessary for the development of anti-Catholicism were as evident in the North East as other places noted for their virulent anti-Catholic cultures. There was, however, no uniform "North East" anti-Catholicism. Indeed, it is the intention of this book to show the variety of ways in which anti-Catholicism influenced, and was influenced by, the political, social and cultural climate inherent in different parts of Tyneside and the county of Durham. Expanding in particular on the theories of Denis Paz in adopting a broader perspective of viewing different expressions of anti-Catholicism, rather than purely a manifestation of one specific form of anti-Catholicism (such as anti-Irishness) it will highlight not only the strength of certain forms, but also the way in which this ideology could be moulded and manipulated in different areas even

---

[27] Adrian Green and S. Pollard, 'Introduction: Identifying Regions', Green and Pollard, *Regional Identities,* p. 23. For the opposing viewpoint, see N. McCord, 'The Regional Identity of North East England in the Nineteenth and Early Twentieth Centuries', *Issues of Regional Identity,* ed. by E. Royle (Manchester: Manchester University Press, 1979), pp. 102-17.
[28] A.W. Purdue, 'The History of the North-East in the Modern Period: Themes, Concerns, and Debates Since the 1960s', *Northern History,* 42.1 (2005), p. 108.

within regions. It will therefore not posit a theory of a "regional anti-Catholic culture", but instead suggest the existence of a variety of different anti-Catholic "cultures" within the area of study. It will also argue that the context of the "North East" did not, as has previously been suggested, act as a bar to anti-Catholic expression, but, on the contrary, may even have assisted in the developments of certain forms of it. Finally, it will highlight the proactive role of the local Catholic community in sectarian controversy. Catholics did not remain passive in the face of anti-Catholic extremism. Indeed, the strength and conduct of the local Catholic community in defence of their religion may have actively assisted in the development of local anti-Catholic cultures.

In order to try to show this, the study will take a thematic approach, examining the ideological, political, cultural and social aspects of anti-Catholicism. Chapter One will concentrate on the ideology of popular anti-Catholicism in the North East of England in order to highlight the various strands of thought which provided the backdrop to the events examined in subsequent chapters. It will demonstrate the way in which these different strands did not represent a single unifying ideology but were often contested and moulded by peculiarly Victorian concerns. Indeed, these strands were as prevalent in the North East of England as they were elsewhere.

The next three chapters will examine anti-Catholicism's political dimension and the local response to the different politico-religious events of the period that drew upon different aspects of anti-Catholic ideology. Chapter Two will examine the local response to the biggest anti-Catholic political event of the period: the Restoration of the Hierarchy in 1850. It will suggest that the hysteria generated by this event occurred because it enabled a broad range of all political and religious groups to unite, however briefly, in a common hatred of the Papal measure. In the North East, not only were town meetings and petitions initiated just as readily as other areas of the country but were, in certain areas, also just as likely to be directed against those Anglicans who had adopted the "Popish" practices of Tractarianism. Chapter Three will concentrate on the local response to political events which played on "Conservative" and/or Anglican interpretations of the "Protestant Constitution", such as the parliamentary "concessions" granted to Catholics in the form of the Maynooth Grant and Irish disestablishment, as well as a raft of changes designed to relax the laws on Catholics generally. Given the Liberal/Dissenter dominance of much of the North East, it would be expected that this aspect of anti-Catholic ideology would hold little sway. However, this chapter will show that, although there were clear weaknesses, many places responded just as vehemently as other areas of the country. Chapter Four will examine the local response to political events which played on Liberal notions of anti-Catholicism. Events such as the campaign for Italian independence, with its charismatic leader Giuseppe Garibaldi, as well as the campaigns for the inspection of convents and the release of the Madiai, infused the "Liberal" ideologies of internationalism and religious liberty with a specifically anti-Catholic outlook. The Liberal slant on anti-Catholicism may have appeared less bigoted than its Conservative equivalent, but its arguments were just as likely to infuriate the Catholic community. Indeed, not only will this chapter highlight the popularity of Liberal anti-Catholicism in certain parts of the North East, but will also show the way in which the strength of the local Catholic communities could be just as militant in combatting these attacks on their religion, most notably in defence of their spiritual leader, the Pope.

Anti-Catholicism was more than just apparent in the response to political events, particularly when the Catholic threat appeared to be closer to home. Chapter Five will, therefore, investigate the Protestant reaction to the growth of the Catholic community in the North East of England. Generally speaking, the outward signs of "Popery", such as the building of churches and public processions, with a few notable exceptions, passed off with little comment, so long as their activities did not directly affect the Protestant community. The real battleground, however, was fought over the souls of Catholics. Indeed, local Protestant evangelicals of all persuasions saw the influx of Irish Catholics into the industrialised towns and cities of the North East as an opportunity for proselytism. The situation was further exacerbated by the strength of the local Catholic community, who ironically assisted in the development of this anti-Catholic culture by their defence against the Protestant proselytisers. Finally, Chapter Six will turn its attention to religious violence in the North East of England. This region was not immune from the sectarian violence which was the product of large scale Irish immigration. Indeed, this chapter will suggest that there were different forms of religious violence associated with the Irish that were clearly linked to anti-Catholicism and dependent not only on the cultural context of the local area but also the period in which it occurred. For Irish Catholics, violence could be either an expression of a defence of their religion against anti-Catholicism, as victims of the anti-Catholicism of the English working class, or as ritualised theatre against their Irish Protestant countrymen.

CHAPTER ONE

THE IDEOLOGY OF ANTI-CATHOLICISM
IN NORTH EAST ENGLAND

"The great mass of the middle class of the people of England are too much taken up with affairs of trade to examine 'vice versa' the great principles of Catholicity; books they seldom trouble, the daily and provincial newspapers form their political and controversial Bible, thousands upon thousands believe as Gospel truth whatever they read in the newspapers they are accustomed to peruse . . . Some time ago the papers in England kept the pulpits at bay, and restrained the bigots from their occupation, but now both pulpit and press are united in the assault on the church of Christ".[1]

Anti-Catholicism, as a set of ideas and beliefs, represents one of the most consistent and dominant ideologies in the history of post-Reformation Britain. Anti-Catholic ideology remained a prominent feature of Protestant thought well into the nineteenth century[2] and the sustained sectarian tension of the mid-Victorian period in particular brought forth an explosion of popular anti-Catholic opinion throughout the Anglophone world. Combining traditional theological polemic with key elements of Victorian philosophy, anti-Catholicism defined what it meant to be Protestant and British. It was, as David Hempton suggests, "probably the most ubiquitous, most eclectic and most adaptable ideology in the post-Reformation history of the British Isles".[3] While it is possible to unpick the various doctrinal aspects of anti-Catholic thought, the range of studies which have examined anti-Catholicism from varying standpoints is testament to the view that there can be no single unifying theory which can wholly explain the continuing prevalence of these ideas and beliefs among

---

[1] From the Northumberland and Durham correspondent of the *Tablet*, 2 October 1852.

[2] For the pre-nineteenth century period, see Wiener, 'The Beleaguered Isle', pp. 27-62; Loades, 'English Protestant Nationalism', pp. 297-307; Haydon, *Anti-Catholicism*.

[3] D. Hempton, *Religion and Political Culture in Britain and Ireland: From the Glorious Revolution to the Decline of Empire* (Cambridge University Press: Cambridge, 1996), p. 145.

the Victorian population. These studies include Victorian anti-Catholic ideology as an essentially reactionary phenomenon (Best, Norman); or as a form of prejudice (Wallis, Sidenvall); or through psychological interpretations of Protestant identity and the Catholic 'Other' in Victorian art and literature (Wheeler, Griffin).[4] This opening chapter will examine the key elements of this ideology within these varying frameworks to argue that the North East shared many of the major tenets of anti-Catholic ideology evident in other parts of the country. It will determine to what extent its tenets represented a continuation of traditional anti-Catholic ideas and how far these ideas were moulded by specific Victorian concerns.

So what were the major tenets of anti-Catholic ideology and to what extent were they evident in the North East of England? At its most basic level, the broad tenets of mid-Victorian anti-Catholic thought can be viewed as simply a continuation of the polemical conflicts of the Reformation era, albeit coloured by a specific Victorian worldview, in which dogmatism and misrepresentation were the defining characteristics of debates.[5] This is evident in the most fundamental of all disagreements between Protestants and Catholics: the rule of faith. Both creeds agreed that faith stemmed ultimately from God, but that this was transmitted in different ways. For Protestants of all persuasions, the Scriptures were the ultimate authority. In the North East of England, the authority of the Bible was a particularly important issue because it enabled the wide range of Protestant denominations that existed throughout the region to unite under a shared "Protestant" heritage and outlook. In a local tract celebrating the power of the Holy Scriptures, the Methodist minister, the Rev. William Cooke, argued that the Bible was the only infallible guide. "It is", he added, "the instrument God employs to enlighten, to save, and to bless our benighted and ruled world".[6] In a Newcastle meeting of the supporters of

---

[4] G.F.A. Best, 'Popular Protestantism in Victorian Britain', *Ideas and Institutions in Victorian Britain: Essays in Honour of George Kitson Clark*, ed. by R. Robson (London: Bell, 1967), pp. 115-42; Edward R. Norman, *Anti-Catholicism in Victorian England* (London: Allen and Unwin, 1968); Frank H. Wallis, *Popular Anti-Catholicism in Mid-Victorian Britain* (Lewiston: Edwin Mellen, 1993); E. Sidenvall, *After Anti-Catholicism: John Henry Newman and Protestant Britain, c.1845-1890* (London: T. and T. Clark, 2005); M. Wheeler, *The Old Enemies: Catholic and Protestant in Nineteenth-Century English Culture* (Cambridge: Cambridge University Press, 2006); Susan M. Griffin, *Anti-Catholicism and Nineteenth-Century Fiction* (Cambridge: Cambridge University Press, 2004).
[5] Wheeler, *The Old Enemies*, p. xii; Wolffe, *Protestant Crusade*, p. 110.
[6] W. Cooke, *The Inspiration and Divine Authority of the Holy Scriptures* (London: John Bakewell, 1846), p. 47.

the extremist anti-Catholic Evangelical organisation, the Protestant Reformation Society, the eminent eschatologist, the Rev. Dr. John Cumming, concurred with this view that the Bible and Protestantism were inextricably linked. It was a belief, he argued, "that they could not let go without lifting the very anchors of their faith and being drifted upon a boat without compass or star and without Him to guide them".[7] In 1866, the Durham Evangelical, the Rev. George Fox, preached on what he saw as the crucial difference in the Protestant and Catholic perception of the Word of God. While the Bible was central to the transmission of faith for Protestants, the Church of Rome was not only an "unscriptural" Church but had an "unceasing enmity to God's Word", denying its followers personal access to the Bible because it was believed to be potentially subversive:

> "Under the pretext that the people cannot understand it, and are apt to pervert it, she has robbed   mankind of her noblest birthright—an open Bible. According to her law, no one may read the   Bible   without   priestly permission; and she hath declared that 'more harm than good comes of it'".[8]

This was certainly an exaggeration in Britain where an English Roman Catholic translation of the Bible had been available since the sixteenth century. From the Roman Catholic perspective, though, allowing the individual the right to *interpret* the Bible without the guidance of the Church was not a part of its teachings. Indeed, in a popular lecture in Sunderland on the subject of 'Church Authority and the Bible' in October 1851, the Catholic priest of the town, the Rev. Philip Kearney, argued that "to give up the Bible to the interpretation of each individual is the most effectual plan to propagate infidelity".[9] Kearney argued that the Bible only "becomes life to those who seek it" through the interpretation of the Church, arguing that it was read by only a comparatively few people until the advent of the printing press and "if Christ wished the salvation of all through the means of the Bible only, he would surely have adopted a system which would necessarily include the masses" before this period.[10]

---

[7] *Hartlepool Free Press*, 2 June 1866.
[8] Fox, G.T., 'The Doctrines of the Bible Contrasted With Those of Rome', *Sermons Preached in St. Nicholas Church, Durham* (London: James Nisbett & Co., 1866), pp. 175-6.
[9] Philip Kearney, born in County Meath, Ireland, o. 1829, d. 1856. *English and Welsh Priests, 1801-1914: a working list*, compiled by Charles Fitzgerald-Lombard (Bath: Downside Abbey Trustees, 1993), p. 42.
[10] *Sunderland Herald*, 31 October 1851.

While the Protestant claims to the authority of the Scriptures were vulnerable in an age of criticism, the Roman Catholic rule of faith was "based upon the Petrine rock of the Church of Rome" which interpreted faith and doctrine through both the Bible and the concept of tradition, i.e. that faith is prominent in those teachings of Christ not committed to writing at the time.[11] To Protestants, particularly Liberals, this emphasis on tradition was "unscientific" and at odds with the empiricism of the Victorian period. It was, as the Rev. George Fox stated in a further sermon, essentially "sayings handed down by word of mouth from father to son and from age to age". The central role played by tradition in the Catholic Church was vehemently attacked by the Anglican minister who saw it as "absurd . . . to attach the least weight to the correctness, or truth, of such flooding irresponsible statements, which may have survived the wreck of ages, and the thick of medieval darkness".[12] Fox believed that as a result of this emphasis on tradition, the Church of Rome had been able to introduce a number of "superstitious" beliefs into the Catholic mind. He argued that the practice of idolatry, in the form of worshipping saints and images, was not only unscriptural but also explicitly forbidden in the Ten Commandments. Fox was clearly irritated by this practice:

> "Nothing can be more disgusting than to walk through the churches and cathedrals on the Continent, and see crowds of deluded persons, bowing down before and worshipping the images of dead men and women, who can no more hear what they say, than the idols of the heathens. This is the crowning iniquity of Rome".[13]

The *Newcastle Journal*, an Anglican High Church paper with a notable anti-Catholic stance, appeared to share the Durham clergyman's view. It regularly printed articles from abroad purporting to be examples of the "gross superstitious practices" of Roman Catholics. An 1846 article entitled "Popish Superstitions" detailed the alleged miracles that occurred after the Chevalier Stewart's body was temporarily placed in a coffin in the Church of Santa Maria in Italy: The story led the paper to conclude: "This is popery in the nineteenth century. What was it in the twelfth? The same".[14]

---

[11] Wheeler, *The Old Enemies*, p. 187.
[12] G.T. Fox, *The Bible the Sole Rule of Faith: A Sermon Preached in St. Hilda's Church, South Shields on Sunday Morning, December 8th 1850* (Durham: Andrews, 1850).
[13] Fox, *Doctrines*, pp. 181-82.
[14] *Newcastle Journal*, 12 September 1846.

For anti-Catholics, the most blasphemous element of this idol worshipping was in the Roman Catholic veneration of the Virgin Mary.[15] Catholics saw Mary as a "universal mother" who sympathised with human suffering; only the Pope commanded more obedience.[16] In contrast, Protestants believed that Marian devotion was sacrilegious. At a meeting of the Evangelical Alliance in Newcastle in June 1847, the chairman of the organisation, Sir Culling E. Eardley, caused controversy when he suggested that an alternative version of the Lord's Prayer, with the substitution of "Our Father" with "Our Mother", was being widely circulated on the continent. This caused an angry response from Matthias Dunn, a local and respected Newcastle Catholic, who entered into a correspondence with Sir Culling to vehemently deny the claim. The *Newcastle Journal* subsequently assisted in the publication of a tract on the dispute, the title of which is indicative of the particular viewpoint that the local paper favoured.[17] The Newcastle paper was again at the forefront of criticism when Pope Pius IX, published an Encyclical on the *Immaculate Conception of the Virgin Mary* in 1849 (a dogma he formally defined in 1854). In commenting on a passage from the *Encyclical*, the paper described it as "remarkable for its blasphemous substitution of the Virgin Mary in the place of that of Christ".[18] Marian devotion continued to incense anti-Catholics as it grew in popularity from mid-century, as is evident in this extract from an 1866 sermon by Fox:

> "The language which she (Church of Rome) makes her votaries address to the Virgin Mary is blasphemous in our ears. There is hardly an attribute belonging to the Deity that she does not ascribe to Mary. There is no solemn worship, no adoration, no penitent confession, no cry for help, which man can offer up to God, that she does not present to Mary".[19]

The claims of the Roman Catholic Church to be an "infallible" Church were also criticised by Protestant polemicists. The Protestant critique of Catholic infallibility was once again due to the locus of the latter being undefined and uncertain.[20] This was a concept that again transcended the

---

[15] John Singleton, 'The Virgin Mary and Religious Conflict in Victorian Britain', *Journal of Ecclesiastical History*, 43.1 (1992), p. 23.

[16] H. McLeod, *Religion and Society in England 1850-1914* (Basingstoke: MacMillan Press, 1996), p. 45.

[17] Newcastle Journal, *Blasphemy, Idolatry and Superstition of the Roman Catholic Church* (Newcastle: Bell, 1847) .

[18] *Newcastle Journal*, 24 March 1849.

[19] Fox, 'Doctrines', p. 182.

[20] Wolffe, *Protestant Crusade*, p. 109.

denominational divide in the North East. According to the High Church Anglican minister and Vicar of Newcastle, the Rev. Richard Charles Coxe, in the second of a series of popular lectures on various church subjects, the concept of infallibility had serious implications for the nature of truth because "as truth is one and the same at all times, she must be altered and unalterable".[21] In another lecture on the subject, the Congregationalist, the Rev. Samuel Goddall, suggested that the power of infallibility had been decided by the Pope who, he argued, was "no more the successor of St Peter than the Queen of England was the successor of Alexander the Great or the Khan of Turkey".[22] The Darlington Anglican clergyman, the Rev. Howell Harries, published a sermon arguing that there was no evidence in the Bible to support this contention.[23] For Catholics, however, the infallibility of their Church was bestowed as part of God's creation. In a defence of the doctrine of infallibility during a sold-out lecture at South Shields, the Irish Catholic priest, the Rev. Dr. Daniel Cahill, argued that God had created "unchangeable physical laws" in relation to the "government of the body". It therefore followed that he must have made "infallible laws for the government of the soul".[24]

For Protestants, the infallible authority of the Catholic Church was epitomised in the sinister figure of the priest who appeared to hold a distinct "apartness" from the bulk of the Catholic laity. The priesthood was particularly abhorrent to Protestants because it reacted against a strong English tradition of the equal relationship between clergy and laity.[25] This "apartness" was maintained by a tremendously powerful psychological hold. Delivering a lecture on infallibility and the priesthood during a tour of the North East in 1852, the renowned Manchester Evangelical lecturer, the Rev. Hugh Stowell[26], who was also Canon of Chester Cathedral, argued that priestly power was reinforced through a number of different mediums. Firstly, this can be observed in the alleged retention of the Bible.

---

[21] R.C. Coxe, *Thoughts on Important Church Subjects, Seven Lectures* (Newcastle: St. Nicholas, 1851), p. 49.

[22] *Durham Chronicle*, 9 December 1864.

[23] H. Harries, *'The Holy Catholic Church, Out of Which None can be Saved'. A Sermon Preached at Trinity Church, Darlington, on Sunday September 19, 1852* (Darlington: Harrison Penney, 1852), pp. 12-13.

[24] *Shields Gazette*, 11 November 1853. For a brief biography of Daniel Cahill, see Sheridan Gilley, 'Cahill, Daniel William (1796–1864)', *Oxford Dictionary of National Biography* (Oxford University Press, 2004).

[25] Best, 'Popular Protestantism', p. 124.

[26] For a brief biography of Hugh Stowell, see John Wolffe, 'Stowell, Hugh (1799–1865)', *Oxford Dictionary of National Biography*, Oxford University Press, 2004.

As it was only ignorance that enabled priestly power to maintain its influence, the Bible—an essential key to knowledge—was kept from the laity and retained by the priest. This enabled him to hold a monopoly over religious knowledge, upon which his congregation became entirely dependent. Secondly, the confession allowed the priest to create a culture of dependency through luring his "subjects" into divulging their greatest secrets and taking them into his confidence. Stowell described this system as one that "could have only been the device of the devil to enable the priests to enslave the people". Thirdly, absolution of sins, the result of confession, exalted the priest "above the Saviour of Mankind" by the power to forgive sins. Finally, Stowell argued, the priest was able not only to "enslave the body, but (also) the conscience of man" through making him believe that they can "haunt him in the unseen and dark shades of purgatory", of which he could only be saved once the "money was heard to tinkle in the box" through the sale of indulgences.[27]

It was the celebration of Mass that particularly caught the attention of anti-Catholics.[28] A pamphlet by the Anglican minister, the Rev. Robert Taylor of Hartlepool, simply entitled 'The Mass', described it as a "*pantomimic* representation of all Christ's labouring and sufferings from the commencement of the Last Supper to his death upon the cross, and his ascension into Heaven".[29] Similarly, in a popular lecture on 'The Sacrifice of the Mass', the Rev. John Sheills alleged to a Newcastle audience that the Mass effectively "invalidated the great sacrifice that Christ made, once for all, upon the cross".[30] Above all, it was the doctrine of transubstantiation and the notion that Christ is corporeally *present* in the Eucharist which particularly horrified many Protestants. The Rev. Samuel Dunn, in a tract entitled "An Exposure of the Mummeries, Absurdities and Idolatries of Popery", saw the consumption of the Body of Christ as cannibalism because the Catholics believed that the disciples ate the body of Jesus, including the "blood, bones, sinews etc." Given this absurdity, Dunn argued, "should a mouse devour a consecrated wafer, it would really eat the body of Christ".[31] The Rev. Mr. Taylor went further in suggesting that the circular shape of the wafer presented to the communicant was, in fact, an old pagan symbol representing "Satan's cypher (sic)".[32] For Roman

---

[27] *Newcastle Courant*, 5 March 1852.
[28] Wallis, *Popular Anti-*Catholicism, p. 23.
[29] Extract quoted in *Newcastle Journal*, 18 September 1847.
[30] *Durham Advertiser*, 5 December 1862.
[31] Samuel Dunn, *An Exposure of the Mummeries, Absurdities and Idolatries of Popery* (Newcastle: Blackwell & Co., 1846), pp. 2-3.
[32] *Newcastle Journal*, 18 September 1847.

Catholics, though, transubstantiation was a doctrine that was closely linked with their individual and communal Catholic identity. In a lecture in Sunderland in December 1851, the Rev. Mr. Kearney acknowledged that the Real Presence of Christ in the Eucharist was a mystery calculated to defy understanding, but he countered the Church's critics by arguing: "was not the Trinity a mystery? The Incarnation a mystery?—a God in a manger! A God under the carpenter's roof! A God mocked by the Jews, and dying on Cavalry!"[33]

The ideology of anti-sacerdotalism (hatred of priests) was also linked to a further popular topic in the anti-Catholic imagination: the role of the nun and the convent. An examination of the appeal sent to the local press during the anti-convent campaigns of the 1850s reveals that this tenet of anti-Catholic thought worked on a number of different levels. To begin with, there was a genuine fear that nuns were physically imprisoned in convents against their own will. "If the inhabitants remain there willingly", cried the appeal, "why are they shut in with high walls and iron bars". Certainly there was a belief that the convents themselves gave the physical appearance of a prison or "dungeons which the light of day cannot penetrate". This reference to the convents as dungeons implies a torture chamber analogy, linked in the idea of the Inquisition and persecution, which were allegedly staples of Roman Catholic justice. The nuns were not merely trapped physically, but also psychologically. It was believed that females were "allured" into nunneries under a trance-like "dream of blessedness", only to discover too late the "fearful reality of desolation". Convents also played on Victorian obsessions with the patriarchal family model. In particular, it has been argued that convents represented a real threat to the Protestant ideal of womanhood which was reflected in the attempted replication of the family model in the convent.[34] The Appeal therefore, was directed towards mothers and their inability to protect their daughters once they were "allured" into these nunneries—"How can she (the mother) bear to think that the voice which once gladdened her fireside may cry for help, where the only reply shall be the echo of the dismal vault". Behind this, lies the popular Jesuitical anti-Catholic stereotype of the Roman Catholic system working its way secretly into the very heart of the Victorian family—"Rome's emissaries . . . may be acting unseen in the

---

[33] *Sunderland Herald*, 12 December 1851.
[34] This is reflected in the use of the term 'Mother' and 'Sister'. S. O'Brien, 'Terra Incognita: The Nuns in Nineteenth Century England', *Past and Present*, 121 (1988), p. 136; S.P. Casteras, 'Virgin Vows: The Early Victorian Portrayal of Nuns and Novices', *Religion in the Lives of English Women*, ed. by Gail Malmgreen (1986), p. 137.

most happy families, to convert them into scenes of weeping and disorder".[35]

The sexual mores of priests and nuns were favourite topics of the more vulgar aspects of popular anti-Catholicism. As D. Peschier has argued, convents "were regarded as the locus for all kinds of perversions, sexual perversions in particular".[36] Celibacy and chastity were particularly repugnant to anti-Catholics who believed them to have immoral consequences.[37] From the 1830s, stories of sexual misdemeanour in "confessional and convent" sprang up in response to a growing market for such works. Ingram suggests that the longevity of the convent question and the recurring popularity of priests and nuns in pornographic print lay in the fact that "Protestant society from top to bottom . . . was deeply harassed by the idea of the Catholic priest as a sexual threat to all women".[38] These ideas were no better expressed than in *The Confessional Unmasked*, a tract that formed the basis of the lectures of No Popery demagogues such as Patrick Flynn and William Murphy, who both toured the North East in the late 1860s.[39] *The Confessional Unmasked* was allegedly based on a manual for Catholic priests on how to deal with taboo subjects in the confessional and is symptomatic of the Protestant obsession with priestly sexuality. The priest is required to interrogate his penitent who he feels may have committed the sin of adultery as this extract shows:

> "If the penitent be a girl, let her be asked—Has she ornamented herself in dress so as to please the male sex?, or for the same end, has she painted herself; or bared her arms, her shoulders, or her bosom?"[40]

---

[35] *Newcastle Journal*, 24 January 1852.

[36] D. Peschier, 'Religious Sexual Perversion in Nineteenth-Century Anti-Catholic Literature', *Sexual Perversions, 1670-1890*, ed. by J. Peakmen (Basingstoke: Palgrave Macmillan, 2009), p. 202.

[37] Wallis, *Popular Anti-Catholicism*, p. 24; C.M. Mangion, *Contested identities: Catholic women religious in nineteenth century England and Wales* (Manchester: Manchester University Press, 2008), p. 56.

[38] P. Ingram, 'Protestant Patriarchy and the Catholic Priesthood in Nineteenth-Century England', *Journal of Social History*, 24.4 (1991), pp. 783, 785.

[39] Wolffe, *Protestant Crusade,* p. 124.

[40] [B.C.]., *The Confessional Unmasked Showing the Depravity of the Priesthood, Questions Put to Females in Confession, Perjury and Stealing Commanded and Encouraged etc. Being Extracts from the Theological Works of Saint Alphonso M. De. Liguori, Peter Dens, Bailly, Delahogue, and Cabassutius* (London: Johnston, 1851), p. 40.

The quote above is mild in comparison to the second half of the tract, which deals with subjects such as *coitus interruptus*, masturbation, ejaculation and impotence and the various scenarios in which they can be categorised as a sin are discussed in lurid detail. This obsession with the sexual activity of his penitents was derived from the priest's forced vow of celibacy, which was not only "unnatural" but could lead to the priest becoming a "super-virile seducer and rapist".[41]

Anti-Catholicism was more than just prurient pornography or theological polemic to the Victorian Protestant. K. Kumar has suggested that anti-Catholicism survived into the eighteenth and nineteenth centuries primarily because of its political and cultural associations.[42] Certainly in the Victorian period, Protestantism and anti-Catholicism were fundamental facets of English national identity as Britain's industrial greatness became inextricably linked to her religion. According to Denis Paz, this perception was closely connected to the idea of Providentialism—Britain had been chosen to carry out God's will. In return, for its evangelical work, it enjoyed superior political and economic status.[43] This idea of Providentialism certainly influenced the views of the Scottish anti-Catholic journal, the *Bulwark*:

> "To her religion, under God's blessing, Britain is principally indebted. But God never works without a purpose, and He would not have given her so much power and influence had she no mission to accomplish. Like the Jews of old, Britain has been chosen as a repository of God's word. She is almost the only light in the midst of surrounding darkness".[44]

The link between British nationalism and Protestantism was also evident at the local level. The editor of the *Newcastle Journal* saw his native country as "the parent of modern industry, enterprise, improved arts . . . and in one word-civilisation", of which her religion played a crucial role.[45] According to the Rev. T. Pottinger, in a local sermon entitled 'The Bible is the Glory of Our Land', the source of Britain's greatness was in her morality and religious devotion, developed through reading and following the Word of God:

---

[41] Ingram, 'Protestant Patriarchy', p. 790.

[42] K. Kumar, *The Making of English National Identity* (Cambridge: Cambridge University Press, 1993), p. 165.

[43] Paz, *Popular Anti-Catholicism*, p. 3.

[44] *Bulwark*, 1 December 1859, p. 148.

[45] *Newcastle Journal*, 18 October 1850.

"In proportion as the people of this country love and revere the Bible they reap the benefits of a *moral and religious training* . . . secular education may make men scholars, citizens, merchants, senators, but it overlooks the Christian *which is the highest state of man*. The Bible claims authority to stamp its own beautiful image upon the education of all classes amongst us . . . Such a training would be the best guarantee for peace, order, liberty, justice, good-will, and national prosperity".[46]

The effects of a return to Popery would, it was believed, be disastrous for the country as a whole. For many who shared these views, it was not merely a matter of opinion. This could be "proved" both geographically and historically. Of the former, they only needed to look to the Catholic countries of Europe to see the material effects of the "Popish" religion.[47] The usually tolerant Newcastle alderman, Sir John Fife, saw no contradiction in his attitude when he spoke at the Newcastle meeting for the liberation of the Protestant Madiai family in Tuscany (see Chapter Four). "The working man in Roman Catholic countries", he argued, "was badly fed, badly clothed, badly lodged, broken in spirit and degraded by the habit of kneeling to his fellow-men (hear, hear) and transplanted to the earth by the cloven foot of tyranny".[48] The people of Catholic countries, it was believed, lived in a climate of fear and oppression that was symptomatic of their religion. "Religious and Civil Liberty" may have been a rather overworked phrase in the nineteenth century[49], but for many it was undeniably the main benchmark that divided Protestant and Catholic countries. Thus, the Italian evangelist lecturer Alessandro Gavazzi, in his popular lectures in the North East, argued that his native country had "neither liberty of thought, liberty of action, liberty of meeting, nor liberty

---

[46] T. Pottinger, *The Bible is the Glory of Our Land: The Substance of a Sermon Delivered in Tulhill Stairs Chapel, Newcastle, on November 15th 1849* (Newcastle: [n. pub.] 1849).
[47] The eminent sociologist Max Weber argued that Protestant countries were at the forefront of industry and culture because Protestants had a 'work ethic' which Catholics lacked. M. Weber, *The Protestant Ethic and the Spirit of Capitalism* (London: Unwin, 1930). In the North East, however, the central role played by Catholic families in local industrial development is an effective rejoinder to this argument. See Leo Gooch, 'Papists and Profits: The Catholics (Silvertop, Brandling and Salvin Familes) of Durham and Industrial Development', *Durham County Local History Society Bulletin*, 42 (1989), which is based on his MA thesis, 'The Durham Catholics and Industrial Development, 1560-1850', (unpublished master's thesis, University of York, 1984).
[48] *Newcastle Guardian*, 19 March 1853.
[49] W.G. Addison, *Religious Equality in Modern England* (London: SPCK, 1944), p. 5.

of conversation".[50] The Rev. J.A. Wylie concurred with this viewpoint in a lecture to the Protestant Alliance. Indeed, Wylie believed there was "far more toleration of the Christians in Pagan times than was in the case in Papal Rome".[51]

Ireland was a particularly special case in this respect. Hugh McLeod has suggested that for nineteenth century British Protestants, "the supreme embodiment of the Catholic Other was not France but Ireland".[52] This negative perception was cultivated by a mainland image of the Irish as lagging behind their "Saxon" contemporaries in mental capacity.[53] A letter writer to the *Newcastle Journal* suggested that this was reflected in the role of the Irish immigrant in his new society:

> "You do not find near Newcastle that Irishmen rise to any station or influence in society, generally they are not proficient in any sort of science, not teachers of music, or drawing, or languages, not employed in superior offices in trade, manufacture, gardening, or engineering . . . the Irishman ends as he began, a day labourer, devoid of skill and knowledge, and even of manual dexterity".[54]

The link between the degrading effects of the Catholic religion and the "subhuman" Irish mindset was not always made clear by contemporaries. The contemporary historian and Whig politician, T.B. Macaulay, certainly thought that English and Irish animosity arose from religious, rather than racial differences[55] and there were attempts by some local commentators to link Catholicism and Irish degradation with Ireland itself. During the Irish Rebellion of 1848, the Liberal *Durham Chronicle* believed that

---

[50] *Newcastle Journal*, 18 October 1851. For Gavazzi's life, see B. Aspinwall, 'Rev. Alessandro Gavazzi and Scottish Identity: A Chapter in Nineteenth Century Anti-Catholicism', *Recusant History*, 28.1 (2006), pp. 129-52; and B. Hall, 'Alessandro Gavazzi: A Barnabite Friar and the Risorgimento', *Studies in Church History*, 12 (1975), pp. 303-56.

[51] *Newcastle Journal*, 30 October 1852.

[52] Hugh McLeod, 'Protestantism and British National Identity, 1815-1945', *Nation and Religion: Perspectives on Europe and Asia*, ed. by Hartmut Lehmann (Princeton: Princeton University Press, 1997), p. 47.

[53] L.P. Curtis, *Anglo-Saxons and Celts: A Study of Anti-Irish Prejudice in Victorian England* (Bridgeport: University of Bridgeport, 1968), p. 64.

[54] *Newcastle Journal*, 14 June 1848.

[55] Hickman, *Religion, Class and Identity*, p. 51. The debate on whether anti-Irish prejudice constituted a form of racism is also propounded by Hickman. See also, Sheridan Gilley, 'English Attitudes to the Irish in England, 1780-1900', *Immigrants and Minorities in British Society*, ed. by C. Holmes (London: Allen and Unwin, 1978), pp. 81-110; and Curtis, *Anglo-Saxons and Celts*.

Ireland's woes rested in the Catholic priests "who seem to have become rather a curse than a blessing, forgetting alike their duty to God and the responsibility of that sovereignty which they hold over men".[56] The Liberal *Sunderland News* reflected on the relative tranquillity of Ireland in 1852, believing it to be based on the increase in Protestantism in the country. This, the paper argued, was evident in the "greater energy, self-reliance and independence" to which the Protestant religion "generates wherever it prevails".[57] The *Newcastle Journal* also grabbed the opportunity to attack the present state of Ireland itself, and agreeing with Admiral Sir Joseph Yorke, that "it would be to the exceeding benefits of society . . . that Ireland should be let into the sea for some 24 hours".[58] Evangelicals believed that the conversion of Ireland and the Irish Catholics to Protestantism provided the only means of escape from their spiritual and material destitution.[59] Not every commentator concurred with the view that the "misery" of Ireland could be blamed solely on the Catholic religion. Indeed, the Liberal *Gateshead Observer* described this theory as "sheer nonsense", quoting Belgium as an example of a prosperous Catholic country where "Catholics (lay and clerical) are as rife as Ireland".[60]

This perception of Catholic countries as harbingers of despotism and the antithesis of liberty was vehemently denied by the Roman Catholics. In a speech during a Roman Catholic festival in Sunderland in 1851, the Rev. Philip Kearney was again active in denying the stereotype of the Catholic poor as "miserable" and "wretched":

> "Don't believe those who say this. I have been abroad for eleven years and I can tell you that the poor people in other (Catholic) countries are happier and more comfortable than the poor people in England. They are better educated, there are no reasoners among them, no infidels who go on in mathematics till they deny the existence of the supreme being. They are good and simple beings . . ."[61]

The consequences of Popery could also be shown by referring to the course of history. This was a particularly favoured tactic of anti-Catholic lecturers, who employed what Herbert Butterfield was later to term, the

---

[56] *Durham Chronicle*, 4 February 1848.
[57] *Sunderland News*, 18 September 1852.
[58] *Newcastle Journal*, 7 June 1851.
[59] Wolffe, *Protestant Crusade*, p. 122.
[60] *Gateshead Observer*, 22 January 1849.
[61] *Sunderland Herald*, 28 November 1851.

"Whig Interpretation of History". This was a positive underlying narrative to history writing, charting what was believed to be a "certain form upon the whole historical story, and to produce a scheme of general history which is bound to converge beautifully upon the present—all demonstrating throughout the ages the workings of an obvious principle of progress".[62] The style was made popular by T.B. Macaulay's *History of England* series (1848-59), which was enormously influential in forming the Victorian perception of its past.[63] From this perspective, many popular anti-Catholic lecturers saw the development of Protestantism as "an obvious principle of progress". As society developed, Protestantism would eventually eradicate Catholicism. An example of this form of historical determinism can be seen in a report of a public lecture at the Wesleyan Chapel in Fawcett Street, Sunderland, on the 'Perils of Protestantism'. Here the Wesleyan minister, the Rev. George Sergeant, had a clear perspective on the direction history was proceeding in:

> "In an interesting sketch he (Sergeant) traced the rise of Protestantism from the teachings of Wycliffe in the 14th century, through the next century until the reign of Henry the Eighth, through that of Mary to Elizabeth, and the final ascendancy of the Protestant faith, pointing out the dangers it had gone through".[64]

Lectures were also delivered on specific historical events which included such favoured anti-Catholic signifiers as the 'English Reformation'[65] and the 'Martyrs of Smithfield'.[66] These helped to fashion a narrative of history into which Protestants and Catholics were heroes and villains respectively. Wolffe has noted that mid-Victorian Evangelicals generally acquired their knowledge and their sense of Protestant history from the same sources. These included Joseph and Isaac Milner's *History of the Church of Christ* (published in the 1790s) and J.H. Merle d'Aubigne's *Historie de la Reformation* (published in Geneva in 1835 and translated into English three years later).[67] Nevertheless, it was a history which many anti-Catholics believed had contemporary validity, particularly as sixteenth-century anti-Catholic works such as Foxe's *Book of Martyrs,*

---

[62] H. Butterfield, *The Whig Interpretation of History* (London: G. Bell and Sons, 1931), p. 12.
[63] Wheeler, *The Old Enemies*, p. 96.
[64] *Sunderland News*, 3 April 1869.
[65] *Shields Daily News*, 24 April 1865.
[66] *Durham Advertiser*, 10 December 1869.
[67] Wolffe, *Protestant Crusade*, p. 111.

were continually reprinted for a new audience in the Victorian period.[68] This created an anti-Catholic worldview which was deeply connected to past conflict and thus explains the intensity and urgency of anti-Catholic polemical thought throughout the Victorian period.[69]

The anti-Catholic historical worldview was not only a purely selective interpretation of history, but it was one in which Catholics found little difficulty in pulling apart at every opportunity. However, Catholics themselves similarly employed a teleological model of historical interpretation when defending their religion against Protestant attacks. The Catholic Rev. Dr. Henry Marshall, in a lecture in Durham, attacked the anti-Catholic notion that the Catholic Church was against the concepts of civilisation and liberty.[70] Indeed, he argued, the very mission of the Church throughout history has been one of civilisation by laying down the principles of common and civil law and bringing "those rights and privileges which have proved our noblest boast, and which are the palladium of our liberties".[71] The Reformation was, of course, abhorred by Catholics so for many it was the pre-Reformation period which constituted a golden age. According to the Catholic orator Charles Larkin, "there never was a time when there was so much gold, silver, and every possible species of furniture, so many rich men, so much contentment, and so much wealth in England, as there was immediately preceding the Reformation". For Larkin, the legacy of the Reformation was one of only "bitterness and misery".[72] A letter writer to the *Newcastle Journal* in 1862 appeared to concur with Larkin. He complained of a recent anti-Catholic lecture by an Anglican layman, a Mr. Addison, in Durham, wherein the orator saw the Reformation as a triumph of liberty:

> "Let him (Addison) study the character of Luther, the lewd and discarded priest, who trampled upon his own solemn vows, whilst he seduced a poor unfortunate nun. Let him scan the character of Queen Elizabeth, who murdered her cousin Mary. Let him peruse the base and bloody pages of the penal laws against Papists during three successive centuries".[73]

---

[68] Norman, *The English Catholic Church*, p. 18; Wolffe, *Protestant Crusade*, p. 112.

[69] Wolffe, *Protestant Crusade*, p. 111.

[70] Henry Johnson Marshall, b. 1818 (Somerset), o. 1848, d. 1875. *English and Welsh Priests*, p. 129.

[71] *Durham Advertiser*, 17 March 1865.

[72] *Newcastle Guardian*, 9 May 1857.

[73] *Newcastle Daily Journal*, 31 October 1862.

The historical determinism associated with the rise of Protestantism was not a single unifying interpretation of the past but a contested area that brought together different anti-Catholic meta-narratives, although they were not mutually exclusive and often overlapped. An example of this is evident in readings of historical development following the Glorious Revolution of 1688.[74] This rested on the belief that the Protestant King of Holland, William of Orange, had guarded English civil and religious liberties by winning the Battle of the Boyne against the Catholic James II. It was at this stage that the "Protestant Constitution" of Great Britain was first promulgated, enshrining these liberties in the legislature of the country and, according to one historian, helping to formulate the "invention of Great Britain and its identity as a Protestant nation".[75] Throughout the nineteenth century, some contemporary commentators believed that the Protestant elements of the constitution were gradually being eroded by concessionary legislation towards Roman Catholics. This had begun with the Catholic Relief Acts of 1778, 1791 and 1829 but continued with the increase in the Maynooth Grant, Irish Disestablishment and a host of other laws that seemed to favour Catholics. This "truckling to Popery" was abhorrent and undermined the very nature of Church and State. These militant Protestants saw it as their duty to protest against any measure which afforded greater rights to their religious adversaries. Edward Norman has suggested that the No Popery movement associated with the "Protestant Constitution" was essentially a dying theory in the nineteenth century, although it still retained some validity, mostly among Conservatives and Anglicans and some Liberal-Dissenters (from a non-Establishment standpoint).[76]

An alternative anti-Catholic narrative of history and, as we shall see, a particular popular one on Tyneside, also took the Glorious Revolution as its starting point, although it placed less emphasis on defending what it perceived to be a backward theory of the "Protestant Constitution". Indeed, it suggested that the legacy of the Revolution was in the foundation of "civil and religious liberty", in which toleration was the key

---

[74] The Protestant Constitution played a large role in the ideology behind the opposition to the Roman Catholic Relief Act of 1829, see G.F.A. Best, 'The Protestant Constitution and its Supporters, 1820-29', *Transactions of the Royal Historical Society*, 8 (1958), pp. 105-27.

[75] J. Epstein, "'Our Real Constitution": Trial Defence and Radical Memory in the Age of Revolution', *Re-Reading the Constitution: New Narratives in the Political History of the Long Nineteenth Century*, ed. by J. Vernon (Cambridge: Cambridge University Press, 1996), p. 43.

[76] Norman, *Anti-Catholicism*, p. 21.

element of government.[77] This anti-Catholic ideology was closely aligned with the development of Liberalism which gradually became accepted into the political mainstream from the 1830s onwards, as well as the growing influence of Dissenters following the repeal of the Test and Corporation Acts. "Liberal" anti-Catholicism departed significantly from the traditionalists in perceiving the No Popery movement of old as the very antithesis of progress and toleration. The No Popery movement was also accused of "disgusting hypocrisy" by the *Eclectic Review* (a Radical Dissenter journal) because of its associations with the interests of the Tory party and the defence of the Established Church.[78] Liberal Dissenting anti-Catholics were happy to concede basic human rights to Roman Catholics within reason because they shared a similar history of persecution. In a popular lecture on the Reformation and its consequences in Newcastle by the notable Liberal Dissenter, Henry Vincent, in 1856, raised the thorny issue of the Acts of Uniformity which "enacted severe persecutions against the Dissenters from the Established Church".[79] Nevertheless, they were still keen to stress their role in the creation of a national identity based on the Protestant religion.[80]

Liberal anti-Catholicism was instead expressed in a more abstract form, presenting Roman Catholicism as a tyrannical and despotic religion that was ultimately opposed to liberty. Indeed, most Liberals were involved in various campaigns which played on fears of persecution in the Catholic system (the anti-convent campaign, the release of the Madiai) or the "despotic" political institutions of Catholic countries (Italian independence).[81] They saw Roman Catholicism as a persecuting and backward religion whose ideas and institutions would inevitably be stamped out by the march of progress of the human mind, in which the Bible played a large part in liberating the minds of those who experienced

---

[77] Bertrand Russell has noted that the theoretical and practical foundations of Victorian toleration were laid down at the end of the seventeenth century by William III who brought the practice over from Holland and John Locke's treatise on toleration. B. Russell, 'Toleration', *Ideas and Beliefs of the Victorians: An Historic Revaluation of the Victorian Age*, compiled by the British Broadcasting Corporation (London: Sylvan Press, 1949), p. 270.

[78] Wolffe, *Protestant Crusade*, p. 134.

[79] *Newcastle Guardian*, 22 March 1856.

[80] Simon Gunn, *The Public Culture of the Victorian Middle Class: Ritual and Authority and the English Industrial City* (Manchester: Manchester University Press, 2000), p. 123.

[81] The latter was clearly influenced by Edward Burke's theory on the balance between arbitrary government and anarchy. E. Burke, *Reflections on the Revolution in France*, ed. by J.C.D. Clark (Stanford: Stanford University Press, 2001).

"priestly tyranny". This paradigm of "progress" was associated with the Protestant religion as the ultimate example of freedom.

The Liberal form of anti-Catholicism highlighted the importance of toleration towards Roman Catholics which was central to Victorian philosophy. While the system of Popery was to be feared, those individuals who practised the Catholic religion should be allowed the liberty to do so without fear of discrimination. Somewhat ironically, therefore, an essential facet of moderate anti-Catholic ideology was toleration for individual Catholics to practice their religion as they pleased. This was closely linked with the ideas of John Stuart Mill, who believed that all individuals had the right of freedom of action and belief, so long as they did not encroach on the rights of others.[82] This was often contrasted with Catholic countries in which Protestants did not receive the same level of toleration. While it was perfectly acceptable to criticise the Catholic religion as a system, the idea of persecution of the ordinary Catholic was abhorrent to all but the most extreme anti-Catholics.

This concept of toleration also extended to anti-Catholic gatherings where the speakers of popular meetings and lectures always seemed to be "at great pains to avoid offending their Roman Catholic fellow subjects". Indeed, virtually all anti-Catholic gatherings paid lip-service to toleration in this sense, a caveat which allowed them to launch subsequently into an aggressive attack on the Roman Catholic system itself. Thus, the Chairman of the Papal Aggression meeting in Newcastle in 1850 wished to speak of the Roman Catholics with the "greatest respect", while a speaker, Ralph Walters, hoped that the Roman Catholics would be encouraged to speak at the meeting for which they would undoubtedly have "a fair and proper hearing".[83] Even the medical practitioner, Dr. William Sleigh, who toured the region in 1851 and was notorious for his vitriolic denunciations of Roman Catholicism, hoped that his lectures would not offend the Roman Catholics themselves. His lectures, he argued, would not "violate or . . . caricature the Catholic religion" and therefore ordinary Catholics need not be angered by his orations:

> "His Catholic-fellow countrymen would, therefore, he hoped, look upon him as their friend, as no man could be more friendly to civil and religious liberty than himself, and he not only abhorred persecution, but denounced

---

[82] J.S. Mill, *Utilitarianism, On Liberty, and Considerations on Representative Government* (London: J.M. Dent and Sons Ltd, 1972), p. 136.
[83] *Newcastle Courant*, 29 November 1850.

it as wholly impolite and directly opposed to the fundamental principles of genuine Christianity. Nor did he stand there to attack men, but principles".[84]

Roman Catholics were perceived as simply the passive and unfortunate victims of a corrupt and evil system. In an anti-Catholic tract on the priesthood, the Rev. James Crozer blamed the priests for the exploitation of their flock:

> "It is very singular that the Roman Catholic laity, who are as rational in all respects as others, and are naturally as good civil neighbours also, should be so changed when their religion interferes, and should suffer themselves to outrage their own good feelings at the notoriously selfish instigation of their designatory priesthood; for they know, from fatal experience, that they will take the last farthing they have from them, and leave themselves and families to starve for all that they care".[85]

The Catholic and ultramontane *Tablet* was evidently unconvinced by this seemingly contradictory Protestant idea of toleration. The paper printed an article on a speech made by Joseph Pease, a Darlington Quaker whose family had a long tradition of good social relations with local Catholics.[86] Pease spoke of his experiences in a recent visit to the cathedral in Lyon. This allowed him the opportunity to condemn the peculiar characteristics of the Roman Catholic system while defending the rights of Roman Catholic individuals to worship as they pleased. The paper described his speech as "an excellent specimen of the strange medley of opinions by a man who is evidently disposed to be good-natured and kind towards the faith of his Catholic neighbours; struggling to be liberal yet still bound in the chains of prejudice".[87]

There is evidence, however, that more extreme anti-Catholics did not even try to shake off the "chains of prejudice", refusing to consent to any idea of toleration towards Roman Catholics. This was a view shared amongst some militant Protestants in the North East of England. In 1851, the opposition of Catholics towards the Ecclesiastical Titles Bill gave rise to suspicion for many Protestants. The *Newcastle Journal* claimed the Catholics had "deliberately and boastfully broken their oath of 1829, an oath which the paper referred to as the "putting of Papists . . . on their

---

[84] *Newcastle Guardian*, 7 October 1851.

[85] J. Crozer, *A Glimpse of all the Denominations of the Priesthood...* (Newcastle: W.B. Leighton, 1845), p. 35.

[86] For a general history of the Pease family, see Orde, *Religion, Business and Society.*

[87] *Tablet*, 8 July 1852.

good behaviour".[88] As a member of the Protestant Alliance, the Newcastle Presbyterian minister, the Rev. Thomas Duncan, spoke of the Roman Catholics in far harsher terms to a meeting of the organisation. He believed they had been "found wanting". "It was only fair", he asserted, that "the large concessions formally made to them should be recalled".[89] This view outlasted the Papal Aggression agitation and there is evidence to suggest that it was still in vogue well into the 1860s. In September 1865, a letter writer to the *Sunderland Herald*, a Liberal newspaper normally sympathetic to Catholics, blamed the 1829 Roman Catholic Relief Act for conceding too many rights to Catholics:

"There is an old proverb, 'Give the mouse a hole and she will become your heir', which is alarmingly verified by the present progress and impudence of Popery in this realm. The Emancipation Act of 1829 gave this mouse a hospitable hole in the dwelling of old England, and ever since then the cunning creature has been growing more and more bold, till now, in 1865, she has abandoned possession of the hole and taken possession of the room".[90]

Towards the end of the 1860s, however, there is also evidence to suggest that a more tolerant attitude was taking hold. Even the Conservative press were moderating their opinions. After a warmly written article on the laying of the foundation stone of a Roman Catholic chapel at Tudhoe in 1869, the Anglican High Church *Durham Advertiser* received strong criticism from a letter-writer who believed that it had betrayed its political and religious principles:

"The *Durham Advertiser* used to be looked upon as the representative of Conservatism in politics, and of the Church of England, which, let me remind you, is a Protestant Church, in religion. In common with many others, I am sorry to have observed for some time past that it has ceased to be so, and that no interests are so warmly received by you as those of Rome".[91]

A recent book by E. Sidenvall has criticised the accepted "Liberal 'master narrative'" that perceives the history of religious freedom in the Western world as one of "progress" towards a growing toleration of other faiths. Instead he suggests that attitudes towards the Catholic religion in

---

[88] *Newcastle Journal*, 6 December 1851.
[89] *Newcastle Journal*, 10 December 1851.
[90] *Sunderland Herald*, 15 September 1865.
[91] *Durham Advertiser*, 18 June 1869.

the nineteenth century included both sentiments of growing toleration *and* traditional prejudice which came to live side by side with each other.[92] The examples above from the *Durham Advertiser* and the *Sunderland Herald* suggest that these two competing discourses are evident in the regional setting.

Sidenvall's ideas, as well as F. Wallis's theory that the Protestant perception of Catholicism was ultimately based on prejudice, are also apparent in the language adopted by the anti-Catholics towards Roman Catholics.[93] An examination of the terms "Romanism"/"Popery" and "Romanist"/"Papist", and the context in which they are employed, may help to support this. These terms were in common usage amongst Protestants during the eighteenth century but were gradually dying out by the mid-Victorian period. Nevertheless, they were still being used in certain sections of the mainstream press and were deeply offensive to Catholics. In an article in August 1851, the *Bulwark* set out to discuss why these labels were used. The paper argued that Catholics were incorrect in using the term "Catholic" because it conveyed "the doctrine that they and they alone are members of the true Church of Christ". Thus, the paper argued, Protestants should not use the term Catholic:

> "Papists then insult and injure us when they assume to themselves, and refuse to us, the designation of Catholics; and when we call them Catholics, we unthinkingly approve of the insult and the injury which they inflict upon us, and concede the validity of the claims on which the treatment of us is based".

As for the use of the terms "Romanist" and "Papist", the paper stressed that it did not do so to "represent these designations as nicknames, and . . . to insult or wound the feelings of those to whom we apply them. The terms imply what they are: subject to Rome (Romanist) and subject to the authority of the Pope (Papist)".[94] It is important to note, however, that these terms are only used when spoken in a negative context. In an editorial shortly after the announcement of the Restoration of the Hierarchy, the *Newcastle Journal* could barely conceal its anti-Catholicism, arguing that "the Romanists were designedly kept very far behind Protestants in mental cultivation". When speaking of them in one of its

---

[92] Sidenvall, *After Anti-Catholicism*, pp. 2-3.
[93] Wallis, *Popular Anti-Catholicism*, p. 11. For a discussion on prejudicial labelling, see G.W. Allport, *The Nature of Prejudice* (Cambridge, Massachusetts: The Beacon Press, 1954), pp. 50, 181.
[94] *Bulwark*, August 1851.

rare moments of toleration, however, the term "Roman Catholic" is used— "We regard Roman Catholics as brothers".[95] This clearly confirms both the theories of Sidenvall and Wallis in the local setting.

While toleration towards Roman Catholics was a key component of Victorian philosophy, for many anti-Catholics there were also real dangers in encouraging the spread of Popery. According to F. Wallis, Protestants perceived Popery as a "vast spiritual and temporal conspiracy against liberty and lawful authority, whose goal was dominion over all Christians".[96] Though the Catholic religion might be weak, it was certainly expanding and a complacency and lack of activity on the part of Protestants would only result in the former gaining strength and usurping the strong position held by the latter. Apocalyptic scenarios promoted by influential Evangelicals, such as Dr. John Cumming, aligned their anti-Catholicism with prophetic and millenarian conceptions of the Second Coming.[97] W.H. Oliver believed that these ideas declined in importance after the 1840s but there is evidence in the local context to suggest otherwise. Indeed, the Rev. George Fox still believed that Popery was on the march in the late 1860s:

> "There never was a period when the nation required more to be warned on this head than the present, for the experience of the past seems to be rapidly passing into oblivion, and those bulwarks which the wisdom of our forefathers caused them to erect for the protection of the nation, are with unwise haste being dismantled, exposing us year by year to the assaults of the enemy, which hath ever produced itself alike unfriendly to civil and religious liberty".[98]

The Rev. George Sergeant argued that this was part of the aggrandizing spirit of Popery, where she could be "found in every region where

---

[95] *Newcastle Journal*, 25 October 1851; 10 December 1850.

[96] Wallis, *Popular Anti-Catholicism*, p. 22.

[97] For the role of Cumming and eschatological thought, see D. Hempton, 'Evangelicalism and Eschatology', *Journal of Ecclesiastical History*, 31.2 (1980), pp. 179-90; and R.H. Ellison and C.M. Engelhardt, 'Prophecy and Anti-Popery in Victorian London: John Cumming Reconsidered', *Victorian Literature and Culture*, 31.1 (2003), pp. 373-89. For a general discussion on millenarianism, see W.H. Oliver, *Prophets and Millenarianists: The Use of Biblical Prophecy in England from the 1790s to the 1840s* (Auckland University Press: Auckland, 1978); and for its social and economic impact: Boyd Hilton, *The Age of Atonement: The Influence of Evangelicalism on Social and Economic Thought, 1785-1865* (Oxford: Oxford University Press, 1992).

[98] Fox, 'Doctrines', p. 174.

Protestantism resides, seeking in every way to advance her power over that of Protestantism".[99] In his tract on the priesthood, the Rev. James Crozer warned that the priests "will not be satisfied until they can grasp universal power and . . . send the whole into eternity in fiery chariots, or in vast rivers of blood".[100] For some, the rise of Roman Catholicism in the mid-Victorian period was predicted in the Bible. The Rev. John Sheils of Durham, in a British Reformation Society lecture in Newcastle, drew parallels with biblical references from the seventh chapter of Daniel, comparing the Pope to the "Man of Sin" and the Romish Church as the "False Apostasy".[101] Not everyone was willing to concur with these views however. The *Durham Advertiser* saw the "ascendancy of Popery in this country" as "either the dream of an exaggerated fear or the illusory anticipation over its linguine professors".[102]

Anti-Catholicism was, to a large extent, mirrored in the Evangelical and Dissenter attitude towards the Tractarian clergy. It has been asserted that the Church of England was declining in importance during the nineteenth century. Its inability to cope with the pressures of industrialisation to which the various Dissenting organisations were clearly more adaptable, coupled with the growing strength of the Catholic Church, led some High Churchmen to believe that the Anglican Church could return to its catholic roots.[103] Many wished to see the Church of England return to its former status, authority and power by re-adopting its "former conservative, traditional values in determined opposition to the blatant corrosive tones of Radicalism and Liberalism in their various guises".[104] It was suggested by the Tractarians that the Church of England was not a Protestant Church but possessed continuity with the Church of the Middle Ages. England was therefore not a Protestant country, but had shared catholic roots, traditions and identity.[105] This had serious implications for the theory of the confessional State and the very foundation of "Protestant" England. It is

---

[99] *Sunderland News,* 3 April 1869.

[100] Crozer, *A glimpse of all the denominations*, p. 35.

[101] *Newcastle Guardian*, 1 November 1862.

[102] *Durham Advertiser*, 3 January 1851.

[103] Gilley, 'The Church of England', p. 292. See also G. Parsons, 'A Question of Meaning: Religion and Working-Class Life', *Religion in Victorian Britain*, II, pp. 63-87.

[104] K. Hylson-Smith, *High Churchmanship in the Church of England From the Sixteenth Century to the Late Twentieth Century* (London: T. and T. Clark, 1993), p. 125.

[105] W.S.F. Pickering, *Anglo-Catholicism: A Study in Religious Ambiguity* (London: Routledge, 1989), p. 25.

no surprise, therefore, that many viewed the movement to re-introduce traditional doctrines into the Church with the utmost suspicion. It was not enough for the Tractarians to deal in theoretical implications; many were also starting to introduce innovations in their churches by the late 1840s, such as placing lighted candles on the "altar" and bowing at the name of Jesus.

Anti-Tractarian ideology targeted those individuals who had introduced "Popish" innovations into Anglican churches. In particular, it was the pretensions to "priestly" authority claimed by these incumbents which really angered commentators. Indeed, the Tractarian emphasis on clerical authority brought a particularly unsavoury element of "Romish priestcraft" to the Anglican rural parish, where power-hungry clergymen could find an easy justification for imposing their will.[106] The Tractarian objective was, according to the *Newcastle Guardian* to "chain down thought, to make the mind a mere instrument for the clergy to play upon, and to dispense with that inalienable birth-right of humanity, the matter of private judgement in all matter religious or political".[107] Paz suggests that this was primarily a Nonconformist fear, because "Anglo-Catholic vicars could practice what English Roman Catholics priests only dreamed of: the persecution of Dissenters".[108] Nevertheless, there is evidence to suggest that lay Anglican Evangelicals shared this concern. An article in the *Sunderland Herald* during the Tractarian controversy in Houghton-Le-Spring accused the "Pope of Houghton", John Grey, as acting like "priest supreme, disregarding alike his venerable diocesan and his parishioners", regrettably forcing many to attend Dissenting chapels.[109] Similarly, at the Wallsend anti-Tractarian meeting, the Anglican William Bainbridge framed the resolutions against the incumbent, the Rev. William Armstrong, in such a way as to play on fears of the tyranny of priesthood.[110] Tractarian clergymen were labelled "Puseyites", a term which not only designated their belief in following the ideas of the leading Anglo-Catholic of this period, E.B. Pusey, but was also a term of "disapprobation and mockery, suggesting troglodytic crankiness and unpatriotic oddity".[111] Of course, the innovations themselves greatly concerned the parishioners and the wider

---

[106] J.S. Reed, *Glorious Battle: The Cultural Politics of Victorian Anglo-Catholicism* (Vanderbilt University Press: Nashville, 1996), p. 32.

[107] *Newcastle Guardian*, 30 March 1850.

[108] Paz, *Popular Anti-Catholicism*, p. 132.

[109] *Sunderland Herald*, 24 January 1851.

[110] *Newcastle Guardian*, 21 December 1850.

[111] R.W. Franklin, 'Pusey and Worship in Industrial Society', *Worship*, 57 (1953), p. 389.

community, but it was the underlying fear that the Tractarians were
mimicking the sacerdotal element of the Roman Catholic clergy which
played primarily on the anti-Catholic mind. However, the threat posed by
Tractarians did not appear to be as pronounced in the North East where,
with the exception of the late 1840s and early 1850s, Tractarianism, and
later Ritualism, held little sway in the predominantly Evamglical and
Dissenter-dominated region.

Clearly then, the North East shared the major tenets of anti-Catholic
thought that were evident in other areas of the country. Anti-Catholicism
was not a single unified set of beliefs but an ideology that could align itself
with other tenets of Victorian philosophy which helped to explain both its
wide appeal and longevity. An examination of the ideology of anti-
Catholicism in the North East of England, however, does not reveal the
extent to which the complex interplay of these ideas helped to influence
anti-Catholic cultures in various parts of the region. Indeed, for many anti-
Catholics, actions spoke louder than words and the next chapter will seek
to examine the nature and extent of the North East's response to an anti-
Catholic event of some magnitude: the so-called "Papal Aggression".

CHAPTER TWO

PETITIONING THE POPE:
THE RESPONSE TO THE RESTORATION
OF THE HIERARCHY, 1850

On 29 September 1850, Pope Pius IX issued a proclamation which created a territorial hierarchy of twelve bishoprics in England and Wales. Intended merely as an administrative measure to manage more effectively the expanding Catholic population of the country, the bull nevertheless caused a storm of Protestant protest, with writers and speakers throughout the country denouncing this "Papal Aggression" as an insidious attempt of a "foreign Power to fasten its authority upon our divisions".[1] The agitation was further encouraged by the newly-appointed Roman Catholic Archbishop of Westminster, Nicholas Wiseman, issuing a pastoral letter to his flock in which he spoke of "Catholic" England being "restored to its orbit in the ecclesiastical firmament from which its light had long vanished"[2], and Lord John Russell, the Prime Minster, publishing an open letter to the Bishop of Durham, within which he virulently attacked the Papal measure.[3] These opinions ensured the revival of anti-Catholicism as a legitimate method of popular expression in every locality throughout the country during the latter months of 1850 and well into the following year. Town and county meetings were initiated, Anglican and Dissenting ministers preached from their pulpits, popular firebrands capitalised on the anti-Catholic agitation by charging for lectures on the evils of the Papacy, and effigies of the Pope and Cardinal Wiseman were burned in the streets on November 5th. Not all anger was directed towards the Catholic community however. The Prime Minister explicitly stated in his Durham

---

[1] *The Times,* 19 October 1850.
[2] *English Historical Documents, 1833-1874,* ed. by G.M. Young and W.D. Handcock, *English Historical Documents*, ed. by David C. Douglas (gen. ed.), 12 vols (New York, 1956), XII, pt 1, pp. 365-6.
[3] The full text of the Durham Letter is printed in Norman, *Anti-Catholicism*, pp. 159-61.

Letter that the real threat lay not in the actions of "Pio Nono" but in the perils of Tractarianism.[4] Throughout the country, any High Churchman who was even remotely perceived to be introducing what Russell termed as the "mummeries of superstition" into the Anglican Church was singled out as a "Puseyite", experiencing regular and sometimes violent abuse in their parish.[5] The indignation against the Papal measure produced a total of 2,616 memorials, bearing 887,525 signatures, comprising roughly five per cent of the total population.[6]

The reaction to the restoration of the Catholic Hierarchy in October 1850 provides an example the way in which different anti-Catholic standpoints could be unified against the perceived threat posed by the Catholic religion. Indeed, the "Papal Aggression", as it was termed, received an unprecedented amount of attention precisely because it transcended the boundaries of zealous anti-Catholic opinion. It was a question which tugged on the heart strings of every loyal British citizen regardless of political or religious stance. The North East of England played its own part in the agitation, and it is the purpose of this chapter to show that the regional response to this event was as passionate as elsewhere. Local Protestant relations with the Catholic community disintegrated as meeting after meeting unashamedly attacked the Catholic religion. Moreover, the Evangelical/Dissenter composition of the political agitation ensured that not only were Catholics much maligned but there was also an assault on the small clique of Anglican clergy whose "Puseyite" practices brought them unwanted attention in the post-Papal Aggression period.

The Reaction of the Local Newspaper Press

It is important to firstly examine why the Restoration of the Hierarchy was so vehemently opposed. The sheer scale of the protests indicated more than just token gestures from anti-Catholic zealots. Undoubtedly, the issue provided a number of reasons for those who shared extremist views to oppose it but what is especially remarkable about the crisis was the way in which the Papal bull attracted almost universal opposition, reacting as it

---

[4] Norman, *Anti-Catholicism,* p. 160.

[5] The most serious examples occurred in St Barnabas, Pimlico, where the Rev. W.J.E. Bennett experienced almost constant physical opposition to his services in the months following the Papal Aggression. See J. E. Pinnington, 'Bishop Blomfield and St. Barnabas, Pimlico: The Limits of Ecclesiastical Authority', *Church Quarterly Review,* 168 (1967), pp. 289-96.

[6] Paz, *Popular Anti-Catholicism,* p. 11.

did with other key ideological cornerstones of Victorian society, i.e. nationalism and Liberalism. The nationalist dimension of a threat from a foreign power, twinned with perceptions of a violation of civil and religious liberties, allowed those of a more Liberal persuasion, who generally tended to stay clear of "No Popery" baiting, to enter the fray. Undoubtedly, the perceived encroachments of the Pope on British liberties acted as means by which these views could be expressed legitimately but an examination of the local Liberal and Conservative papers dominant in the North East of England reveal just how blurred views were at the outset of the crisis.

The initial reaction from the Liberal weeklies was somewhat muted. The local press either chose to ignore the issue or attempted to play down the significance of the Papal bull. The *Sunderland Herald*'s initial editorial on 26 October found the reaction incomprehensible. "After all", it opined of the new bishoprics, "what is in a name, beyond an impertinence?"[7] Similarly, the Liberal and Anglican *Shields Gazette* stated confidently that it saw as much chance of the Pope obtaining absolute spiritual dominion of England "as there is of the conversion of India, or China, or any other heathen community, to the faith of the gospel".[8] It was the publication of the Liberal Prime Minister's Durham Letter which brought a hardening of attitudes. For a leader who was a self-proclaimed follower of the principles of civil and religious liberty the Durham Letter seemed an odd statement of intent.[9] It appeared that Russell had abandoned these principles in favour of the "political possibilities" of a "No Popery" policy which in the past had been the exclusive preserve of the Ultra-Protestant worldview.[10]

Whether the Prime Minister's outburst was a spontaneous expression of anti-Catholicism[11] or a calculated political manoeuvre[12] is perhaps immaterial. It only succeeded in encouraging a nationwide revival of popular anti-Catholicism. Indeed, for many Liberals, the publication of the Durham Letter was a cause for celebration. Their Liberal leader had

---

[7] *Sunderland Herald,* 26 October 1850.

[8] *Shields Gazette,* 26 October 1850.

[9] Usherwood, S., '"No Popery" Under Queen Victoria', *History Today,* 23.4 (1973), p. 278.

[10] R.J. Klaus, *The Pope, the Protestants, and the Irish: Papal Aggression and Anti-Catholicism in Mid-Nineteenth Century England.* (New York and London: Garland Publishing, 1987), pp. 172-3.

[11] D.G. Paz, 'Another Look at Lord John Russell and the Papal Aggression, 1850', *The Historian,* 45.1 (1982), p. 48; Wolffe, *Protestant Crusade,* p. 244.

[12] J.B. Conacher, 'The Politics of the "Papal Aggression" Crisis, 1850-51', *Canadian Catholic Historical Association Report,* 26 (1959), p. 17.

produced, as the *Durham Chronicle* observed, a manifesto which is a "matter of great congratulation and undeniable importance, and clearly evinces that . . . it is a truly Protestant spirit that guides the helm of the State".[13] The *Sunderland Herald* now felt free to express indignation "at the assumptions of a power, which has ever been the enemy of unfettered thought and free enquiry, in all fields of knowledge, and all matters of life".[14] A leader in the *Newcastle Chronicle*, an influential Liberal newspaper, saw the issue as a matter for ridicule that "this free and glorious realm of England . . . should stoop from her proud position and voluntarily place her neck beneath the foot of a foreign priest".[15]

In the question of who was to blame for the Papal measure, the Liberal press followed their leader's example to look no further than the "Puseyite" Anglican clergymen, whose "Romanist" innovations were destroying the Established Church from within.[16] The *Shields Gazette* saw a clear relationship between Papal Aggression and Puseyism. "The Puseyites", it argued, ". . . who have been coquetting so long with Rome, and affecting to bewail the Reformation as a mistake, have been startled from their medieval dream by the bellow of a real Vatican bull". Indeed, the *Newcastle Chronicle* believed that the Papal Aggression had given "Puseyites" a choice—either remain true to Anglican principles or convert to Catholicism. Of the latter, the paper had few worries. "If all those who are Romanists in heart, become Romanists by profession", it believed, "Protestantism will gain rather than lose".[17] The Puseyite factor was also of central importance to the Liberal *Darlington and Stockton Times*. Its initial leader focused its attentions firmly on this grouping, arguing that the high clergy have no right to "complain of any aggressive movements of the Roman Catholic church" given that their (high church) teachings have "tended towards Rome".[18] Indeed, the paper defended the Durham Letter precisely because it exposed the "apostasy of a large number of the English clergy, who have prepared the way by secret . . . for this open attack upon our Church and Crown".[19] Even the *Gateshead Observer*, a paper notable for its toleration towards other religious groups, could not resist an attack on the Popery in the Established Church. "No doubt of it!"

---

[13] *Durham Chronicle*, 15 November 1850.
[14] *Sunderland Herald,* 8 November 1850.
[15] *Newcastle Chronicle*, 16 November 1850.
[16] Wallis, *Popular Anti-Catholicism*, p. 65.
[17] *Newcastle Chronicle*, 8 November 1850.
[18] *Darlington and Stockton Times,* 26 October 1850.
[19] *Darlington and Stockton Times*, 9 November 1850.

it exclaimed, "The Protestantism of this country is in more danger from the Anglican than from the Romish Church . . ."[20]

The Tractarian factor also played a part in how the Conservative newspapers of the region viewed the agitation. While the Liberal newspapers presented a united front against the Papal Aggression in the initial stages of the crisis, the opinions of the two Conservative newspapers in Newcastle and Durham were influenced by the pro-Tractarian views of their editors. They were faced with a clear dilemma. If the agitation had concentrated solely on Roman Catholicism, then the Conservative press would have had little difficulty in expressing anti-Catholic opinion. As it was, the fury was also directed towards the Tractarian party, of which the *Newcastle Journal* and *Durham Advertiser* were both keen supporters. The *Newcastle Journal* managed to avoid the issue entirely by ignoring the Tractarian element and focus its energies on the Papal bull and the Roman Catholics. It saw the matter as an aggressive act of invasion by the Pope. "No foreign priest", it argued, "possesses . . . any ecclesiastical power or authority in this free and enlightened country".[21] The patriotic dimension of its anti-Catholicism was also evident in another early leader which argued that "the corrupt and idolatrous Romish church is at this moment engaged in a crusade to recover the supremacy she lost in the sixteenth century", while a later polemic attacked the Papal measure as "a general and deeply planned conspiracy against the religious freedom of Europe".[22]

The *Durham Advertiser*, however, chose to proceed down a different route. The paper was very much an organ for local Tractarian opinion. The paper took the unusual stance of attacking the anti-Catholic agitation itself, believing that the majority of the comments made against the Papal bull were "angry and senseless".[23] If the Pope was to blame for anything, the paper argued in a further editorial, it was the holding back of those souls who "were struggling into the glorious light of catholicity from the vague negations of Protestantism".[24] Not surprisingly, the *Durham Chronicle* pounced on its "semi-Popish" contemporary and saw the *Advertiser's* views as proof that Tractarianism wanted nothing more than "to undermine and destroy the Protestant Establishments of this kingdom".[25] Lord John Russell's letter was met with a stern rebuke by the *Advertiser*

---

[20] *Gateshead Observer,* 9 November 1850.

[21] *Newcastle Journal,* 22 November 1850.

[22] *Newcastle Journal,* 26 October and 9 November 1850.

[23] *Durham Advertiser,* 26 October 1850.

[24] *Durham Advertiser,* 22 November 1850.

[25] *Durham Chronicle,* 22 November 1850.

for stirring Protestant passions "to their lowest depths" and the paper denounced the local Anglican clergy who took part in the agitation. Indeed, the virulent anti-Catholic language of the *Durham Chronicle* could be seen as a reaction against its contemporary—as the *Advertiser* refused to wield the "No Popery" banner, its Liberal rival took up the mantle. Examples of this nature show the way in which the role of the provincial press was more than just a retread of the opinions of the metropolitan papers, as R.J. Klaus has suggested, and were often affected by local circumstances.[26]

Political Agitation

For many Protestants, the opinions of the Prime Minister and the press had left no doubt in their minds of the necessity of responding in some way to the perceived Papal threat. At the forefront of the agitation were the Anglican clergy. This is not surprising given that the Papal bull appeared for many Anglicans to be a direct attack on the jurisdiction of their bishoprics. Owen Chadwick has noted that the Bishop of London, for the first time in centuries, encouraged his clergy to preach controversial sermons during the opening months of the agitation[27] and it seems likely that the Bishop of Durham gave a similar consent, owing to the amount of anti-Catholic sermonising among the North East clergy throughout November and December.[28] The Vicar of Newcastle, the Rev. R.C. Coxe, adopted this stance in his Sunday morning services to lecture on the errors and corruptions of the Roman Catholic Church, beginning with the doctrine of purgatory in which he "proved" that "there was not a tittle in the Word of God to support it". He also attacked the Papal Aggression itself, believing that it would either make the Pope "the despot of the world" or "precipitate Rome's sure impending doom . . ."[29] A similar course was adopted by the Rev. William King, Rector of St Mary-Le-Bow in Durham, taking the text from his first discourse from Matthew 13:8-10 to show that St Peter was never Bishop of Rome and, therefore, neither

---

[26] Klaus, *The Pope*, p. 221.

[27] Owen Chadwick, *The Victorian Church,* vol. I (London: Adam and Charles Black, 1971), pp. 293-94.

[28] M.E. Burstein notes that the anti-Catholic sermon could be hugely influential because it had 'the ability to respond almost instantly to the ebb and flow of particular Protestant causes'. M.E. Burstein, 'Anti-Catholic Sermons in Victorian Britain', *A New History of the Sermon in the Nineteenth Century,* ed. by R. H. Ellison (Boston: Brill Academic, 2010), p. 233.

[29] Coxe, *Church Subjects*, p. 4.

should the Pope claim such a title. At the end of the sermon *God Save the Queen* was played on the organ.[30] The more active Evangelicals also took it upon themselves to tour the region. For example, the notorious Durham Evangelical, the Rev. George Fox, preached on such controversial topics as the "The Bible: The Sole Rule of Faith" at St. Hilda's, South Shields.[31] The preaching of the Rev. Alex Howell at St. Cuthbert's Church, Darlington, to a "crowded and attentive auditory" on the "Errors of Romanism" won the backing of the *Darlington and Stockton Times* who saw the local clergymen preaching against the Papal Aggression and Roman Catholicism as performing a duty "which seems to be imperatively required of them by this present emergency".[32]

Indeed, the fact that the recipient of the Prime Minister's letter was Edward Maltby, the Bishop of Durham, ensured that the issue was a particularly prominent one for the local diocesan clergy.[33] The Dean and Chapter of Durham, comprising both High Churchmen and Evangelicals, sent an address to their Bishop declaring their "unabated attachment to the Reformed Church of England". The address was so worded as to appeal to all groups within the Anglican Church but it proved to be one of the few occasions in which the Evangelical and High Church groups in Durham were united during this episode.[34] Numerously-signed addresses were also sent to the Bishop of Durham from clergymen and parishioners. An address from the clergy and laity of Sunderland regarded the Papal measure as "an aggression upon the Protestant Constitution of this realm" and promised to "unite in doing whatever lawfully and charitably may be done to uphold the prerogative of the Crown, and defend the rights and privileges of the Church".[35]

It soon became clear, however, that the issue was more than just a clerical affair affecting the Anglican Church and its parishioners. As John Wolffe has noted, the Papal bull was, for many people, an attack not just on their religion but also on their identity and conception of nationhood.[36]

---

[30] *Durham Advertiser*, 22 November 1850.

[31] G.T. Fox, *The Bible the Sole Rule of Faith*.

[32] *Darlington and Stockton Times*, 23 November 1850.

[33] Edward Maltby was a 'Whig' Bishop who had supported the 1829 Catholic Relief Act but who had no sympathy for Roman Catholicism or Tractarianism, see H.C. Fowler, 'Edward Maltby: His Episcopal Superintendence and Views as Bishop of Durham, 1836-1856' (unpublished master's thesis, University of Durham, 1989), pp. 55, 80.

[34] *Durham Chronicle*, 15 November 1850.

[35] *Newcastle Journal*, 22 November 1850.

[36] John Wolffe, *God and Greater Britain* (London: Routledge, 1994), pp. 113-4.

It seemed essential that they respond in some way to this perceived aggression and public memorials to the Queen were drawn up in all parts of the country. In some major towns in the North East, such as Sunderland, Gateshead and Hartlepool, door-to-door petitioning proved to be a very popular mode of obtaining signatures. With the exception of Gateshead, the petitions drawn up were fairly similar in style; attacking the Papal Bull as a threat to the British Constitution, as well as civil and religious liberty, and declaring loyalty towards the monarch. In this activity, clergymen were also active in organising the protest. Mary Raine wrote to her grandson describing the way in which her husband, the Rev. William Raine, "was busy now going from home to home to get a Paper signed by all the People about the saucy Pope".[37]

In other areas, there was a requirement for a more visible form of protest in the shape of that great Victorian institution, the public meeting. However, those responsible for organising the various meetings had underestimated the truly overwhelming response generated by this issue. In Newcastle, the Guildhall was originally chosen as the venue for a meeting at the end of November 1850. Handbills were posted around the town, calling upon the "Protestant inhabitants to rally round the faith of their forefathers . . . and upon the Catholics to maintain their rights".[38] However, it soon became apparent that it was far too small for the purpose. Long before the appointed time of 2pm, every seat was filled and the upper portion of the hall crammed as over two thousand people jostled for places. The Mayor, seeing that only one-tenth of those in the council room could enter the room, adjourned the meeting to the Corn Exchange. What followed next, according to the *Newcastle Journal*, clearly shows the hysterical atmosphere generated by the issue of the Papal Aggression:

> "There was a general rush down the staircases into the street, and a large body of persons running up the Side and Dean Streets, in their anxiety to secure places, presented a curious spectacle . . . Every gate of the Corn Exchange was soon besieged. In a few minutes, the north gates were opened and there was a great rush, in which several persons were roughly handled".[39]

The conduct of the Mayor, in arbitrarily deciding to adjourn to the Corn Market, was later called into question by the *Newcastle Chronicle*:

---

[37] DCRO, Letter from Mary Raine (Mrs William Raine) to Crozier Surtees Raine, 12 December 1850, D/X 332/171.
[38] *Shields Gazette*, 29 November 1850.
[39] *Newcastle Courant*, 29 November 1850.

"Had a few minutes consideration been given, and the sense of the meeting taken, it would have been seen how improper it was to adjourn to such a place, which is entirely unfitted for the purpose, and where a great deal of damage has been done".[40]

A similar situation occurred at the Durham town meeting where the "most numerous meeting held in the City of Durham since the era of the Reform Bill" was forced to adjourn to the New Hall after it was found that the Town Hall was insufficient for the occasion: "As the doors were thrown open, a dense crowd pressed in . . . (and) every corner was completely crammed, and not only so but the lobby and entrances only".[41] At South Shields, the Seamen's Hall was "quite crowded and many were unable to gain admission"[42] and at Stockton, the Town Hall was "completely filled" by a "large and very enthusiastic meeting".[43] From the reports of meetings elsewhere, it is possible to see that the popularity of the issue was not only confined to the larger urban areas. A meeting at Shildon was described as "numerously attended"[44] and at Hetton-Le Hole "a very large meeting of the inhabitants" took place.[45] Nowhere was this issue treated with indifference, and it is clear the local correspondent of the *Tablet's* assumption that the "the people (of the North East) are not responding to the 'No Popery' cry"[46] was little more than wishful thinking.

The meetings themselves were filled with expressions of bellicose patriotism and self-confident triumphalism emanating from a number of different quarters. Caroline Scott suggests that the Newcastle meeting was "Anglican-dominated"[47] but this assumption is clearly incorrect as the meeting was not dominated by clergy of any denomination. The organisers of the meeting were a mixture of Anglican and Dissenting ministers, with a small proportion of laymen[48] and the social composition of the meeting itself, or at least those who spoke during them, reveals the extent to which the Papal Aggression had transcended the boundary from being purely a religious issue concerning Anglican clergymen, to one in which laymen

---

[40] Ibid.
[41] *Durham Chronicle*, 6 December 1850.
[42] *Shields Gazette*, 29 November 1850.
[43] *Sunderland Herald,* 22 November 1850.
[44] *Darlington and Stockton Times*, 29 November 1850.
[45] *Newcastle Journal,* 14 December 1850.
[46] *Tablet*, 9 November 1850.
[47] Scott, 'Comparative Re-examination', p. 101.
[48] *Newcastle Journal* , 22 November 1850.

took an active part.[49] The Mayor opened the meeting with an unashamedly partisan speech, describing the Papal Bull as "an attack upon the free, tolerant and happy constitution under which the people of England had so long lived together in harmony". Ralph Walters, an alderman, saw the issue as "an attempt . . . against the just prerogative of the Crown" and Mr. Blackwell, a journalist, hoped that "Englishmen would never allow any foreign power to devise enactments and make bishops, and say that the souls of all classes should be under them". Other speakers included further members of the council as well as a respected local surgeon.[50]

Meetings held elsewhere also expressed the sentiments of the town or city's financial and religious elite. Durham's status as a bishopric saw a more Anglican-dominated platform. The three most prominent anti-Catholic Anglican ministers of the town, the Rev. Dr. George Townsend, the Rev. George Fox and Canon William S. Gilly all made long and impassioned speeches, as did Professor Johnson, who was Professor in Chemistry at the (essentially Anglican) University of Durham. It is notable that no High Churchmen spoke on the platform given the Low-High alliance in the formation of the address to the Bishop of Durham. Indeed, High Churchmen were actively critical of their Evangelical contemporaries for their appearance in the meeting. Two laymen, Mr. Spearman and Mr. Bramwell, and a Congregationalist minister, the Rev. Samuel Goddall, were the other speakers.[51] Other areas reflected the composition of the Newcastle meeting by drawing support from influential civic, industrial and religious notables. Of the 14 speakers at the South Shields meeting, seven were ministers (four Anglicans and three Dissenters), with the other seven speakers comprising of the "principal inhabitants of the town" including ship-owners and councillors.[52] Similarly at the Stockton meeting, where the Mayor opened the proceedings, only four ministers (out of twelve) were present as either speaker or seconder to a resolution. These included the Anglican vicars of Trindon, Stockton and Norton, although Dissenters were present among the laymen, such as a Mr. Samuel who was described as a Methodist.[53]

While the meetings and addresses expressed a range of anti-Catholic opinions, not everyone supported their objects, not least the Dissenting groups. As shown in the last chapter, Dissenters could often be found

---

[49] It seems that this social composition was evident in other areas too. See O'Leary, 'When was Anti-Catholicism?', p. 314.
[50] *Newcastle Journal*, 22 November 1850.
[51] *Durham Chronicle*, 6 December 1850.
[52] *Shields Gazette*, 29 November 1850.
[53] *Sunderland Herald*, 22 November 1850.

sympathising with the Catholic cause, or at the very least with Catholics as individuals with basic rights.[54] Furthermore, many Dissenters did not recognise the authority of the Queen in spiritual matters and there is some local evidence to suggest that this caused a dilemma in responding to the Papal Bull. At the Newcastle meeting the Congregationalist minister, the Rev. John Rogers, was unable to recognise the Queen's spiritual authority and at the South Shields meeting the Presbyterian minister, the Rev. John Storie, refused to sign the requisition for this reason also. A meeting in Blaydon was attended by thirty Dissenters, who signed the requisition purely on "political grounds". One gentleman present could not understand why any Dissenter should sign the requisition as there was essentially no difference between the Queen and the Pope.[55] These hesitations from Dissenters did not go unnoticed, and the *Newcastle Journal* lost no opportunity in attacking them. A letter to the newspaper questioned why the Dissenters chose to be present at all in the Newcastle meeting, given they were "bound both by need and position to oppose all alliance between Church and State".[56]

It is important to note that a refusal to acquiesce with the view that the Queen was the spiritual head of the Church did not mean that those Dissenters who shared this view were pro-Catholic, or against the idea of a monarchy *per se*. Indeed, for many Dissenters, this dilemma only made them more determined to defend their Protestant identity against the Papal threat. It was, as Timothy Larsen put it, "a moment when the dissenting community failed to live up to its own noble principles".[57] This was particularly the case in the Dissenter-dominated North East. Both the Rev. John Storie and the Rev. John Rogers were notable organisers of anti-Catholic activity in South Shields and Newcastle respectively and thus were determined to find a way around the dilemma. Both saw the solution in defending the Queen's *temporal* rights against the Pope. Storie had a reputation as a strict Presbyterian with strong opinions,[58] and this is apparent in a letter to the *Shields Gazette*. "There can be no dispute,"

---

[54] According to John Bossy, Catholics and non-Protestant Dissenters shared such a similar outlook in the post-reformation period that Catholicism should even be regarded as a strand of Nonconformity. John Bossy, *The English Catholic Community 1570-1850* (London: Darton, Longman and Todd, 1975), pp. 391-401.

[55] *Gateshead Observer*, 9 November 1850.

[56] *Newcastle Journal*, 7 December 1850.

[57] Timothy Larsen, *Friends of Religious Equality: Nonconformist Politics in Mid-Victorian England* (Woodbridge: The Boydell Press, 1999), p. 243.

[58] W.B. Robertson, *St. John's Presbyterian Church, South Shields Tercentenary Year Book, 1662-1962* (South Shields: [n. pub.] 1962).

Storie wrote, "that in the Queen alone is vested, by law, the power to make diocese, to nominate bishops and bestow dignitaries. It may be the law is fuddy, but if the power is bad when vested with the Queen, it becomes intolerable if the Pope usurp it . . ."[59] The Rev. John Rogers would have agreed with Storie, commenting at the Newcastle meeting that the Queen was a far more favourable alternative to the Pope, seeing her as a "warm supporter of civil and religious liberties". Rogers therefore disagreed with the views of the *Nonconformist* newspaper which urged Dissenters not to join forces with other denominations on this issue.[60]

Indeed, the Congregationalists in the North East of England seemed to follow the views expressed by Rogers. At the Durham meeting, the Rev. Samuel Goddall, a Congregationalist minister and another notable anti-Catholic, considered the Papal Bull as an act of civil aggression. He was, therefore, "fully persuaded to act" in asking "all faithful and loyal subjects to raise the voice of loud and indignant remonstrance, and to say that it should not be".[61] Similar views were expressed at the annual meeting of the Independent church connected with St James's Congregational Chapel in Newcastle. The Rev. Alexander Reed remarked that he "gloried in being a protestant dissenter, but he gloried still more in holding those peculiar doctrines which distinguished the Reformation from Popery". D.H. Goddard further suggested that the Papal Aggression "behoved protestants to be true to their principles, and to be earnest and persevering in their efforts".[62] In Sunderland, the Congregationalist minister, the Rev. R.W. McAlt, even held a public meeting in his own chapel to protest against the Papal Aggression.[63]

The Presbyterians were no less active in agitating against the Pope. The Newcastle Presbytery were actively involved in discussing the matter in their internal meetings and passing resolutions against the "Popish movement at present agitating the earth"[64] and at the Trinity Free Church in Durham, a meeting was assembled to "have a word with the Pope about his recent line of conduct" wherein the minister of the Church, Mr. Duncan, designated the Bull as "bold and singularly audacious".[65] Moreover, at a Presbyterian meeting in South Shields it was even decided

---

[59] *Shields Gazette*, 22 November 1850.
[60] G.I.T. Machin, *Politics and the Churches in Great Britain, 1832-68* (Oxford: Clarendon Press, 1977), p. 222.
[61] *Durham Chronicle, 6* December 1850.
[62] *Newcastle Chronicle*, 27 December 1850.
[63] *Sunderland Herald*, 6 December 1850.
[64] TWAS, 'Minutes of Newcastle Presbytery', 17 November 1850, II (1832-1855).
[65] *Durham Chronicle*, 22 November 1850.

to form a committee to "watch over this movement" by organising petitions and memorials as well as arranging the delivery of lectures on "the position of the Romish body, and its chief mission agencies".[66]

The Methodists, with a long tradition of anti-Catholicism, could react clearly and consistently against the Papal measure in spite of their internal problems.[67] At a meeting of expelled Methodists in South Shields in December 1850, the Rev. William Griffiths attacked his former church, believing that if the Pope "was a Methodist preacher (Wesleyans) would kiss his toe". He also stated that he "hated Popery and would use all his strength on putting it down".[68] Nor were Methodist preachers willing to be outdone by their Anglican rivals in the field of sermonising and lecturing against the Papal Bull. In Darlington, the Rev. George Jackson gave a lecture on 'The Errors of Popery' in the Bondgate chapel consisting of "a happy selection from the works of talented protestant writers".[69]

In general, the Papal Aggression proved a successful issue on which Evangelicals and Dissenters could unite against a common enemy. According to D.M. Lewis, the episode provided a "significant advance in pan-evangelical cooperation" between the two groups.[70] Only the Quakers and the Unitarians avoided the anti-Catholic baiting of their other Dissenting contemporaries. In the Newcastle meeting, the Unitarians questioned the purpose of the gathering. The Rev. G. Harris followed the stance of the Congregationalists and Presbyterians in attacking the power of the Queen. He believed that "to get up a memorial to the sovereign was sheer folly. . .(as) no human authority had the right to dictate in matters of belief".[71] He was, however, more tolerant to the Catholics than either Rev. John Storie or Rev. John Rogers in moving a resolution to the memorial, to the effect that the "blessings of civil and religious liberties which they enjoyed" should be given to his "fellow countrymen of all persuasions".[72] The Quakers remained very quiet publicly throughout this controversy, but the fact that Darlington, a town with a strong Quaker influence, was one of the few places in the region neither to petition nor memorialise the Queen on the subject is perhaps indicative of Quaker opinion on this matter. It is important, however, not to assume that all Quakers shared the same

---

[66] *Shields Gazette,* 13 December 1850.

[67] Paz, *Popular Anti-Catholicism*, p. 172.

[68] *Shields Gazette*, 13 December 1850.

[69] *Darlington and Stockton Times*, 30 November 1850.

[70] D.M. Lewis, *Lighten Their Darkness: The Evangelical Mission to Working-Class London, 1828-1860* (Connecticut: Greenwood Press, 2001), p. 194.

[71] *Newcastle Journal*, 22 November 1850.

[72] *Newcastle Courant*, 29 November 1850.

opinions in their toleration towards Roman Catholics. Edward Pease, part of the Quaker family dynasty which controlled Darlington, wrote in his diary for 6 November 1850 that he hoped the "arrogance of the (Papal) measure . . . would be indignantly repelled by the people and the legislature".[73] In spite of what they thought privately, though, the Quakers generally kept aloof from the agitation.

The addresses sent to the Queen throughout the country were published by Parliament the following year.[74] This published document is particularly important in revealing evidence of which towns and villages responded to the Papal Aggression, as well as the numbers who added their signature to them. Denis Paz has tabulated these signatures to compare regional fluctuations in the responses of the 42 counties of England. Given the amount of interest in the subject of the Papal Aggression in the North East, it is perhaps surprising to learn that the county of Durham is ranked at number 34, with Northumberland (which included Tyneside) faring only slightly better (30).[75] However, there could be several possible reasons for this. Firstly, there is a clear Anglican bias in the majority of addresses sent to the Queen which may have dissuaded Dissenters and others from signing them. For example, a number of addresses claim to be signed by the churchwardens, the rector/vicar, and the inhabitants. Even the seemingly innocuous phrase "from the inhabitants of the parish" may have been disagreeable to Dissenters because of the use of the word "parish". In the North East, where the Anglicans were the minority religion in many places (at least in terms of practise), this would have presented a dilemma for those Dissenters who would have wanted to express their disapproval at the Papal Bull but would have felt compromised in signing an "Anglican" address. Indeed, it is noteworthy that addresses framed in this way were only successful in certain areas which had a large Anglican presence, such as Tynemouth, where 3,800 signed the address from the "clergy, churchwardens and parishioners". Secondly, Paz has conceded that the figures are distorted because, in some town meetings, the address is only signed by the chairman of the meeting.[76] In the North East, the town meetings would

---

[73] Alfred E. Pease, *The Diaries of Edward Pease: The Father of English Railways* (London: Herdley Brothers, 1907), p. 286.
[74] 'Return of the Number of Addresses which have been presented to Her Majesty on the Subject of the Recent Measures taken by the Pope for the Establishment of a Roman Catholic Hierarchy in this Country', *Parliamentary Papers*, 1851, 59 (84), pp. 649-739.
[75] Paz, *Popular Anti-Catholicism*, p. 43.
[76] Ibid, p. 41.

have been particularly important in not only uniting the various denominations under a shared "Protestant" banner, but in representing a broad base of lay opposition to the Papal Bull. However, it appears that all the major town meetings in Newcastle, Durham and Stockton were only signed by the Chairman, thereby only contributing three signatories to the total for the counties of Durham and Northumberland. Paz believes that his method is a "broadly accurate measure" of measuring public sentiment against the Papal Bull. This is questionable given that those meetings expected to contribute the greatest numbers of signatories to the total in reality only contributed a single signature.[77] It is also not possible to gauge the strength of popular feeling (whether Anglican or Dissenter, lay or religious) that the Papal Bull generated in the localities without closer examination of the local sources.

The Reaction of the Catholics

The majority of speakers in the meetings and the language of the petitions made great pains to avoid offending their "Roman Catholic fellow-subjects", arguing that it was merely a protest against the Papal measure and not an attack on the Catholics themselves. However, there were instances which show how the Papal Aggression episode was stretching the limits of toleration. At the Durham meeting, the notoriously anti-Catholic Anglican minister, the Rev. Dr. Townsend, was astonished at the reaction of the audience who responded with "loud and continued cheers", when he made the controversial suggestion that the Penal Laws should be re-enacted against the Roman Catholics. He had expected this suggestion to be met with strong opposition.[78] At the South Shields meeting, Mr. Swinburne spoke as a "friend of toleration" to Roman Catholics, but then appeared to blame them for awakening the "spirit of religious controversy and intolerance".[79]

There is also evidence to suggest that this episode was affecting the treatment of Catholics in the wider society. At the election of governors for the Gateshead Dispensary it was alleged that the local Roman Catholic, Dr. Charlton, had lost because a fellow governor, Dr. Robinson, had "create(d) a prejudice against him".[80] Nor was it safe for Roman Catholics to walk the streets in Gateshead, where they were regularly "greeted with

---

[77] Ibid, p. 42.
[78] *Durham Chronicle*, 6 December 1850.
[79] *Shields Gazette,* 29 November 1850.
[80] *Gateshead Observer,* 18 January 1851.

cries from the walls of 'Beat the Pope!', 'To Hell with the Pope!' and 'The Devil take the Pope!'".[81] In May 1851, the Northumberland and Durham correspondent for the *Tablet* noted with dismay that "society is undergoing an unfavourable change; bigots, whose language would have called forth the most indignant reproof from their more intelligent neighbours, now are sanctioned and supported". This observation was made after a report of a Catholic student of "a town in the diocese" harassed by boys shouting 'Down with the Pope!' and 'Down with Popery!'"[82] Similarly, the *Tablet* reported the following year of the "considerable annoyance" caused by a set of Protestant boys in Darlington, who regularly collected together outside the Catholic school of the town, shouting insults such as "Papists" and "Romanists" and "not infrequently making use of sticks and stones by way of emphasis".[83]

So how did the Catholics themselves respond to the reaction of what was essentially an internal matter? Some Catholics who were notable figures in the region managed to obtain a platform at the public meetings to air their views, particularly in the larger urban areas where the influence of Catholicism was strong. Their presence as speakers at these meetings had given the organisers a dilemma—allowing them to speak could cause further incitement to both Protestants and Catholics present, but to prevent them from doing so would threaten to break the moral code of freedom of speech that was so beloved of the Victorians.[84] The celebrated local orator Charles Larkin was a case in point.[85] His appearance on the platform at the Newcastle meeting suggested that the organisers had given him the opportunity to speak though they probably wished they had decided against it. Mr. Larkin could not resist the opportunity of infuriating the Protestant section of the audience. He attacked those who supported the memorial as "intolerants and persecutors", arguing that they would re-enact the penal laws against Catholics given the chance. Most damning of all, he claimed that he would support the Pope and "trample on the royal prerogative of the Queen of England". This latter comment caused uproar

---

[81] *Gateshead Observer,* 23 November 1850.

[82] *Tablet,* 24 May 1851.

[83] *Tablet,* 23 October 1852.

[84] This is typified in the ideas of John Stuart Mill. See Mill, *Utilitarianism.*

[85] Charles Larkin appeared to be something of a local celebrity in the area, not only for his outspoken opinions, but also for the flamboyant language he employed. He had spoken in favour of Catholic Emancipation in 1829, as well as being an agitator for the Northern Political Union, a local body in favour of the Reform Act. See T. P. Macdermott,, 'Charles Larkin, Radical Reformer, 1800-1879', *Northern Catholic History,* 28 (1988), pp. 13-7.

in the audience and his attempts to continue were met with "yells, shouts and whistles", eventually forcing him to stand down.[86]

Whatever the reason for Larkin's outburst, there is no doubt that his appearance visibly stirred a large number of Newcastle's sizable Irish Catholic community, many of whom turned out in support of their spiritual leader. The Conservative *Newcastle Courant* reported several vocal disturbances from Irish Catholics throughout the meeting. Thus, when Charles Rogue mentioned Lord John Russell in his speech, an Irish voice was heard to shout "Down with him and up with the Pope!" The anti-Irish attitude of the press is apparent in their descriptions of the Irish response. The *Shields Gazette*, reporting on the meeting, believed the Irish "set up the most unearthly howls ever heard in Newcastle, or any other civilised town in the kingdom . . . producing a . . . compound resembling wind that had got into an old farm chimney and could not get out again, and Wombwell's wild beasts at feeding time . . ."[87] In spite of the turbulence of the meeting and the potential for serious trouble, there was no repeat of the Birkenhead public meeting in which clashes between Irish Catholics and English Protestants led to a full-scale riot.[88]

Larkin continued his tirade against the "No Popery movement" with a successful lecture tour throughout the country in the subsequent weeks and months, outraging the Protestant community even further. He lectured in Newcastle in February 1851 on the subject of the 'Temporal Power of the Pope', asserting that it was the duty of all Christians to "prevent all kings and queens from daring to usurp any domination or dominion in the church of Christ". He felt the wrath of the usually tolerant *Newcastle Guardian* whose reporter indicated that though Mr. Larkin was a "masterly speaker . . . his address was interspersed with the most foul and abusive language, that a report of it would defile the columns of any

---

[86] *Newcastle Courant*, 29 November 1850. In his autobiography written over 50 years later, J.G. Rogers believed that Larkin was attempting to delay the meeting until late afternoon when it would be impossible to continue in the darkness of the unlit Corn Exchange, thereby forcing the abandonment of the meeting. Rogers, *Autobiography*, pp. 95-6.

[87] *Shields Gazette*, 29 November 1850.

[88] Neal, *Sectarian Violence,* p. 131-3. In other towns and cities with an Irish presence, vocal disturbances from Irish contingents in Papal Aggression meetings were more the norm. For example, the response of the Catholic Irish in the York Papal Aggression meeting corresponds more with Newcastle. Marion Emes, 'Anti-Catholicism in York from the General Election of 1826 to the Opening of the New St. Wilfrid's Church in 1864' (unpublished master's thesis, York University, 1996). pp. 61-2.

newspaper".[89] When Larkin's lecture tour reached Hartlepool in July 1851, he was met by Mr. Lamb, an equally zealous No Popery lecturer, who proceeded to hold his own lectures attacking Larkin and the Papal Bull. These inflammatory speeches caused a "Boyne Day" riot amongst the Irish immigrants of the town.[90] Leo Gooch's assertion that Larkin's public lectures helped "to moderate the anti-Catholic hysteria" underestimates the anger caused by the Catholic speaker.[91]

Larkin was not the only Catholic to take a militant stance against the heightened anti-Catholic feeling in the locality. In Gateshead, the Roman Catholic priest of the area, Father Betham, was able to influence proceedings in quite a different way.[92] In October 1850, Betham circulated an appeal around Gateshead and Newcastle, calling for aid for the purpose of building a Catholic Church and parochial building in the former town. This would be a fairly standard request from a new priest who wished to begin a mission in a town with a large Catholic population and no means of worship. It was, however, his signature attached to his appeal which caused controversy. Betham signed himself as the "Parish Priest-Elect of Gateshead", seeing himself representing a parish that had been "too long left a widow deprived of a Church or resident pastor".[93] This was a direct attack on the Anglican clergyman of the town, the Rev. Dr. Davis, and caused a great deal of anger among the Protestant portion of the town, who saw this as yet another example of Romish tyranny. The *Newcastle Journal* believed that Betham's ultimate aim was to displace Davis of his incumbency at St Mary's, and thus "obtain possession of that venerable and substantial edifice". The paper even went as far as declaring that the "Parish Priest" had committed an act of felony, and was therefore subject to transportation.[94] Not surprisingly, Davis was particularly incensed. "So far as is known to me", Davis stated in a speech delivered to the Gateshead Church of England Young Men's Society, "Gateshead enjoys the enviable distinction of being the first parish in England of which a Romish priest has taken unceremonious possession".[95] The Anglican Rector capitalised on this heightened sense of religious feeling during the Papal Aggression

---

[89] *Newcastle Guardian*, 18 February 1851.

[90] See Chapter Six.

[91] Morris and Gooch, *Down Your Aisles*, p. 10.

[92] Father Frederick Betham was a convert born in Lincolnshire and trained at the English College in Rome. Morris and Gooch, *Down Your Aisles*, p. 140.

[93] RCHNDA, *Appeal by Fr. Betham for the funding of a new church in Gateshead*, October 1850, RCD 1/11/86.

[94] *Newcastle Journal*, 9 November 1850.

[95] *Gateshead Observer*, 7 December 1850.

by delivering a course of lectures under the heading of 'Scriptural Truth contrasted with Romish Error'. This was partly a response to a sermon preached by Betham at St Mary's, Newcastle, in which he attacked the "insidious and unjust outcry that has been raised against the Church by its enemies" following the Papal Bull.[96]

The Gateshead controversy was so great it even managed to influence the wording of the town's Papal Aggression petition sent to the Queen. A sentence was inserted in the middle which made explicit reference to the episode:

> "As indicative of the ultimate designs of the unscrupulous usurpation, an ordained functionary of the Roman Catholic Church has announced himself, in terms peculiarly unseemly, disloyal and offensive, as 'Parish-Priest Elect of Gateshead' and has stated his plans in such language as manifestly implies that he considers himself as invested with parochial functions".[97]

The fact that this petition was signed by 2,000 people, at least three-quarters of the population of the town[98], shows clearly the indignation of its inhabitants.

In general, the Catholics of the region were well organised in combating what they re-labelled as the "Protestant Aggression". Just as Protestants were willing to send memorials and petitions to the Queen showing their attachment to the throne, addresses were also sent from Catholic communities throughout the region, eager to show that their loyalty to the monarchy was not as suspect as some Protestants believed. At a Catholic Soirée in Darlington, the attachment to the Queen from the Catholic community was self-evident as the newly-appointed Roman Catholic Bishop of Hexham[99], William Hogarth, was received with loud applause when he mentioned the name of the Queen. In proposing "health, long life, and prosperity to the Queen, Prince Albert and all the Royal Family", he was also met with "unbounded enthusiasm". "Catholics at all times and in all ages", he argued, "had been remarkable for loyalty to their

---

[96] *Tablet,* 30 November 1850.

[97] *Gateshead Observer,* 16 November 1850.

[98] *Gateshead Observer*, 7 December 1850.

[99] It was originally intended for Newcastle to be the name of the diocese but Hogarth preferred Hexham because it was "by far the most central and easy access by means of railroad from all parts of the District and as to the idea of gratifying the people of Newcastle, I think it is of little value. A bishop may go into Newcastle occasionally on great occasions, but no-one should be condemned to live there . . .", quoted in Morris and Gooch, *Down Your Aisles,* p. 11.

sovereign".[100] Addresses were also sent to Cardinal Wiseman by the Catholics of the region, congratulating him on his appointment as Archbishop of Westminster and indicating just how much anger the Protestant response to the Catholic Hierarchy was causing in the Catholic community, as is evident in the address sent from the Catholic Clergy of the diocese to Wiseman:

> "We cannot, indeed, but feel sorrow and shame, for those of our deluded countrymen who have taken occasion from this event to reiterate calumnies against our holy religion which have been a thousand times refuted . . ."[101]

A similar sentiment can be observed in an address to the newly-installed Bishop of Hexham from the Catholic Clergy of South Durham, expressing the hope that the "storm of calumny and abuse which has of late raged so violently against our most Holy Father, and our venerable Bishop" had not affected him greatly.[102]

The response of both Wiseman and Hogarth to these addresses was typical of both men's aggressive determination and uncompromising zeal to overcome adversity and to further a sense of mission in the Catholic Church. For Wiseman:

> "The trials of the last few months have served, indeed, like a crucible, to cement more precisely the hearts of the clergy into a holy and happy union of zeal and love. The strength of the church has always been in her sufferings and we have no cause to fear that she is less able now than hencetofore to cope with the enmity of the world".[103]

Hogarth expressed similar sentiments in a more metaphorical way:

> "The raging tempest, which is now passing away, has but reminded us that our Church is founded on the Rock of Ages, and that although the winds may howl, and the waves may dash against it with never ceasing fury, the rock will remain unmoved until the end of time".[104]

---

[100] *Darlington and Stockton Times*, 12 January 1851.
[101] *Catholic Standard*, 15 February 1851.
[102] *Catholic Standard*, 1 March 1851.
[103] *Catholic Standard*, 15 February 1851.
[104] *Catholic Standard*, 1 March 1851.

"No Semi-Popery!": Targeting the "Puseyites"

The Catholic community were not the only religious grouping experiencing the full force of Protestant prejudice. As has been shown, the outcry against the Papal Bull saw a concentration of attack not only on the Roman Catholic Church, but also against those who wished to introduce "Popish" practices into the Anglican Church. Indeed, as Walter Ralls has suggested, it could be argued that the Tractarians (often disparagingly referred to as "Puseyites") faced more actual antagonism than the Roman Catholics in the backlash against the Papal measure.[105] This was in no small part due to the language of Lord John Russell's Durham Letter laying the blame for the encouragement given to the Papal Bull firmly on the Tractarians who wished to imitate the "mummeries of superstition". By doing this, it has been argued that Russell was attempting to deflect attention away from the Catholics onto the Tractarians.[106] However, according to Denis Paz, Russell's attempt to redirect the public hatred towards Tractarians only worked if the local conditions were right, i.e. Tractarianism only became a factor in meetings and petitions if the organisers were especially concerned about its growth.[107]

It has been suggested that Tractarianism had nothing more than an academic hold on the North East. This claim has been strengthened by a number of historians. W.B. Maynard has argued that the Durham clergy were rarely involved in Tractarian disputes[108] and further research by Nigel Yates has suggested that, by 1870, Ritualism (a later offshoot of Tractarianism) was notable by its absence in the parishes of the North East.[109] Given this supposition, it would be perfectly reasonable to

---

[105] Ralls, 'The Papal Aggression' p. 122.

[106] This was certainly a popular view at the time, so much so that even the Queen, who rarely commented on political issues, was pleased to see the 'unfortunate papal aggression direct the people's attention to the alarming tendency of the Tractarians'. Klaus, *The Pope*, p. 181.

[107] Paz, *Popular Anti-Catholicism*, p. 148.

[108] W.B. Maynard, 'The Ecclesiastical Administration of the Archdeaconry of Durham, 1774-1856' (unpublished doctoral thesis, University of Durham, 1973), p. 88.

[109] The diocese of Durham had only six Tractarian incumbents in 1870. This compares to 57 in the diocese of Oxford. Indeed Yates argues that Durham had the lowest number of Ritualist churches of all the dioceses. Nevertheless, the controversy surrounding the Bishop of Durham's treatment of the overtly Ritualist Durham clergyman, J.B. Dykes, in the 1860s and 1870s, suggests that Ritualism did have a small pocket of support in Durham City. See Nigel Yates, *Anglican Ritualism in Victorian Britain, 1830-1910* (Oxford: Oxford University Press,

presume that the nationwide vilification of Tractarians would not have found a voice in the North East as there was no culture to react against. Further research, however, reveals that Tractarianism maintained a small but defiant pocket of support throughout the North East, evident in the negative reaction to the continued growth of the movement. This initially took the form of clerical opposition. As early as 1837, the notoriously anti-Catholic George Townsend was issuing anti-Tractarian Charges to his clergy and in the following decade, when anti-Tractarian agitation had been building up something of a head of steam in response to the publication of John Henry Newman's Tract 90, Archdeacon Thorp followed suit.[110] Similarly, the Bishop of Durham was just as indignant at the seemingly unstoppable march of Tractarianism. In a Charge to his clergy in 1841, he stressed the importance of keeping a watchful eye on the dangers from "within" the Church of England:

> "So far from adding to the purity of our faith, as contrasted with those errors from which we believe that the reformation has set us free, the tendency appears to have been in a opposite direction . . . (and) to uphold them with such earnestness as to threaten the revivals of the evils of by-yore superstitions".[111]

In spite of the Bishop's warning, Tractarianism began to make its presence felt in some local Anglican churches from the late 1840s. As Pickering has suggested, once it moved out of Oxford, the movement began to "grow rapidly" in the parishes of England[112], the North East being no exception. Any sign of this "semi-Popery" was immediately acted upon, regardless of whether there was any substance in the accusations. The adorning of churches with the latest "Puseyite fashion", such as stained-glass windows featuring "our Saviour and the Virgin Mary" at Walker parish church[113], or the purchasing of an "altar" cloth for

---

1999), pp. 84, 113-4; and J.T. Fowler, *Life and Letters of John Bacchus Dykes* (London: John Murray, 1897).

[110] Gooch, 'From Jacobite to Radical', p.275; P. Toon, *Evangelical Theology, 1833-1856: A Response to Tractarianism* (London: Marshall, Morgan and Scott, 1979), pp. 36, 38.

[111] E. Maltby, '*Salutary Cautions Against the Errors Contained in the Oxford Tracts': A Charge to His Clergy, Delivered at St Nicholas' Church, Newcastle-upon-Tyne on Mon. August 9th 1841, by the Lord Bishop of Durham* (Newcastle: Blackwell & Co, 1841), p. 7.

[112] Pickering, *Anglo-Catholicism*, p. 42.

[113] *Newcastle Guardian*, 14 April 1849.

St Cuthbert's in Darlington[114], did not go unnoticed by those who feared the Church of England was returning to its Roman roots. It was not purely the outward signs of decoration which infuriated many church-goers. In Frosterley, Weardale, the local Rector and his curate were accused of observing the doctrines and devotional practices of "that qualified Romanism prescribed by Dr. Pusey". A letter to the *Durham Chronicle* described what this entailed:

> "(T)hey favour a dramatic form of worship, with the bowings, bendings, and wheel-about antics of scenic sanctity: they seek to exalt the authority of the Church, by enslaving the understandings of the people, and foisting upon the public mind the dogmas and deceits of a spurious religion".[115]

Similar accusations were levelled at Jarrow, where it appeared that the church was revisiting its pre-Reformation nadir. The Anglican minister, the Rev. John Carr, was accused of simony in allegedly purchasing his incumbency for £700.[116]

When the Papal Aggression burst onto the scene it was hardly surprising that anti-Tractarianism became a major issue in the region. Indeed, given that Evangelicals and Dissenters played a large part in the organisation of Papal Aggression memorials and petitions, the High-Church Tractarians were unlikely to escape vilification. Klaus's notion that, with the encouragement of the Durham Letter, High Churchmen received "psychological terrorizing"[117] is certainly as true of the North East as it was elsewhere. With the exception of one or two examples, all memorials and petitions in the locality made, at the very least, a passing mention to the detrimental effect of those "Puseyite" practices which were undermining the Protestant Church. The Newcastle memorial stated quite categorically the worrying influence of Tractarian doctrines introduced "by a considerable number of clergy in the Church of England".[118] Paz also suggests that references to Tractarianism in the memorials were based on local experience—its appearance suggesting fears brought about by the appearance of "Puseyite practices" in the local area.[119] Tractarianism was clearly a factor in the immediate vicinity of many towns, perhaps explaining its appearance in the memorials and petitions. These meetings

---

[114] *Darlington and Stockton Times*, 8 July 1848.
[115] *Durham Chronicle*, 14 April 1848.
[116] *Newcastle Guardian*, 10 February 1849.
[117] Klaus, *The Pope*, p. 180.
[118] Ibid.
[119] Paz, *Popular Anti-Catholicism*, p. 148.

and petitions were therefore reflecting these fears and it is likely that they gave encouragement to neighbouring anti-Tractarian agitation. This can be observed by a number of local accusations of "Puseyism" against High Churchmen. Although the agitation never reached the levels of St Barnabas, Pimlico, in which months of rioting took place against the Tractarian services of the Rev. W.J.E. Bennett[120], the number and range of disputes in the region suggests that the Prime Minister's attempt to deflect attention away from the Catholics was just as successful in the North East as anywhere.

Anti-Tractarian agitation was particularly acute in Durham[121]. The city had been a haven for the small pocket of Tractarian support in the region. Its clique of High Church clergy, who included Rev. Hugh James Rose and Rev. William Palmer and centred on the cathedral and the university, helped to foster an unpopular set of beliefs which ran counter to the prevailing religious culture.[122] Indeed, the Papal Aggression in the city effectively diverted anti-Catholic energies elsewhere as the Durham meeting against the new hierarchy was initially dominated by the Tractarian issue. This was assisted by the appearance of a locally-renowned Tractarian and his supporters. Before the meeting, a placard had been circulated announcing the intention of a Tractarian to oppose the objects of the meeting. This Tractarian turned out to be the Rev. Samuel Harper, who had been refused a licence by the Bishop of Durham because of his "Popish practices" at Newburn. Harper had written a pamphlet in support of the "Puseyite" party against the "No Popery" movement, and calling on the working classes to rise up against it.[123] He had also allegedly refused to stand up at a recent concert in Durham when the National Anthem was sung, arguing on the occasion that "if it had been God Save

---

[120] Pinnington, 'Bishop Blomfield', p. 293. As Morris has pointed out however, incidents of this type were extremely rare. J. Morris, 'The Regional Growth of Tractarianism: Some Reflections', *From Oxford to the People: Reconsidering Newman and the Oxford Movement*, ed. by P. Veiss (Leominster: Gracewing, 1996), p. 153

[121] Indeed, Durham University was at the centre of a Tractarian dispute after the publication of Tract 90 when attempts were made to suppress favourable opinions among the Durham students and masters to Newman's theories. See Louis Allen, 'Tract 90 and Durham University', *Notes and Queries*, 212 (1967), pp. 43-7.

[122] R. Lee, 'Class, Industrialization and the Church of England: The Case of the Durham Diocese in the Nineteenth Century', *Past and Present*, 191.1 (2006), p. 169.

[123] S. Harper, *Do Not Be Duped! A Letter of Counsel to the Labouring Classes on the No Popery Movement by the Writer of 'A Voice from the North'* (Newcastle: Kaye, 1850).

the Pope, I would have stood up!" However, a clergyman with such strong Tractarian sympathies was keen not to take a back-seat in the proceedings of the Papal Aggression meeting. As the crowds began to gather, Harper positioned himself in the main body of the hall and, once he was discovered, ignited the fury of the crowd who, according to the *Durham Chronicle*, "seemed determined to pull him in pieces". With some difficulty, he managed to pull over a temporary barricade, effectively blocking him from his adversaries. Harper and his supporters made frequent interruptions throughout the speeches. Cries of "Put him out!" followed as the speakers made reference not only to Tractarianism but also the conduct of Harper himself. The Rev. George Fox described him as a man who was "so extravagant in his ideas, so wild and self-sufficient, as justly to be entitled to be called the Buffoon of the Tractarians" and an "ill-bred, wretched creature".[124] Harper's sanity was also called into question by the *Durham Chronicle* in an editorial on the meeting, believing that he was "labouring under some disease of the mind".[125]

Other meetings were essentially anti-Tractarian, rather than anti-Roman Catholic, and clearly moulded by grievances against local Anglican clergymen which outlasted the initial hysteria surrounding the Papal Aggression. At the Wallsend meeting the attendees had a special reason to be wary of Puseyism. The Vicar of the parish, the Rev. John Armstrong, had long been accused of Puseyite practices and disparagingly referred to as the "Pope of Wallsend". It appeared to be a personal crusade of Mr. Bainbridge[126], a barrister who spoke at the Newcastle meeting, to "unmask" the real intentions of the Vicar, and the "Puseyite" practices of the High Church.[127] "Who was it that commenced the strife throughout the land?" he questioned, "Let them ask at Rome and if they found no answer there, let them ask at Oxford". Mr. Ralph Walters, who also spoke at the Newcastle meeting, continually attacked the vicar. "In the Scriptures, they

---

[124] *Durham Chronicle* , 6 December 1850.

[125] Ibid.

[126] William Bainbridge was a notable Liberal in Newcastle provincial life. "Lawyer Bainbridge", as he was known, was a "powerful and fervent speaker" who wrote pamphlets and delivered lectures on a variety of subjects. R. Welford, *Men of Mark 'Twixt Tees n' Tweed*, I (London: Walter Scott, 1895), pp. 169-72.

[127] This is in direct contrast to the Bainbridge's attitude to Armstrong nearly two years earlier. The barrister held a dinner for the choir of Armstrong's church in Wallsend, speaking in flattering terms of the difference between the choir in this parish and the "lugubrious psalmondy" in other, more Puseyite, churches. After the meal, Armstrong expressed his gratitude to Bainbridge for his kind words. *Gateshead Observer*, 20 January 1849. It appears, therefore, that the Papal Aggression may really have "awoken him from his slumber".

were commanded not to hear not man, but God", he argued, "and whether it was the Pope of Rome or the Pope of Wallsend (hear, hear), they would never find him bending to any one of these earthly pontates (sic)". Not surprisingly, given the atmosphere, Armstrong had declined to attend this meeting.[128] At a further meeting to consider "the general conduct of the incumbent (and) the manner in which the services are conducted". Seven hundred people squeezed into the parish church after the vestry was found to be too small to accommodate the overwhelming interest of the village's inhabitants. Resolutions were passed against the intolerance of Armstrong, "the overbearing demeanour towards his parishioners", calling for the Bishop of Durham's assistance in "this unhappy emergency".[129] However, the momentum ebbed away and little more was said on the matter following this meeting.[130]

In Tynemouth, the activities of the "Puseyite" vicar actually prevented the organisation of the Papal Aggression meeting. Although a numerously-signed petition had been forwarded to the Bishop of Durham from the inhabitants of Tynemouth, no town meeting was called to discuss the matter. The issue even reached the town council, who normally steered clear of religious matters. In a council meeting of the 4th December, an attempt was made by a Mr. Tinley to pass a resolution on the Papal Aggression. This proved to be unsuccessful as many councillors believed it was not the right place to discuss an issue of this nature.[131] It did, however, raise the question of why a public meeting had not been called by the Vicar and Churchwardens.[132] After all, the *Shields Gazette* argued, the Vicar and Churchwardens had the full authority to call a meeting of the parishioners. Indeed, the newspaper added, once a public meeting is called, "we do not doubt the Protestant followers of our fellow parishioners of Tynemouth will be expressed quite as plainly against the Puseyism within, as the Popery without, the Church"[133], a clear reference to the Puseyite activities in the town. This was further encouraged by an address which

---

[128] *Newcastle Guardian,* 28 December 1850.

[129] Ibid.

[130] Bad feeling continued to exist between the parishioners and Armstrong and by the end of the 1850s, many were refusing to pay the church rate in protest. W. Richardson, *History of the Parish of Wallsend* (Newcastle: Northumberland Press, 1923), p. 133.

[131] Successful memorials against the Papal Aggression from town councils were apparent in some other areas of the country, such as Southampton and York. Matthews, "'Second Spring'"; and Emes, 'Anti-Catholicism in York', p. 61.

[132] TWAS, Tynemouth County Council Minutes, 4 December 1850.

[133] *Shields Gazette*, 6 December 1850.

appeared in the same paper, calling on the inhabitants of the town to put a stop to the activities of the local Tractarian clergy:

> "It is now high time that a stop was put to these disgraceful fooleries, you must maintain a bold front, and by every lawful means compel these infatuated men to retrace their steps. Apply to your diocesan, and represent to him respectfully, but firmly, that it is your conscientious belief, that these unfaithful and Romanizing teachers are driving from the Establishment her best supporters, her most pious worshippers".[134]

In spite of this earnest appeal, it was not until 1853 that action was taken against one of the Anglican curates of the town, the Rev. John Blunt. In April, a memorial was sent to the Bishop of Durham, "protesting against the Puseyistic practices of the Rev. Blunt".[135] He was accused of preaching "Romish" doctrines and services, such as bowing to the communion table. Blunt published a sermon defending his views on the controversial subject of the Real Presence in the sacrament of the Lord's Supper, the introductory note of which stated: "this sermon was preached and published for the purpose of refuting a charge made against the Author of holding and teaching the doctrine of Tractarianism".[136] After an investigation, Blunt, who was a member of Durham University and was in the process of applying for ordination from the Bishop, was suspended for 12 months. The Bishop rejected the allegations against him of preaching "Romish doctrine" but suggested that his language was "mystical and confused" and he could not therefore be ordained.[137]

In some areas, the issue of Puseyite clergymen appeared to dwarf the agitation against the Papal Bull completely. Indeed, it was a particularly acute one in villages where the only alternative for the Anglican parishioner was to attend a Methodist chapel.[138] In Heworth, near Gateshead, the parish priest, the Rev. Matthew Plummer, was a long-standing clergyman of the village but was caught up in the wave of anti-Tractarian hysteria in the post-Papal Aggression period. That Plummer was influenced by Tractarian ideas can be seen by a section of his pamphlet written by his son, who cited the Oxford Movement as a huge influence on his father, suggesting that he was one of the earliest

---

[134] Ibid.

[135] *Shields Gazette*, 29 April 1853.

[136] J.H. Blunt, *The Real Presence: A Sermon by John Henry Blunt, Curate of Tynemouth, in the Diocese of Durham* (Durham: Andrews, 1853), p. 1.

[137] *Durham Chronicle*, 22 July 1853.

[138] Reed, *Glorious Battle*, p. 32.

clergymen in the North of England to "begin the work of restoring due order and decency to the Services of the Church".[139] Others were not quite so complimentary. In an editorial entitled "Another Clerical Exposure!" at the height of the Papal Aggression crisis, Plummer was accused by the *Newcastle Guardian* of "Romanizing" tendencies:

> "There are lighted candles upon the altar, and muttering and bowing most confounding to simple-minded parishioners of a rural township. But why do the churchwardens and people tolerate this? The Bishop of London has shown how it can be put down, and our own diocesan will not, we imagine, be less prompt and decisive".[140]

Following a crowded meeting to discuss the matter, it was decided to open a correspondence with the Bishop of Durham and to request that he use his authority to put an end to the current services in Heworth church.[141] Bishop Maltby ordered Plummer to abstain from these practices. Plummer was infuriated by the Bishop's conduct. In a letter to Maltby, the Heworth minister not only defended the innovations he had brought into the church services on the grounds that they were legally based on Edward VI's First Prayer Book[142], but also attacked the Bishop's partisan stance on the issue:

> "I cannot conceive, my Lord, why you should join a set of brawling agitators in their ungodly work. Why are such men allowed to annoy a peaceable and respectable congregation? . . . I need hardly say, that I trust your Lordship will see the necessity of acting strictly according to law, and that you will not attempt to exercise a power which you do not possess".[143]

A full scale investigation was launched by Archdeacon Thorpe for the purpose of "inquiring into the differences between the incumbent and the

---

[139] Charles Plummer, 'In Memoriam', Matthew Plummer, *Letter to the Lord Bishop of Durham, in Reference to the Late Proceedings in the Parish of Heworth* (Newcastle: Robert Robinson, 1852).

[140] *Newcastle Guardian*, 18 January 1850. Plummer was also accused of non-residency which was seemingly a familiar charge in the diocese of Durham, where the bishop was forced to issue 463 licenses for non-residence to 126 individuals. W.B. Maynard, 'Pluralism and Non-Residence in the Archdeaconry of Durham, 1774-1856: The Bishop and Chapter as Patrons', *Northern History*, 26 (1990), p. 123.

[141] *Newcastle Guardian*, 18 January 1851.

[142] Appealing to the First Prayer Book was a popular defence used by the Tractarians. Reed, *Glorious Battle*, p. 41.

[143] Plummer, *Letter to the Lord Bishop of Durham*, pp. 16-7.

churchwardens", although this came to nothing.[144] The enquiry appeared to be the last word on the subject officially, although a burglary in July 1853, in which the surplices and scarfs were thrown down and the candles smashed to pieces[145], suggests that popular feeling against Plummer's innovations still existed.

One of the more intense examples of the way in which popular passions could be stirred by the issues of Tractarianism and anti-Catholicism occurred in the Durham pit-village of Houghton-Le-Spring. The agitation proved to be particularly severe here because the issue became embroiled in other grievances, most notably the thorny issue of church rates and the creation of a new burial ground. Here, as elsewhere, the issue received its initial impetus from the Prime Minister's Durham letter and the Papal Aggression agitation but its roots can be located much earlier. The incumbent of Houghton Church was the Rev. John Grey, a member of the influential and aristocratic Grey family.[146] He was, in the vein of his Heworth counterpart, well known for his Tractarian leanings. Indeed, a letter from his brother Charles Grey to his wife, Caroline, on the subject of his appointment as Rector of Houghton in 1847, expressed the hope that John "will do nothing to harm the prejudices of the people but that he will be content to perform the service according to the old custom", as Maltby was particularly concerned with the "violence of his Tractarianism".[147] This was to be a forlorn hope. Grey was already making his presence felt with his introduction of new innovations to the parish services as early as the following year. The *Gateshead Observer* reported that although Grey had greatly improved the church choir with a number of scholars with good voices, "some of the good folks in the parish smell Puseyism in the reverend gentlemen's reforms".[148]

It was, as in other places, the Papal Aggression which acted as a catalyst to anti-Tractarian agitation in the village. In January 1851, eyebrows were raised when it was reported in the *Sunderland Herald* that Grey had placed a petition for signature in a stationer's shop against the Papal Aggression and in support of "the Reformed principles of the

---

[144] *Newcastle Guardian*, 15 May 1852.

[145] *Shields Gazette*, 22 July 1853.

[146] Support for the "Tractarian party" by the local gentry in the mid-nineteenth-century was also evident in south-east Lancashire. See C.S. Ford, 'Pastors and Polemicists: The Character of Popular Anglicanism in South East Lancashire, 1847-1914' (unpublished doctoral thesis, Leeds University, 1991), p. 86.

[147] DULSP, Letter from General Charles Grey to Caroline Grey, *4* March 1847, GRE/D/V/2/1-15.

[148] *Gateshead Observer*, 31 August 1848.

Established Church". This angered the Dissenters, who refused to sign it on the grounds that it was offensive to their beliefs. The controversy brought the opportunity to examine the Rector's alleged Tractarian beliefs and accusations were levelled at him for his "Puseyite" innovations and forcing the children of the parish to stay up late on Christmas Eve to stitch crosses to an "altar" cloth. In a collection for the relatives of 28 miners who lost their lives in a recent pit explosion in the village, the Rector caused controversy by introducing "scarlet bags with crosses" as collection bags. As a response to Grey's petition, a counter-petition against "the Papal Aggression and Puseyism" was currently "going the round at Houghton" and receiving numerous signatures.[149]

The controversy rumbled on for several years until, in November 1853, a church rate contest provided the ideal excuse for tempers to boil. Until their abolition in 1868, church rates were a constant bone of contention for the Anglican minister and his parishioners. They were particularly opposed by Dissenters, who were forced to pay a rate to maintain the upkeep of a church they did not belong to.[150] Church rate meetings were therefore notoriously hot-headed affairs but the meetings in Houghton in November 1853 were particularly volatile, owing to the Rector's unpopular plan of increasing the rate to fund the building of a burial ground.[151] Following accusations against Grey of vote-rigging, however, the vote was declared illegal and a second poll was to be instigated the following week.

The excitement generated by the issue was immense and anti-Catholicism and anti-Tractarianism proved to be a particularly effective stick with which to beat the Rector. Large handbills, such as "No Popery!", "No priestly domination!", "Down with Puseyism" and "Popery in disguise!" were posted through the village. Once again the Rector attempted to use underhand tactics to win the vote. Mr. Welford and Mr. Hopper accused him of altering votes "by reducing the number given by a voter after his vote had been recorded". Hopper, owner of the Iron Works at Sunderland Lane, decided that if the Earl of Durham could use his pitmen to influence the vote then he would do likewise. A procession of workers heeded his call and the influence of anti-Catholicism in stirring

---

[149] *Sunderland Herald*, 10 January 1851.
[150] J.P. Ellens, *Religious Routes to Gladstonian Liberalism: The Church Rate Conflict in England and Wales* (Pennsylvania, Pennsylvania State Press, 1994); Paz, *Popular Anti-Catholicism*, p. 16.
[151] The Rector's plan proved particularly unpopular, owing to the increase of the charge made for gravestones from 5 shillings to £3. *Newcastle Guardian*, 5 November 1853.

the energies of these men is evident in the *Sunderland Herald's* description of this parade:

> "At this period a procession of 100 men was formed at Mr. Hopper's Iron Works, Sunderland Lane, headed by the Marquis of Londonderry's band. These stalwart sons of Vulcan carried a number of flags and banners. On the largest was inscribed, 'No Popery'; on another, 'Down with the semi-Pope', and 'No priestly domination'; the band played 'All the Blue Bonnets are over the Border' and the procession marched off under a heavy shower of rain amid the greatest excitement".[152]

When the procession arrived a rush was made towards the Rector, who retired into the corner of the room to take the poll. A tall blacksmith asked the Rector to record his vote against the rate "an' if ye divena poul ma vote awll stick ye agyen the wall". As a result, Grey duly complied. The votes of the ironworkers were taken amidst great confusion in which "a number of people climbed upon the higher benches, and the crowd were roaring and yelling against the rector in dismal chorus". At half-past four, the poll was declared closed. This announcement was met with cries of "down with the semi-Pope" and "No Popery John". Grey was then attacked as he tried to leave the room. He managed to escape injury although his coat was ripped to pieces and his hat destroyed. In spite of the best efforts of Hopper's men to turn the vote, the Rector had still succeeded in raising enough support by 21 votes (318 to 297). [153]

The editorial in the *Sunderland Herald* failed to condemn the violence against the Rector, appearing to be more concerned with what it saw as the "tyrannical" conduct of Grey and his Puseyite tendencies, and suggesting that Grey only had himself to blame:

> "The Puseyite rector of Houghton is one of those types of a bye-gone gloom, which linger to chide our tendency to regard the pillory and the Inquisition as historic fables, and to convince us that such things might be again if we had many rectors of Houghton. For years Mr. Grey's popish predilections and meddlesome propensities have kept his parish in hot water and made himself a bye-word and a scoffing in the district. And last week, on demanding a rate, in his usual despotic fashion, for the formation of a new cemetery, this pent-up hostility burst forth . . ."[154]

---

[152] *Sunderland Herald,* 4 November 1853. This description bears striking similarities to an Orange parade, although the song chosen, *All the Blue Bonnets are over the Border* is of Scottish origin.
[153] *Sunderland Herald,* 4 November 1853.
[154] Ibid.

The Rector himself appeared deeply shaken by the recent events, so much so that in a letter to his churchwardens and other parishioners he conceded that the new rate would not be pressed permanently. This was, he argued, owing to the "violence and disorderly conduct of some of the opponents of the rate" and his lack of desire to pursue "long and painful litigation".[155] Peace was finally proclaimed in February 1854, when it was agreed that a burial board was to be organised by the ratepayers and to be independent of the Rector's control.[156] Nevertheless, accusations of Tractarianism still lingered in the air. At the annual meeting of the Houghton Bible Society in November 1854, the *Sunderland Herald* noted that the speakers offered encouragement to the audience "under the Tractarian practices which were carried on at their own doors".[157] Never again, however, was the spectre of Tractarianism to dominate the mood of the village of Houghton-Le-Spring as it had so successfully done in the early 1850s.

"A Damp Squib": The Ecclesiastical Titles Act

Thus the Papal Aggression brought out deep-seated prejudicial opinions not only towards Catholics, but those who seemed to be imitating them in the Church of England. Indeed, it could be argued that the Tractarians faced far stronger popular opposition than the Catholics. Yet the Durham Letter implied that it was the Catholics, not the Tractarians, who would receive the full brunt of legislative measures.[158] Local Catholics were divided over what possible effect a parliamentary measure could have. While there were those, such as Rev. Robert Tate who wrote to John Lingard expressing his hope that the Liberals would not "call upon Parliament for any new law", others were more bullish.[159] In a published letter to the Bishop of Durham, a "Catholic clergyman resident in the Diocese of Durham" was confident that Catholics should have little reason to feel anxious:

> "I believe that Catholics entertain but little apprehension as to the final issue of coming events. Enactments may ensue, such as your Lordship

---

[155] John Grey, *Letter to the Churchwardens and Other Parishioners of Houghton-Le-Spring* (Durham: R. Robinson, 1853).
[156] *Sunderland Herald*, 10 February 1854.
[157] *Sunderland Herald*, 15 September 1854.
[158] Machin, *Politics and the Churches*, p. 210.
[159] Martin Haile and Edward Bonney, *Life and Letters of John Lingard, 1771-1851* (London: Herbert and Daniel, 1911), p. 362.

rehearses, but the indomitable spirit of English liberality will suffer *no species of aggression* on the birth rights of a British Subject".[160]

When Parliament reconvened in February 1851, Russell faced a serious dilemma. The public demanded that "something be done to repeal the Papal Aggression and Russell, by the Durham Letter, appeared to have promised that something, indeed, would be done".[161] In February 1851, he introduced the Ecclesiastical Titles Bill—a measure designed to make the assumption of territorial titles illegal. The measure did not satisfy anti-Catholics; nor did it pacify Roman Catholic and moderate Liberal opposition in Parliament, with debates holding up the measure for 5 months. Indeed, the debates surrounding the Ecclesiastical Titles Bill encouraged an anti-Catholic petitioning drive throughout the country. Thus, 1,914 petitions, bearing 348,590 signatures, were sent to Parliament asking for the bill to be made more stringent.[162]

There was a limited attempt to try to garner public support in the North East of England. In Newcastle, a meeting of about 30 "clergymen, dissenting ministers and laymen of various congregations" was held in Anderson and Garland's Sale Room to discuss the form of the petition. However, the discussions broke down and both the Congregationalist minister, the Rev. John Rogers and the Presbyterian minister, the Rev. Thomas Duncan, left in protest. The form of the petition was eventually agreed upon and it was decided to send the petition door-to-door.[163] It appears that the organisers at South Shields were more successful in framing the petition to target synods. As well as calling for the suppression of territorial titles "in every part of the British dominions, and the exercise of territorial jurisdiction and delegation from a foreign power" the petition also wished "to prevent synodical action on the part of the Romish clergy under colour of any authority from the Bishop of Rome".[164]

It was the Wesleyan Methodists who were the most active in campaigning for stringent measures. They had a long history of organised petitioning in relation to religious matters. Indeed, Hempton argues "that anti-Catholicism was the most consistent principle in Methodist political

---

[160] Anon., *Protestant Aggression. Remarks on the Bishop of Durham's Letter to the Archdeacon of Lindisfarne by a Catholic Clergyman Resident within the Diocese of Durham* (Newcastle: G.B. Richardson, 1851), pp. 8-9.

[161] Paz, *Popular Anti-Catholicism*, p. 11.

[162] Ibid, p. 12.

[163] *Newcastle Guardian*, 15 March 1851.

[164] *Shields Gazette,* 9 May 1851.

involvement from Wesley's lifetime until 1846".[165] Petitions against the
1839 Education Act and the 1843 Factory Bill, as well as opposition to the
Maynooth Grant, are clear examples of the way in which the Wesleyans
developed a unified petitioning culture against Catholicism.[166] The
Ecclesiastical Titles Bill granted this group a further incitement to political
agitation. The petitioning drive was organised around a central body—the
Committee of Privileges—who prepared a standard petitioning form in
early March 1851, distributing it around local circuits. The Wesleyan
paper *The Watchman* urged Wesleyan congregations to support the drive,
but "without the parade and needless labour of a public meeting".[167] The
petition declared that "all assumptions, use or recognition of any
Ecclesiastical Titles . . . may be declared illegal, and made punishable by
sufficient penalties".[168] Given the large Wesleyan congregations in the
region, it is not surprising to learn that Wesleyan congregations of almost
every village and town contributed to this petition.[169] In the last week in
March, petitions were presented from, to name but a few, Wesleyan
Methodist communities in Houghton-Le-Spring, Easington, Newbottle,
Haswell, Coxhoe, Cassop, Witton Gilbert, Thornley, Shincliffe, Littletown,
Philadelphia and Hetton-Le-Hole.[170] The Wesleyan dominance of the
Durham pit villages may help to explain why County Durham was more
active in petitioning the Ecclesiastical Titles Bill than it was in
memorialising the Queen against the Papal Bull. Indeed, in Paz's
tabulation based on Ecclesiastical Titles Bull petitions, County Durham
was ranked 25th out of the 42 counties.[171]

The Catholic community was clearly incensed by an attempt to
introduce what was essentially a legitimate promotion of "No Popery"
through a legislative measure. Irish Catholic MPs, or the "Irish Brigade"
as they were mockingly dubbed, continually opposed the measure from the
outset in Parliament and compelled the ministry to waste almost the entire
session on this one measure.[172] The Catholics of the region were no less
active in defending their religion. William Hogarth was among the

---

[165] D. Hempton, 'Methodism and Anti-Catholic Politics, 1800-1846' (unpublished
doctoral thesis, University of St Andrews, 1977), p. 7.
[166] Ibid, pp. 247-66, 276-89, 315.
[167] Quoted in Paz, *Popular Anti-Catholicism,* p. 173.
[168] *Newcastle Guardian*, 15 March 1851.
[169] *Newcastle Courant.*, 22 March 1851.
[170] *Newcastle Guardian*, 29 March 1851.
[171] Paz, *Popular Anti-Catholicism*, p. 43.
[172] J.H. Whyte, *The Independent Irish Party, 1850-59* (Oxford: Oxford University
Press, 1958), p. 23.

signatories of a declaration of Catholic Bishops, protesting on what they saw as "a moral persecution . . . against the religious liberties of the Catholics of England" and "appeals to the passions and prejudices of men, to influence the public mind, and induce the Government to re-enact the penal laws".[173] More locally, Catholic Defence Societies sprang up in North Shields and Gateshead with the intention of opposing this "Protestant persecution". The Catholics of North Shields, Stockton and Durham also sent petitions to Parliament against the Bill.[174]

In general, the Ecclesiastical Titles Act, and petitions sent to Parliament regarding it, certainly did not ignite anti-Catholic passions amongst the laity in the same way as the announcement of the Restoration of the Hierarchy.[175] The call for legislation against the Catholics was only supported by those who shared extreme opinions against the Catholic religion. However, those who had been hoping for strict penalties, spurred on by Lord John Russell's letter to the Bishop of Durham, were thoroughly disappointed. *The Times*'s assertion of the measure being "inadequate to what the emergency requires and the opinion of England demands"[176] seems moderate in comparison with the language of the localities and the universal condemnation of the measure. "Such a damp squib after such a crushing peal!" cried the *Newcastle Journal*. "Why the deafening swell of the Premier's artillery", it concluded, "has ended in the flash of a pop gun".[177] The Liberal *Shields Gazette* saw matters in a similar light:

> "The roar of the bull has been answered, indeed, by the bleat of a calf, but that, faint enough at first, is now dying away in the poor creature's throat, not most musical, but most melancholy".[178]

The Roman Catholics, however, were incensed when the bill was eventually passed in July 1851.[179] At a Roman Catholic festival in

---

[173] RCHNDA, *A Declaration of the Catholic Bishops of England*, 1850, RCD 1/11/89.

[174] *Newcastle Courant,* 21 March 1851.

[175] This appears to have been the case throughout the country. Paz refers to a "second round of meetings" in response to the Ecclesiastical Titles Bill (p. 12). However, the chapter in his book which examines public meetings draws examples solely from the Hierarchy meetings at the end of 1850, thus suggesting that the Ecclesiastical Titles Bill meetings were not popular in nature.

[176] *Times*, 9 February 1851.

[177] *Newcastle Journal*, 15 February 1851.

[178] *Shields Gazette*, 21 March 1851.

Sunderland four months later, the Rev. Philip Kearney, denounced the
Ecclesiastical Titles Bill as one which "will stamp this country for ever in
the eyes of every human being with bigotry and fanaticism". "At this
moment", Kearney added, "the English nation exhibits itself to all the
civilised countries on the face of the earth as guilty of the greatest piece of
folly that ever disgraced any nation".[180] Kearney need not have worried.
The bill proved hopelessly ineffectual and almost impossible to carry out
in practice. This can be observed by local controversies in the decade
following the passing of the act. In June 1855, the Anglican incumbent of
Stella, the Rev. William Brown, attempted to raise the "No Popery" cry
among his parishioners when a placard announcing the visit of the "Lord
Bishop of Hexham" appeared in the village. Mr. Brown argued that in the
eyes of the law, there was no bishopric of Hexham and that anyone
assuming such a title could be prosecuted. Despite his protestation, the
Newcastle Journal wryly observed that "the government which passed the
law never intended it to take effect, and Romish ecclesiastics are therefore
left to claim titles and bishoprics as they please".[181] No further action was
taken. Similarly, the notorious firebrand, Andre Massena, unsuccessfully
attempted to bring a lawsuit against Hogarth in 1860. Massena stated his
case at the Sunderland Police Court, in which he argued Hogarth was
illegally using his title of "Bishop of Hexham" in placards announcing the
laying of a new foundation stone of a Catholic church in Church Street.[182]
The magistrate promised to look into the case for Massena, although the
lack of reference in the following weeks tends to suggest that his request
was ignored.

The Papal Aggression, therefore, had as little lasting effect in the
region as it had elsewhere. It could be argued, as Roger Cooter has, that
the agitation surrounding it was merely a temporary aberration of sectarian
hysteria brought to surface by the outpouring of nationalistic sentiment
and was not genuinely indicative of underlying tensions between the local
Protestant and Catholic communities. Nevertheless, it does suggest that the
capacity for anti-Catholicism, pitched at the right levels, could be a highly
persuasive ideology for generating mass support.

---

[179] The Ecclesiastical Titles Act was the last measure of religious discrimination
passed by a British Government. Machin, *Politics and the Churches*, p. 227.
[180] *Sunderland Herald*, 28 November 1851.
[181] Newcastle Journal, 2 June 1855. It is difficult to see how a case could be
brought in this instance given that Hogarth was not assuming an Anglican title.
[182] *Hartlepool Free Press*, 10 March 1860.

CHAPTER THREE

"NO POPERY!":
THE DEFENCE OF THE "PROTESTANT CONSTITUTION"

The last chapter examined the response to the Restoration of the Hierarchy in the North East and how the issue could successfully generate political agitation from a number of different and often competing quarters. However, the Papal Aggression was only one of a number of political events which animated anti-Catholics during the mid-Victorian period and, for many, the real danger lay closer to home in the seemingly pro-Catholic policies of the governments of the period. The Ecclesiastical Titles Act was something of an anomaly in an age in which increasing toleration towards the Catholic religion was the norm. This was reflected by various parliamentary measures during this period designed primarily to afford Catholics greater religious equality. These legislative "concessions" proved to be particularly abhorrent to many Conservatives and Anglicans who believed that Church and State was inexorably linked to the idea of the "Protestant Constitution" and that this must be defended at all costs. This chapter therefore seeks to address how far this primarily Conservative/Anglican form of anti-Catholicism influenced anti-Catholic thought in the predominantly Liberal and Dissenter North East. It will provide an examination of the main political issues and the mechanics of agitation employed, illustrating how these issues were only successful in stirring powerful opposition in some towns if they were able to garner Liberal-Dissenter support for other reasons.

The Maynooth Grant and the Irish Question

The political campaign against the Maynooth Grant was evidence of the way in which Catholic concessions to the "Protestant Constitution" could cause a sustained anti-Catholic backlash. An annual grant from the British government to the Catholic seminary at the Royal College of St Patrick at Maynooth, County Kildare, had been a constant source of irritation for anti-Catholics since 1795.[1] However, it was only in April 1845 when the Conservative leader, Sir Robert Peel, introduced a measure to increase its annual subsidy to over £26,000 and to allow the grant to be automatically drawn from the Consolidation Fund that a major political backlash occurred. Peel hoped that the measure would help to pacify the Irish Catholic clergy[2] and make them more amenable to further reform. The introduction of the bill by a Conservative leader, however, caused outrage among the "Ultra" Tories, Evangelical Anglicans, Wesleyan Methodists and even many Congregationalists, who believed the Premier had compromised the Protestant principles of his party and his country.[3] Although not as significant or as all-encompassing an issue as the Papal Aggression in terms of its capacity to provoke large-scale demonstrations, the anti-Maynooth campaign nevertheless proved to be a more persistently thorny issue.[4]

Opposition to the bill was unusually large because the anti-Maynooth campaign initially had the support of a group of "Voluntaryists". These were Liberal Dissenters, who, as Norman states, "believed that the cardinal sin lay in the establishment principle, and that the cardinal virtue resided in the voluntary payment of their pastors by those electing to form their own congregations".[5] Voluntaryists wished to sever the connexion between Church and State and therefore their opposition to the bill was based on a general dislike of all religious endowments. In spite of their contrasting approaches to the issue, there was an attempt to unite churchmen and Dissenters under the banner of a shared Protestant heritage against the evils of Popery. A great conference was organised by the Central Anti-Maynooth Committee to meet in Exeter Hall from 30 April-3 May but this ended in disarray after many Congregationalists and Baptists walked out. In spite of huge efforts from various groups and a massive petitioning campaign which saw 10,000 petitions into Parliament between

---

[1] D.A. Kerr, *Peel, Priests and Politics: Sir Robert Peel's Administration and the Roman Catholic Church in Ireland, 1841-1846* (Oxford: Clarendon Press, 1982), p. 224.

[2] K.B. Nowlan, *The Politics of Repeal, 1841-50* (London: Routledge and Kegan Paul, 1965), p. 81.

[3] Michael R. Watts, *The Dissenters, Vol II: The Expansion of Evangelical Nonconformity* (Oxford: Oxford University Press, 1995), p. 549.

[4] Frank Wallis has noted that the Maynooth question, in its ability to absorb parliamentary time, transcended the debates over the Corn Laws, the 1848 Revolutions, the Crimean War, the Indian Mutiny, the American Civil War and the debates over the Second Reform Act. Wallis, *Popular Anti-Catholicism*, p. 115.

[5] Norman, *Anti-Catholicism*, p. 40.

the months of February and May, the Maynooth Bill was passed by an enormous majority and given royal assent in June.[6]

In the North East, the divisive nature of the agitation was evident in the opinions of the local press who could not agree on what action to take. As was to be later apparent in the crisis over the Papal Aggression, both Conservative papers in Durham and Newcastle were divided on the matter. The *Durham Advertiser*, which was yet to succumb to the support of a Tractarian editor that undermined its anti-Catholic stance five years later, pursued a vigorously traditional anti-Catholic line against Maynooth in 1845. It saw the Maynooth Bill as a "direct encouragement and sanction of Popery", of which "there is nothing more fatal to the constitution of this country". The paper called on "every sincere and enlightened Protestant to join immediately in petitioning the legislature to refuse its sanction".[7] The *Newcastle Journal*'s initial leader on the subject followed a similar line, holding little back in its attack on the College:

> "The very name of Maynooth is looked upon, and deservedly looked upon, as a term of reproach—as a synonym for all that is violent, illiterate, and course; and, unquestionably, the stream of ill-bred, ill-taught, and ill-conditioned priests, which it annually sends forth, is anything but calculated to give one a favourable opinion of it as a seminary for education, much less an ecclesiastical establishment".[8]

The paper urged Protestants not to be "apathetic or indifferent spectators" while the Maynooth Bill was being debated in parliament. This outburst of vitriolic anti-Catholicism is all the more surprising given that in the following week, after reading Peel's statement on the issue, the *Journal* appeared to reverse its opinion on the subject and toe the party line. It now saw the endowment as the "lesser of two evils", believing that "a large and liberal addition to the grant was required, if the establishment were to be kept up at all by the expense of the state".[9] Indeed, throughout the following weeks it became a staunch defender of the Premier's bill, seeing it as a necessary evil to pacify Ireland.

The Liberal press were just as divided as their Tory adversaries. The *Sunderland Herald* opted for a Voluntaryist line, attacking the Maynooth Grant on the basis of a campaign against all state endowments. The paper

---

[6] Richard Brown, *Church and State in Modern Britain: 1700-1850* (London: Routledge, 1991), p. 277.

[7] *Durham Advertiser*, 7 February, 28 March 1845.

[8] *Newcastle Journal*, 5 April 1845.

[9] *Newcastle Journal*, 12 April 1845.

stated that its stance was not against Maynooth or its students, but merely a protest "against the State endowing *any* college for training either Protestant clergymen or Catholic priests".[10] Perhaps with the *Newcastle Journal* in mind, the paper also attacked those that placed party loyalty before religious principle and "who like Peel so well, that they will support anything he may choose to bring forward".[11] The *Newcastle Chronicle*, however, was an unambiguous supporter of the grant. The *Chronicle* saw the bill in a pragmatic light describing it as a "bold and important measure" in allaying the "popular feeling of ill-will towards the country (from Ireland)". Indeed, argued the paper, if it is advisable that such a College be maintained by the legislature then it "ought to be placed in a more respectable and efficient state".[12]

Throughout the region during April and May 1845, meetings were held and petitions were drawn up to protest against the grant from a variety of standpoints. A number of meetings were dominated by Dissenters with Voluntaryist principles. On 30 April, a meeting in Bethel Chapel, Sunderland, contained "nearly all the Dissenting ministers of the town" with numerous denunciations of the endowment principle. The first resolution, introduced by the Rev. Mr. Wilson, objected to "all State interference with religion, and . . . to all grants of public money, in whatever form it be distributed, for the support of either truth or error, as unscriptural, unjust, and injurious to the cause of truth".[13] A similar meeting was held in Newcastle, under the banner of "the friends of civil and religious liberty". The Rev. James Pringle described endowing Maynooth as "essentially unjust" because it was "at variance with the nature of Christ's kingdom, and the legitimate aims of civil government".[14] Similar public meetings were held at Gateshead, South Shields, and other places.[15]

In some towns, meetings were held protesting against the grant with a more blatant anti-Catholic agenda. In Hartlepool, a town renowned for its anti-sacerdotal culture, the meeting against the endowment was notable for its ecumenical and influential attendance; even the Mayor of the town, William Manners, was involved in chairing the meeting. With the obvious exception of a Roman Catholic priest, all the other speakers denounced Maynooth and the Catholic religion. The Presbyterian minister of the town, the Rev. James Douglas, described the Maynooth priests as

---

[10] *Sunderland Herald*, 11 April 1845.
[11] *Sunderland Herald*, 25 April 1845.
[12] *Newcastle Chronicle*, 18, 25 April 1845.
[13] *Sunderland Herald*, 2 May 1845.
[14] *Newcastle Journal*, 19 April 1845.
[15] *Newcastle Courant,* 25 April 1845; *Newcastle Journal*, 26 April 1845.

"agitating priests and most deeply imbued with a persecuting and intolerant spirit", while Alderman Worthy was concerned that if the bill was passed, "it would speedily be followed by a proposal to endow the Roman Catholic Church".[16] In Newcastle, a crowded meeting of Protestants was held on 29 May in the Music Room, Nelson Street in order to protest to the House of Lords. The speakers were comprised of Anglican, Presbyterian and Wesleyan ministers, with a number of notable laymen. The solicitor, Thomas Davison, noted his presence at the meeting in his diary[17] and it was even observed that the music gallery was completely occupied by ladies. The petition adopted received over six hundred signatures from this meeting alone. It was then left for signature at various Presbyterian and Methodist chapels in the town.[18] Petitions against the grant were also sent from North and South Shields, Darlington, Great Stainton (signed by the entire adult populace) and Houghton-le-Spring[19] as well as Wesleyan congregations in Durham, Bishop Auckland, West Auckland, Shildon, New Shildon, Totthill, Southchurch, Crook and Escombe.[20] The Newcastle Presbytery also unanimously agreed to petition Parliament against the Grant.[21]

The response of towns to the Maynooth Question was sometimes dependent on specific circumstances. In South Shields, an inordinate amount of interest in the issue was created after an Anti-Maynooth Committee was formed and the town was one of the few places to hold a successful joint meeting of Voluntaryists and anti-Catholics in April. It was decided to form a committee to put pressure on local MP's in Parliament to vote against the grant. A memorial, signed by a portion of the electors of the town, was presented to the MP, J.T. Wawn. It asked for Wawn to vote against the bill, although he refused and voted in favour of it.[22] The local Committee also sent a deputation headed by John Mather and the Rev. H. Lawson to London in order to attend the national Anti-Maynooth Conference.[23] When the deputation returned, it presented its

---

[16] *Sunderland Herald*, 19 April 1845.
[17] TWAS, DX55/1/2, Diary of Thomas Davison, 29 May 1845.
[18] *Newcastle Courant*, 6 June 1845.
[19] *Newcastle Courant* 18 April 1845.
[20] *Newcastle Courant*, 6 June 1845.
[21] TWAS, Minutes of Newcastle Presbytery, II, 25 March 1845.
[22] *Sunderland Herald*, 2 May 1845.
[23] The anti-Maynooth conference featured twelve laymen and ministers from the north-east (six from Newcastle and three from Durham and South Shields respectively). Central Anti-Maynooth Committee, *Proceedings of the Anti-Maynooth Conference* (London: Blackburn and Pardon, 1845), pp. 219-32.

findings in front of a crowded public meeting of electors and other inhabitants in the Town Hall.[24] In contrast, there appeared to be a marked lack of interest in the subject at Durham. In presenting a petition from the inhabitants of Great Stainton to the House of Lords, the Marquis of Londonderry remarked that "it was singular in itself as it was creditable to the clergy, that . . . no public agitation of any kind" had been organised against the bill in Durham.[25] The main reason for this was the stance of the Bishop of Durham, who voted in favour of the bill in the Lords. The Bishop explicitly requested his clergy not to take any part in any local demonstrations, much to the frustration of Canon George Townsend who, in spite of adding his name to a Cambridge petition and a list of subscribers for the payment of Sir Culling Eardley Smith's expenses, could not lead the local clergy in the agitation.[26]

For the Catholic community, the anti-Maynooth agitation appeared as yet another example of Protestant bigotry. Indeed, as G.I.T. Machin has argued, it is unlikely that Catholics would have seen any difference in ultra-Protestant and Voluntaryist opposition, in spite of the latter's claim to the contrary.[27] Caroline L. Scott has suggested in Manchester that an anti-Maynooth meeting organised by the Evangelical anti-Catholic, the Rev. Hugh Stowell, ended in uproar after "O'Connell-cheering Irish" managed to move an amendment in favour of the Grant.[28] Scott, however, failed to note that a similar tactic was attempted by the local Repeal Association in other Tyneside towns. Indeed, the appearance of a local Irish Repealer, Thomas McNally, ensured that the Catholic community was well represented in many of the major anti-Maynooth meetings in the region. He was particularly successful in the Voluntaryist meetings where Liberal opinion was generally open to allowing a Catholic onto the platform. In the Newcastle Voluntaryist meeting, McNally almost managed to overturn the anti-Maynooth resolution when he moved an amendment to the effect that "this meeting is of the opinion that the measure adopted by the Government, regarding the College of Maynooth, is but a small concession of justice to the Catholics of Ireland . . ." The measure was seconded by another Irish Catholic, John McShane, and put to a show of hands. The chairman caused uproar among the Irish Catholics present by declaring against the amendment and the proceedings had to be quickly terminated. A similar attempt was made in the Sunderland

---

[24] *Durham Advertiser*, 16 May 1845.

[25] *Durham Advertiser*, 2 May 1845.

[26] *Durham Advertiser,* 9 May 1845.

[27] Machin, *Politics and the Churches*, p. 174.

[28] Scott, 'Comparative Re-examination', p. 100.

meeting, where a group of Irishmen employed at the Pier took early possession of the seats in front of the platform. This time McShane and McNally were unsuccessful.[29] In Gateshead, however, these tactics bore fruit as the meeting adopted an amendment approving of the grant that was passed by a very large majority.[30] By the time of the Newcastle Ultra-Protestant meeting at the end of May, the organisers were in no mood for concession and McNally's attempt to speak at this meeting was met with immediate ejection.[31] Nevertheless, McNally and his band of Irish followers clearly had a good understanding of the mechanics of political agitation and this episode is indicative of a strongly politicised Irish culture on Tyneside, before the famine immigration "sapped the political libido".[32]

The government's policy in subsidising the education of Roman Catholic priests in Ireland was not extended to the provision of education among the Roman Catholics on the mainland. In 1847, Lord John Russell intimated his willingness to exclude Roman Catholic schools from a proposed Education Grant which planned to subsidise schools of all denominations.[33] This caused outrage, with many seeing the measure as a blatant example of persecution. The *Sunderland Herald* was fairly typical of Liberal opinion on the matter, believing the act to be "the very essence of bigotry and injustice".[34] Indeed, the North East in general appeared to be firmly against the Government measure, and the Catholic community in particular were vocal in their denunciations. A number of clerical and lay meetings were held by Catholics in most towns, including Newcastle and Sunderland, which also received great deal of support from non-Catholics.[35] Support for the exclusion of Catholic schools appeared to be rare in the region and largely came from Dissenters who were in favour of voluntary education and who therefore wished to see the Government abandon the Grant altogether. At the Sunderland meeting, the Congregationalist minister the Rev. John Rogers, argued that "the Government had no right to interfere in the teaching of religion and therefore he was compelled to offer to it strong and uncompromising

---

[29] *Sunderland Herald*, 2 May 1845.
[30] *Newcastle Journal*, 26 April 1845.
[31] *Tyne Mercury*, 31 May 1845.
[32] Cooter, *Paddy*, p. 145.
[33] D.G. Paz, *The Politics of Working Class Education in Britain, 1830-50* (Manchester: Manchester University Press, 1980), p. 134.
[34] *Sunderland Herald*, 16 April 1847.
[35] Ibid; *Newcastle Guardian*, 17 April 1847, 24 April 1847, 15 May 1847.

opposition".[36] Support for the exclusion of Catholics based on anti-Catholic grounds was rarer still and largely confined to internal meetings of particular denominations. Thus, at a meeting of the Presbyterian Synod in Sunderland, an overture was read out declaring that the State "ought to assist in educating the people, and that such education should be strictly Christian and Protestant".[37]

The agitation surrounding the Maynooth Grant, as well as the Education Grant, helped to ensure that religious issues played a prominent part in the general election of 1847. Other topics, such as Chartism, Poor Law Reform and the Game Laws were undoubtedly important electoral issues but the religious questions essentially dominated the hustings.[38] Certainly, for many Conservative and Anglican anti-Catholics, election time was a dangerous period for the advance of Popery. The prospect of MP's returning to Parliament sharing pro-Catholic views and undermining the "Protestant Constitution" had become a reason to be fearful since Catholic Emancipation. In August 1846, the National Club, a Tory/Anglican organisation, called on Anglicans and Dissenters to unite against the common foe in the coming election and to organise into local Protestant Associations and vote for no man who would not align himself with Protestant principles.[39]

In the North East, there is no evidence that local anti-Catholics followed the lead of the National Club in organising Protestant Associations, or certainly no such organisation was ever publicised in the local press. However, the issues of Maynooth and, to a lesser extent the Education Grant, still dominated elections in the main constituencies. In Newcastle, the anti-Catholic climate not only enabled the local Conservative Party a rare opportunity of putting forward a candidate but it also caused a split in the local Liberal Party. The Conservative candidate, Richard Hodgson, spoke decidedly against Catholic endowments in election speeches, believing them to be inconsistent with the "Protestant Constitution" and promising to offer a "strenuous opposition to any such proposal" in Parliament.[40] This won the support of the *Newcastle Journal* but the Liberal press were outraged. The *Newcastle Guardian* described him as the "avowed champion of bigotry" in "professing to defend the citadel of Protestantism" and describing his principles as of an "unenlightened

---

[36] *Sunderland Herald*, 16 April 1847.
[37] *Gateshead Observer*, 1 May 1847.
[38] Machin, *Politics and the Churches*, p. 186.
[39] Wolffe, *Protestant Crusade*, p. 221.
[40] *Newcastle Journal*, 10 July 1847.

character".[41] The second candidate, the Liberal William Ord, was a well-known advocate of Catholicism and therefore declared himself favourable to the extension of the Education Grant to Catholics.

It was the third candidate, the Liberal Thomas Headlam, who caused the most controversy. At a meeting of the local Liberal Committee, Headlam declared that, as a member of the Church of England, he could not vote in favour of the separation of Church and State and the abolition of church rates, two policies on which Liberals were normally united. For these reasons Mr. Crawshay, the Chairman of the Liberal Committee, and 200 political Dissenters, had great difficulty in supporting Headlam as a candidate. However, at a further deputation meeting, Headlam retracted his statement against church rates and stated that he would in fact vote for their abolition. Some of the Dissenters agreed to defend him, but his views on Church and State remained a bone of contention. He considered "any measure for the payment of the Roman Catholic priesthood in that country (Ireland) as wholly impractical" although he had earlier spoken to a meeting of Catholic electors, declaring it "absolutely necessary" that the minutes of the Education Grant should include Roman Catholics.[42] It is worth noting that they did not appear overly concerned with Headlam's anti-Catholic views.[43] An editorial in the *Journal* described Headlam as executing a country dance in his addresses, "for he changes sides with amazing dexterity, crosses over, and passes down the middle, in admirable accordance with the rules of the art. He is first a Churchman, then a Dissenter, then a Roman Catholic".[44] In the end, the two Liberal candidates won the election but, at least in Headlam's case, it was not through the cause of religious toleration.[45]

Anti-Maynooth agitation also played a part in the election in other constituencies, with both Liberal and Conservative candidates exploiting the cause for their own ends. In South Shields, where Maynooth was a prominent issue generally, the *Newcastle Journal* appealed to both Anglican and Dissenter to vote for the Conservative candidate, W. Whateley, who was "attached by an adherence to sound Protestant principles" in voting against Catholic grants.[46] The Liberal candidate, J.T. Wawn, however, was not pro-Catholic. The *Newcastle Guardian* was forced to issue an apology after misprinting a speech from Wawn, in

[41] Ibid; 24 July 1847.
[42] *Newcastle Guardian*, 10 July 1847.
[43] Ibid.
[44] *Newcastle Journal*, 17 July 1847.
[45] *Newcastle Journal,* 31 July 1847.
[46] *Durham Advertiser*, 19 June 1847.

which he stated that he was in favour of the Education and Maynooth Grants. [47] On the contrary, the candidate appeared to be strongly against both and was elected with twice as many votes as Whateley.[48] A similar situation occurred in Sunderland where the Conservative candidate, George Hudson, and the Liberal, D. Barclay, both adopted anti-Maynooth policies from respective Ultra and Voluntaryist stances, and were elected to Parliament at the expense of the pro-Maynooth Liberal candidate, W.A. Wilkinson.[49] In the county elections, a Conservative and a Liberal, Lord Seaham and James Farrer, were elected for their respective counties of North and South Durham with anti-Maynooth views.[50] Where pro-Maynooth candidates did succeed, it was not always clear that their real motives were to support the Catholic religion. In the Gateshead election, the Liberal candidate William Hutt replied to a memorial from a deputation of 39 people asking him to vote against the Maynooth Grant on doctrinal grounds, by stating that he would in fact vote for it on the basis that the Roman Catholic priesthood should be educated. However, he also stated that he wished to find some way to "convince the Catholic population that, in maintaining . . . (certain) points of faith, they were in error".[51]

Anti-Maynooth agitation, however, was not so prominent in the Durham City election. This was largely due to the internal wrangling of the local Conservative Party. The Conservatives were relatively numerous and influential in Durham. The Cathedral Chapter was composed almost entirely of Conservatives. However, the Durham Conservatives were largely dependent on the support of the aristocratic Londonderry family who used their influence to try to put forward Tory candidates favourable to their own interests.[52] This had caused a rift in the 1841 election when Lord Londonderry managed to secure the election of an "ultra-Radical Leaguer", much to the dismay of the local Conservatives. As a consequence, many Conservatives refused to vote for Londonderry's chosen candidate, Captain Wood, in the 1847 election.[53] Wood's situation was not helped by his vague religious policies. In his address to the electors, he announced that he did not want to pledge himself on any issue,

---

[47] *Newcastle Guardian,* 26 June 1847.

[48] *Newcastle Journal,* 31 July 1847.

[49] *Newcastle Journal,* 7 August 1847.

[50] Ibid.

[51] *Gateshead Observer,* 12 April 1845.

[52] Nossiter, *Influence,* pp. 122-3.

[53] *Durham Advertiser,* 6 August 1847.

other than "to uphold the Established Constitution in Church and State".[54] The Liberal candidates, T.C. Granger and H.J. Spearman, were more specifically in favour of the Maynooth Grant. Indeed, in a heated speech on the day of the election, Granger attacked the resurgence of No Popery in general:

> I look upon it as a most disgraceful thing that, at the present day, years after the admission of our Roman Catholic fellow-subjects to all the privileges of citizenship—that cry should be persevered in.[55]

Unsurprisingly, Granger and Bright were elected at the expense of the Conservative candidate.[56]

The Maynooth issue essentially lay dormant until the Papal Aggression stimulated renewed interest in the early 1850s. The issue was once again brought to the fore of political debate in June 1851 when the MP Richard Spooner spoke out against it in Parliament. The emergence of the Protestant Alliance in November 1851, along with the activities of the Protestant Association and the newly founded anti-Catholic newspaper *The Bulwark*, saw a revival of the petitioning campaign against this "training school of heresy and sedition".[57] The campaign received a total of 951 petitions with 325,000 signatures from localities around the country.[58] In the North East, as elsewhere, the agitation appeared to be localised and centred on the activities of newly-formed Protestant Alliance auxiliaries. The Protestant Alliance was originally established as a national body in November 1851 by the Earl of Shaftesbury in order to "combine all classes of Protestants" to combat "against all encroachments of Popery" and promote "the doctrines of the Reformation and the principles of religious liberty".[59] Unlike its rival bodies the Evangelical Alliance and the Protestant Association which were either exclusively Dissenter or Anglican dominated, the vagueness of the Protestant Alliance's main object helped it to attract support from all denominations.[60] Indeed, the Alliance's aims seem particularly tailored to the North East, where

---

[54] *Durham Advertiser*, 30 July 1847.
[55] Ibid.
[56] The result was as follows: Granger – 595; Spearman – 519; Wood – 450. The *Durham Advertiser* calculated that 130 electors did not vote, the 'chief part of these the Conservative party' who had refused to vote for the Londonderry candidate. *Durham Advertiser*, 6 August 1847.
[57] *Bulwark*, October 1851.
[58] Wallis, *Popular Anti-Catholicism*, p. 126.
[59] Quoted in John Wolffe, *Protestant Crusade*, p. 251.
[60] Wallis, *Popular Anti-Catholicism* , p. 126.

ecumenical co-operation was possible in resisting the encroachments of Popery. Organisations were therefore established in Newcastle, Durham, Darlington and Sunderland.

The Maynooth issue was chosen by the Alliance as the most likely to elicit an effective anti-Catholic response[61] but it was ill-conceived for three reasons. Firstly, as evident in the 1845 campaign, combining two entirely different views on the subject (Voluntaryist and Ultra-Protestant) was always likely to be a difficult task. This difficulty was somewhat reduced by the Protestant Dissenting Deputies decision not to petition on the subject[62] and thus taking the Voluntary camp out of the equation, but it meant that a huge body of support was removed as the agitation against Maynooth became more anti-Catholic and less anti-establishment.[63] Not all Dissenters were Voluntaryists but, with the exception of the Methodists, there was a substantial number of Nonconformists who shared these principles. Secondly, because of the nature of ultra-Protestant support, the agitation changed from one in which both Conservatives and Liberals could unite, to a purely Conservative issue. This was in part encouraged by Lord Derby's administration which appeared to be pursuing a vigorously anti-Catholic line in the run up to the 1852 general election, as well as Conservative MP's who were exploiting the agitation for their own political benefits. This led many to believe that the anti-Maynooth meetings were nothing more than Tory electioneering rallies. To a Liberal Dissenter, therefore, there was little incentive to join in the agitation. Thirdly, the aims of the agitation had changed. In 1845, the issue was whether or not the Maynooth Grant should be increased; in 1852, however, the agitators were seeking its complete abolition. This may have dissuaded many moderate anti-Catholics from pledging their support.

The limitations of the Alliance's narrow anti-Maynooth campaign can be observed in Newcastle. There was certainly no lack of support in the town for the formation of a local Protestant Alliance *per se*. In its inaugural meeting in December 1851, virtually every Evangelical and Dissenting minister of the town and neighbourhood were present, with the organisation also attracting numerous and influential lay members. When the Alliance tried to elicit support for a public meeting against Maynooth in April of the following year, however, the results were disastrous. On 22 April 1852, an announcement was made by placard that a public meeting was to be convened for the purpose of courting the support of the "men of Newcastle, (who were) opposed to the maintenance of the endowment of

---

[61] Wolffe, *Protestant Crusade*, p. 262.
[62] Larsen, *Friends of Religious Equality*, p. 240.
[63] Wolffe, *Protestant Crusade*, p. 263.

Maynooth College". However, at the appointed time, only 100 people had shown up. The Rev. Thomas Duncan moved to adjourn the meeting to a more favourable time as a large number of ministers who, he argued, were particularly interested in the subject, could not make it that night. He also pointed to the lack of support from the local press. However, when a petition against the Grant was sent to the Dissenting chapels many refused to sign. Roger Cooter has suggested that this incident is symptomatic of the lack of anti-Catholic feeling in the town[64] and this is certainly true of the type of political anti-Catholicism which the Alliance was peddling at this time. An Ultra-Protestant and seemingly Tory-baiting anti-Maynooth campaign was unlikely to receive the backing from a place which had a large Liberal/Dissenter presence. That the meeting was held at the end of April when the election campaign was in full swing did little to diminish the accusations of electioneering.

The Alliance's campaign fared better in Durham and Darlington. Both towns had large Liberal Dissenting populations, but they also had a strong Anglican and Wesleyan presence and thus the agitation received some measure of support. In Durham, where the issue had failed to ignite anti-Catholic passions in 1845, the independent organisation of the Alliance indicated that support for a public meeting was no longer reliant on the Bishop of Durham's acquiescence. Cooter has suggested that the attendance at the anti-Maynooth meeting in the Town Hall was poor.[65] However, reports in the local press suggest a far more respectable attendance, although mass support was notable by its absence. The *Durham Advertiser* described the attendance as "pretty numerous", while the *Chronicle*, which had no reason to exaggerate the attendance, believed the Town Hall was two-thirds full. On the platform were a number of men who had spoken in the recent Papal Aggression meeting including Professor Johnson and the Rev. George Fox. Accusations of electioneering, however, were rife and not entirely without foundation. The *Durham Chronicle*, no supporter of the anti-Maynooth agitation, thought that the most interesting thing about the meeting was the "expressed mention of some of the principal members of the Alliance in reference to the disposal of their votes" in the forthcoming general election. This was based on the Rev. George Fox's promise to use all his influence in securing the election of the South Shields Conservative candidate, Henry Liddell, "on account of his opposition to the grant to Maynooth".[66] The local Darlington Alliance managed to escape similar

---

[64] Cooter, *Paddy*, p. 78.
[65] Cooter, *Paddy*, p. 78.
[66] *Durham Chronicle*, 26 March 1852.

accusations and indeed its meeting was one of the few notable successes, presumably because it had the support of a large number of anti-Catholic Dissenters. The meeting contained, according to a report in the *Advertiser,* "the largest we ever remember having seen in the Central Hall, the large hall being crammed almost to the very door".[67] Ministers and laymen were observed "representing all the different communions existing in the place".[68] The speakers were generally Anglican, including the Liverpool clergyman, the Rev. Samuel Minton. However, the appearance of the Congregationalist minister, the Rev. R. Macbeth and the Baptist minister the Rev. Mr. Lewis, is again indicative that Dissenters could sometimes adopt an anti-Catholic and non-Voluntaryist stance.

In South Shields, the formation of a local Protestant Association ensured that the agitation in the town was more exclusively based along Anglican/Tory lines. The Protestant Association was set up in 1835 to oppose Roman Catholicism on theological and constitutional grounds.[69] It saw the defence of the "Protestant Constitution" as its main priority and therefore attracted a great deal of Anglican support. It disavowed allegiance to any political party, but its open support for Protestant candidates during elections meant that it veered towards Conservatism.[70] Local auxiliaries were formed throughout the country although the North East was generally lacking in organisations where the more Dissenter-friendly Protestant Alliance dominated. Indeed South Shields was the only town in the region where the Association gained a foothold. In November 1851, an auxiliary was set up under the banner of the South Shields and Westoe Protestant Association. It was dominated by Anglicans and Tory notables such as the ship-owners Robert Anderson and J.C. Stevenson although it was also able to attract support from the more Conservative Presbyterians and Wesleyans. Its inaugural meeting, chaired by the Mayor of the town, John Clay, saw speeches made and resolutions passed in favour of "the discontinuance of the national encouragement given to Popery".[71] It was clear that, unlike the Protestant Alliance, the Association had clear political aims. A circular appeared in the *Shields Gazette*, calling for the abolition of all aid for "Popish" schools in England, the enforcement of laws against "Romish religious orders" and the granting of an endowment to the Church Education Society in Ireland, as well as the

---

[67] *Durham Advertiser,* 12 March 1852.
[68] *Darlington and Stockton Times,* 12 March 1852.
[69] Paz, *Popular Anti-Catholicism,* p. 104.
[70] Ibid, p. 198.
[71] *Shields Gazette,* 22 November 1851.

abolition of the Maynooth Grant. The *Shields Gazette,* in spite of its Liberal stance, appeared to fully support these objects.[72]

When the Maynooth issue began to dominate in the early months of 1852, the South Shields Association was not behind its contemporaries in organising a meeting and there appeared to be a strong feeling in the town on the subject as the requisition to the Mayor was signed by over 200 people.[73] Once again, however, the issue of the forthcoming election was again to cause controversy. The speakers of the meeting, held in the Central Hall of the town, were essentially those who had taken a central role in the formation of the Protestant Association and, therefore, the speeches reflected their stance in defending the "Protestant Constitution". The petition adopted attacked the government's support for Maynooth as "inconsistent with the principles of the British Constitution, and opposed to the dictates of sound policy and the revealed will of God". The Rev. Samuel Brasher called upon all election candidates "not to compromise their Protestant principles for some fancied good". Mr. Strachan caused considerable uproar in the hall by his assertion that the Maynooth question was "brought up to affect the next general election". Indeed, he argued, "What did one of the speakers mean by speaking of the next election, but to get them to support the protectionist party?" In spite of this dissension, the petition was put and adopted by a considerable majority.[74]

The anti-Maynooth agitation in the North East was further encouraged by the activities of the Anglican Rev. Hugh Stowell of Manchester. Stowell was invited by the Protestant Alliance to lecture in a number of towns on their behalf in the early months of 1852. Although Stowell's lecture tour was not directly linked to the anti-Maynooth campaign, his choice of topic-the "Romish Priesthood"-clearly complemented the Alliance's political aims. Stowell was something of a national celebrity noted for his powerful oratory. His popularity among ministers and laymen alike ensured that there was considerable interest in the "champion of the cause of evangelical truth"[75]. He did not disappoint his audiences. In Newcastle, he spoke for over two and a half hours with an "overpowering eloquence, clearness, energy and effect". [76] The *Sunderland News* described his actions during his lecture at Sunderland:

---

[72] Ibid. The editor of the *Shields Gazette* was an avowed Liberal but he was also a member of the Church of England.

[73] *Sunderland News*, 21 February 1852.

[74] *Shields Gazette*, 20 February 1852.

[75] *Sunderland News*, 9 April 1853.

[76] *Newcastle Journal*, 6 February 1852.

> "Mr. Stowell when addressing his audience, frequently holds forth his right
> hand and tosses it fervently . . . On these occasions his head (is) thrown
> backward, one foot elevated and stomping furiously, his right hand waving
> warrior like (grasping) the blade of battle".[77]

Stowell employed millennial language to heighten the effect of his oration.
Thus, at the conclusion of his speech, he stressed that "the prophecy of the
Revelation was nigh its fulfilment, a voice could be heard crying,
'Babylon, the great is fallen, is fallen'". [78] It was a combination of these
factors which helped to command the attention of his audience with
"breathless interest, excepting at such times when the Rev. gentleman's
remarks were met with a response in the hearts of his hearers, and elicited
unanimous bursts of applause".[79] Not everyone was so convinced
however. A letter from a "High Churchman" to the *Advertiser* chastised
Stowell for using "the most stale and common place arguments, with very
little novelty of illustrations" although the letter appeared to be more
concerned about Stowell's attack on church music.[80] The Catholic
community were far from satisfied either. A letter to the *Darlington and
Stockton Times* from a Roman Catholic described Stowell's Darlington
speech as unrivalled for "rampant bigotry, false, odious, representation and
uncharitable expression".[81]

Unsurprisingly given its prominence in earlier months of 1852, and the
accusations of Tory electioneering which followed it, the Maynooth issue
again dominated the general election contests of that year. Indeed, it has
been suggested that the 1852 general election represented perhaps the most
"anti-Catholic" of all elections in the Victorian period. Though these
elections often "did not yield the fruits for which ultra-Protestants had
hoped"[82] they did produce "the most success for the anti-Catholics of any
election before or since".[83] Maynooth was again the main topic for
discussion, but there were other issues, such as the Ecclesiastical Titles
Act, which helped to play their part in increasing sectarian tension. In May
1851, the newly-created *Bulwark* led the cry.

> "The fate of our beloved country is, humanly speaking, in the hands of our
> electors. The Parliament about to be chosen may last for seven years, and

---

[77] *Sunderland News*, 9 April 1853.

[78] *Newcastle Courant*, 6 February 1852.

[79] *Darlington and Stockton Times*, 2 April 1852.

[80] *Durham Advertiser*, 13 February 1852.

[81] *Darlington and Stockton Times,* 16 April 1853.

[82] Machin, *Politics and the Churches*, p. 241.

[83] Paz, *Popular Anti-Catholicism*, p. 203.

do immense damage to the Protestant cause and to all that is dear to us as Christians and brothers".[84]

This was further encouraged by the Ministry of Lord Derby which attempted to walk a tightrope of conciliation to all Conservative groupings including Protectionists, ultra-Protestants, Peelites and even Irish Catholics who were angered by the previous Liberal government's anti-Catholic policy during the Papal Aggression crisis. However, on 15 June 1852, Derby issued an ill-timed proclamation against the wearing of Catholic vestments and ornaments in public which helped to cause a serious sectarian riot in Stockport.[85]

"No Popery" became a dominant feature in many local election contests throughout the country[86] and the North East was no different. This was particularly the case in Newcastle, where feeling was strong amongst an anti-Catholic clique against any candidate who had espoused a pro-Papal policy in his past parliamentary conduct. All three candidates, Messrs Headlam, Watson and Blackett, were Liberals, but it was only Watson who had voted against the Ecclesiastical Titles Bill in Parliament[87], helped to repeal certain penal laws against Irish Catholics and received the personal endorsement of the *Tablet*. This convinced many that Watson was actively assisting the Catholic cause. A series of placards were displayed around the town as early as March claiming, amongst other things, that Watson was "a Papist, and a friend of Papists, an abettor (sic) of the Jesuits and an advocate for Roman Catholic supremacy".[88] In a canvas to the electors, Watson denied "ever harbouring the idea of supporting or defending their (Catholic) religious views", arguing that he had only repealed the penal statutes "from an honest conviction that he was conferring an act of justice upon them".[89] The residence of the local subsidiary for the Protestant Alliance in this town also saw the Maynooth Grant as a local issue in the build-up to the election. Indeed, the opinions of the candidates on this subject were not indicated in their canvasses, and it was only the intervention of Protestant Alliance members during the

---

[84] *Bulwark*, May 1851.

[85] Machin, *Politics and the Churches*, pp. 237-38; Millward, 'The Stockport Riots. Legislation against the wearing of vestments in public remained in place until 1926.

[86] For examples in the localities, see Paz, *Popular Anti-Catholicism*, chapter 7.

[87] Of the other two, Mr. Headlam had voted in favour of it, while Mr. Blackett was a newcomer to politics.

[88] *Newcastle Guardian*, 26 March 1852.

[89] *Newcastle Courant*, 26 March 1852.

question and answer sessions at the end of the candidates' speeches that actually brought this issue to the fore. Thus, in response to questioning from the Alliance, all the candidates declared identical attitudes on the subject—they all agreed they would vote for no increase or new endowment, but would maintain the existent one as a legal contract between the government and the college.[90] The frustration of the Protestant Alliance with the lack of an anti-Maynooth candidate almost led them to introduce one of their own. However, the chosen contender, Captain Ryder Burton, declined to come forward due to ill health.

In contrast to the previous contest in 1847, the newly-formed Durham Protestant Alliance ensured Maynooth became a major election issue in the city, although not in the way most anti-Catholics hoped. Whether it was the intention of the Alliance, its anti-Maynooth meeting earlier that year had drummed up enough anti-Catholic feeling in the town to ensure that it could not be ignored by candidates in their speeches at the hustings. The chosen Conservative candidate was the son of the Marchioness of Londonderry, Lord Adolphus Vane, who understandably felt few doubts in declaring in a speech that he was "averse to the Maynooth Grant" and that "if the measure was properly brought forward I could not, with my opinions, politically or conscientiously, oppose its repeal". Both Liberal candidates, T.C. Granger and W. Atherton, chose to declare their support for the Grant.[91] In the end, Vane narrowly lost the election by four votes[92] but his defeat was made all the more disappointing for his supporters when it was discovered that many of the Liberal electors in the Protestant Alliance had seemingly betrayed their Protestant principles for party loyalty. This had been apparent during the campaign itself when some members openly declared their support for the pro-Maynooth policy of the Liberal candidates in the city. Speaking at a meeting of Granger's friends, Mr. Shadforth, the secretary of the local Alliance, defended Granger whilst attacking those members of his organisation who refused to vote for him on the grounds of their religious opinions. Indeed, Granger himself called on Alliance members to support him. "What is the use of withholding their votes from me if no government can be formed . . . that would for one moment think of proposing this question (Maynooth) to the House of Commons?" Furthermore, many of Granger's other policies such as free trade, were seductive to many of the Alliance's Liberal members who

---

[90] *Newcastle Courant*, 26 March 1852.
[91] *Durham Advertiser*, 30 April 1852.
[92] The results were as follows: Granger 571, Atherton 510, Vane 506. *Durham Advertiser*, 16 July 1852.

could not agree with the Vane's Protectionist stance.[93] This caused outrage amongst those members of the organisation who believed that religion should be the ultimate determining issue in any decision.

There were a number of "guilty" Alliance members, but Ultra-Protestant wrath in particular singled out the Rev. Samuel Goddall for attack. Goddall represents a perfect case study for the difficulties faced by the Alliance in influencing elections. He was a prominent Congregationalist minister in the city but was drawn to the organisation as a staunch anti-Catholic, taking part in the Papal Aggression agitation as well as the Maynooth issue, the latter on doctrinal as well as Voluntaryist grounds.[94] Although he was, like many of his Congregationalist peers, a staunch Liberal, because of his public face in the organisation of anti-Catholicism in the city it was nevertheless all the more surprising when Goddall voted for both Granger and Atherton and therefore against the anti-Catholic Conservative candidate Adolphus Vane. In an open letter to Vane printed in the *Durham Chronicle*, Goddall attempted to justify his stance by arguing that Alliance members should not feel pressurised into voting for a particular candidate and that the organisation "was not formed for electioneering purposes".[95] This, however, brought a long and stinging reply from the Anglican Rev. Thomas Ebdon in the *Durham Advertiser*. The clergyman was incensed by Goddall's views:

> "You seem to forget that our Protestant Establishment is founded on the *Union of Church and State*. Thus, members of Parliament become our representatives in the House of Commons, and electioneering concerns are of necessity mixed up with the proceedings of the Alliance. This Society strongly recommends that candidates offering their services to Parliament shall be required to give a pledge that they will support certain measures calculated to maintain the Protestant cause".

Edbon therefore accused Goddall of "not merely sleeping on your post, but what is far worse—aiding the enemy".[96]

In the following weeks, the question of whether the Alliance was effectively an electioneering machine for the Tory party or whether its

---

[93] *Durham Advertiser*, 23 April 1852.

[94] As stated earlier, Goddall spoke at the Papal Aggression and anti-Maynooth meetings in the city. He also delivered lectures on a number of anti-Catholic topics throughout the early 1850s. For example, in December 1850, he lectured on the subject of 'The Supremacy of the Pope' at Claypath Chapel before a 'large and attentive audience'. *Durham Chronicle*, 27 December 1850.

[95] *Durham Chronicle*, 28 July 1852.

[96] *Durham Advertiser*, 6 August 1852.

members had freedom of choice to choose between candidates was debated in the columns of the two Durham newspapers. The *Durham Chronicle*, siding with Goddall, suggested that the Conservatives had "relied on trapping Liberal votes by means of the Alliance".[97] A letter in the same paper from "A Protestant Dissenter" asserted that the Alliance had now "degenerated into a political engine for the support of a Ministry supposed to be favourable to illiberal and selfish principles".[98] Even the Anglican minister, the Rev. George Fox, who seemed to forget that he had openly pledged his vote for a Conservative candidate at the anti-Maynooth meeting in the town earlier that year, defended Goddall in his belief that "the Durham Protestant Alliance was not to be a political institution, much less to furnish an arena for electioneering purposes".[99] The end result was a serious division in the Durham Alliance, in particular the resignation of one of the Secretaries of the Alliance, George Moor,[100] and, with it, a decline in the relationship between Anglicans and Dissenters in the city.[101]

   In other constituencies, the Protestant organisations played less of a role in the proceedings, but the Maynooth issue still remained an important one for Conservative candidates. In South Shields, the local Protestant Association was unusually quiet throughout the election campaign which suggested that it had quietly disbanded. However, the Conservative candidate, H.T. Liddell, was a staunch supporter of the anti-Maynooth campaign. Liddell had voted for the grant in 1845, but now felt that the measure had failed in its original aim of conciliation of the Irish priesthood and, therefore, he pledged that he would now vote against the measure but only on the grounds of doctrinal, rather than Voluntaryist, reasons. The Liberal candidate, R. Ingham, took the opposite view and stated that he would not vote for the abolition of the grant, believing "that a conciliatory course towards our Roman Catholic fellow subjects would gradually alter their feelings towards Protestantism".[102] It was the Liberal candidate, however, who was victorious in the election.[103] There were some notable

---

[97] *Durham Chronicle*, 13 August 1852.
[98] Ibid.
[99] *Durham Advertiser*, 13 August 1852.
[100] *Durham Advertiser*, 20 August 1852.
[101] Controversy over whether to support a 'Protestant' candidate was not unique to the North East. In the sectarian battleground of Liverpool, the Conservative Anglican (and explicitly anti-Catholic) the Rev. Hugh McNeile appeared to compromise his Protestant principles by supporting a Protectionist candidate with "unsound" religious opinions; see Wolffe, *Protestant Crusade*, p. 264.
[102] *Newcastle Journal*, 10 April 1852; *Shields Gazette,* 19 March 1852.
[103] *Durham Advertiser*, 9 July 1852.

successes for anti-Maynooth Conservatives in other constituencies. In Sunderland, Tynemouth and North Durham, the Conservatives George Hudson, Hugh Taylor, and T.H. Liddell saw off the challenges of the Liberal candidates with their anti-Maynooth views.[104] To what extent Maynooth proved to be the deciding factor for voters is difficult to ascertain.[105]

The 1852 general election also saw the emergence of widespread bloc voting by the Catholic community for candidates who supported their interests. In the country as a whole, their political strength was not as numerous as their population would suggest. Two-thirds of the Catholics in England were Irish immigrants but only a small proportion were enfranchised.[106] Moreover, the Catholic converts after 1845 were not sufficiently numerous nor were they active in politics.[107] Nevertheless, this did not stop them from trying to influence various electoral contests to their own ends, particularly in the North East where the Catholic community was strong and bloc voting was commonplace. Who they would vote for, however, was a different matter. Traditionally, the Catholics had sided with the Liberals but, as the *Tablet* pointed out, the recent activities of the Liberal Government had left them facing something of a dilemma:

> "(The Catholic electors) cannot vote for Whigs, who supported the penal bill (Ecclesiastical Titles Bill) but who, in other respects, conform most near to the electors' political principles: and on the other hand . . . regular Tory hacks, pledged to support bigotry, and a stringent application of the penal bill, and in whose political creed the Catholic elector has no sympathy".[108]

This may explain why the Catholics of the North East generally appeared divided in pledging their votes. In South Shields, the choice was straightforward as they chose to support Robert Ingham in South Shields

---

[104] *Sunderland Herald*, 9 July 1852; *Durham Advertiser*, 23 July 1852.

[105] In a recent article, W.F. Matthews ignores the subject of religion completely when examining the Sunderland election. W.F. Matthews, 'The Sunderland Election of 1852', *Northern History*, 48.2 (2011), pp. 315-36.

[106] O'Day, A., 'The Political Representation of the Irish in Great Britain', *Governments, Ethnic Groups and Political Representation: Comparative Studies on Governments and Non-Dominant Ethnic Groups in Europe, 1850-1940*, ed. by G. Alderman, 4 vols (New York University Press: Dartmouth, 1993), IV, p. 35.

[107] J.L. Altholz, 'The Political Behaviour of the English Catholics, 1850-67', *Journal of British Studies*, 4:1 (1964), p. 90.

[108] *Tablet,* 13 March 1852.

who, according to the *Tablet*, "has for many years evinced much liberality and kindness to his Catholic fellow countrymen".[109] Ingham also received the support of the Catholic lecturer, Charles Larkin, who congratulated him particularly on his eloquent defence of the Catholics of Ireland in Parliament.[110] Across the river in Tynemouth, the Catholics electors were said to be "sufficiently numerous, in a close contest, to decide the election".[111] However, in this contest, they were generally divided with some voting for the successful Conservative candidate, Hugh Taylor, and others for the Liberal candidate George Grey. The *Tablet* bemoaned the fact that had all the Catholics voted for Grey, "they would have been sufficiently numerous to put in the Whig by a majority of two".[112] In Sunderland, in which there were about 40 Catholic electors, the Irish Catholic priest, the Rev. Philip Kearney, was active in organising the Catholics in a bloc to assist those candidates who supported the repeal of the Ecclesiastical Titles Bill and were in favour of the Maynooth Grant. Here, Kearney followed the example of his clerical contemporaries from his native country where, according to one historian, the priest was one of many "wheeler-dealers, suppliers of favours, and orchestrator of pressure groups" in the political arena, holding enormous sway over the outcome of elections.[113] Nevertheless, he failed to make use of his flock as there appeared to be no obvious candidate for the Catholics of Sunderland. Both Liberals, Fenwick and Seymour, were far from perfect candidates, as the former opposed the abolition of the Maynooth Grant but refused to support the repeal of the Ecclesiastical Titles Bill, while the latter supported the repeal of this measure but not the Maynooth Grant.[114] Although Fenwick was eventually victorious, the indecision of the Catholics may partly explain why the Conservative, George Hudson, was eventually elected with him.

Although the Maynooth issue continued to stir anti-Catholic passions well into the 1860s, it would never again generate the same amount of interest as in 1845 and 1852. The MP, Richard Spooner, continued his anti-Maynooth crusade in Parliament much to the increasing derision of his colleagues, but the issue declined in support throughout the country as the 1850s progressed. This was particularly the case after 1854, when a

---

[109] Ibid.

[110] *Tablet*, 27 March 1852.

[111] *Tablet*, 3 May 1851.

[112] *Tablet*, 6 August 1851.

[113] K.T. Hoppen, *Elections, Politics, and Society in Ireland, 1832-1885* (Oxford: Clarendon Press, 1984), p. 232.

[114] *Tablet*, 27 March 1852; *Sunderland News*, 27 March 1852.

Royal Commission appointed to investigate Maynooth failed to prove the anti-Catholic fantasies of political dissension and moral depravity.[115] Petitions still continued to arrive from some localities including County Durham, notably Stockton, Hartlepool, Norton, Darlington, Hetton-le Hole and Houghton-le-Spring, as well as Wesleyan chapels in Weardale.[116] The Durham clergyman, the Rev. George Fox, was also active in trying to resurrect the anti-Maynooth campaign in a national meeting of Protestants on the subject in London, where the minister said of the report of the Royal Commission that it was drawn up "in a Popish spirit, and was altogether a one-sided document".[117] Indeed, Fox was so committed to the anti-Catholic cause that he was unable to spend time on assisting with his temperance movement duties.[118] Nevertheless, as Wolffe has pointed out, the agitation during these years was based "more on energetic action and less on public sympathy" than earlier in the decade, particularly as the Crimean War and the Indian Mutiny vied for the attention of evangelicals.[119] By the end of the 1850s the issue had lost so much support that the Protestant Alliance even considered dissolving itself.[120] During the 1860s, the Maynooth issue increasingly receded into the background, eventually disappearing from view after the Irish Disestablishment Act effectively depoliticised it.[121]

Strange Bedfellows? Catholics and Conservatives, 1852-68

Part of the reason for the decline of the Maynooth issue during the 1850s and 1860s was due to the attempts of the Conservatives to court the Catholic vote. In the years 1852-68, the public attitude of Conservatism towards Catholicism was not the defence of the "Protestant Constitution" but a superficial attempt to defend Catholic rights. This essentially became party policy after 1852 when Conservative candidates were becoming increasingly nervous about playing the No Popery card. Where Conservative MPs did contest elections, references to sectarian issues were made sparingly or indirectly. At Durham in 1857, the Conservative MP, John Mowbray, stated his "determination to uphold those Protestant principles to which under the blessing of Divine Providence, we are

---

[115] Wallis, *Popular Anti-Catholicism*, p. 144.
[116] *Sunderland Herald*, 11 May 1854; *Durham Chronicle*, 4, 11 May, 8 June 1855.
[117] *Durham Advertiser*, 20 April 1855.
[118] DCRO, Letter from G.T. Fox to [unknown], 17 March 1855, D/X 487/10/16.
[119] Wolffe, *Protestant Crusade*, p. 276.
[120] Wolffe, *Protestant Crusade*, p. 282.
[121] Wallis, *Popular Anti-Catholicism*, p. 153.

indebted as well for our civil as our religious liberties".[122] At Sunderland, the Conservative MP, George Hudson, made a similar speech in defence of the Established Church, which he saw as a "great barrier against intolerance and bigotry".[123] The only role played by the Maynooth Grant in the Newcastle election was from a Liberal Voluntaryist viewpoint, in which the candidate P. Carstairs pledged his determination to repeal the Grant. This was, however, only on the pretext of abolishing all endowments including the Irish Church.[124] In the county elections, similarly vague speeches were made from Conservatives. Lord Adolphus Vane, who was contesting North Durham in 1857, stated only that he would "support the interest of the Protestant Church". Only James Farrer, in the contest for South Durham, appeared willing to air his anti-Maynooth views by pointing to his votes in Parliament on the subject and pledging to continue supporting for a repeal of the Grant.[125]

In both the 1859 and 1865 elections, anti-Catholicism played virtually no part in the proceedings with both parties unwilling to raise the increasingly unfashionable "No Popery" cry.[126] Indeed, the Conservative policy of encouraging the Catholic vote appeared to be paying dividends, particularly after Garibaldi's crusade against the Pope began to receive staunch Liberal support.[127] For the Catholic electors, the Italian Question was "the central consideration of Catholic politics" and the Liberal support given to Italian independence effectively cemented the Tory-Catholic partnership.[128] This was further enhanced by the Pope's attack on Liberalism in his *Syllabus of Errors* published in 1864 which received universal condemnation in the Liberal press which considered it to be another example of the unenlightened and despotic thinking of the Catholic Church.[129] The Tories therefore were more than willing to form a partnership with a religious grouping they had effectively shunned in the years before 1852.

---

[122] *Durham Advertiser*, 13 March 1857.

[123] *Sunderland Herald*, 3 April 1857.

[124] *Newcastle Guardian*, 28 March 1857.

[125] *Durham Advertiser*, 13 March 1857.

[126] This appeared to be the situation nationwide as Wolffe has noted that anti-Catholicism was only a "minor force" in the 1859 election; Wolffe, *Protestant Crusade*, p. 280.

[127] K.T. Hoppen, 'Tories, Catholics and the General Election of 1859', *The Historical Journal*, 13 (1970), p. 50.

[128] D. Quinn, *Patronage and Piety: The Politics of English Roman Catholics, 1850-1900* (Basingstoke: Macmillan, 1993), p. 10.

[129] Ibid, p. 13.

The effects of this partnership were even felt in the more traditionally Liberal-dominated North East, and there were some notable victories for Conservatives during these years. In Tynemouth, where accusations had been raised in the 1859 elections that Roman Catholic priests had been putting pressure on Catholic electors to vote for the Tories[130], the Conservative candidate Richard Hodgson won an important seat in the Tynemouth by-election in 1861 on the back of Catholic votes and the support of the Catholic priest of the town, the Rev. John Bewick.[131] By the time of the 1865 election, Conservative candidates were even found to be *supporting* the Maynooth Grant, as was the case with Somerset Beaumont in Newcastle[132] and the Hon. G.W. Barrington in the North Durham election.[133] The South Shields election was dominated by debates on which party the Catholics should really be voting for and whether it was right to keep repaying the Liberals "for the mere justice they did thirty-five years ago in aiding the carrying of the Emancipation Bill".[134] Others, however, were of the belief that the pro-Catholic policy of the Tories would prove as "baseless as sand".[135]

In Sunderland, the wooing of the Catholic electorate and the subsequent victory in 1865 of the Conservative candidate, J. Hartley, had a profound effect on the Liberal Party and, in particular, the defeated Liberal Alderman John Candlish. When a by-election was announced early in 1866, Candlish took the unprecedented step of adopting an extreme No Popery canvas. After losing the election in 1865, he appeared to take defeat gracefully and was even willing to absolve the Catholic electors from the charge of "folly and inconsistency" made by many of his supporters in voting for Hartley.[136] By the early months of 1866, however his mood had changed. In preparation for the contest, Candlish had invited Alessandro Gavazzi to Sunderland to lecture on the topic of 'No Popery'. He also issued placards to be placed all over the town, one of which described scenes of nuns being immured alive in locked underground

---

[130] *Durham Chronicle*, 20 May 1859.

[131] *Durham Chronicle*, 26 April 1861. John William Bewick, 3rd Bishop of Hexham (1882), b. 1824 (Northumberland), o.1850, d. 1886. *English and Welsh Priests*, p. 38.

[132] He also stated that he was in favour of equal treatment for Catholics and Protestants in workhouses. *Newcastle Guardian*, 7 July 1865.

[133] *Durham Advertiser*, 30 June 1865.

[134] *Shields Daily News*, 27 June 1865.

[135] *Shields Daily News*, 30 June 1865.

[136] *Sunderland Herald*, 1 September 1865.

basements at Roman Catholic convents.[137] In his speeches he made frequent attacks on the other Liberal candidate in the contest, Henry Fenwick. Candlish believed that Fenwick was secretly a Catholic because of his pro-Catholic stance in Parliament in support of the Maynooth Grant and other legislative measures. In contrast, Candlish pledged at a meeting to the electors his support against all state endowments "and especially and double to Papal endowments", accusing Fenwick of advocating a policy that is likely to be "destructive to civil and religious liberty (loud cheers)". Candlish turned the screw even further by accusing Fenwick's wife of being a secret Roman Catholic.[138]

Not surprisingly, Candlish faced a large amount of opposition for his views, particularly among Fenwick's supporters. The *Sunderland Herald*, who sided with Fenwick, was particularly vocal against Candlish, bemoaning the increase in sectarian intolerance that his canvass had brought to the town:

> "To use the No Popery cry for the purpose of gaining popularity is contemptible in the extreme, and the constituency can hardly fail to see how little right to the name of Liberal is possessed by the narrow-minded and bigoted individuals who employ it, and how unscrupulous the party who seek to elevate themselves by prejudices so entirely opposed to the principles they profess to be desirous of promoting".[139]

Fenwick himself attacked Candlish's canvas as "illiberal" and "full of so many mis-statements calculated to deceive".[140]

The end result was victory for Candlish, much to the outrage of the more tolerant Liberals of the town. Fenwick had been a long-standing MP in the constituency but he was ultimately defeated, according to the *Sunderland Herald*, due to "industrious and persistent mis-representation of his conduct". Indeed, the fact that Candlish eventually ended up winning the election on the back of a blatant exploitation of No Popery suggests that, given the right set of circumstances, a strong feeling existed in Sunderland for the more extreme elements of anti-Catholicism. Candlish was at least true to his word as the "champion of Protestantism", causing outrage in Parliament by introducing a motion to disqualify a Roman Catholic from filling the office of Lord Lieutenant of Ireland.[141]

---

[137] *Sunderland Herald*, 9 February 1866.
[138] *Sunderland Herald*, 16 February 1866.
[139] *Sunderland Herald*, 9 February 1866.
[140] *Sunderland Herald*, 16 February 1866.
[141] *Sunderland Herald*, 25 March 1866; *Durham Chronicle* 24 May 1867.

The canvass of Candlish in Sunderland is perhaps an isolated example, but it does reveal the way in which Liberals as well as Conservatives could sometimes exploit the ideology of No Popery for their own ends.

The Conservatives, however, were not entirely pro-Catholic throughout these years either. Indeed, if the Conservative public face was one of toleration, the reality was rather different. Local Conservative MPs reverted to type in their defence of the "Protestant Constitution" once they secured their seats and were active in opposing the raft of pro-Catholic legislation. The bill intending to alter the parliamentary Oath for Roman Catholics is a case in point. Opposition to altering the Oath of Supremacy to make it less offensive to Catholics, as well as to abolish the Oath of Abjuration, were indeed rare. This opposition rested on the premise that these measures effectively safeguarded the Protestant faith and the Protestant succession to the throne. Liberals had nothing but disdain for this opposition to what they essentially saw as progressive legislation. Larsen has noted that campaigns in favour of the Roman Catholic Oaths Bill won the support of Liberal Dissenters who sympathised with Catholics on the grounds of religious equality. The Protestant Dissenting Deputies even petitioned in favour of the bill.[142] This may help to explain why public opposition was rare in the Liberal-Dissenter dominated North East. The *Darlington and Stockton Times* was typical of other Liberal papers in reaction to this effort in 1865, describing the oath as a "disgrace to our Protestant Christianity, an insult and a sham".[143] In Parliament, the Liberal MPs of the region all voted for the alterations to legislation while the few local Conservatives opposed it.[144] At any rate, the political response towards these measures was always likely to be coloured by the Liberal dominance in the region's politics and consequently there appears to have been little attempt to organise a meeting or even a petition from the Conservatives and Anglicans in any part of the North East. Indeed, the Liberal elite were primarily responsible for the eventual passing of the bill in 1866, after the local Liberal aristocrat, Sir George Grey, reintroduced the measure into parliament.[145]

The traditional Conservative/Liberal divide on "No Popery" legislation is also evident in the response to the introduction of Roman Catholic chaplains in the armed services, prisons and workhouses. Irish Catholics

---

[142] Larsen, *Friends of Religious Equality*, pp. 227, 240.

[143] *Darlington and Stockton Times*, 27 May 1865.

[144] In June 1865 legislation to amend the Roman Catholic Relief Bill amounted to support from eight Liberal MP's and opposition from the three Conservatives in the North East. *Durham Chronicle*, 13 July 1859.

[145] Machin, *Politics and the Churches*, p. 336.

comprised a sizeable minority in these institutions and many believed it was perfectly acceptable that they should be provided with amenities to practise their religion.[146] The measure was first brought before Parliament by Lord Palmerston in December 1853. Opposition was immediately declared from the Scottish Reformation Society in March 1854 and, partly as a result of their campaign, the motion was defeated in June 1854.[147] Local Conservative MPs were active in voting against it, such as Lord Adolphus Vane and Messrs Farrer, Hydson, Liddell and Mowbray. The local Liberals, such as Atherton, Forster, Ingham, Majorbanks, Seymour and Shafto, all voted in its favour.[148] As with the Parliamentary Oaths Bill, opposition in the localities was rare and limited to extremists. The Newcastle Protestant Alliance, which had become more narrowly anti-Catholic by the 1860s, held a meeting in the Temperance Hall on the subject in 1863 to organise a petition against a new proposal to introduce Roman Catholic chaplains in prisons.[149] This proposal was designed to improve the facilities of non-Anglican prisoners in England and Scotland and was successfully passed in spite of this opposition from the Protestant Alliance.[150] Nevertheless, resistance continued from internal bodies long after legislation received the royal assent. The Durham County Magistrates voted down a proposition from Henry Fenwick to appoint a Catholic chaplain in Durham gaol.[151] In the Newcastle Gaol, the town council discussed increasing the salary of the Roman Catholic chaplain. His salary was £30 in comparison to the Anglican chaplain who was paid £250 for his services. However, the council voted against an increase on financial grounds.[152] As will be shown in Chapter 5, the local Board of Guardians also provided continuous opposition to the appointment of a Roman Catholic chaplain in the workhouse.

The general trend, however, was towards a greater toleration of Roman Catholics and these measures received the support of a number of influential Liberal newspapers. After the defeat of the Roman Catholic Chaplains Bill in 1854, the *Sunderland Herald* believed it a victory for "narrow-minded bigotry and religious intolerance".[153] When the matter

---

[146] Gilley, 'The Roman Catholic Church in England', p. 357.

[147] Wolffe, *Protestant Crusade*, p. 271.

[148] *Durham Chronicle*, 16 June 1854.

[149] *Newcastle Guardian*, 28 February 1863.

[150] Machin, *Politics and the Churches*, p. 305.

[151] *Darlington Stockton and Times*, 9 April 1864.

[152] TWAS, *Newcastle Town Council Minutes*, I, 13 April 1868.

[153] *Sunderland Herald*, 16 June 1854.

was raised again in the early 1860s, the *Newcastle Guardian* defended the bill as a matter of fair play to their Roman Catholic contemporaries:

> All advocates of civil and religious equality . . . must admit that so long as Protestant clergymen   are paid for their services, Catholic priests, when employed by the State, should not be excluded from State pay. We know not then what objection can be raised to this measure.[154]

Indeed, most of the political activity surrounding the measure came from the Catholics themselves. Throughout the 1860s, Roman Catholic congregations from Newcastle and Durham, as well as smaller towns such as Birtley, Blaydon, Consett, Croxdale, Stella, Seaham Harbour, Broom, all petitioned the legislature in favour of the bill.[155]

Irish Disestablishment and the 1868 General Election

By the late 1860s, it appeared that the tenets of anti-Catholic ideology associated with the defence of the "Protestant Constitution" were becoming a spent force. Conservative MPs were no longer reaping the benefits of playing the anti-Catholic card in elections, the Maynooth issue was all but dead in the water, and political anti-Catholicism in general was being directed towards narrower ends. However, the supporters of "No Popery" were to wage one last campaign against the Irish Disestablishment Bill in 1868. This issue ensured that the ideology of anti-Catholicism associated with a "Protestant Constitution" did not, as Wolffe has suggested, end with the failure of Spooner's anti-Maynooth campaign in 1860. That year, according to Wolffe, should be viewed as "marking the end of the rearguard action in defence of exclusively Protestant constitutional norms which had been fought over the three decades since 1829".[156] However, the campaign against Irish disestablishment reveals that this was far from the case.

For Irish Catholics, the Church of Ireland had been a symbol of oppression since the sixteenth century. It was originally perceived as "an instrument for making the Irish people Protestant" in the vain hope that it would provide better security for England against foreign invasion. Power was concentrated in the hands of the Church of Ireland, much to the anger

---

[154] *Newcastle Guardian*, 25 April 1863.

[155] *Durham Chronicle*, 24 April 1863; *Newcastle Daily Journal*, 3, 24 May 1865; *Durham Advertiser*, 5 May 1865; *Durham Chronicle*, 6 May 1865; *Shields Daily News*, 6 May 1865; *Newcastle Courant*, 11 May 1866.

[156] Wolffe, *Protestant Crusade*, p. 288.

of the Irish Catholic Church. During the sixteenth and seventeenth centuries, the newly-created Protestant communities flourished in the North.[157] However, it had failed in its ultimate aim of the mass conversion of Ireland and, by the nineteenth century, its privileged position in Irish society was becoming more and more questionable. The 1861 Irish Census was an embarrassment for the Irish Church. Its members accounted for only 11.9% of the population in contrast to the Roman Catholics who amounted to over 77.6%,[158] Calls for its disendowment began in December 1864 with the formation of the National Association of Ireland and, in July 1867, the Liberation Society took up the cause.[159] By this stage many Liberal MPs were calling for disestablishment and, in March 1868, Gladstone introduced the very proposal into Parliament in the hope that it would act as unifying principle for all Liberals in his party.[160]

The parliamentary campaign for disestablishment was a long and protracted affair, lasting well over a year and coinciding with a general election at the end of 1868. The battleground was more or less divided into two clear-cut groupings—those who were in favour of disestablishment and those who were against it. Those who were in favour included Liberals of various factions, Dissenters and Irish Catholics. They believed that it was a wrong for a Church, which comprised such a small proportion of the population, to possess the levels of privilege and wealth it enjoyed.[161] Dissenters also exploited the issue to attack all state endowments and the Anglican Church in general. Still revelling in the abolition of church rates from the previous year, many Dissenters saw Irish disestablishment as a precursor to disestablishing the Church in England. Even Wesleyans, who had been generally happy to side with the Anglicans in defence of the "Protestant Constitution" in the past, joined the pro-disestablishment side.[162] For Irish Catholics, they had a particularly

---

[157] P.M.H. Bell, *Disestablishment in Ireland and Wales* (London: SPCK, 1969), p. 26. It is worth noting that a substantial number of these Protestant communities were Presbyterian rather than Church of Ireland.

[158] Ibid, pp. 40-1.

[159] Ibid, p. 42. For a history of the Liberation Society, see D.M. Thompson, 'The Liberation Society, 1844-1868', *Pressure From Without in Early Victorian England*, ed. by P. Hollis (London: Edward Arnold, 1874), pp. 210-38.

[160] Machin, *Politics and the Churches*, p. 358.

[161] Bell, *Disestablishment*, pp. 45-7.

[162] H.J. Hanham, *Elections and Party Management: Politics in the Time of Gladstone and Disraeli* (London: Harvester Press, 1959), p. 212; Ian Machin, 'Disestablishment and Democracy, c.1840-1930', *Citizenship and Community: Liberals, Radicals and Collective Identities in the British Isles, 1865-1931*, ed. by Eugenio F. Biagini (Cambridge: Cambridge University Press, 1996), pp. 123-4.

personal grievance. They felt that the land held by the Irish Church had been unjustly seized from its rightful Catholic owners. The Church of Ireland was effectively a symbol of the Protestant Ascendancy. Both Catholics and Dissenters felt that they could work together to achieve Irish disestablishment, so much so that the Liberation Society abandoned its opposition to the Maynooth Grant in order to obtain Catholic support.[163] Nevertheless, the Catholic community remained quiet in the affair, perhaps assuming that any opposition could prove counterproductive.[164] Those who were against disestablishment saw the matter rather differently. Comprising mainly of Conservatives and Anglicans, they were horrified at the idea of conceding the Irish Church and undermining the "Protestant Constitution". Many, of course, had much to lose by this course of action, not just financially but symbolically also. They believed that the Established Church was the true Church of Ireland and to give up the Irish Church would weaken the Establishment principle. They also pointed to the fact that if the Irish Church was weakened, the Catholic Church would seize the opportunity for proselytising Irish Protestants.[165] This was supplemented by a feeling of paranoia within the Irish Church, as no contingency plan was in place if the disestablishment act was successfully passed.[166]

In the North East of England, where Dissenters and Roman Catholics formed the majority of the religious population, it would have been expected that the disestablishment question would be a very much one-sided affair in favour of those who supported it. It is certainly true that there appeared to be a great deal of support for disestablishment in the region. Many of the Liberal papers, in particular the *Newcastle Chronicle*, threw their weight behind the cause. The *Chronicle,* edited during this period by the influential Radical, Joseph Cowen, saw the Irish Church Question as one involving a "fundamental change in our national life" and as an example of the "blast of popular will".[167] The *Darlington and Stockton Times* also praised Gladstone for framing his resolutions in such a way that "no man, who earnestly wished to remove the great grievance of the Irish people, and to make the nation really and peacefully united, could gainsay them".[168] Other papers drew attention to the weakness of the Church of Ireland, questioning its purpose in the first place. The

---

[163] Machin, *Politics and the Churches*, p. 322.
[164] Hugh Shearman, *Privatising a Church: The Disestablishment and Disendowment of the Church of Ireland* (Lurgan: Ulster Society, 1995), p. 26.
[165] Bell, *Disestablishment*, pp. 49.
[166] Shearman, *Privatising a Church*, p. 26.
[167] *Newcastle Chronicle*, 21 March 1868.
[168] *Darlington and Stockton Times*, 4 April 1868.

Sunderland News, called wholeheartedly for Irish disestablishment, perceiving the Ascendancy as "a vile fungus, tumour and cancer of three hundred years' growth".[169] The *Durham Chronicle* was more moderate. It praised the Church of England but saw the Irish Church as "doomed", believing that any attempts to organise an opposition would be "the greatest of blunders".[170]

However, in spite of their numerical disadvantage, the Conservatives and Anglicans in the region were determined to ensure that their voice against disestablishment could be heard also. The two Tory papers both supported the Irish Church and were more than willing to defend what they perceived to be an unjust attack upon the "Protestant Constitution". The *Newcastle Journal* called on the Conservative party to attack the motion "strenuously and openly", describing the opposition as based on "merely a sentimental grievance". Above all, disestablishment would "entirely put off, the time when we may hope, from increased education and cultivation, Ireland may become entirely Protestant". The paper hoped that "not only Churchmen, but Protestants of all denominations will arouse themselves" against the disestablishment cause.[171] For the *Durham Advertiser*, this was nothing more than a shrewd political manoeuvre on the part of the Liberal party to gain office:

"Mr. Gladstone desires the destruction of the Irish Church not as he pretends as an act of political justice, but in order that he may have a chance of reaching the seat Mr. Disraeli occupies on the Treasury benches".[172]

The hopes of the *Newcastle Journal* that the opposition would consist of all denominations of Protestants proved unfounded as the issue developed along specific political and religious lines: Liberals and Dissenters in favour, Conservatives and Anglicans against. Throughout 1868, a series of rival meetings and lectures were organised on the disestablishment question. Meetings against disestablishment were dominated by Anglican clergymen. Thus, at an anti-disestablishment meeting in Gateshead, it was observed by the local paper that all the major Anglican clergy of the area were present.[173] Meetings in favour saw Dissenting ministers dominate, including those such as the active pro-

[169] *Sunderland News*, 4 April 1868.
[170] *Durham Chronicle*, 20 March 1868.
[171] *Newcastle Journal*, 21 March 1868.
[172] *Durham Advertiser*, 3 April 1868.
[173] *Gateshead Observer*, 22 August 1868.

disestablishment Rev. John Rutherford, who had angered Catholics in the past with his sectarian views. Often these meetings advertised the appearance of a notable lecturer who would address the audience on a topic in favour of the objects of the meeting. The Secretary of the Protestant Defence Association, R.W. Gamble, who toured the region during the summer and autumn of 1868 giving lectures against disestablishment in a number of towns, was a notable example.[174] Meetings were held and petitions sent, for and against, from almost every town and village, which was testament to how deeply felt the question was in the region.[175]

Part of the reason for this heightened level of interest was the 1868 general election, whose significance was enhanced by the enfranchisement of a greater proportion of the population following the passing of the Second Reform Act in the previous year. In the urban towns of the North East, the rise in the number of people eligible to vote was spectacular: In South Shields, the register rose from 1,200 in 1865 to 7,000 in 1868; in Sunderland from 3,200 to 11,500 and in Newcastle from 7,500 to 18,600.[176] It had also created a larger number of constituencies—in the North East, the inhabitants of Darlington, Stockton and Hartlepool were given the opportunity to elect their own MP. In this election, the Irish Question was of paramount importance, particularly to those new constituents who felt they could now have a definite say on the important questions of the day. The issue effectively divided the newly-enfranchised working class but there were clearly a large number who were against disestablishment. At St. Stephen's Lecture Room on Scotswood Road near Newcastle, a lecture from the Rev. Graham Norton in defence of the Irish Church was "attentively listened to by a considerable number of working men, who frequently expressed their approbation of the views brought before them".[177] At Gateshead, a barrister, John Bingham, lectured to 200 working men in favour of the Irish Church and calling on them to adopt the motto "No Surrender" at the next general election.[178] The question was particularly acute in the city of Durham, where a local Constitutional

---

[174] He visited Gateshead, Stockton, South Shields, Bishop Auckland, Sunderland, Newcastle and Durham amongstother places. *Gateshead Observer*, 22 August 1868; *Durham Advertiser*, 28 August 1868; *Newcastle Chronicle*, 12 September 1868; *Newcastle Chronicle*, 17 October 1868; *Durham Chronicle*, 23 October 1868.

[175] See local press reports throughout the summer and autumn of 1868.

[176] Nossiter, *Influence*, p. 39.

[177] *Newcastle Daily Journal*, 24 September 1868.

[178] *Gateshead Obserser*, 20 June 1868.

Association was formed by working men on the basis of uniting "the friends of Constitutional principles in resisting any attempt to subvert the Constitution of the country".[179] Meetings were often stormy affairs, particularly those gatherings in favour of the Irish Church. A lecture by a Joseph Barker at Easington Colliery was interrupted by a group of Primitive Methodists, who had a large working class support in the pit villages of County Durham. The lecturer invited discussion and two Primitives and two laymen ascended the platform amidst "a great deal of hissing and other signs of disapproval".[180] At South Shields, a lecture by Dr. Massingham which lasted nearly four hours, was crowded with an audience "evidently determined from the first to be turbulent".[181]

By far the most serious disturbances, however, took place in the Durham and Newcastle meetings. In Durham, a lecture by the Rev. Henry Gamble was organised under the auspices of the Durham Constitutional Association. The *Advertiser* reported that well before the meeting was due to start, the lecture hall was "filled with organised opposition of a very low kind". Throughout the lecture, two working men, Mr. Donnabey of Gilesgate and a packer by the name of Maurice Flinn, hollered and shouted throughout the lecturer's performance. These men stirred a crowd of Irishmen who, at the end of the lecture, rushed towards the platform "and fairly took it by storm", causing the chairman quickly to terminate the proceedings.[182] A similar outcome occurred in a meeting of the Friends of the Irish Church in Newcastle. The meeting had been stormy throughout but it was the decision of Dr. Rutherford to obtain the platform in favour of disestablishment which ensured the issue became more than a merely a heated exchange of words. There was some confusion as to whether Rutherford should be allowed a hearing as his views were contrary to the objects of the meeting. Cries of "Rutherford, get upon the platform" and "Rutherford, get down" rang throughout the hall. Rutherford was eventually carried by the upheld hands of the crowd towards the door. Fights broke out in the main body of the hall, tables and chairs were overturned and men were thrown from the platform onto the ensuing melee below. As the crowd left the building they continued their arguments on the street and a number of "open-air" meetings were attempted although they were quickly dispersed by the police.[183] In the newspaper discussions of the following days, it had been discovered that a

---

[179] *Durham Advertiser*, 14 August 1868.

[180] *Durham Chronicle*, 11 September 1868.

[181] *Newcastle Chronicle*, 27 June 1868.

[182] *Durham Advertiser*, 23 October 1868.

[183] *Newcastle Chronicle*, 6 June 1868.

large number of tickets for the meeting had been circulated to Irish Catholics and Dissenters and a number of "roughs" were able to get in because the policeman stationed at the door left his post.[184] A lecture by the Rev. Graham Norton and Mr. R.W. Gamble in October also caused a near-riot between Orangemen and Ribbonmen. When it was discovered that there were Orangemen present and an organised attempt from a "Roman Catholic guild" to disturb the lecture was about to take place, the chairman attempted to end the meeting. The itinerant preacher David Davies then managed to obtain the platform, taunting the Catholics, and shouting "We will win the day". This caused a sudden surge towards the platform and again chairs and tables were destroyed and windows were broken by huge pieces of clay. The gas was turned out and eventually those still left inside the hall dispersed.[185]

The Irish Question, therefore, was not one to be taken lightly and many local MPs who were contesting the 1868 general election were fully aware of its political advantages. In Newcastle, Joseph Cowan, who had organised and spoke at a number of meetings in favour of Irish disestablishment, received the support of the Irish electors, many of whom were newly enfranchised by the Second Reform Act.[186] The other Liberal candidate, the long-standing MP, Thomas Headlam, also believed in disestablishing the church. However, because his father was a Church of England minister, it was alleged that his heart was not in the cause.[187] The heightened religious feeling also saw the appearance of the first Conservative candidate in Newcastle for over 20 years, although Charles Hammond's stance against disestablishment was to prove fruitless as the two Liberal candidates won the election easily.[188] In Durham, the young Conservative candidate, John Lloyd Wharton, who was also chairman of the Durham Constitutional Association, saw disestablishment as a precursor to the "destruction of all existing Establishments in the Empire".[189] He was, however, defeated by the two Liberal candidates, J. Henderson and J.R. Davison, who were both in favour of disestablishment. Similar results occurred in Tynemouth, Stockton, and the county election of South Durham.

The Conservatives had failed in their attempt to mobilise the new armies of working class support and there was therefore no repeat in the

---

[184] *Newcastle Daily Journal,* 5 June 1868.
[185] *Newcastle Chronicle*, 17 October 1868.
[186] *Newcastle Chronicle*, 31 October 1868.
[187] Ibid.
[188] *Newcastle Chronicle,* 21 November 1868.
[189] *Durham Advertiser*, 6 November 1868.

region of the "Tory triumph" apparent in some areas of the country, most notably in south-east Lancashire where popular Protestantism and anti-Catholicism were successfully employed by the Conservatives to secure nine out of the fifteen seats available.[190] Overall, it was the "worst Conservative performance anywhere in the country".[191] Gladstone's aim to unite the Liberal Party with disestablishment[192] appears to have paid off in the stronghold of the North East. Only in the county election of North Durham and the new constituency of Hartlepool, were there Conservative successes, with George Elliott and Ralph Ward Jackson succeeding respectively. Nossiter has suggested that the North Durham Conservative victory can be partly explained by the reorganisation of the party since 1865. It was divided into central and district committees and working men's associations, with the aim of reducing its dependence on the Londonderry family.[193] Nossiter also points to the standing of Elliott as a coal owner which, in a recession-hit climate, may have helped sway the newly-enfranchised working class vote by the promise of employment.[194] In Hartlepool, Ward Jackson was a similar Conservative industrialist, who had made his fortune and reputation in iron, providing employment for English and Irish alike, and thus would have benefited in the newly created constituency.[195]

However, even in constituencies where there were no Conservative candidates, religion could still cause controversy if the local conditions were right. In South Shields, the two candidates, J.C. Stevenson and the Jarrow shipbuilder Charles Palmer, were both Liberals. Unlike his adversary, however, Palmer refused to vote for the disestablishment of the Irish Church, which, as the *Shields Gazette* pointed out, was "certainly a very strange proposal to announce from a Liberal platform.[196] Because of his views on the Irish Church, it was alleged that the members of the local Orange Order, which had been steadily growing in numbers and influence on the banks of the Tyne since the early 1860s, were ordered by their superiors to vote for Palmer in the forthcoming election.[197] It appears,

---

[190] Lowe, J.C., 'The Tory Triumph of 1868 in Blackburn and Lancashire', *Historical Journal*, 16 (1973), pp. 733-48.

[191] Nossiter, *Influence*, p. 39.

[192] Bell, *Disestablishment*, p. 108.

[193] Nossiter, *Influence*, p. 88.

[194] Ibid, p. 91.

[195] Robert Wood, *West Hartlepool: The Rise and Development of a Victorian New Town* (Hartlepool: West Hartlepool Corporation, 1967), p. 52.

[196] *Shields Gazette*, 23 July 1868.

[197] See Chapter Six for an analysis of the Orange Order and anti-Catholicism.

however that many Orangemen were reluctant to follow the lead.[198] This caused a split in the organisation with many breaking off to form a new Orange Society.[199] Without the united support of Orangemen, Palmer lost the election and Stevenson was elected. In the newly-constituted Darlington constituency, the Irish Question appeared to be of secondary importance to the town's personal battle for power between the two Liberals, the Quaker Edmund Backhouse and Henry Spark. Spark was accused by another Quaker, Arthur Pease, of restricting the educational liberty of Roman Catholic children in the workhouse as a Guardian. This attempt backfired, however, as the *Darlington and Stockton Times* pledged its support for Spark. The paper was eager to break the Quaker monopoly, so much so that it reprinted minutes from a Board of Guardian meeting from May 1867 which appeared to show exactly the opposite.[200] Furthermore, Spark received the full support of the Catholic vote with the celebrated orator, Charles Larkin, giving him his personal endorsement.[201] In spite of this support, however, Backhouse still managed to win the election, much to the anger of the local paper which accused him of bribery:

> "Nothing but villainy could have seduced the hundreds of promised voters—including Committee men—from their allegiances to Mr. Spark . . . and Quaker gold and Quaker tyranny were only too ready to do the infamous work".[202]

Nationwide, the results of the general election proved to have little lasting influence on the campaign against Irish disestablishment as the measure was made law the following year. The anti-disestablishment movement represented the last mass anti-Catholic political movement in the North East, as it did elsewhere. After 1869, political "No Popery" became increasingly marginalised and could no longer stir popular passions to the same extent as in its former years.

It is clear, therefore, that the ideology of "No Popery", associated with the defence of the "Protestant Constitution" in the face of increasing Catholic toleration, was very much a minority ideology throughout this period. Nevertheless, it garnered a certain amount of influential support who wished to make their feelings known at every opportunity. Moreover,

---

[198] *Shields Gazette,* 17 August 1868.

[199] *Shields Gazette*, 25 August 1868.

[200] *Darlington and Stockton Times*, 29 August 1868.

[201] *Darlington and Stockton Times,* 7 November 1868.

[202] *Darlington and Stockton Times*, 21 November 1868.

if the conditions were right, they could sometimes successfully stir powerful ecumenical opposition, as is evident during the anti-Maynooth campaigns. The ideology of "No Popery" in particular acted as a rallying cry for the local Conservative Party by providing the most consistent issue on which the majority of Tory MP's could unite. This was certainly true during 1845-52 and the late 1860s. Without other local studies to compare it with, it is tempting to suggest that this reflected the general trend throughout the country, particularly as the ideology of the "Protestant Constitution" was facing stiff competition from other, perhaps more fashionable, tenets of political anti-Catholicism linked to notions of liberty and tyranny. As will be shown in the next chapter, these Liberal forms of political anti-Catholicism were to prove particularly popular in certain areas of the North East of England.

CHAPTER FOUR

ENLIGHTENED BIGOTRY:
ANTI-CATHOLICISM AND LIBERTY

"For hark! The destruction of Babylon is approaching;
The signs of the times portend its speedy fall,
For the beast on the justice of God is encroaching,
And Garibaldi to avenge it has had a call,

Where then is the beast and he who will slay it?
T'is in Rome they say in the garb of humility,
Let Garri, with the Sword of the Spirit belay it,
For showing to the Light such great hostility".[1]

In the previous chapter, it was shown how perceptions of concessions to Catholics over the "Protestant Constitution" could influence specific forms of anti-Catholic political thought in the North East of England. However, as the first chapter has demonstrated, "Liberal" forms of anti-Catholicism which played on Protestant interpretations of liberty and their opposition to "Popish" tyranny became increasingly popular during the mid-Victorian period. This particular filter of anti-Catholic thought was expressed in the support for a number of seemingly disparate but inter-linked campaigns that were influenced by a combination of Liberalism, Republicanism, internationalism, and anti-Catholicism. Under the banner of international liberty, anti-Catholic campaigners looked particularly towards Italy, where Catholic persecution and political despotism were very much intertwined and were evident in both the outcry against the treatment of the imprisoned Protestant missionaries, Rosa and Francisco Madiai, as well as support for Italian independence. These campaigns also tapped into the currents of anti-Catholicism inherent in Victorian evangelicalism—an evangelicalism that saw its ultimate aim in spreading Protestantism globally which, its supporters believed, would eventually lead to the complete eradication of its "Popish" arch enemy. Tropes of

---

[1] [B.T. Ord], *The Beginning of the End, or the Destruction of Babylon and the Fall of the Beast* (Hartlepool: Hartlepool Free Press, 1864), p.1.

"liberty" and "tyranny" were also evident in an issue closer to home: the campaign for the inspection of convents which reached its peak in the early 1850s.

This chapter will examine the support for these campaigns in the North East of England where, it will be argued, the Liberal-Radical tradition combined with a strongly evangelical religious culture in certain areas (particularly Tyneside) to ensure that this form of anti-Catholicism received a great deal more attention than it appeared to warrant elsewhere.[2] It will also show that the Liberal anti-Catholic campaigns could be as equally offensive to the Catholic community as the more explicitly anti-Catholic campaigns examined in the last chapter. Indeed it will show how these campaigns helped to encourage the formation of a strongly politicised Catholic body in the region, with the Risorgimento's attack on the Pope in particular providing Catholics with a important reason for steadfastly defending their faith.

Constitutional Liberty: The Campaign for Italian Independence

The strength of feeling in the North East, and on Tyneside in particular, towards the nationalist and liberal movements of Europe of the mid-nineteenth century were so well-known to contemporaries that The *Northern Tribune* felt itself able to claim in 1855 that "Newcastle has come to be looked upon as the headquarters of national patriotism".[3] Support was given to fund constitutional democracy in a number of countries, including Poland, Hungary and Russia, but by far the most popular was the campaign for Italian independence which ran intermittently between the years 1848-70. Regional support for the Risorgimento has been well researched[4] but these studies tend to see this support as a purely political one, emphasising the strength of Radicalism, and attending particularly to the role of Joseph Cowen in fostering Italian sentiment in the region. Joan Allen, for example, sees this emphasis on internationalism as a deep-rooted strand of Tyneside Radicalism.[5]

---

[2] This assumption is admittedly based on the limited research conducted elsewhere.
[3] *Northern Tribune*, Vol II, p. 65.
[4] N. Todd, *The Militant Democracy* (Whitley Bay: Bewick Press, 1991); J. Allen, *Joseph Cowen and Popular Radicalism on Tyneside* (Monmouth: Merlin Press, 2007).
[5] Allen, *Joseph Cowen*, p. 35.

However, the religious dimension of the question has largely been ignored.[6] For many contemporaries support for Italian independence was more than just a Radical movement with the aim of achieving international democracy. It was also an attack on Papal power. As John A. Davies suggests, "the republican internationalism of the middle class Radicals played heavily on hostility to England's traditional enemies and Catholicism".[7] This support may not have been *directly* linked to the Catholics themselves[8], but the arguments proposed often invoked latent anti-Catholic ideology. Indeed, as Biagini has argued, popular Radical movements began with what was essentially a "political interpretation of the Bible" and the Italian Question in particular played on the Protestant notion of a direct relationship between man and God.[9] In the eyes of anti-Catholics, Papal power and despotic government was essentially the same thing. The overthrow of the Pope and his replacement with a constitutional form of government was optimistically perceived as a way to usher in a new dawn for Italy. This new dawn was one infused with civil and religious liberty of the kind that Protestant Britain currently enjoyed. Indeed, the model of constitutional government in England provided the blueprint for a new Italy, liberated from "foreigners and priests".[10] This essentially appealed to nationalist notions of the superiority of English institutions over their continental neighbours.[11] However, for the Catholics themselves the attacks on Papal power were attacks on the very foundation of their religion. The Pope was there for a reason, as having been ordained by God. The religious arguments, to a certain extent, cannot be divorced from the political situation.[12] While there were those, such as Joseph

---

[6] The exception to this is D.M. Jackson's study of the Garibaldi riot in Newcastle which acknowledges the loyalty of the Irish towards the Pope as the main cause of ethnic friction and implies the link between the local Liberal press and anti-Catholicism, although this link is not examined in any detail. D.M. Jackson, "'Garibaldi or the Pope!'", pp. 49-76.

[7] John A. Davies, 'Garibaldi and England', *History Today*, 32.12 (1982), p. 24.

[8] Eugenio F. Biagini, *Liberty, Retrenchment and Reform: Popular Liberalism in the Age of Gladstone, 1860-1880* (Cambridge: Cambridge University Press, 1992), p. 16.

[9] This is best summed up in the Italian revolutionary Mazzini's famous war cry against despotism, "God and the People". Ibid, pp. 38, 46.

[10] C. T. McIntire, *England against the Papacy*, p. 7.

[11] G. Clayes, 'Mazzini, Kossuth and British Radicalism 1848-1854', *Journal of British Studies*, 28.3 (1989), p. 231.

[12] John Wolffe has demonstrated how political events in Europe were often perceived by British Protestants in a religious context. John Wolffe, 'British Protestants and Europe, 1820-1860: some perceptions and influences', in *The*

Cowen, who exploited the Italian Question to support his own ideas of political Radicalism and rarely commented on the Catholic dimension, others exploited and infused the cause with anti-Catholic arguments that perceived the issue as a crusade against Catholicism. Catholics in the North East, moreover, were deeply offended by this attack on their religion and stood firmly united against the threat to their Papal leader.

The first attack on Papal Government in Italy came in the late 1840s with the European Revolutions. The reaction amongst the Liberal press throughout the North East of England reveals latent anti-Catholic sentiment.[13] The *Darlington and Stockton Times* blamed Pope Pius IX for what it saw as his own downfall in a land where there was "only the semblance of a fragment of liberty" and where "the priest has his neck upon the people, and in the name of Him . . . whose gospel consecrates the principle of fraternity and humanity, held in pitiable political and mental slavery three millions of men".[14] Indeed, the following year, the paper believed it had found the root of the problem that appeared to infect Italy and other Catholic countries:

> "Whilst the inhabitants of Great Britain, cradled in progressive liberty, cast their eyes towards Italy . . . and find the same baneful influence crippling the civilisation of Spain, Austria and other continental nations, they sometimes overlook the fact that the most fateful poison in the system of Popery is that ascendancy of the Priest . . . that sacerdotal supremacy which is the development of human assumption and arrogance".[15]

The *Sunderland Herald* concurred with its contemporary. It praised the Roman people for fighting "with a valour worthy of their classic sires to rid themselves of the priesthood incubus that has pressed them down for centuries".[16]

The local political reaction was fairly muted at this stage. A meeting was organised in Newcastle in November 1849 to express joint sympathy

---

development of pluralism in modern Britain and France, ed. by R. Bonney and D.J.B. Trim (Bern: Peter Lang Ltd., 2007), pp. 207-25.

[13] The Liberal press were active in promoting this form of anti-Catholicism throughout Britain. Paul O'Leary, suggests that there is evidence of anti-Catholic sentiment on the topic of the 1848 Revolutions in Wales 'which was heavily coloured by the implications of this upheaval for the temporal power of the Catholic Church in the Vatican states'. P. O'Leary, 'When was Anti-Catholicism?', p. 313.

[14] *Darlington and Stockton Times*, 19 May 1849.

[15] *Darlington and Stockton Times*, 31 August 1850.

[16] *Sunderland Herald*, 5 October 1849.

for both the Romans and the Hungarians; the latter experiencing a similar political revolution at this time. The meeting concentrated predominantly on the political side of the question but this did not stop the Catholic orator, Charles Larkin, from denouncing the speakers for their "No Popery" views and defending Pius IX as making other rulers "sink into entire insignificance". In defence, Lord Dudley Smith argued that the question concerned the temporal power rather than the spiritual power of the Pope but this held little sway for Catholics who saw them as essentially one and the same.[17] Indeed, the Catholics of the region had nothing but sympathy for their spiritual leader. In March 1849, an 'Address of the Clergy and Laity of the Northern District' spoke of their unconditional loyalty towards their Holy Father:

> "Wherever our Father is, there are the hearts of his Children, and when our Father is in affliction, then do we love and venerate him the more; and if the ingratitude of some of his Children has inflicted a grievous wound on his Paternal heart, we are the more desirous of renewing to him the offering of our most sincere respect and love".[18]

Moreover, it was agreed at a meeting of Catholics in Newcastle to organise a collection for Pius IX in his hour of need.[19] Two months later, it was announced that Catholics had contributed £92 8s 6d to the collection which was forwarded to Rome.[20] When the Pope eventually returned to Rome the following year, a Te Deum was sung in celebration in every Catholic chapel throughout the region.

In spite of the failure of the 1848 Revolution in Italy, support for the Italian cause appeared to be gathering momentum during the 1850s. Allen and Todd both argue that this was due to the rising influence of the local Radical, Joseph Cowan, whose "enthusiasm for foreign affairs ensured that it retained a high profile on the radical agenda".[21] Cowan was active in providing financial support, seditious literature, arms and even asylum for many Italian revolutionaries such as Mazzini, Orsini and Garibaldi.[22] This is undoubtedly true to an extent but it is surely no coincidence that

---

[17] *Newcastle Guardian*, 24 November 1849.

[18] RCHNDA, 'An Address of the Clergy and Laity of the Northern District', 1 March 1849, RCD 1/11/28.

[19] *Newcastle Guardian*, 10 March 1849.

[20] *Shields Gazette*, 18 May 1849.

[21] Allen, *Joseph Cowan*, p. 40.

[22] Allen, *Joseph Cowan*, pp. 40-43; Todd, *Militant Democracy*, p. 14.

the campaign for Italian independence coincided with the heightened sense of anti-Catholic feeling in the aftermath of period of the Papal Aggression.

Indeed, during the early 1850s, anti-Catholicism and Radical internationalism essentially combined in a number of ways that were particularly evident in the celebrated lecturing tour of the Italian liberal, Alessandro Gavazzi. Gavazzi was a former priest who renounced his Catholicism, leading the liberal crusade against the Pope in 1848 which resulted in his exile. He spent the subsequent years lecturing in Britain with the profits from his tours helping to finance other Italian exiles living in London.[23] Given Gavazzi's anti-popery, his first lecturing tour of England and Scotland in the post-Papal Aggression period of 1851-52 would have undoubtedly proved a profitable one. However, his success, and the reaction towards him, cannot be explained purely in terms of his anti-Catholic views. It was the combination of anti-Catholicism and his preaching for the cause of Italian unification which allowed him to achieve a broad spectrum of support that not only encompassed anti-Catholic evangelicals of all persuasions but also political Radicals.[24]

Gavazzi's tour reached the north towards the end of 1851 where he lectured at Newcastle, Sunderland, South Shields and Durham. For anyone who saw him, Gavazzi's lectures were more than just an evening's edification. Indeed, the announcement of Gavazzi's visit prompted a rush for tickets in every town he visited. Of his lecture in Newcastle, the *Newcastle Journal* reported that demand "was so great that it was found impossible to accommodate all who applied for them" and hundreds of people were disappointed.[25] When he arrived outside the lecture hall in Newcastle, the Padre was greeted by hearty rounds of applause from a crowd of 2,000 working men. In all towns too, the appointed lecture rooms were filled well in advance of the commencement of proceedings and the lecture halls were crowded to excess with a broad range of people.[26] In South Shields, the reserved seats included clergymen of all denominations, magistrates and members of the principal families of the town.[27] The audience in Newcastle included "people of all persuasions and classes"[28], the *Newcastle Journal* even reporting the presence of Italian scholars.[29] He

---

[23] For more background information on Gavazzi, see Hall, 'Alessandro Gavazzi'.

[24] Aspinwall, 'Alessandro Gavazzi', p. 131.

[25] *Newcastle Journal*, 11 October 1851; *Durham Advertiser*, 10, 17 October 1851; *Shields Gazette*, 10 October 1851.

[26] Ibid.

[27] *Shields Gazette*, 10 October 1851.

[28] *Gateshead Observer*, 10 October 1851.

[29] Ibid.

lectured on two subjects: 'Papal Institutions, Errors and Corruptions' and 'Italy and the Italians'. In the latter, the charge for admission was reduced to allow the working classes the "opportunity of hearing the celebrated orator".[30] However, there is no evidence of the "latent 'orangeism'" that one historian believed dominated his audiences.[31] Indeed, other than a few hisses from some Irish Catholics, Gavazzi's visits passed off peacefully.[32]

As Paz has argued, Gavazzi was "more of an opponent of papal claims than a proponent of Evangelical Protestantism",[33] but this did not prevent the use of evangelical techniques in his orations. Certainly a large part of Gavazzi's critical acclaim stemmed from his overriding presence on the platform and his style of oratory gave him an "almost pop-star status".[34] In the lectures in the North East he wore a long black robe with a cross emblazoned on his chest. This was complemented by an overwhelming physical stature. It was his lecturing style, however, that won over many plaudits, made all the more remarkable by the fact that he spoke only in his native Italian.[35] The *Newcastle Chronicle* pointed out that, though he spoke no English, "throughout his lengthened orations, such is the charm, the almost magical influence, that attaches his oratory, that his English audience were awash with admiration".[36] Indeed, what Gavazzi lacked in communication, he made up in his animation. The *Bulwark*'s description of him striding across the platform "with all the grace and majesty of a Julius Caesar, and proclaiming with all the fervour and power of a Demosthenes",[37] was shared by the local Liberal newspapers. The *Durham Chronicle* concurred:

> "His speaking gestures, and kindling energy, more and more attract them (the audience), until in some fiery burst of the Italian soul, their sympathies, their admiration, and confidence, are enthusiastically surrendered at his feet".[38]

---

[30] *Durham Advertiser*, 10 October 1851.

[31] Hall, 'Alessandro Gavazzi', p. 306.

[32] Edward R. Norman's assertion that the lectures of Gavazzi "prompted literally hundreds of No Popery disturbances" now seems a gross exaggeration as there is no evidence of this in England, other than a strong police presence when he visited Wolverhampton. Edward R. Norman, *Anti-Catholicism*, p. 18; R. Samuel, 'An Irish Religion', *Patriotism: The Making and Unmaking of British National Identity*, ed. by R. Samuel, II (London: Routledge, 1989), p. 96.

[33] Paz, *Popular Anti-Catholicism*, p. 28.

[34] Aspinwall, 'Alessandro Gavazzi', p. 131.

[35] Paz, *Popular Anti-Catholicism*, p. 124.

[36] *Newcastle Chronicle*, 10 October 1851.

[37] *Bulwark*, October 1851.

[38] *Durham Chronicle*, 10 October 1851.

His dominance of the public platform was also complemented by an expert employment of evangelical language.[39] It has been suggested that Gavazzi's importance lay in "his quickness in assimilating views current in his time".[40] Thus, like any successful evangelical, he was able to play on the religious fears of his audience by combining concepts of millenarianism with contemporary events to heighten the power of his message. The Papal Aggression, according to Gavazzi, had brought about a situation in which "peace has disappeared, hatred increases . . . for the day of battle draws nigh . . . see the riots of Liverpool, of Manchester, of Birmingham . . . they may be considered as the fore-runners of still more severe contests". Evangelical lecturers were known for their colourful and often fiery metaphors and Gavazzi was no exception. Thus, of the influence of Jesuits in Roman Catholic countries, he believed that "these countries are now swarming with filthy reptiles, all full of poison . . . they at times conceal themselves in slime, or in the dust, to work undetected". Gavazzi also evoked powerful, metaphorical imagery in his speeches: "No! I dream not!—there—there—I see it . . . Who is he? It is the great Scottish Reformer—it is John Knox . . . He looks not at me—he looks no more to his native land—he has fled to the heavens!"[41]

As expected, Gavazzi's oratories were met with thunderous applause. The *Newcastle Courant* perhaps best sums up the local feeling generated by his lectures: "Few will forget the enthusiasm which the Father's oration . . . produced among the audience and perhaps such an overpowering specimen of eloquence they will never hear again".[42] Not everyone, however, believed that Gavazzi's speech was "an overpowering specimen of eloquence". In spite of praising some of his anti-Catholic views and "his roar when demolishing Pio Nono", the *Durham Advertiser* believed that Gavazzi was nothing more than a charlatan:

> "The address . . . considered as a piece of argument was a failure. It consisted merely of scraps from newspapers respecting the Papal Aggression, the conversion of the Duke of Norfolk and a few sentences of abuse of the Papacy. We had looked for some unmasking of the iniquities of Rome, and of the devastating effects of her superstitious idolatry. But we looked in vain for something of this sort".[43]

---

[39] Though he spoke only in Italian, Gavazzi's speeches were translated at various points for the benefit of his English audience.

[40] Hall, 'Alessandro Gavazzi', p. 307.

[41] *Newcastle Journal*, 11 October 1851.

[42] *Newcastle Courant*, 17 October 1851.

[43] *Durham Advertiser*, 17 October 1851.

Gavazzi's republican views particularly concerned the Conservative newspaper, believing that he "cares nothing about Popery, except so far as he can make it self-serving to his own object of modernising Italy".[44]

For the Liberal press there appeared to be no such paradox. In its report of the Newcastle lecture, the *Gateshead Observer* described Gavazzi in glowing terms, believing that "every passion and emotion of the heart—anger, contempt, indignation, pity, scorn, commiseration, defiance—he truthfully and firmly expressed". Furthermore, it seemed to forget its usual stance of toleration towards Catholicism when it commented on Gavazzi's statement that the Pope had prevented a Protestant church being built in Rome. Without confirming the truth of the Padre's opinion, the paper lambasted the Pope for this, offering him an alternative of providing "a church for English Protestants in Rome or no church for the Italian Catholics in London".[45] The Catholic orator, Charles Larkin, however, challenged the fawning praise Gavazzi had received in the region. Larkin described Gavazzi as a "hypocrite who conceals his Protestantism under the garb of a monk". Larkin lambasted the *Gateshead Observer* in particular for showing, as he put it, "unfairplay" to the Catholics and stating that there were, in fact, two or three Protestant churches in Rome. The *Observer* was forced to issue something of a partially disguised apology, arguing that it had seen the words of Catholics themselves justifying the lack of Protestant churches in that city and believed "till now, that the fact was as Father Gavazzi stated".[46]

Throughout the 1850s and 1860s, Alessandro Gavazzi became a regular fixture in the lecturing season. His popularity ebbed and flowed depending on the particular context of the topics he professed. Thus, his next lecturing tour in 1854 was not as successful as his previous visits. The *Shields Gazette* reported that the audience in his Newcastle lecture "was not as good as expected".[47] His Durham lecture was equally disappointing, the *Durham Advertiser* stating that the attendance was "not nearly so large as on the last occasion of the Rev. Gentleman's visit".[48] This was due to the decline in interest of anti-Catholicism in general during the mid-1850s and also partly because the Italian Question was superseded by the Crimean War in importance among the British public. Ironically, Gavazzi's decision to lecture in English may have also had an impact on his mystique among his audience. The *Durham Advertiser*

---

[44] Ibid.
[45] *Gateshead Observer*, 10 October 1851.
[46] *Gateshead Observer*, 24 October 1851.
[47] *Shields Gazette*, 8 December 1854.
[48] *Durham Advertiser*, 8 December 1854.

certainly took this view, arguing that his spoken English "detracted from the bold, dramatic, and stirring style of his oratory" because it "frequently renders what he says unintelligible to the greater portion of the audience".[49] As the movement for Italian independence gathered renewed momentum in the late 1850s, so did Gavazzi's popularity. In November 1857, he preached three times on a Sunday in the Music Hall, Newcastle, to "crowded congregations" and was even invited by Joseph Cowan to lecture in Blaydon where he was warmly received by a "large and enthusiastic audience".[50] He addressed similar audiences in Sunderland, Stockton and Durham, and for the next three years made annual visits to the region.[51]

Gavazzi managed to retain popularity throughout the 1860s through his ability to tailor the content of his lectures to cover current topics of interest. Thus when General Garibaldi arrived in England with the intention of visiting the North East in October 1864, Gavazzi delivered a lecture in Stockton on 'Garibaldi's Reception in England' to a large audience.[52] The following year, he lectured in Newcastle on the subject of the current political situation in Italy with the arrival and departure of the French troops in Rome.[53] He was also hired to lecture on anti-Catholic topics that were not necessarily linked with the Italian Question but were influenced by local circumstances. Thus, the week after a self-styled "Tractarian monk" had lectured in Newcastle, Gavazzi delivered a counter-lecture on the topic of 'Monks and Nuns, Real and Sham'.[54] He was also prepared to speak on more traditional forms of anti-Catholicism, lecturing by the invitation of John Candlish (before the latter's 1866 election victory in Sunderland) on a discussion of No Popery in defending "the glorious Protestantism" of the Constitution.[55] Gavazzi often donated his earnings to worthy local causes, such as a fund for the building of a new Temperance Hall and Working Man's Club in Stockton in January 1864.[56] He also conducted a number of religious services in various churches around the region. In his autobiography, James Dillow, who was present at a meeting in the Trinity Presbyterian Church in Newcastle,

---

[49] Ibid.
[50] *Newcastle Guardian*, 7 November 1857.
[51] *Durham Advertiser*, 24 December 1858; *Newcastle Guardian*, 21 December 1858, 17 December 1859.
[52] *Darlington and Stockton Times*, 15 October 1864.
[53] *Newcastle Guardian*, 20 October 1865.
[54] *Newcastle Guardian*, 13 October 1865.
[55] *Sunderland Herald*, 10 February 1866.
[56] *Durham Chronicle*, 15 January 1864.

remembered how appalled he was at the audience for applauding Gavazzi in such a "sacred edifice" but as the sermon continued, he found himself "doing it as frequently as others".[57]

Gavazzi was not the only lecturer to visit Tyneside and Durham to combine anti-Catholicism with support for Italian independence. Joseph Cowen's support for political exiles ensured that the region was well stocked with Italian émigrés wishing to draw attention to the despotic system of government in Italy. Another Italian, Felice Orsini, who had risen to fame with the publication of his account of escape from an Austrian prison where he was incarcerated for his insurrectionist activities, toured the region in October 1856. Orsini had nothing of the charisma of Gavazzi. Indeed, a report in the Conservative *Durham Advertiser* described his lecture in West Hartlepool as "tame" and read "without the slightest animation or elocutionary grace".[58] Nevertheless, his tour was successful because his reputation as an Italian insurrectionist seemed to command respect from the large audiences who attended his lectures. Orsini spoke in his lectures of the present condition of Italy, and in particular the priests and Jesuits who acted as spies for the Papal Government:

> "Spies are present everywhere, and the Italians were obliged to bow their heads—but with haughtiness and not in humility, as they had to bear on their shoulders the whole despotism of Europe (applause)".[59]

Committees were formed in the conclusion of his lectures to "aid the rescue of Italian liberty", which appealed directly to the working classes.[60]

Another lecturer who toured the country in association with the movement for Italian independence was Jessie White (later known as Madame Mario). White, according to John Wolffe, could "tap extensive reservoirs of sympathy" for Liberal anti-Catholic sentiment.[61] White was unique among British Victorian women, breaking popular conceptions of the role of females as passive and domestic. She worked as a war correspondent, a medical officer in Garibaldi's army and was arrested several times for subversion in Italy.[62] She lectured with one of Mazzini's

---

[57] James Dillow, *Memoirs of an Old Stager* (Newcastle: A. Reid 1928), p. 52.

[58] *Durham Advertiser*, 14 November 1856.

[59] *Newcastle Guardian*, 15 October 1856.

[60] A committee in Sunderland was organised to meet in the Mechanics Institute. *Sunderland Herald*, 31 October 1856.

[61] Wolffe, *Protestant Crusade*, p. 283.

[62] Todd, *Militant Democracy*, p. 16.

assistants, Seignior Saffi, and both used arguments denouncing the Catholic system. At a lecture in Newcastle, Saffi argued that those who had died on the battlefields for the cause of Italian independence were "like the martyrs of Christianity, with a sublime, unquenchable faith in the right and justice of their cause" and that it was "foreigners and priests" who "strove to make them ignorant". White, dressed in the red army jacket of Garibaldi's army, hoped that one day they would be able to enjoy the liberty "of which we are proud" and liberty that Italy is currently denied. For the chairman of the meeting, Sir John Fife, this constitutional liberty was the hallmark of Protestantism.[63]

Joseph Cowen's support for political émigrés hostile to the Roman Catholic Church was not confined to Italy alone. He was also instrumental in bringing the German exile Johannes Ronge to the region. Ronge was a particularly adept self-publicist who wrote a tract of his life to advertise his forthcoming lecture tour in the North East in January 1852. The autobiography explains Ronge's former vocation as a Roman Catholic priest in Silesia. Growing increasingly frustrated with the corruption of the Church, Ronge set up his own organisation, the New Catholics, which abolished priestly celibacy, auricular confession and excommunication, as well as placing a renewed emphasis on the teachings of the Bible. For this, Ronge was excommunicated from the Roman Catholic Church and fled to London.[64] Like Orsini, Ronge was not a natural public speaker but all his lectures (entitled 'The Influence of the Jesuits in Europe') were sold out. Following the Newcastle lecture, the Chairman, George Crawshay, believed that Ronge had "made a strong case for the argument that religious tyranny and political freedom could not exist together". "The policy of this country", he added, "was to support religious liberty all over the world".

However, it was primarily the Italian Question that cemented the link between political despotism and the Roman Catholic religion. Some extremist anti-Catholic lecturers naturally jumped on the bandwagon of the Italian cause in order to promote attacks on Catholicism. The notorious anti-Catholic firebrand, the Rev. J.A. Wylie, delivered a series of lectures in the region in the 1850s with Italy as their theme. The clergyman saw the real designs of Popery, arguing in a lecture sponsored by the Protestant Alliance in Newcastle in February 1854 that "Popery was inseparable from despotism—it ruled the whole of the despotism of the continent, and a crusade had been preached for the conversion and subjugation of Great

---

[63] *Newcastle Guardian*, 9 May 1857.
[64] J. Ronge, *Autobiography of Johannes* Ronge (Newcastle: [n. pub.] 1850).

Britain".[65] Wylie returned in 1859 with the Italian Question regaining popularity once again. He lectured on the topic of 'Italy under the Papacy', "proving" that the Papal Government had made the Romans beggars by ruining their trade; slaves by crushing their liberties; and atheists by depriving them of the Scriptures.[66]

The successful lecturing tours of Gavazzi, White, Orsini and others were all the more remarkable given the general lull in the Italian Question during much of the 1850s. As the decade drew to a close, however, Protestant evangelicalism and political Liberalism merged again when popular support for the Risorgimento intensified after a new attempt at revolution. In March 1859, Papal monarchy was effectively overthrown in most of Central Italy, first in the Romagna in June 1859, then in the Marches and Umbria in November 1860.[67] Of all the European countries, England provided the most effective and consistent supporter for the Risorgimento[68], and this was reflected in the language of the local press. The *Newcastle Guardian* could hardly contain itself:

> "The dark cloud which has over-spread Central Italy, like a pall, is now fringed by a silver light, harbinger of the dawn which is to usher in the clear and full light of the morn of her redemption and deliverance".[69]

The following week, the paper even suggested that the erosion of Papal temporal power was necessary, as "a constitutional government, with a Pope at Rome, would be simply ridiculous".[70]

For Liberals, the Risorgimento was personified in the glorification of one man, the charismatic leader of the movement, Giuseppe Garibaldi. According to Wolffe, the popular support for Garibaldi reveals "broad linkages between anti-Catholicism and liberal attitudes".[71] Davies has also asserted that anti-Catholicism was certainly not the only factor in support for Garibaldi, but it "played an important part in both the radical and popular image" of the man.[72] Furthermore, Garibaldi, along with Mazzini, epitomised the Liberal Dissenting ideal as a modern-day Oliver Cromwell

---

[65] Wylie also delivered a similar lecture in Sunderland the following month. *Sunderland Herald*, 24 February 1854.

[66] *Shields Gazette*, 3 May 1859.

[67] McIntire, *Papacy*, p. 1.

[68] McIntire, *Papacy*, p. 2.

[69] *Newcastle Guardian*, 8 January 1859.

[70] *Newcastle Guardian,* 15 January 1859.

[71] Wolffe, *Protestant Crusade*, pp. 283-4.

[72] Davies, 'Garibaldi and England', p. 25.

in his "Leveller zeal, Puritan moralism, and reformed religiosity".[73]
Certainly, the *Bulwark's* opinion that "every Christian must rejoice in the
triumphant march of Garibaldi over the prostrate despotisms of one of the
fairest portions of the earth, and in the prospect of a united Italy under a
reign of comparative liberty"[74] was taken up by the local Liberal press.
The *Sunderland Herald* opined that "it was impossible to read the
accounts of Garibaldi's . . . progress without feeling the deepest sympathy
with the hero in this hour of triumph". Indeed, the paper argued, "Heaven
itself appears to fight for him".[75] The *Shields Gazette* shared similar
sentiments: "the sympathies of mankind are with the Garibaldians; and we,
in England, in particular, rejoice at the brightness of their prospects".[76]
Even the Conservative press momentarily joined in the jubilation.
Garibaldi was, according to the *Durham Advertiser*, the "true hero of the
war beyond all doubt".

The popularity of Garibaldi was particularly acute on Tyneside because
links with the General dated as far back as 1854. In March of that year he
sailed into the Tyne on the American ship *Commonwealth* and was
received by a number of notable Liberals of Newcastle but declined a
banquet in his name for fear that it might give rise to a public
demonstration.[77] It was resolved at a public meeting in Newcastle to
present an address and the gift of a sword to the General before he left the
port.[78] Five years later, Blaydon, under the guidance of Joseph Cowan,
was one of the first to send Garibaldi an address wishing him well in his
campaign against the Pope.[79] In 1860, with the *Risorgimento* well under
way, the *Newcastle Guardian* was able to opine:

> "It would be strange indeed if the revolt in Sicily did not excite interest and
> awaken enthusiasm in the metropolis of the North. With us the name of
> Garibaldi is a household word . . . It is true that success has increased the
> number of admirers even here; but in the days of comparative seclusion
> and privacy . . . there were a few on Tyneside who not merely lauded the
> hero but loved the man".[80]

---

[73] Biagini, *Popular Liberalism*, p. 49.

[74] *Bulwark*, October 1860.

[75] *Sunderland Herald*, 7 September 1860.

[76] *Shields Gazette*, 25 October 1860.

[77] *Newcastle Guardian*, 25 March 1854.

[78] *Newcastle Guardian*, 1 April 1854.

[79] *Newcastle Guardian*, 17 September 1859.

[80] *Newcastle Guardian*, 23 June 1860.

Indeed, in the early 1860s, popular support for Garibaldi and the Italian Revolution reached an unprecedented level on Tyneside. Concerts were held in order to raise funds for those injured in Garibaldi's army. In Newcastle, £50 was raised at a concert and cheers for Garibaldi were "enthusiastically given at the close".[81] In most of the major towns, Garibaldian Volunteer organisations were formed, and suppers held in their honour, for those locals who wanted to offer their services in the Italian army.[82] Meetings were held in Newcastle, Sunderland and South Shields in response to the latest twist in the story of the Risorgimento. These sometimes provoked blatant anti-Catholic opinions. A crowded meeting in Newcastle in September 1862, called to express sympathy with Garibaldi after the French had retaken Rome, was addressed by a number of lay and clerical speakers. One of the latter, the Rev. J.H. Rutherford, a Liberal Dissenting minister who played a large part in agitating in support of Italy, saw Garibaldi's campaign as the "cause of freedom against despotism, of unity against division . . . of the people against the tyrants, of a free Gospel against a crushing and deadening form of religion, of order against anarchy (applause)".[83]

Garibaldi's crusade against the Pope was not universally welcomed by all sections of the community and this was the case even on Tyneside. A recent article by M. P. Sutcliffe has argued that Garibaldi's republicanism made him particularly unpopular amongst the Conservatives of Tyneside.[84] However, it was equally the questionable nature of Garibaldi's secularist opinions that prevented the Tyneside Conservatives from supporting his campaign. One letter writer to the *Newcastle Daily Journal* even saw the movement as "anti-Christian" and appealed for the public to "renounce all complicity with such a cause as this before it saps all belief, all morality, all honour between man and man, all worship between man and God".[85] This was something of a minority view, however, and the appearance of Protestant ministers on the platform and in the lecture theatre is testament to the feeling that Garibaldi's movement was as much a Protestant campaign against Popery as support for democracy against

---

[81] *Newcastle Guardian*, 15 September 1860.

[82] *Newcastle Guardian*, 21 January 1861.

[83] *Newcastle Guardian*, 13 September 1862. Meetings were also held in Sunderland and South Shields, see *Sunderland Herald*, 10 September 1862; *Durham Chronicle*, 19 September 1862.

[84] M.P. Sutcliffe, "'Negotiating the 'Garibaldi Moment'' in Newcastle upon Tyne (1854-1861)', *Modern Italy*, 15.2 (2010), pp. 129-48.

[85] *Newcastle Daily Journal*, 25 October 1862.

absolutism.[86] Indeed, Garibaldi was seen as "the Lord's battleaxe", chosen by God to rid the earth of the Papacy on account of his high moral character.[87] At a meeting of the Newcastle Evangelical Alliance in April 1863, the Rev. James Davis believed that Garibaldi was in the process of a "great mission" in which "the Bible was to be the canon to liberate Italy".[88]

Moreover, the response of the Catholic community is indicative of the fact that they saw Garibaldi and his movement as a direct attack on their religion. Indeed, Catholics were unlikely to feel anything other than derision for a man who wished to see the downfall of their spiritual leader[89] and as McIntire has argued, the Catholics of Great Britain and Ireland provided the Pope with his most effective support.[90] Dr Cullen, the Archbishop of Dublin and the Papal Legate for the Catholic Church in Ireland, described the English press and the people as "brutalised" for supporting the cause of the Italian Liberals and denouncing in strong terms the activities of Victor Emmanuel and Garibaldi.[91] This was reflected at the local level. The *Newcastle Guardian's* attempt to justify its stance as one not designed "to offend the profound religious sentiments of many of our Roman Catholic friends" [92] proved ineffectual as many Catholics did feel very aggrieved at the situation. The Lenten Pastoral of Bishop Hogarth in February 1860 condemned the "rebels and revolutionists of the Papal States, who are endeavouring to rob the Pope of his patrimony".[93] At Catholic Soirées, priests were active in defending their Pontiff. In Sunderland, Canon Bamber attacked those who had joined in the agitation in Italy, arguing that "to subvert the power of the Pope was to subvert the very foundations of society".[94] The Rev. Henry Coll of Darlington, in an

---

[86] Many lectures in praise of Garibaldi featured Protestant ministers, such as the Gateshead minister, the Rev. J. Jeffery, lecturing in Newcastle in March 1863. The lecture was also chaired by the Rev. Robert Thomson of Newcastle. *Newcastle Guardian*, 21 March 1863.

[87] D.E.D. Beales, 'Garibaldi in England: The Politics of Italian Enthusiasm', *Society and Politics in the Age of the Risorgimento. Essays in Honour of Denis Mack Smith* ed. by J. Davis and P. Ginsborg (Cambridge: Cambridge University Press 1991), p. 186.

[88] *Newcastle Guardian*, 18 April 1863.

[89] Beales, 'Garibaldi in England', p. 193.

[90] McIntire, *Papacy*, p. 7.

[91] *Durham Chronicle*, 19 October 1860.

[92] *Newcastle Guardian*, 29 September 1860.

[93] RCHNDA, William Hogarth, 'Lenten Pastoral', February 1860, RCD 1/16.

[94] *Sunderland Herald*, 12 October 1860.

impassioned speech also at Sunderland, presented a defence of Papal
Government as a rejoinder to certain Liberal anti-Catholic opinions:

> "It is not intent on aggrandisement and worldly glory, it is not reckless of
> blood and treasure, it seeks not the prosperity of a few, but the happiness of
> the many and the welfare of *every individual,* it prefers to reign over a
> *family* rather than a troop of slaves!"[95]

The Catholic clergy throughout the region were also active in
reminding their flock of their obligation to the Holy Father. At Crook, the
Rev. S. Brooke addressed his parishioners after Mass, urging them to
denounce "the perpetrators and abettors of the injuries inflicted upon him".
"It shall not go forth to the world uncontradicted by us", Brooke
concluded, "that England is unanimous for the overthrow of the Pope's
temporal power".[96] The strength of feeling towards the Pope was evident
in the Durham pit villages well into the following decade. Louis Casartelli,
a student at the nearby Ushaw College and later the Bishop of Salford,
wrote to his father that a pro-papal volunteer regiment had been formed in
Bishop Auckland and the Rev. Thomas Wilkinson was currently helping
to organise a similar initiative in Crook with the support of the College.[97]
Casartelli later noted that a number of former college students had enlisted
to fight for the Pope.[98] In October 1860, all Catholic churches in the
region, in line with the rest of the country and the world, were to offer
prayers for the defence of the Pope "against the plots and machinations of
bad and wicked persons in the various countries in Europe who are
leagued together to degrade the Sovereign Pontiff by exciting revolt and
bloodshed in the States of the Church".[99] The Bishops of Hexham, both
Hogarth and Chadwick, took leading parts in speaking out in sympathy
with the Pope. The latter, in one of his first speeches as Bishop, spoke at
length in a Soirée in Sunderland of the need for Catholics to be vocal
against the harm being committed to their spiritual head.[100]

---

[95] *Darlington and Stockton Times*, 27 February 1864. Henry Coll, b. 1837
(Scotland), o. 1861, d. 1878. *English and Welsh Priests*, p. 39.
[96] *Tablet*, 24 December 1859.
[97] Ushaw College Library, Casartelli Papers, Letter from Louis Casartelli to his
father, 15 December, 22 December 1867, UC/P4/A1/30,33-34. Thomas William
Wilkinson, 5th Bishop of Hexham and Newcastle (1889), b. 1825, o. 1848, d.
1909. *English and Welsh Priests*, p. 47.
[98] Letter from Louis Casartelli to his father, 31 March 1868, UC/P4/A1/60.
[99] *Durham Chronicle*, 14 October 1859.
[100] *Sunderland Herald*, 30 November 1866.

Altholz has argued that the Italian Question became "the major political issue for Catholics throughout Europe".[101] Indeed, a definite determination to make their feelings known resulted in feverish political organisation amongst the Catholic body. 'A Declaration of the Lay Members of the Catholic Body in England and Scotland' was drawn up and signed by a great number of notable Catholics, among whom included the names of many from the North East. The Declaration was controversial in the sense that it deemed rebellion against the Pope "unjustifiable". The *Newcastle Guardian* was perhaps not the only Liberal paper to suggest that this had important repercussions if followed to the letter but nor was it, according to the paper, completely surprising:

> "Human rights, according to their dogma, are to be set aside, violated, or destroyed, whenever they stand opposed to Papal supremacy. We are not yet prepared in England for these slavish dogmas, and all that the Catholics can accomplish by attaching their signatures to a document affirming such a monstrous proposition, is to separate themselves from those friendly Protestants who are in favour of civil and religious liberty everywhere as well as here . . ."[102]

In other parts of the country, it has been noted that Catholics were often divided between Liberal members who supported the Revolution as a necessity for constitutional democracy and those who were fully behind the Pope.[103] In the North East of England, there appears to have been no such division as is evident by the strength of feeling amongst the Catholic community at a meeting held in Newcastle Town Hall.[104] Nearly 6000 Catholics were present from around the neighbouring areas and further afield. These included all classes of Catholics, the Bishop of Hexham, all the local clergy, notable Catholic families and a great portion of "the labouring classes"; the seats on the floor being removed to accommodate

[101] Altholz, 'The Political Behaviour', p. 99.
[102] *Newcastle Guardian*, 24 December 1859.
[103] Those who supported the Italian Revolution were part of a group known as Liberal Catholics. They were primarily converts, such Lord Acton, who wished to liberalise the Catholic religion. See J. L. Altholz, *The Liberal Catholic Movement in England: The Rambler and its Contributors 1848-1864* (London: The Ditchling Press, 1962). In the context of the Italian Question, they wished to restore "the ecclesiastical democracy of early Christianity". Biagini, *Popular Liberalism*, p. 224.
[104] There appears to be few other large gatherings of this nature. Altholz cites only four (Newcastle, London, Birmingham and Manchester). Altholz, 'Political Behaviour', p. 99.

as many of them as possible. A large contingent of females were present, who were "as enthusiastic in their applause (and) as vehement in their demonstrations", particularly when they spotted the pro-Garibaldi minister, the Rev. J.H. Rutherford "taking a few notes". They pelted him with orange peel while the "sterner sex" proceeded to "expel" the minister from the meeting. The meeting itself saw impassioned defences of Papal authority, and it was proposed that an address be sent directly to Pius IX himself.[105] Other Catholic congregations in the region followed suit, drawing up memorials to express their sympathy with the Sovereign Pontiff. Indeed, it was estimated that between 20,000-30,000 signatures would be attached to these memorials from the Diocese of Hexham alone.[106]

The Catholics of the region contributed financially as much as politically to the Papal cause. The parish of St. Andrew's in Newcastle was one of the first in the country to re-establish the ancient tribute to the Pope, Peter's Pence, on a weekly basis in early December 1859 and other churches in the region closely followed.[107] The following year, a campaign was orchestrated to collect donation money for the Pope in every chapel in the diocese.[108] The Bishop of Hexham ordered a pastoral to be read in every church and chapel in the diocese on Sunday May 17, with collections planned for the principal services of Whit Sunday. Hogarth also directed all the priests in his diocese to "solicit the offerings of the faithful during one month, beginning with Whit-Monday, and ending on Monday the 25th day of June".[109] This, and other donations to the cause, amounted to a total of over £1,042 by October, made all the remarkable given that this was the only Papal Fund of its kind in the country.[110]

The Roman Catholics themselves were not without their defenders in the lecturing circuit either. In June 1860, the Rev. Robert Belaney, who was formerly a Church of England minister but now a Roman Catholic

---

[105] *Newcastle Guardian*. RCHNDA, 'Address to the Holy Father from Catholics in Newcastle and Gateshead', 28 January 1860, RCD 1/16.

[106] *Durham Chronicle*, 20 January 1860.

[107] *Tablet*, 3 December 1859. The church at Crook introduced this practice just three weeks later. *Tablet*, 24 December 1859.

[108] *Durham Chronicle*, 25 May 1860.

[109] RCHNDA, William Hogarth, 'Pastoral Letter', 1st May 1860, RCD 1/16.

[110] *Tablet*, 13 October 1860. There is evidence to suggest that this initiative continued well into the next decade. The papal official, George Talbot, thanked the Catholic priest at Crook, the Rev. Thomas Wilkinson for sending a £40 Peter's Pence donation in August 1864, and a further donation of £60 the following year. Wilkinson Papers, Letter from George Talbot to Thomas Wilkinson, 20 August 1864 and 24 October 1865, UC/P16/9,11

convert, lectured on the 'Temporal Sovereignty of the Pope' in Sunderland.[111] Belaney had recently published a lecture he had delivered to the Roman Catholic Young Men's Society in Dublin and this publication was presented as a gift to Pius IX himself. Belaney argued that the Pope, unlike Victor Emmanuel, had obtained his throne without fraud or violence and "any attempt to rob the head of the Church of his crown would be to rob the Almighty". He believed the Pope's rule was "mild and humane", and, in turning the anti-Catholic argument on its head, argued that "in no other country was there so much happiness and so little misery as in his dominions".[112]

The Tyneside Irish in particular had other ways of showing their support for their spiritual leader as the campaign progressed. For the Irish Catholics, the Pope represented the supreme symbol of Catholicism and a man to whom they declared their undying loyalty.[113] In a similar way to the large numbers of English who volunteered to join Garibaldi's Redcoats, many Irish Catholics saw it their duty to the Pope to enlist in defence of him, seemingly with support from the Catholic Church.[114] At Catholic chapels in the region, Requiem Masses were regularly sung to those Irish Catholics who had lost their lives fighting for the Papal cause.[115] Tensions were clearly growing between the Irish and English communities over the issue and this is evident in seemingly trivial incidents. In July 1860, the *Durham Chronicle* printed an article entitled 'Irish Intolerance' concerning a group of Irishmen who threatened to destroy a boat moored on the Tyne because it bore the name *Garibaldi*. The paper warned the Irishmen that they "may get their hands broken if they attempt to meddle with the boat, as the blood of the Tynesiders is up on the matter".[116] Garibaldi also became a battle-cry for the Durham miners in their continual struggles against the Irish blacklegs headed by Lord Londonderry.[117] Irish Catholics were also responsible for destroying the statue that Cowan erected to Garibaldi.[118] More serious, however, was a riot on the Town Moor, Newcastle, during Race Week in 1866. Events in Italy, where Italian forces had recently occupied Venice, were clearly

---

[111] Robert Belaney, b. 1804 (Berkshire), o. 1857, d. 1899, *English and Welsh Priests*, p. 2.

[112] *Sunderland Herald*, 8 June 1860.

[113] H. McLeod, *Religion and Society*, p. 45.

[114] *Durham Advertiser,* 25 May 1860.

[115] *Tablet*, 29 September 1860.

[116] *Durham Chronicle*, 6 July 1860.

[117] Davies, 'Garibaldi and England', p. 25.

[118] Ibid, p. 25.

having an impact on local affairs, as is evident when one Irish rioter was heard to shout "Down with Garibaldi!".[119]

By the time of the Italian army's capture of the city of Rome in 1870, attentions had been diverted elsewhere to other political upheavals in Europe. Indeed, the Liberal view of democratic internationalism was becoming more infused with secular nationalism and less concerned with the role of religion within it. The local reaction was surprisingly muted and the *Durham Chronicle*'s opinion on the matter epitomised Liberal views at this time, which could even evoke sympathy at the Pope's temporal demise:

> "There is help in no quarter for the old man who, in his time, has been called upon to suffer very heavily in defence of the temporal power; but there will be a very widespread sympathy with his misfortunes; and in the event of his resolving to depart from the scene of his troubled pontificate, he will not be left without a very practical manifestation of England's good will to those who fall in political turmoil. A British frigate, it is understood, will be ready to receive him if he should decide upon leaving Rome".[120]

In the end, the frigate was not needed and the Risorgimento was effectively completed.

International Liberty and the Madiai Controversy

The support for Italian independence described above cannot be divorced from the context of a general increase in evangelical support for global Protestantism and anti-Catholicism during the Victorian period. Protestant evangelicals believed it was their destiny to rid the world of Popery and they adopted a particularly aggressive approach to those who did not share this vision. Catholic countries in Europe, such as France and Belgium, were felt to be particularly ripe for conversion. Support for evangelical organisations of this nature was apparent in a number of different places in the North East of England. In July 1849, public meetings were held in South Shields, North Shields and Newcastle to form

---

[119] For a thorough examination of this riot see Jackson, "'Garibaldi or the Pope!'". Jackson shows how Cowenite support for Italian nationalism helped to drive a wedge between the English and Irish communities. Similar riots occurred earlier in the decade in Birkenhead and London where, in the former case, the campaign was hijacked by the (essentially) Conservative Orange Order. Gilley, 'Garibaldi Riots', Neal, 'Birkenhead Garibaldi Riots'.

[120] *Durham Chronicle*, 16 September 1870.

auxiliaries to the Evangelical Society of France. Its aim was to support the spread of "the simple and pure message of the Gospel" among the Catholic population in that country.[121] In January 1851, the Presbyterian minister of North Shields, the Rev. George Duncan, commenced a series of papers on the 'Progress of Protestantism in Belgium'.[122] In July 1853, a more general auxiliary was formed in Newcastle by a number of Nonconformist ministers. The Evangelical Continental Society's aim was to promote "pure evangelical principles upon the Continent". This society wished to give aid and encouragement to similar organisations on the Continent, with particular emphasis on France and Belgium. The contributions were not to be issued to English missionaries, whose "imperfect pronunciation" might fail to excite a French audience, but the French missionaries themselves.[123] The chairman of this organisation, the Hon. and Rev. Baptist Noel, continued to lecture throughout the 1850s in the region in promotion of this society.[124] Indeed, the organisation was active well into the 1860s.[125] This support for Protestantism encouraged lecturers from the continent to visit the area in order to obtain financial assistance for spreading Protestantism in their own country. Thus, a French Protestant, Monsieur Fisch from Lyon, delivered a lecture to congregations in the various Nonconformist chapels of Newcastle with the aim of garnering support for the building of a Protestant Church in the French town.[126]

Spreading Protestantism was also becoming an intrinsic part of the broader aims of the larger and more traditional missionary societies, such as the Society for the Propagation of the Gospel in Foreign Parts, the Church Missionary Society, the British and Foreign Bible Society and the Religious Tract Society.[127] Many of these societies had existed as a means

---

[121] *Shields Gazette,* 6, 13 July 1849; *Newcastle Guardian,* 14 July 1849.

[122] *Gateshead Observer,* 4 January 1851.

[123] *Newcastle Guardian,* 23 July 1853.

[124] *Newcastle Guardian,* 26 July 1856; *Shields Gazette,* 24 July 1856. For a biography of Baptist Noel, see David W. Bebbington, 'The Life of Baptist Noel', *Baptist Quarterly,* 24 (1972), pp. 390-401.

[125] The *Newcastle Guardian* reported a society meeting in its 3 February 1866 edition.

[126] *Newcastle Guardian,* 12 May 1855.

[127] These societies had their origins in the evangelical movement of the late eighteenth and early nineteenth century. The Society for the Propagation of the Gospel in Foreign Parts and the Church Missionary Society were both Anglican organisations while the British and Foreign Bible Society and the Religious Tract Society were primarily Nonconformist. Often, however, they worked together as co-operation in non-Christian environments became essential. C.P. Williams,

of spreading the Bible throughout the world since the eighteenth century and auxiliaries to these societies were apparent in every town in the region.[128] They may have all had different motives for carrying out their missions as P. Hinchcliffe has observed,[129] but their survival throughout the Victorian period is testament to the public's interest in this form of religious activity. Indeed, the emphasis on millenarianism and the belief that conversion of the heathen was part of God's great design was an essential element in evangelical thinking "across the denominational divide".[130] The notion of Protestantism as a civilising force was an integral part of Anglican-dominated organisations such as the Church Missionary Society. At a meeting of the Sunderland Auxiliary in May 1852, the Rev. Charles Hodgson spoke of the organisation's efforts in New Zealand. "Twenty five years ago", he argued, "the place was a den of cannibals". However, the Society's efforts had reaped rewards with "fully three-fourths of the people . . . Protestant Christians".[131] The key element in the conversion process was the Bible. For these societies, Gospel dissemination was the main weapon in not only combating infidelity around the world, but also against false religions such as Roman Catholicism. At the Jubilee meeting of the Durham Bible Society, a largely ecumenical organisation, in May 1853, the Rev. Mr. Wilson believed that the preaching of the Word was having an enormous impact throughout the globe:

> "(T)he stream of divine truth was wide-spreading and increasing—that river of the waters of life was intended to spread, bearing down in its onward course everything opposed to truth as it was in Jesus; sweeping away every form of idolatry, and snapping even the foundations of Popery itself".[132]

'British Religion and the Wider World: Mission and Empire, 1800-1900', *A History of Religion in Britain*, p. 401.

[128] S.G. Green, *The Story of the Religious Tract Society* (London: The Religious Tract Society, 1899), p. 1

[129] Peter Hinchcliffe, 'Voluntary Absolutism: British Missionary Societies in the Nineteenth Century', *Studies in Church History*, 23 (1986), p. 364.

[130] Elizabeth Elbourn, 'The Foundation of the Church Missionary Society: the Anglican Missionary Impulse', *The Church of England, c. 1689-1833: From Toleration to Tractarianism*, ed. by John Walsh, Colin Haydon and Steven Taylor (Cambridge: Cambridge University Press, 1995), p. 255.

[131] *Sunderland Herald*, 28 May 1852.

[132] *Durham Advertiser*, 15 April 1853.

It was, indeed, the spectre of Roman Catholicism that loomed largest. This
was, of course, particularly the case in Italy. D. Raponi has noted that
missionary activity in Italy was based on a desire not only to convert the
population to Protestantism for religious reasons, but also to unite and
develop the disparate and backward country whose growth had been
stunted by the Catholic religion.[133] These societies faced stiff opposition
and were often hampered by "priestly interference". The Rev. John Bruce,
a prominent member of the Newcastle Protestant Alliance, spoke at a
meeting of the Newcastle Bible Society of the difficulties the organisation
experienced in spreading the Gospel in Rome, where "the eagerness of
many to obtain the Bible had called forth the angry remonstrance of the
priesthood".[134]

The dangers that Protestant evangelicals faced when confronted with
the mask of Popery in Italy is no better illustrated than with the
imprisonment of Francesco and Rosa Madiai in 1852. The Grand Duke of
Tuscany had pursued a policy of anti-Protestantism since the 1848
Revolution. He banned Protestant worship and Protestant proselytism, but
it was his actions in 1852 which were to cause the most controversy. In
August 1852, he imprisoned two Tuscans, Francesco and Rosa Madiai, for
allegedly holding a Protestant meeting in their home in an attempt to
proselytise the local Catholic population. This was a bold move,
particularly as the Madiai's had some influential connections in the
Foreign Office and the British Government. The subsequent campaign for
the release of these two prisoners became something of a *cause célèbre* for
Liberals and Protestant evangelicals who saw the affair as highlighting the
limits of religious liberty in a country where the temporal power of the
Pope remained unchecked. In the mid-Victorian period, Liberal opinion
abhorred intolerance, particularly religious intolerance, and anti-Catholics
were quick to exploit this. Indeed, the Protestant Alliance took a central
role in the proceedings and the Madiai's eventual release was, according to
Wolffe, "one of the Protestant Alliance's most notable achievements".[135]

In the North East of England, the campaign was no less keenly felt
and, in fact, may have surpassed other places. The Liberal press, in
particular, were outraged over the affair. Anger was expressed at
imprisoning people over their religious beliefs, which as Anne Lohrli has
suggested, was an affront to the Englishman's "traditional espousal of

---

[133] D. Raponi, 'Religious Reformation and National Unity: British Protestants and
Italy, 1860-1870', *New Perspectives in British Cultural History*, ed. by R. Crone,
D. Gange and K. Jones (Newcastle: Cambridge Scholars, 2007), p. 80.
[134] *Newcastle Guardian*, 28 August 1851.
[135] Wolffe, *Protestant Crusade*, p. 268.

liberty". Primarily, however, it was opposed because it was a "Protestant people's indignation at the persecution of fellow Protestants",[136]and thus arguments soon degenerated into bigoted anti-Catholic attitudes. In the *Darlington and Stockton Times*, a letter from the incumbent of St Cuthbert's Anglican Church in Darlington, the Rev. Howell Harris, spoke of this as yet another example of persecution by the Roman Church and quoting further examples of the way in which "Rome carries out her merciless logic with demonical consistency".[137] The normally tolerant *Gateshead Observer* agreed with the notion that the persecution of the Madiai could only emanate from the nature of the Roman Catholic system, which had "shown herself as unrelenting as in the worst ages of her dominion".[138] The *Sunderland Herald* believed that the problem lay in the nature of the two religions, and their respective opinions on heresy:

> "It is hardly necessary to remark that Protestantism involves no such principle as that of persecution of heresy, and that this principle lies at the very root of Romish claims to infallibility in matters of faith".[139]

Furthermore, the paper could hardly contain itself when the campaign led to the eventual release of the Madiai, seeing it in the nature of the superior morality guiding Protestant England:

> "Her (England's) power is great among the nations on earth, and it cannot fail to be otherwise so long as her policy is directed by liberal hands—so long as she hesitates not to hold out a helping hand to the oppressed; refuses not the right hand of fellowship to her persecuted neighbour, without asking of what religion, sect or party, colour or clime, he may be".[140]

The outrage was not solely confined to the Liberal section of society. The two Conservative papers, the *Durham Advertiser* and the *Newcastle Journal*, predictably could not resist the opportunity to lambast the Catholics of Britain for their silence in this issue. The *Journal* somehow managed to interweave arguments concerning the "Protestant Constitution" into its polemic blamed the removal of the penal laws for admitting "rank

---

[136] Lohrli, 'The Madiai', p. 30.

[137] *Darlington and Stockton Times*, 22 January 1853.

[138] *Gateshead Observer*, 15 January 1853.

[139] *Sunderland Herald*, 25 February 1853.

[140] *Sunderland Herald*, 26 March 1853.

idolators, professing obedience to a foreign power, into a Christian legislature".[141]

It was, however, where Liberal feeling was greatest that the Madiai issue received its strongest anti-Catholic support. In Newcastle, where there was a great deal of support for Italian independence and Liberal anti-Catholicism, meetings were organised in order to protest against the Madiai imprisonment. The town's Protestant Alliance, staffed in no small part by Liberal Dissenters, took the lead, and the organisation held its own meeting to protest against what it saw as another example of Catholic injustice.[142] What is more surprising, however, is that the public of the town felt so aggrieved by this affair that they felt it their duty to pressure the authorities to organise a town meeting in protestation.[143] The meeting was well attended and addressed by many of the leading Liberals of the town, including the Mayor and members of the town council, along with the usual suspects in anti-Catholic meetings, such as the Rev. Richard Clayton. Here, speakers including Alderman Headlam and Sir John Fife, who would probably not have been present at other anti-Catholic meetings, felt it their duty to "express themselves in terms so moderate and gentle, and to frame their resolutions in a frame so unsectarian, and truly liberal, and so undeniably Christian, that no conscious Roman Catholic fellow citizen . . . need be debarred . . . from joining in the petition for the liberation of the Madiai".[144] However, Sir John could not resist an attack on the state of Roman Catholic countries vis-à-vis their Protestant neighbours which deeply offended the Catholic contingent present at the meeting. Charles Larkin, who once again took up the mantle of defending his faith, attacked Sir John as an individual allegedly "honourable in character and distinguished for his political liberality" but seeming to side with the Rev. Mr. Clayton, "the leader of the bigots". He continued:

---

[141] *Newcastle Journal*, 22 January 1853; *Durham Advertiser*, 25 March 1853.

[142] Protestant Alliance meetings also took place in other towns, such as Durham. *Durham Advertiser*, 21 January 1853.

[143] Newcastle was only one of a handful of towns to hold a meeting on the subject, which is testament to its support for Liberal anti-Catholicism, although Lord Malmesbury described the interest in other major cities such as London, Birmingham and Manchester as 'notorious' also. Lohrli, 'The Madiai', p. 36.

[144] *Newcastle Guardian*, 19 March 1853. The stance of Roman Catholics in general varied. Some, such as Frederick Lucas, appeared to justify their imprisonment because of their "wicked acts of proselytism" but others, such as the Catholic MP Thomas Chisholm, saw the imprisonment as a grave injustice. Catholics could not attend meetings on the subject, however, because of the 'narrow and sectarian spirit of the conveners'. Lohrli, 'The Madiai', pp. 39-40.

"This meeting was not a proof of any sympathy, on the part of the inhabitants who had called it, in favour of religious liberty, for from the whole course of observations that had been made it was clear that the great object in view was to hold up the Catholic religion to derision and odium".[145]

Larkin denounced the motives of the speakers "for in advocating toleration they did it in the spirit of intolerance". After being voted off the platform by those present he bid farewell to the "tolerant Christians". Another notable Catholic, William Dunn, who had never before taken part in a public meeting, felt it his duty to speak in support of Larkin's views, criticising the Protestant speakers for being "totally at variance with the principles of freedom". After a number of further speeches, James Watson urged all who supported the meeting to support the European Freedom Fund and the meeting finally broke up after three hours.[146] In spite of the disturbances from the Catholics, the *Newcastle Guardian*, who devoted copious column spaces to the proceedings, proclaimed the meeting "a most successful as well as influential demonstration on behalf of liberty of conscience at home and abroad".[147]

Support for the Madiai can also be observed in a number of other towns in the region. Crowds flocked to hear the lecture of the local Durham minister, the Rev. George Fox, the subject of which was very relevant to the times: 'The Bible: How Popery Hates It'. Fox's lectures were sponsored by the Protestant Alliance and coincided with its direct involvement in the Madiai affair between December 1852 and March 1853. As shown above, anti-Catholic lecturers were popular in the post-Papal Aggression period, but Fox's choice of subject touched a nerve with a public who were eager to hear tales of Popery's alleged prohibition of the Scriptures. Fox lectured to crowded audiences at Durham, Sunderland, South Shields, Stockton and Darlington. The popularity of the lecture was overwhelming in some places. In Sunderland, "one of the largest audiences ever known" assembled at the Lyceum theatre. It was estimated that the crowd was around 2,300, with hundreds more disappointed at not being able to obtain a reserved seat.[148] Similarly, in Stockton, the Borough Hall was "crammed to suffocation".[149] His lectures were not without

---

[145] *Newcastle Guardian*, 19 March 1853.
[146] Ibid.
[147] Ibid.
[148] *Sunderland News*, 3 December 1852.
[149] *Durham Advertiser*, 28 January 1853.

controversy. At Durham, Fox caused outrage when he implied that a Catholic priest of the city had burned a Bible.[150]

The local Protestant Alliance auxiliaries clearly benefited from their involvement in the Madiai affair. The negative image of the group in 1852 as an electioneering organ of the Conservatives, along with the dissensions over the anti-Maynooth campaign, had given way to more positive perceptions of the organisation as being at the forefront of the cause for international liberty. This internationalist dimension to anti-Catholicism was particularly popular among the members of the Protestant Alliance's Liberal Dissenters, many of whom had been uncomfortable with the accusations of Toryism the year before. In many parts of the North East, where Liberalism was arguably the dominant ideology, the local Alliance auxiliaries experienced an evident upturn in fortune. Annual meetings of the amalgamated North of England Protestant Alliance in 1853 and 1854 saw a rapid increase in the organisation's annual income. In 1853, the treasurer reported that the auxiliary had made a profit of £60. This allowed them to spend more the following year in spite of their expenditure being £70, 10s in 1854. Even taking into account a £10 donation to the London Alliance, the local organisation was able to bring forward a balance of £66, 18s, 5d for the following year.[151] Furthermore, there was evidence in 1854 that the Alliance was willing to expand its operations. The Secretary of the national body, G. H. Evans, was active in touring the region and helping to form new societies in various towns, including Sunderland and North Shields.[152]

The Alliance's promotion of Protestant liberty overseas was further enhanced by one of its principal members taking an active part in campaigning in favour of rights for a group of Italian Protestants in Piedmont, known as the Waldenses. The Rev. William S. Gilly, a prominent member of the Durham Protestant Alliance used the local

---

[150] *Durham Chronicle*, 11 February 1853.

[151] *Newcastle Guardian*, 11 November 1854. The fact that the full annual report for this year appeared in the *Newcastle Guardian*, a Liberal paper which had refused to support the organisation when it was first established at the end of 1851, is evidence of the broad range of support the organisation was now attracting for its anti-Catholic activities.

[152] *Bulwark*, June 1854. Indeed, the Newcastle Protestant Alliance was so successful in tapping into this form of anti-Catholicism that, unlike many of its contemporaries, it survived relatively unscathed into the 1860s; the *Bulwark* noting in 1863 that it was one of only seven auxiliaries still in existence. *Bulwark*, June 1863.

Protestant societies to help him promote his cause.[153] His lectures and other works assisted in raising awareness and finance for this persecuted group. In a pamphlet entitled *The Waldenses and Evangelists of Italy*, he saw the defence of this group as integral to the political campaign of constitutional government for Italy: 'Liberal international enactments, and free religious action, must go together', he argued, 'Fetter the one and you must restrict the other'.[154] Unfortunately for the Waldenses, Gilly's death in 1856 effectively ended local involvement in this campaign, although the subject still maintained a large amount of interest to the public well into the next decade, as is evident by the large and respectable audience who listened to the Rev. C. Brewster's eloquent defence of the Waldenses in North Shields in March 1864.[155]

Liberty of Conscience: The Convent Campaign

The classic anti-Catholic stereotype of incarceration against one's will that epitomised the Liberal perception of the Madiai is also evident in the Protestant Alliance's campaign in favour of Roman Catholic convent inspections. The organisation's campaign of anti-Catholicism and liberty abroad in the 1850s was therefore consistent with its activities closer to home. A bill proposing inspection was first introduced into Parliament in 1851 by the MP Henry Drummond, who notoriously described convents as "either prisons or brothels"[156]. The agitation was ignited, however, by the Protestant Alliance's petitioning campaign in localities throughout the United Kingdom. In a similar way to the anti-Maynooth campaign, anti-Catholics never succeeded in abolishing convents, though the agitation surrounding it brought a wave of anti-Catholic petitioning from localities throughout the country.[157]

The local dimension of the anti-convent movement was initially aimed at the female population. An 'Address to British Protestant Females' was

---

[153] Rev. W.S. Gilly had a history of involvement in similar campaigns. As early as 1823, he was championing the cause of another persecuted Italian Protestant sect, the 'Vaudois'. Indeed, it was his involvement in this campaign, along with his subsequent publications and platform speeches, which helped to make Gilly a "leading anti-Catholic polemicist" in his day. *The Blackwell Dictionary of Evangelical Biography: 1730-1860*, ed. by D.M. Lewis (Oxford: Blackwell Publishing, 1995), pp. 443-4.

[154] *Durham Advertiser*, 3 March 1854.

[155] *Shields Gazette*, 12 March 1864.

[156] *Hansard*, 115 (1851), p. 266.

[157] Paz, *Popular Anti-Catholicism*, pp. 16-7.

issued in Edinburgh at the end of 1851 and the central body of the
Protestant Alliance adopted this appeal with the support of other women's
groups.[158] The petition called for a measure that would "effectively open
these establishments to regular inspection, so that no person may be
received into, or detained in, or dismissed from them, without the
knowledge of the proper authorities". [159] The main thrust of the argument,
therefore, was to give nuns freedom of action and impose safeguards for
those detained against their will. There were those who wished for their
total abolition but, as Wolffe has pointed out, this would have been
inconsistent with the assertion of individual liberty that the campaign
relied upon.[160] This allowed the petition to be framed in such a way as to
appeal to as broad a range of views as possible and thus explains its initial
success.

In the North East of England, the convent issue was a particularly
prominent one in a number of places. In comparison with its parallel anti-
Maynooth campaign, the local Protestant Alliance in Newcastle seemed to
have far more success with this appeal. A memorial to the Queen, signed
by 4,808 females of the town and the immediate neighbourhood, was
forwarded by the organisation, to the Earl of Shaftsbury for presentation in
May 1852.[161] The method of this petition appears to have been door-to-
door, the Alliance clearly a little apprehensive about calling a meeting
following the humiliation of their disastrous anti-Maynooth meeting. The
agitation was also surprisingly prominent in North Shields. This was a
town where no protest took place either against the Maynooth Grant or
Papal Aggression and where no Protestant society existed. Yet as early as
April 1851, the town's Liberal newspaper, the *Shields Gazette*, was calling
for a public meeting on the subject of "nunneries" and seeking legislation
either for their "total suppression, or efficient superintendence".[162]
Although no public meeting took place on the matter, there was clearly a
strong anti-convent feeling in the town and in May 1852, nearly 1,000
women signed a petition "against Nunneries".[163] In Durham, the petition
signed by 1,300 ladies was framed slightly differently, describing convents
as inconsistent with "the constitution of these lands" although issues of
individual liberty were prominent also. A further petition was also sent

---

[158] Wolffe, *Protestant Crusade*, p. 269.
[159] *Bulwark*, July 1852.
[160] Wolffe, *Protestant Crusade*, p. 269.
[161] *Newcastle Journal*, 2 October 1852.
[162] *Shields Gazette*, 11 April 1851.
[163] *Durham Advertiser*, 7 May 1852.

from the town in the following year.[164] Petitions were also sent from South Shields and Hartlepool, the latter obtaining an "almost countless number of signatures"[165]; as well as Darlington, where the appearance of an actual convent fuelled Protestant fears.[166]

The local press reporting the horror stories of convent life also did little to discourage the agitation. The Talbot case, in which the young Miss Talbot had allegedly been "imprisoned" against her will in a convent, provided a practical example of the horrors of the nunnery. It received extensive coverage in the national and local press and, as the *Newcastle Journal* argued, offered an "awful commentary on the foul profligacy and heartlessness of Romish Priests and the penalties of the Roman Church".[167] There was, however, a more localised case of convent imprisonment. The *Sunderland News* reported that the young Lady Stourton of Hartlepool had succumbed to convent life, reporting that she had "become insane" after joining a convent.[168]

These towns highlight the way in which certain forms of anti-Catholicism could be stronger than others in different areas, as well as demonstrating that anti-Catholic ideology could merge with other ideologies which were prominent in particular areas. These petition drives are all the more remarkable once differences in population with major anti-Catholic centres are taken into consideration. Petitions were received in a number of towns and cities throughout the country during 1852, including 19,000 from Liverpool.[169] The 4,808 women who signed the Newcastle petition for the inspection of convents represented 5.5% of the town's population. Even Liverpool's 19,000 petitioners had produced a slightly lower tabulation of 5.1%.

Just as strong, however, was the political campaign of the Roman Catholics against the Convent Inspection Bill. A draft counter petition was framed in the *Tablet* as early as April 1851 when the first stirrings of a debate took place in Parliament. The petition was fairly moderate in language, denying that females were forcibly detained against their will in convents, seeing little need for any form of inspection, and attacking the move as a "violation of the liberty of unoffending British subjects".[170] However, it was not until the anti-convent campaign was in full swing

---

[164] *Durham Advertiser*, 12 March 1852; 13 May 1853.
[165] *Shields Gazette,* 15 April 1853; *Durham Advertiser*, 24 June 1853.
[166] *Darlington and Stockton Times,* 18 June 1853.
[167] *Newcastle Journal*, 14 March 1851.
[168] *Sunderland News*, 7 May 1852.
[169] Wallis, *Popular Anti-Catholicism*, p. 191.
[170] *Tablet*, 12 April 1851.

during 1852-53 that the Catholic community decided to act. A more
strongly worded petition was issued, attacking the bill as one "calculated
to destroy the liberty of the subject" and describing the provision to allow
Protestant visitors to inspect convents as a "disgraceful and revolting
exercise of power". The petition was intended to lie for signature at the
door of every Catholic Church in the country and to be sent from door-to-
door. It was hoped that as many people would sign the petition as
possible—the collectors were even expected to write the names
themselves of those who were illiterate—as there was a belief that the
absence of a strong protest "would unhappily furnish the supporters of the
Bill with a plausible argument in its favour".[171]

In the North East of England, the Catholics of the region certainly
answered this call. Leo Gooch has suggested that the protest against the
Inspection Bill was the first national political campaign mounted by the
Victorian Catholics and that Tyneside contingents were strongly active in
opposition.[172] There is certainly enough evidence to confirm this assertion.
In Newcastle, matters were initiated in a meeting of Catholics in St
Andrew's Church in the town in June 1853, in which all the major
Catholics of the area took part. Addresses were made by Dr. Charlton,
William Dunn, Mr. Fenton, John Young and Mr. Duffy, and the above
petition was adopted which, according to the *Tablet*, soon received a large
number of signatures. Local Catholic Defence Societies were also active in
promoting this protest. In North Shields, where, as has been shown, the
issue had received a large amount of attention, the Catholic Defence
Society in the town contributed in the assistance of a petition that received
460 signatures. A similar petition assisted by the Gateshead Catholic
Defence Society garnered 840 signatures. Counter petitions were also sent
from the Catholic communities in South Shields and Durham.[173] Although
the North East had significantly fewer convents than other areas of the
country, the few areas where nuns were active helped to provide a focus
for anti-Catholic agitation.[174] In Sunderland, the appearance of a convent
of the Sisters of Mercy is a good example.. As early as January 1851, the
town received the orations of Samuel Day, a former Roman Catholic monk
who lectured on the subject of 'Life in a Convent'. Day adverted to the

---

[171] RCHNAD, 'Petition Against the Convent Bill', RCD 1/12.
[172] Morris and Gooch, *Down Your Aisles*, p. 19.
[173] *Tablet*, 18 June 1853; *Shields Gazette*, 24 June 1853.
[174] B. Walsh has noted that the county of Durham only contributed between 2-4%
of the number of convents in England and Wales in 1857. B. Walsh, *Roman
Catholic Nuns in England and Wales, 1800-1937: A Social History* (Dublin: Irish
Academic Press, 2002), p. 66.

way in which convents and monasteries assisted the "prostration of the human intellect" and, at the close of the lecture, three cheers were given for Mazzini and three groans for the Pope.[175] The local Liberal paper also adopted a stance against convents, calling for inspection in the belief that "if there can be no such thing as bodily coercion, excessive rigour, or forcible detention in such places, inspection can enable the visitors to certify the fact".[176] However, the local convent may have actually helped to allay fears, as the pro-convent movement was unusually strong. C.M. Mangion has noted that anti-Catholic prejudice towards the convent dissipated with the philanthropic efforts of local nuns.[177] Indeed, many would have experienced first-hand the benevolent works of the local Sisters of Mercy in Sunderland and this may explain why upwards of 2,000 women of the town, as well as a further petition signed by a 1,000 people, were presented to Parliament against the bill.[178]

After 1854 the anti-convent agitation declined in support throughout the country when Dr. Thomas Chamber's bill of this year was defeated in Parliament. The Crimean War had effectively transformed the negative perception of nuns, further encouraged by Lord Aberdeen's government seeking the alliance of Roman Catholic France against the Russians.[179] It was not until the 1860s that convents once again became a focus for anti-Catholic agitation but it was primarily a parliamentary, rather than localised, issue. In the late 1860s the attention, particularly of the Liberal press, was concentrated more on Anglican sisterhoods and monasteries than Roman Catholic institutions, although the *Durham Chronicle* saw no distinction in introducing legislation for the protection of inmates, whether it be a "Protestant college or a Catholic nunnery".[180] Newdegate's eventual success in 1870 for an inspection of convents did win some support in the local Tory press[181] but, like the Maynooth Committee before it, the inspectors did not produce the required evidence that anti-Catholics

---

[175] *Shields Gazette*, 13 January 1851. The choice of Mazzini is interesting because it highlights the ideological link between the anti-convent agitation and support for Italian independence.

[176] *Sunderland Herald,* 1 July 1853.

[177] Mangion, *Contested identities*, p. 99.

[178] *Durham Chronicle*, 1 July 1853. It is also interesting to note that no petition was raised in Sunderland supporting the Convent Bill. V. Fetherston, 'Irish Social Catholicism', p. 76.

[179] Arnstein, *Protestant Versus Catholic*, p. 63.

[180] *Durham Chronicle*, 12 February 1870.

[181] *Durham Advertiser*, 6 May 1870; *Newcastle Courant*, 1 April 1870.

required and, after 1871, the "convent question was increasingly seen as a joke".[182]

In a similar way to its Tory adversary, then, Liberal anti-Catholicism effectively died a death from the 1870s as political Liberalism embraced more and more the ideals of secular nationalism. Nevertheless, it proved a particularly powerful force for political agitation in a region in which Liberalism and anti-Catholicism were not axiomatic. The strength of a Liberal culture in the area therefore did not, as Roger Cooter has suggested, act as a buffer in reducing sectarian feeling. Religious tensions between Protestants and Catholics in the North East were not solely motivated by political events. Indeed, at grass roots level, the fear of the Catholic "Other" was more than just one of abstract political ideas. It was the seemingly unstoppable growth of the local Catholic communities which really frightened Protestants, as hordes of Irish Catholics and numerous ultramontane priests transformed the built environment and cultural landscapes of Protestant England. Therefore, the next two chapters will reveal the way in which the response of the Protestant community towards this Catholic "invasion" helped to bring about an equally defensive and united Catholic front that did little, at least in the short term, to provide a smooth transition towards religious toleration.

---

[182] Paz, *Popular Anti-Catholicism*, p. 18.

CHAPTER FIVE

"POPERY" UNLEASHED:
IRISH IMMIGRATION
AND THE CATHOLIC REVIVAL

The previous three chapters examined the response of the North East of England to national and even international controversies associated with anti-Catholicism, as well as the reaction of the Catholic community to these events. However, for many who shared anti-Catholic views, the Catholic threat was more apparent closer to home as the visible growth of Catholicism in localities during this period appeared to threaten the very fabric of English (i.e. Protestant) society. The outward signs of "Popery", such as church buildings and processions, were complemented by a heightened sense of militancy among the Catholic clergy. This led to an evangelical battleground in which the souls of Catholics were fought over as the Catholic clergy struggled to preserve their flock from proselytism. This chapter seeks to examine how this conflict was played out in the North East of England, arguing that the growing strength and confidence of the Catholic community in the region assisted in the development of an anti-Catholic evangelical culture which, in turn, had the effect of increasing the militancy of the Catholic community in defence of their religion.

The Changing Landscape

By the 1850s, the Roman Catholic Church in England had experienced something of a dramatic resurgence. The extent to which this was attributable to Irish immigrants or whether it was merely a natural process within the English Catholic Church has been a matter of some debate among historians.[1] However, there can be no doubt that the Catholic Church was becoming increasingly more assertive in the period after Catholic Emancipation, as is evident in the proliferation of churches and

---

[1] Bossy, *English Catholic Community*; G. Parsons, 'Victorian Roman Catholicism', pp. 146-68; Gwynn, *Second Spring*.

religious practice. In 1850, there were 587 churches in England and Wales, and 788 clergy. By 1870, however, there were 1151 churches and 1528 clergy.[2] This was complemented by the aggressively ultramontane attitudes of Catholic leaders, such as Cardinal Nicholas Wiseman in England and Cardinal Cullen in Ireland.[3] For many Protestants, this only served to show the true nature of Popery. Francis Close, the notorious Cheltenham anti-Catholic, complained of the consequences of Catholic Emancipation:

> "We give them civil and religious liberty *usque ad nauseum* and yet they go on bit by bit . . . beautiful cathedrals spring up, and the pomps and ceremonies of Popery, with its priests and bishops prevail, until at length comes a scarlet cardinal to take possession of the land. This is Romish ingratitude".[4]

In localities throughout the country, the march of Popery seemed unstoppable to those who feared not only the decline of Protestantism but also of the very fabric of the cultural landscape.

In the North East of England, the Catholic resurgence was just as evident and Catholic communities grew rapidly in most of the region's major towns and villages during the mid-Victorian years. The days of small meeting houses, hidden away from the public gaze, were long gone. In their place were clear signs of the growth in self-confidence of a resurgent Catholicism: large and ornate Gothic churches, influenced by the ambitious architectural designs of A.W. Pugin, that were situated as close to public life as possible.[5] Churches were given dedications, such as St Patrick in the east end of Sunderland and in some places, such as St Michael's in Esh Laude, the name of the local Anglican parish was adopted if it pre-dated the Reformation.[6] The worship within these churches highlighted the growing trend towards Ultramontanism with continental forms of Italianate piety, such as devotions to the Blessed Sacrament and the Blessed Virgin Mary.[7]

---

[2] Norman, *The English Catholic Church*, p. 205.

[3] Ibid, p. 110.

[4] *Protestant Magazine*, 12 (March 1850), p. 40, quoted in Paz, *Popular Anti-Catholicism*, p. 100.

[5] Morris and Gooch, *Down Your Aisles*, p. 13.

[6] Ibid, p. 13.

[7] Horton Davies, *Worship and Theology in England*, vol. IV, *From Newman to Martineau, 1850-1900* (Princeton: Princeton University Press, 1962).

For the most part, this increase in the Catholic community passed off without much comment from the Protestant population.[8] Direct opposition to expressions of Catholic worship was rare but this reflected the trend throughout the country.[9] As Norman has suggested, there was a general movement towards an acceptance of Catholicism in the country as a whole.[10] Many believed that Catholics were entitled to worship as they wished and only extreme anti-Catholics were prepared to deny them this right. There was, however, controversy surrounding the building of Catholic churches in some places in the North East. The Seaham Harbour dispute, in which Lady Londonderry wielded her influence to ensure that the continued demands of Irish Catholics for a church were denied to them[11], was perhaps the most famous local example of Protestant opposition to Catholic worship, but it was not the only example as difficulties were experienced in other areas too. In Esh, the Catholics of the village were constantly thwarted by opposition from the staunch Anglican clergyman, Rev. Temple Chevallier who, in a letter to his Cambridge friend, Rev. George Corrie, Rector of Newton, complained of the Catholics "spreading their nets with too much success... neighbourhoods have either fallen into their hands or been purchased.".[12] In Jarrow, the Catholics priest of the town was eventually reduced to purchasing a disued Baptist chapel. The foundation of St. Augustine's, in Darlington, was sabotaged on several occasions.[13] In September 1854, a foundation stone was laid by the Bishop of Hexham for a new Catholic church at Shotley Bridge which, according to the local correspondent of the *Tablet*, had been previously opposed by anti-Catholic prejudice:

"The bigotry displayed by the landed proprietors in the immediate neighbourhood has been so great that for several years past, every effort to obtain a site on which to build a church has been baffled. Not a piece of land could be purchased, even by a Protestant, without allowing the

---

[8] For example, Father Ignatius Spencer could walk in his full Passionist dress without fear of molestation, "even when he was urging people to say a Hail Mary each day for the conversion of England". Morris and Gooch, *Down Your Aisles*, p. 10.

[9] See Emes, 'Anti-Catholicism in York', p. 88.

[10] Norman, *English Catholic Church*, p. 204.

[11] This has already been examined in detail. R.J. Cooter, 'Lady Londonderry and the Irish Catholics of Seaham Harbour: "No Popery" Out of Context'. *Recusant History*, 13.4 (1976), pp. 288-98.

[12] DUASC, Letter from the Rev. Temple Chevallier to the Rev. George Corrie, 11 May 1850, Add. MSS.837/109.

[13] Morris and Gooch, *Down Your Aisles*, p. 13.

insertion in the deeds of a clause preventing the alienation of any portion of it to a Catholic".[14]

At Hartlepool, a Catholic church was finally opened in 1851 by Cardinal Wiseman after various attempts to sabotage its erection.[15] Although the opening passed off without incident, bad feeling was evident in the town towards Wiseman and the building of this church. The No Popery lecturer, Mr. Lamb, issued a public challenge to Cardinal Wiseman to debate a series of controversial subjects in the Town Hall in July. Although Wiseman declined, the sectarian tension generated by this issue led to a serious riot in the town.[16] A letter from W.G. Harrison in the *Durham Advertiser* complained of the support of the Catholics of the town for this project, when the Protestants themselves could not raise enough money to complete the building of a Protestant church holding 774 people. Harrison stressed the necessity of erecting this church in order to meet "the strenuous efforts that the Roman Catholics are making to gain the ascendancy".[17] Some Protestants even saw the method of raising money from the Catholic laity for church building projects as evidence of the ultimate designs of Popery. In February 1854, a letter to the *Darlington and Stockton Times* complained of a recently published pastoral letter from the Bishop of Hexham, which requested one half-penny a week from those Catholics in employment. The letter-writer saw this appeal as "well calculated to enlist the sympathies of the humblest" and typical of the aggressive nature of the Catholic Church:

> "Thus it has ever been with the Roman Catholics—they are always on the move. If the voluntary system fails they have recourse to authority—if authority is out of their reach then they always fall back on the voluntary system. They are always aggressive—always either insinuating, or openly advancing".[18]

---

[14] *Tablet*, 2 September 1854.

[15] Morris and Gooch, *Down Your Aisles*, p. 13.

[16] See Chapter Six.

[17] *DA*, 5 September 1851. How exactly Protestant churches could act as a bulwark against Roman Catholicism was questioned in June 1853 when the Anglican church of High Conniscliffe appeared to be ringing its bells in support of Cardinal Wiseman's carriage as he passed through the village on a tour of the region. As it turned out, the bells were ringing for Wiseman's passenger, the landowner Phillip Howard, who owned, according to a letter-writer in the *Darlington and Stockton Times*, "every acre of ground, and almost every home in the parish". *Darlington and Stockton Times*, 9 July 1853.

[18] *Darlington and Stockton Times*, 18 February 1854.

Rituals and other outward expressions of Catholic life were tolerated so long as Protestants were not affected in some way. When they were, however, anti-Catholic outrage was not far behind. An example of this can be seen with an increase in the bell-ringing of Catholic institutions. Few Protestants could escape from the "clamour" which often affected their daily lives. Thus, the *Bulwark* complained that the Catholics of Hartlepool had made themselves very unpopular with their Protestant neighbours by ringing the bells of the Catholic chapel and drowning out the sermon of an Anglican clergyman. Indeed, the journal suggested, it was not merely the noise that was the problem but also "the consciousness of the act of gross idolatry being perpetrated".[19] Similarly, in Sunderland, where a contingent of the Sisters of Mercy resided in Green Street, the noise generated by the convent bell was a cause for complaint among the Protestant population. One letter writer to the *Sunderland Herald* protested about the way in which the "unmusical wagging of this intolerable convent clapper" affected his daily existence:

> "Morning, noon, and night it is heard wailing out its church-yard like notes, disturbing people in their beds, and in their sitting rooms. Often I am aroused in the morning although living a full-quarter of a mile from Green Street, long before the hour at which I feel inclined to get up, by the mournful ding-dong of this excruciating bell".[20]

Renewed signs of confidence were also evident in the outward expression of Catholic Soirées. Their popularity as a social event amongst different sections of the Catholic community is evident by the vast crowds who assembled for an evening's entertainment of dinner, speeches and music. At a crowded meeting of Catholics held in the Newcastle Town Hall in January 1859, Canon Eyre remarked that there was such an enormous assembly, "they must arrange to have their next public meeting on the Town Moor" as that was the only place which could hold them.[21] Often Protestants themselves were attracted to these events and were welcomed by Catholics. Press reports of speakers thanking Protestants for their attendance were commonplace. In September 1848, the *Sunderland Herald* printed a report of a Catholic Soirée in the town at which the Chairman gave a toast of "Prosperity to the Protestants who had honoured the meeting with their company".[22] Nearly two decades later, the

---

[19] *Bulwark*, December 1854.
[20] *Sunderland Herald*, 22 January 1858.
[21] *Newcastle Guardian*, 15 January 1859.
[22] *Sunderland Herald*, 29 September 1848.

attendance of Protestants at these events was still commented upon by the Catholic contingent. At a Soirée in South Shields in April 1866, Mr. Turnbull stated that it afforded him "great gratification to see present at that social gathering so many of their Protestant brethren".[23]

The speeches made at these events were generally good-natured but often allowed the expression of clerical opinion that would have raised a few eyebrows among those Protestants present. At a meeting of Catholics in the Music Hall, Newcastle, in February 1853, the Rev. John Bamber of Sunderland caused outrage by stating that if justice were not done to Ireland, he would, along with the Catholics of the United Kingdom, be prepared to "welcome a French invasion".[24] This caused a storm of protest led by the *Gateshead Observer*, which condemned the priest's speech. A Catholic wrote to the paper, hoping that Bamber's sentiments were not a reflection of Catholic opinion in general for, if they were, "even the most liberal of our Protestant fellow-countrymen would be justified in believing that a Catholic cannot be a good citizen in a *Protestant* country, and that, therefore, the Emancipation Act of 1829 was a mistake".[25] A similar response was generated at a Catholic Soirée in Durham in January 1859. In his speech, Father Consitt stated that every Catholic must feel sadness when casting eyes on the Cathedral in the city as it is "now in the hands of those who were quite unsuited to hold it".[26] If it were a Catholic cathedral, Consitt argued, then it would be "fill to overflowing".[27] This caused an angry rebuke evident in a number of letters printed in the *Durham Advertiser* the following week.[28]

In the minds of some Protestants, Catholic priests cut an even more sinister figure as they became more militant in their outlook. At a Soirée in Newcastle, the Rev. John Bamber complained that there were Protestants in the town "whose prejudice ran so high that they would not look a priest in the face".[29] The Rev. Thomas Wilkinson, who later became the Bishop of Hexham and Newcastle, faced a hostile reception from his own family

---

[23] *Shields Daily News*, 10 April 1866.

[24] John Bamber, b. 1819 (Lancashire), o. 1843, d. 1902, *English and Welsh Priests*, p. 38.

[25] *Gateshead Observer,* 12 February 1853.

[26] Edward Consitt, b. 1819 (Canada), o. 1842, d. 1887. *English and Welsh Priests*, p. 39.

[27] *Durham Advertiser*, 31 December 1858.

[28] *Durham Advertiser*, 7 January 1859.

[29] *Tablet*, 9 June 1855.

when he converted to Catholicism in 1847.[30] His father, George, in a letter to Thomas, made it perfectly clear what he thought of his son's decision by instituting a codicil to his will that effectively reduced Thomas's annual allowance to £100 p.a.[31] When Thomas later became the parish priest at the nearby Durham village of Tow Law, George warned him to abstain from using his influence to try to convert any family members to the Catholic religion.[32]

Accusations were also levelled at Catholic priests in a number of court cases which served to highlight Protestant suspicions of a morally corrupt "priestcraft", thus helping to reinforce "the image of the perverted Roman Catholic" and, in particular, the image of the priest as a murderer "or sexual corrupters of young women".[33] In the town of Stockton in 1854, the local Catholic priest, the Rev. Richard Singleton was accused of bastardy by the daughter of an Anglican incumbent, Miss Jane Jones.[34] Other charges were levelled against him by Miss Jones, including bestiality with his dog. In the subsequent trial that followed, lurid details of the priest's affair with Miss Jones were dramatised in the local and even national sectarian press and devoured by a public who watched the proceedings with keen interest. The Rev. George Fox, always willing to capitalise on the popular mood against the Catholic religion, delivered a sold-out lecture at Stockton and subsequently printed a pamphlet on the subject that was even circulated in America.[35] The priest was declared innocent by the magistrates who, in the end, could not convict him for lack of corroborative evidence.[36] Miss Jones appealed to other judges the following year but was still unsuccessful and the case was even reopened in Stockton when it was revealed that new evidence had come to light and

---

[30] For more information on Thomas Wilkinson, see L. Gooch, 'Thomas Wilkinson 1825-1909, Bishop of Hexham and Newcastle 1889-1909', *Northern Catholic History*, 13 (1981), pp. 26-31

[31] UCL, Wilkinson Papers, Letter from George Wilkinson to Thomas Wilkinson, 12 January 1847, UC/P16/4

[32] UCL, Wilkinson Papers, Letter from George Wilkinson to Thomas Wilkinson, 2 October 1848, UC/P16/6

[33] Peschier, 'Religious Sexual Perversion', p. 205.

[34] Richard Singleton, b. 1825 (Lancashire), o. 1848, d. 1880. *English and Welsh Priests*, p. 46.

[35] This pamphlet was dedicated to the Scottish anti-Catholic newspaper the *Bulwark* "as a tribute of respect for the energy and talent with which they have defended the cause of Protestant truth against Popish aggression in Great Britain". G.T. Fox, *Priestly Celibacy Exposed: A Lecture, Delivered in the Borough Hall, Stockton-upon-Tees. . .* (Stockton-on-Tees: Jennett & Co., 1854).

[36] *Tablet,* 7 October 1854.

a new character witness appeared, but to no avail. The failure to convict the priest was met with incredulity by one Protestant magistrate in a letter to the *Durham Advertiser*:

> "Surely seeing the unhappy and ill-used girl leave the man's bedroom at two o'clock in the morning, and on another occasion witnessing them in a situation that admitted no doubt of their intimacy—his arm encircling her waist—were abundant confirmatory evidence, superadded to her own solemn oath, to satisfy the requirements of an Act of Parliament".[37]

Anti-sacerdotalism was also present in the town of Hartlepool throughout the 1850s. The Catholic priest of the town, the Rev. William Knight, appears to have been victimised on a regular basis in a town where a rabid anti-Catholicism seemed to be ingrained amongst the local Protestant community.[38] His very existence seemed to excite at best curiosity and at worst outright hostility. At a Soirée in Sunderland, the *Sunderland Herald* reported the Rev. Mr. Knight recalling his first entry into the town by horseback:

> "On entering the town, he observed a crowd of people assembled, and though he never imagined for a moment that they were waiting of him, yet he was soon made sensible of it. An old woman advanced, and, taking the horse by the bridal, she stared at him a short time. Then turning to her companions, in evident disappointment and disgust, she exclaimed, 'Oh— he's nowt but any other man'. (Laughter) He verily believed they expected to see him enter the town on four legs, with long ears, and a tail of his own (Loud laughter)".[39]

During the 1850s, the Rev. Mr. Knight became an increasing figure of hate for the local anti-Catholics. After narrowly escaping a lynching in July 1851, Knight found himself the target of sustained abuse, so much so that he was forced to appeal to the magistrates of the town. He complained that men and children "had called him by very opprobrious names, and using such language as he would not repeat in court". The driving force behind this campaign was allegedly the Rev. George Fox of Durham, whose "fiery discourses" against Catholicism in a sermon at the local Anglican church had generated renewed distrust of the priest. Knight also complained that his sister had been assaulted while out riding. The controversy reached the attention of the *Bulwark*, whose correspondent

[37] *Newcastle Guardian*, 14 July 1855; *Durham Advertiser*, 15 July 1855.
[38] William Knight, b. 1808, o. 1833, d. 1874. *English and Welsh Priests*, p. 42.
[39] Reprinted in the *Darlington and Stockton Times*, 27 October 1860.

believed that Knight and the Catholics were hypocritical in complaining of discrimination when true persecution was carried out regularly in the "dungeons of Rome, and the prisons of Florence".[40]

It was, however, Knight's alleged behaviour towards a respectable young lady which caused the most controversy. In October 1851, the priest accused the local solicitor, John Hines, of assaulting him. Mr. Hines, who acted as his own defence lawyer, argued in return that Knight had attempted to seduce his daughter, Henrietta. It was alleged that Knight put his arm around Henrietta and told her she was "a pretty girl". The report of the case seemed to revolve around whether Knight had seduced Miss Hines or not, rather than the actual assault. Indeed, Mr. Hines appealed to the jury to consider carefully his motivations for attacking the priest:

> "If any of you gentlemen are fathers and having daughters, and you found that a man, more especially a minister of the gospel, as he is styled in the summons, is trying all in his power to pollute them, how would you act? Draw your own inferences whether I discharged him or not".[41]

In the end, the case was dismissed on a technicality and Hines escaped punishment for assault.

This local anti-sacerdotal culture was often fuelled by individual personalities. The local Hartlepool orator, A.H. Lamb, delivered popular lecturers on the evils of Popery, some of which he subsequently published in pamphlet form. In a pamphlet entitled *Popery Opposed to the Laws of Nature and Revelation*, he lambasted the confessional in uncompromising language:

> "By its means . . . the priest is made one with Satan. Operating in the very origin of the will, he can vitiate the purest mind . . . It seems a doubt whether Satan ever brought his ancient system of Paganism to such a state of maturity as his priesthood, in the counterfeit system of the Christian church, have brought his   system of auricular confession".[42]

Similarly, the editor of the Conservative and Evangelical *Hartlepool Free Press*, Benjamin T. Ord, directed his energies towards exposing the sinister designs of the priesthood, publishing two aggressively anti-

---

[40] *Bulwark*, December 1854.
[41] *Sunderland Herald*, 2 October 1857.
[42] A.H. Lamb, *Popery Opposed to the Laws of Nature and Revelation* (London: [n. pub.] 1854), p. 11.

sacerdotal pamphlets in the mid-1860s.[43] In the second of these pamphlets, Ord accused priests of coercing dying Catholics into bequeathing their estates to individual priests, concentrating on a particular case in which a local priest was alleged to have donated £100,000 to Ushaw College bequeathed to him by a deceased Catholic. Ord entered into correspondence with William Hogarth, Cardinal Wiseman, and even W.E. Gladstone, to draw attention to this practice but to no avail.

Although anti-sacerdotalism was mostly evident in the southern area of the region, it was not uncommon in other areas. Court cases against priests in Durham City and Felling fuelled Protestant paranoia further north. In February 1863, a young lady, Hannah Hunt, alleged that the Roman Catholic priest of Durham, the Rev. Patrick Matthews, had threatened to assault her.[44] Matthews had originally accosted Hunt in a shop in Framwellgate, telling her that her husband, Patrick Hunt, was to stop deriding the Roman Catholic religion or he (Matthews) would stop him from "walking or talking". A few days later, Hunt told her friend what had occurred but as she was leaving her friend's house, Matthews walked in to speak to her friend's Catholic husband. On seeing Hunt, the priest asked if she was offended by what he had said before. When Hunt replied in the affirmative, the priest then said "If that puts you about I will do far more". The case was dismissed, to the applause from a group of Irish Catholics, owing to the fact that nothing untoward had taken place and the threats were more implied than real.[45]

Perhaps the most famous court case against a priest in the region concerns Father Kelly of Felling.[46] A stolen watch had been given to Kelly by a thief who admitted his guilt in confession to the priest. However, because the thief had surrendered the watch in confession, Kelly could not name the thief in court, much to the incredulity of the judge. After a fruitless attempt to obtain the name of the criminal, the judge felt he had no other option but to send Kelly to Durham Gaol for withholding information. This caused an outcry among Catholics and, after forty hours incarceration, Kelly was freed. The *Bulwark* was incensed, claiming that the confessional effectively "defeats the ends of justice, both by absolving

---

[43] *The Beginning of the End*, which Ord "dedicated to the Catholic priesthood", and *A blue book: or, an Exposition of the Manner in which the Priesthood Plunder and Devour their Flocks* (Hartlepool: Hartlepool Free Press, 1865).

[44] Patrick Thomas Matthews, b. 1833 (County Meath), o. 1862, d. 1899. *English and Welsh Priests*, p. 48.

[45] *Durham Chronicle*, 6 February 1863.

[46] Edmund Joseph Kelly, b. 1794 (Kilkenny, Ireland), o. 1835, d. 1866. *English and Welsh Priests*, p. 42.

and concealing the criminal".[47] Cooter has argued that Kelly's release is an example of a tolerant attitude towards Catholics, but the very fact that the priest was imprisoned in the first place for following the teachings of his faith suggests otherwise.[48]

The battleground between an increasing militant Catholic community and a staunchly defensive anti-Catholicism can be also observed in the arena of the public lecture. The heightened religious tension in the early 1850s was "strongly encouraged" by the culture of No Popery lecturing campaigns that dwelt on the theological errors of Roman Catholicism.[49] This is clearly evident in the North East of England. Newcastle was graced with the presence of a number of evangelical lecturers who exploited the anti-Catholic tension of the period. No fewer than ten No Popery orators visited the town in these years—all of them being met with large attendances. It also appears they were all effective public speakers who knew how to command their audience. Thus Dr. Sleigh, who lectured on the 'Errors and Inconsistencies of Popery', was reported to be a "master of his subject, and his style of oratory is pleasing and effective". In general, these lecturers were cordially received by their audience but, on occasions, the appearance of Irish Catholics often led to disruption. Thus a lecture delivered by Samuel Day on the subject of 'Romanism, the Religion of Terror' was "frequently disturbed" by the presence of Roman Catholics from "the Sister Isle".[50]

While anti-Catholic lecturing was particularly popular in the early-1850s, so too were the lectures of prominent Catholics who saw a clear need to defend the increasing attacks on their faith. The obvious example is the Catholic orator Charles Larkin. As has been shown, Larkin was active in defending Catholicism in political controversies but he was also a recognised authority on doctrinal subjects. He was never afraid to speak in reply to the anti-Catholic lecturing of Alessandro Gavazzi and John Sheridan Knowles. Knowles, a famous playwright who had capitalised on the heightened anti-Catholic feeling of the early 1850s, was sponsored by the Protestant Alliance, as the organisation saw a definite commercial advantage in supporting the lecturing tour of such a famous figure. In North Shields, Larkin replied to Knowles's Newcastle lecture on the 'Romish Apostasy', delivering a long lecture in defence of the Pope to a crowded audience in which one Protestant was almost lynched for trying

---

[47] *Bulwark*, April 1860.
[48] Cooter, *Paddy*, p. 82.
[49] MacRaild, *Irish Migrants*, p. 174.
[50] *Newcastle Journal*, 8 February 1851.

to question the lecturer.[51] Controversial Catholic lecturers could also be clerical. In 1852, both Fathers Kelly and Knight, of South Shields and Hartlepool respectively, delivered a series of controversial sermons in their churches, the latter delivering anti-Protestant orations every Sunday evening for three months.[52] In Sunderland, the lectures of the Rev. Philip Kearney, in which the priest implied that if a penitent was to admit the crime of murder in confession before committing it, the confessor could not notify the authorities, generated an anti-Catholic outrage which went beyond the confines of the North East. Indeed, opposition was even evident from the notable anti-Catholic firebrands, Rev. Hugh Stowell of Manchester and Rev. Hugh McNeale of Liverpool. McNeale argued that if Kearney's statement was true, priests should be given the death penalty as accessory to murder if the penitent carried out his threats.[53]

Some anti-Protestant lecturers came from further afield. Dr. Cahill, a renowned Irish Catholic theologian, toured the region in 1852 and 1853, lecturing in Newcastle, South Shields, Durham, Darlington and Stockton on subjects such as the 'Infallibility of the Church'.[54] The reports in the local press were generally unwelcoming to these anti-Protestant lecturers (in contrast to the somewhat fawning reception offered to their anti-Catholic adversaries), and their attitude to Cahill was no different. In a report of his lecture at Stockton, the *Durham Advertiser* was clearly shocked by Cahill's oration:

> "Such a specimen of Popery, pure and simple, has been seldom heard in Stockton. There was no artificial dressing of the subject to suit the time and place, but a real exhibition of the Papal system in all its extravagancies and deformity".[55]

The appearance of Dr. Cahill, however, often inspired more than just vocal complaints. In Darlington, attempts were made by the "Orange Low Church Party" to placard the town and prevent the lecturer from speaking.[56] A more serious incident occurred in Newcastle. The *Newcastle Journal* reported a "malicious outrage", in which a stone was thrown

---

[51] *Shields Gazette*, 18 March 1853.

[52] *Tablet*, 17 January, 17 April 1852.

[53] *Sunderland Herald*, 12 December 1851.

[54] According to John Wolffe, Daniel Cahill was one of the most controversial of all Catholic lecturers. From the 1820s, he employed language as extreme as his anti-Catholic opponents. Wolffe, *Protestant Crusade*, p. 169.

[55] *Durham Advertiser*, 18 November 1853.

[56] *Tablet*, 10 December 1853.

through the window of St Andrew's Roman Catholic Church where the Irishman was preaching, striking a young female and cutting her "head to the bone".[57]

Anti-Catholic Evangelicalism and the Irish Poor

One facet of the Catholic priest's work which usually received praise rather than scorn from Protestants was their dedication to the Catholic poor. Roger Cooter's assertion that the priest's role in shielding the poor Irish Catholics from intemperance, vice and secret societies, as well as providing social fraternities such as St. Vincent de Paul, helped to "promote an image of the Catholic Church as a valuable social force" to Catholics and Protestants alike is difficulty to dispute.[58] Even the Newcastle Anglican minister, James C. Street, in his pamphlet, *The Night Side of Newcastle*, praised the "fidelity and devotion of the Roman Catholic Church, which never shrinks from ministering to the poor, the sinful, and miserable".[59] In particular the work of the priest in acute times of distress, such as the typhus and cholera outbreaks of the late-1840s and early-1850s won clerical and public praise from all denominations. Priests, who had died in the administration of their duties, such as Bishop Riddell and Canon Henry Gillow, were spoken of warmly in the local press. Cooter suggests the latter example is evidence of a more tolerant attitude towards Catholics in the region and an appreciation of the labours of the priest. However, it was rare for Protestants to criticise Catholic individuals, least of all those who had recently died. In particular, the united response of both Catholics and Protestants to the death of Cardinal Wiseman in 1865 is symptomatic of the general attitude towards the deceased in the country as a whole.[60]

---

[57] *Newcastle Journal*, 31 January 1852. Cahill also returned later that year to preach in the same church, delivering a series of ten orations on different subjects. TWAS, 'Church Notice Book: St. Andrew's, Newcastle', 21-28 November 1852, C/NC/76/8/1.

[58] Cooter, *Paddy*, p. 81.

[59] James C. Street, *The Night-Side of Newcastle...A Lecture Delivered in the Church of Divine Unity* (Newcastle: Joseph Barlow, 1865), p. 4.

[60] Wiseman's funeral cortège was watched with obvious signs of respect by thousands of Protestants and Catholics in London. Norman, *The English Catholic Church*, p. 129 ft. 82. Marion Emes has also noted this attitude towards the Catholic deceased in York in a study of anti-Catholicism in the city. A funeral for the priest, Benedict Raymond, received warm reports in the local press and shops were even closed as a mark of respect. Emes, 'Anti-Catholicism in York', p. 53.

Nevertheless, the *Newcastle Journal's* opinions on the "martyrdom" of Roman Catholic priests during these epidemics is also evidence that not everyone was willing to pay tribute to the self-sacrifice of the Catholic clergy. In an article during the typhus outbreak in 1847, the paper even blamed the death of these priests on the peculiar tenets of Catholic practice:

> "The number of Roman Catholic clergymen that have fallen victim to Typhus fever, which has prevailed chiefly among the poor Irish, is accounted for by the circumstance of the parties being brought into very close proximity, and even contact, with the patients whom they visit. The debilitated sufferer whispers his 'confession' into the ear of his spiritual advisor . . . the latter frequently places himself upon the head of the patient, and thus imbibes the contagious atmosphere by which he is surrounded".[61]

A week later, the paper even aired anti-Catholic views in its report on the funeral service of Bishop Riddell, suggesting that the Catholic chapel in Newcastle was crowded with spectators, "many of whom appeared impressed with superstitious awe" at the performance of the Mass.[62] In 1853, the paper also felt incensed when, during the cholera outbreak in Newcastle, the Newcastle Corporation voted £500 to provide cabs to ferry Roman Catholic priests around the stricken areas. For the paper, there was a clear link between the cholera outbreak and Popery, suggesting that "a great portion of the mortality has been occasioned by the deplorable state into which the demoralising tendencies of the designing Romish priests . . . has either brought them, or in which it has left them to sink, and sicken, and die".[63] In a bitter attack on the recently arrived immigrants, the paper also suggested that the Irish Catholics only had themselves to blame for their plight:

> "(I)f disease and death prevail to so great an extent among the Irish Romanists, who swarm its densely populated lanes and streets, fearfully augmenting the mortality, and adding immeasurably to the rates, it might really become a question whether the local authorities would not be justified in interfering to ascertain and

---

[61] *Newcastle Journal*, 6 November 1847.

[62] *Newcastle Journal*, 13 November 1847.

[63] *Newcastle Journal*, 29 October 1853. The article in which these views emanated was entitled, 'Cholera and Popery' and was a response to an article in the *Tablet*.

remove the presentable causes of the degradation and turpitudes of those impositions from Ireland".[64]

These views contradict Cooter's claim that "the Irish were not held up for public execration" during the cholera epidemic.[65]

The *Newcastle Journal's* views are a clear indication that many were growing increasingly concerned by the seemingly supernatural power which the Catholic priest held over his flock. The increase in the number of resident Irish Catholics in the late 1840s, however, posed its own problems for the Catholic authorities. Not only were they concerned with how to manage the burgeoning Catholic population but also how to prevent "leakage" from the Church. One obvious solution was to build more churches to enable many Catholics to remain within the bosom of the Church, but the pace of church building, although impressive during the mid-Victorian years, was never able to keep up with the needs of congregations.[66] The number of Easter communicants, an essential ritual for Catholics and therefore a reliable indicator of the number practising the faith, indicated that many were lost from the Church, particularly in the years before 1855.[67] There were a number of reasons as to why this was the case, such as the lack of places of worship, the distance required to travel to these places and the temporary residency of migrants. One of the most feared as far as the Catholic clergy were concerned was the loss of their members to a Protestant church.

Although not the most important reason, Protestant proselytism undoubtedly had an impact on Catholic leakage. Protestant evangelicals were not slow to act when confronted with a marked increase in the number of the "perishing class" in the mid-Victorian period and the fact that many of these were Irish Catholics ensured that an anti-Catholic stance was inevitable. As Harrison has argued, religious proselytism had the function of alleviating poverty and ignorance because poverty was viewed largely as a result of moral failure.[68] Conversion to Protestantism was thus seen as a necessary step in the path to enlightenment. With this in mind, a number of societies existed with either a specific or broader aim to convert the local Irish Catholic. By far the largest and most influential was

---

[64] *Newcastle Journal,* 29 October 1853.

[65] Cooter, *Paddy*, p. 39.

[66] Cooter, *Paddy*, p. 59.

[67] Ibid, p. 59.

[68] Brian Harrison, 'Philanthropy and the Victorians', *Victorian Studies*, 9.4 (June 1966), p. 356.

the Town Mission, which was an offshoot of the London City Mission.[69] Its aim was to combat "Popery and Infidelity" and employed a number of Scripture readers who entered Irish areas in order to preach the gospel and distribute tracts in the hope that the "Papists" would see the error of their ways in their religion as well as their immoral ways of life.[70]

The nineteenth-century evangelical had a responsibility to "rebuke bodily those who sin bodily"[71] and there was no greater evidence of this than in the poorest areas of the towns and cities. This was particularly the case in Newcastle with its large working class population. Of the areas which were marked out for special attention by local missionaries in Newcastle, Sandgate appeared to be the most potentially fruitful. Not only did it contain a large portion of the town's Irish population, many of whom were attracted to the area by its close proximity to employment in the shipbuilding industry;[72] its living conditions were arguably amongst the worst in the country. One of the main problems was overcrowding. A report by the *Newcastle Chronicle* stated that 3,000 men, women and children were effectively:

> "crammed into a space which, if properly lived out, would be four or five times more exclusive. There are about twenty-five entries on each side of the street, with from 8 to 10 houses in each, containing on the average, eight rooms in each house . . . from ten to twenty people are very often to be found in one room".[73]

For some anti-Catholics there was a clear link between Catholicism and immorality. At a meeting of the Newcastle Mission, the missionary, Mr. Popley, reported that, in the western part of Newcastle "depravity did not exist to quite so great an extent as in some other places". One reason he cited for this was the small number of Bibles in Roman Catholic homes.[74]

Other towns had their own poverty-stricken areas where infidelity was rife amongst the inhabitants. Sunderland, which was described in one town mission report as the "very Sebastopol of Satan", was in a particularly desperate state. In "twenty-five streets and lanes, out of 3,097 families", the report suggested, "only 635 professed to attend any places of worship,

---

[69] Gilley, 'Protestant London', p. 212.

[70] *Newcastle Guardian*, 15 April 1851.

[71] Lewis, *Lighten their Darkness*, pp. 63-4.

[72] Scott, 'Comparative Re-examination', pp. 262-3.

[73] Newcastle Chronicle, *Inquiry into the Condition of the Poor of Newcastle-upon-Tyne* (Newcastle: M & M.W. Lambert, 1850), p. 23.

[74] *Newcastle Guardian*, 3 April 1847.

leaving 2,042 in entire neglect of even the outward observances of religion".[75] Similarly, Dr. Piper, on commenting on the Darlington Irish in his report for the Darlington Board of Health, also saw a critical link between poor living conditions and immorality:

> "They lived in the depth of squalor, the children working to support their indolent, able-bodied parents, to whom pauperism was hereditary rather than a disguise. Rooms of 10 to 12 feet square were occupied by up to a dozen people".[76]

Lewis has suggested that, in the mid-nineteenth century, Anglicans and Dissenters developed a "shared concern for evangelism" through accepted theological, polemical and practical factors.[77] The Town Missions therefore can be seen as a working case-study of the way in which Anglicans and Dissenters set aside their doctrinal differences in favour of broader evangelical principles. This co-operation is evident in the North East of England, with the Newcastle Town Mission in particular managing to retain ecumenical support throughout the 1840s, 1850s and 1860s. Thus, at the annual meeting of the society in 1860, the *Newcastle Guardian* noted the attendance embraced "ministers of all denominations".[78] Anglican clergymen, such as the Revs Richard Clayton and John Bruce, took a leading role in the Newcastle Mission from its inception in 1846. Indeed, according to his biographer, Bruce was "in the habit of mixing with men of various schools of religious thought, and of taking part in public meetings to promote philanthropic objects, where he met men of all denominations".[79] The reporter of the *Sunderland Herald* was pleased to note a large and attentive gathering at the first annual meeting of the Hartlepool Town Mission, which "comprised a fair sprinkling of all denominations".[80] Similarly, the chairman of the South Shields Town and River Mission praised the fact that the organisation was "not only supported by ministers and members of the Established Church, but also

---

[75] *Sunderland Herald*, 6 May 1853.
[76] Quoted in N. Sunderland, *A History of Darlington* (Manchester: E.J. Morten, 1972), p. 89.
[77] Lewis, *Lighten their Darkness*, p. 2.
[78] *Newcastle Guardian*, 17 March 1860.
[79] Garistord Bruce, *The Life and Letters of John Collingwood Bruce* (Edinburgh and London: William Blackwood, 1905), pp. 216-7. Clayton similarly was "placed at the head of religious and philanthropic movements in which Churchmen and Dissenter were able to cooperate". R. Welford, *Men of Mark*, p. 587.
[80] *Sunderland Herald*, 1 March 1850.

by those of other religious denominations in the town".[81] Not everyone
agreed with the sentiments of the Town Mission. Many Anglicans had
difficulty cooperating with Dissenters and mistrust was increased by the
bicentenary celebration of the Ejection of 1662. Dissenters were found on
the platforms and lecture halls delivering orations which greatly offended
their Anglican adversaries.[82] A letter in the *Newcastle Journal* saw this
event as the turning point in ecumenical organisation:

> "The constitution of the present Town Mission prevents a large number of
> earnest Churchmen from either contributing to its funds or taking any
> interest in it whatever. I have always held that to work with Dissenters
> generally was next to impossible; and the time has arrived, thanks to the
> bicentenary agitation, when those who have worked with them find it their
> solemn duty to come out from among them".[83]

Indeed, in Durham, where the Anglican-Dissenter relationship was always
more precarious than in other places, no such organisation existed. The
reason for this could also lie in the lack of general support given to
evangelical societies by the parochial clergy. The few societies which did
exist had been founded by laymen.[84]

Unlike the London City Mission, there does not appear to be any direct
evidence that the Town Missions of the region were formed in order to
combat the rise of the perceived Catholic threat. Indeed, the Report of the
Newcastle Mission in 1848 placed great stress on the ecumenical nature of
the society:

> "They (the committee) would earnestly urge upon Christians of all
> denominations, that until some better instrumentality presents itself, they
> should lay aside all sectarian differences and minor consideration, and join
> heart and hand in this work of faith".[85]

---

[81] *Shields Gazette*, 12 December 1861.

[82] I.E. Binns, *The Evangelical Movement in the English Church* (London: Methuen
and Co, 1932). A local example can be seen in 1862 when the Congregational
minister, the Rev. Samuel Goddall, who was known throughout Durham for his
role in ecumenical organisations, preached two sermons on the 1662 Ejection in
August 1862. *Durham Chronicle*, 29 August 1862.

[83] Quoted in *Darlington and Stockton Times*, 24 May 1862.

[84] Maynard, 'The Ecclesiastical Administration', p 87.

[85] Newcastle Town Missionary and Scripture Readers Society, *Report of the Town
Missionary and Scripture Readers Society* (Newcastle: [n. pub.] 1848).

Similarly the Stockton mission report of 1857 suggested that the society was "formed on the basis of unsectarianism, and the missionary had fully carried out its principle in its operations".[86] That the society was made up of Protestant ministers and laymen preaching from the King James Bible was hardly likely to endear Catholics to an organisation of this nature, particularly in light of papal pronouncements throughout the nineteenth century that forbade the reading of the Protestant Scriptures by the Catholic laity.[87] As Lewis suggests, anti-Catholicism in the mid-nineteenth century acted as a shared, unifying principle for both Anglican and Dissenter alike.[88]

Indeed, because the anti-Catholic and evangelical communities were so intertwined, it was almost inevitable that an anti-Catholic stance would be adopted, particularly following the Papal Aggression.[89] In the annual meeting of the Newcastle Mission in April 1851, many of the speakers referred to the Papal Aggression and the need for greater action against the Church of Rome. The Congregationalist layman, D. H. Goddard, urged upon the meeting "the importance of all denominations of Christians merging their minor differences to repel the common enemy (i.e. Roman Catholicism)" and the Rev. John Bruce saw that "there was much to be done to check the rapid rise of Popery and infidelity". The visiting deputy, the Rev. E. W. Foley of Derby, saw the solution in "providing education to the masses of the people, not a merely secular education, but an education based on the pure Word of God". The Scripture readers who entered Sandgate were then ordered to preach the gospel and distribute Protestant tracts to "Papists" in the hope they would see the error of their ways.[90] It is telling that many of those involved in the newly-formed Protestant Alliances were also found in the town missionary organisations also.

This anti-Catholic attitude was also notable in other auxiliaries. At the Hartlepool Town Mission meeting in 1853, the Rev. Mr. Douglas believed that there were "various obstacles retarding the progress of the mission". These, he argued, were "intemperance, Popery and infidelity". Similarly, another speaker, Mr. Adam, asked the audience to "give more attention to the subject of Popery".[91] In the same year, an editorial in the *Shields Gazette* promoting the South Shields society called for more religious services for the sailors because "Romanist and Mormonist agents are

---

[86] *Durham Advertiser*, 30 January 1857.
[87] Lewis, *Lighten their Darkness*, p. 64.
[88] Ibid, p. 2.
[89] R. J. Klaus, *The Pope*, p. 305.
[90] *Newcastle Guardian*, 15 April 1851.
[91] *Sunderland News*, 13 March 1853.

doing all in their power to propagate error".[92] Indeed, the *Tablet* had noted with some dismay the previous year that Protestant missionaries in seaport towns were offering Protestant Bibles to Italian, Neapolitan, Austrian and French sailors. These were "frequently accepted" because they were "printed in the language of the nation to which the respective crews belonged".[93]

The town missionaries employed a wide variety of methods to bring their message across to the irreligious poor. Home visits were the most popular but also the most dangerous tactic. Missionaries often entered the homes of the poor uninvited, preaching sermons and distributing tracts against infidelity and Romanism. The town missions often set up their own schools. In Newcastle in 1859, Rev. John Bruce warned that although "Popery was striving to regain its power", a great object had been accomplished in setting up a school for the poor in Prudhoe Street, consisting of 80 scholars.[94] In Sunderland, two missionary Sabbath schools were established in 1852 and, by the end of the decade, 230 scholars were receiving religious instruction from twenty-five teachers.[95] In Stockton, religious services were held by town missionaries every Sunday night in the Ragged School of the town and, in Sunderland, missionaries were making regular visits to the local workhouse to preach the Word of God to the inmates.[96] The Sunderland Mission also distributed evangelical periodicals, such as *Sunday at Home* and the *British Messenger*. The Rev. George Maitland further announced that a copy of the *British Ensign* was to be sent to each public house and beer house in Silver Street.[97] In South Shields, the local port encouraged the missionaries to target seamen as well as the irreligious poor of the town.[98] Here, missionaries were also active in using the Shields ferry service to distribute tracts, including No Popery publications in times of heightened anti-Catholicism.[99]

---

[92] *Shields Gazette*, 29 September 1853.

[93] *Tablet*, 25 September 1853.

[94] *Newcastle Guardian*, 5 March 1859.

[95] *Sunderland Herald*, 15 October 1852, 16 December 1859.

[96] *Durham Advertiser,* 30 March 1860; *Sunderland Herald*, 16 December 1859.

[97] *Sunderland Herald*, 16 December 1859.

[98] The importance of the society's mission to seamen is most evident in the title of the organisation. Whereas other local societies were called Town Missions, the South Shields organisation was referred to as the South Shields Town and River Mission. *Shields Gazette*, 12 December 1861.

[99] *Shields Gazette,* 6 December 1850.

As Lewis argues, missionary organisations measured themselves by statistics and these help to reveal some of the specific goals of the society.[100] Thus the achievements reported in the annual meeting of the Stockton Town Mission in 1854 can be seen as typical of other missions:

> "From the report . . . it appears that 8581 calls and visits had been made during the past year, as well as 602 visits to the sick; portions of the Scripture had been read to 1158 persons; 1611 tracts had been given, and 670 tracts exchanged; 448 English and foreign vessels had been visited; and 1420 tracts given to the seamen on board".[101]

Unlike foreign missionary organisations, the Town Missions were rarely profitable and for this reason they often found themselves struggling to remain in existence. The principal income for the society was charitable donations and these were not always forthcoming. Regular appeals were made to wealthy and benevolent individuals to contribute to a charitable cause. The Sunderland Mission, which in the 1850s could only appoint one missionary to oversee the whole town, constantly used the press as a vehicle for its endeavours:

> "Prosperity is at present flowing in upon our merchants and traders, and from them especially does the Home Mission of Sunderland naturally look for the means of support. Upon the wealthy, and upon the inhabitants generally, do we urge the duty of assisting that mission in its endeavours to add two colleagues to the solitary missionary who now gropes his way in those dreary labyrinths of vice . . ."[102]

Similarly the *Sunderland Herald* reported that the Stockton Mission annual meeting in 1854 was lively and interesting; "the only drawback was the statement that the funds were in arrears".[103]

The organisations were clearly affected by local circumstances as is evident by the number of missionaries employed in each respective organisation. Generally, missionaries were hard to find and most towns were only able to employ one or two.[104] In spite of being labelled as the

---

[100] Lewis, *Lighten their Darkness*, pp. 128-9.

[101] *Sunderland Herald*, 27 January 1854.

[102] *Sunderland Herald*, 6 May 1853.

[103] *Sunderland Herald*, 27 January 1854.

[104] This is in stark contrast to the London City Mission where the organisation employed 631 full-time workers in 1860: Lewis, *Lighten their Darkness*, p. 120. However, it must be borne in mind that the towns of the North East were much

Town and River Mission, the South Shields branch was only able to concentrate on the latter portion of its title before 1861. The organisation's one missionary was not able to increase his operations to the town's inhabitants, and the chairman was glad to announce that year they could now claim their full title in response to the appointment of a missionary dedicated to the poor of the town.[105] The exception was Newcastle. In 1850, the Newcastle Mission employed three missionaries. By 1852 this number had doubled to six and in the 1860s, eight missionaries were on the payroll of the organisation.[106] The Newcastle organisation was the most successful of all the local societies, managing to remain in credit throughout the 1850s and 1860s. This was due in no small part to an annual Christmas bazaar, organised by some of the principal ladies associated with the society. The Society was so reliant on this income that when the ladies protested about holding the bazaar in 1858, they were put under undue pressure and only gave their services "under protest". It was estimated at this stage that 50% of the annual income came from the bazaar. By 1860, the income from the bazaar amounted to 96% of the annual income.[107] By the early years of that decade, the annual report of the organisation was not exaggerating when it stated that the "continued existence of the Newcastle Town Mission" relied on the efforts of the ladies and their bazaar.[108]

Aside from the efforts of the Town Missions, individual denominations also sought to establish societies which were dedicated to religious instruction among the poor of the town. A number of societies were Anglican in their make-up. The Church of England had long been accused of neglecting its duties to the lower classes, but the evident increase in activity among the Catholic clergy had become an area of concern for Anglicans. Many felt they were losing ground with their rivals and a more sustained and direct policy was required if Popery was not to succeed. This was a particular fear of the Church Pastoral Aid Society. Established

---

smaller by comparison and therefore the number of missionaries was relative to this.

[105] *Shields Gazette*, 12 December 1861.

[106] *Newcastle Guardian*, 8 May 1852; Newcastle Town Mission and Scripture Readers Society, *Fifteenth Report of the Town Missionary and Scripture Readers Society of Newcastle-upon-Tyne* (Newcastle, 1861), p. 5.

[107] *Newcastle Guardian*, 17 March 1860. The amount raised by the bazaar was £297 and the annual income was £309.

[108] Newcastle Town Missionary and Scripture Readers Society, *Sixteenth Report of the Town Missionary and Scripture Readers Society of Newcastle-upon-Tyne* (Newcastle: [n. pub.] 1862), p. 10.

in the mid-1850s, the CPAS was essentially an Anglican version of the Town Mission, although it received far less press attention and support than its interdenominational rival. It sent out Scripture readers and organised Bible classes, although it was also responsible for assisting in the maintenance and development of Anglican churches in the region.[109] It was primarily the fear of the Catholic revival which drove many Anglicans to support the society. At a meeting of the organisation in Newcastle, the Rev. A. Irwine of Richmond was particularly critical of the Anglican Church's missionary endeavours, believing that the Church "had not yet shown all the effort she might have shown in this work, while the Roman Catholics and Mormons were unrelaxing in their efforts in that direction".[110]

There were also other Anglican home missionary societies with a more narrow anti-Catholic agenda. In the 1850s, branches of the Church of England Missions to the Roman Catholics were established in Newcastle, Hartlepool, Sunderland and Stockton. They, according to the Rev. J. White in a meeting in Newcastle, "were to preach controversial sermons, hold discussion classes, as well as by other means consistent with the doctrine and discipline of the Established Church, to promote the spread of the religion among Roman Catholics".[111] The society attracted a number of anti-Catholic zealots, such as the Rev. Lewis Paige, who regularly preached sermons in his Anglican church in Hartlepool to promote the organisation.[112] These auxiliaries appear to have had little longevity because there are few reports of CEMRC meetings after 1856, although this reflected the national trend.[113] The British Reformation Society was more successful in this regard. Auxiliaries and missionary stations of the Society had existed in Newcastle, Durham and Hartlepool since 1827[114] and, although the organisation rarely received attention owing to its apolitical stance, scattered press and society reports in the 1840s and 1850s reveal that local branches still existed.[115] However, the aims and

---

[109] Reference was made to these operations at the annual sermon of the South Shields auxiliary. *Shields Gazette*, 28 February 1856.

[110] *Newcastle Courant*, 3 March 1860.

[111] *Sunderland Herald*, 26 September 1856.

[112] *British Protestant*, May 1853, p. 69.

[113] Sheridan Gilley notes that the society went into "disastrous decline" after 1856, dismissing all but two of its missionaries in London due to lack of funding after which it quietly dissolved. Gilley, 'Protestant London', p. 28.

[114] Wolffe, *Protestant Crusade*, p. 153.

[115] The *Newcastle Guardian* and the *Sunderland Herald* reported lectures from the society in the Anglican churches of Newcastle in March 1849 and Hartlepool

religious composition of the above societies were too narrow and in any case were unlikely to make much headway in a region dominated, if not exclusively so, by Nonconformity.[116] Brian Dickey has noted that societies with narrow aims such as the conversion of Catholics only attracted a "predominantly evangelical list of subscribers". The broader the aims, the more likely they were to attract support. [117] This may help to explain why the Town Mission received greater coverage than the more specifically anti-Catholic societies.

It was not only the Church of England which was concerned by the consequences of the growth of Roman Catholicism in the region. The Wesleyan Methodists, whose evangelicalism had been always infused with anti-Catholicism[118], saw Catholic growth as a direct threat to their religious influence in the region. They had played a large role in foreign missions to Catholics but were turning their attention to problems closer to home by the 1860s. Wesleyan Home Mission organisations were set up in a number of towns including Newcastle, Durham, Darlington and Stockton. The aims of these societies were similar to those of the Town Missions, i.e. to deliver religious instruction to the poor and thereby improve their morality. The interconnection of anti-Catholicism and evangelicalism, along with the high proportion of Irish Catholics amongst the poor, meant that the missions also adopted a similar "No Popery" ethic. At a public meeting of the Durham branch, the Rev. S. Cox of Sunderland believed that more attention needed to be paid to the expansionist plans of Popery, "which had doubled its representatives in this kingdom during the last fifty years".[119] The Rev. William Pepperell expressed similar sentiments at a meeting of the Darlington branch. He was particularly concerned with the growth of Catholicism which, he

---

Town Hall in June 1855: *Newcastle Guardian*, 11 March 1849 and *Sunderland Herald*, 29 June 1849. The annual reports of the Reformation Society were printed in the *British Protestant* journal which included a list of auxiliaries. Newcastle appears to be the only branch in operation in the North East in the late 1840s-early 1850s, see *British Protestant*, July 1850, p. 128.

[116] The Reformation Society was generally more popular in the southern cities, specifically Bristol, Portsmouth and Southampton, where Anglicanism was stronger. Matthews, 'Second Spring', p. 93; see also Wolffe, *Protestant Crusade*, p. 136.

[117] Brian Dickey, "Going About and Doing Good': Evangelicals and Poverty, c.1815-1870' in *Evangelical Faith and Public Zeal: Evangelicals and Society in Britain 1780-1980* ed. by John Wolffe (SPCK: London, 1995), p. 42.

[118] Hempton, *Religion and Political Culture*, p. 37.

[119] *Durham Advertiser*, 13 February 1863.

argued, "had done more to falsify truth, as it is in Jesus, than any other system fabricated by Satan".[120]

So how did the Catholics respond to this threat to their religious beliefs? One solution was to fight back, with many local Catholic organisations adopting increasingly militant attitudes. Paz has pointed to the lack of funding in Catholic organisations when compared with their Protestant equivalents but they clearly saw that there was a need to defend their faith at the local level.[121] In 1845, it was announced at the annual meeting of the Newcastle upon Tyne Catholic Tract Society that several valuable Catholic books had been purchased and 1,360 volumes were circulated throughout the year.[122]   This organisation developed along similar lines to their Protestant rivals, redoubling their efforts in response to anti-Catholic evangelical behaviour. They were particularly concerned with the conduct of the Scripture readers ("Ranters"), believing they were "making use of every species of black art and magical and necromantic incantation to invoke the long laid demon of bigotry with the half shout of 'No Popery'!"[123]

Elsewhere, Catholic organisations developed in response to the heightened religious tension surrounding the Papal Aggression. In North Shields and Gateshead, Catholic Defence Associations were formed with the intention of providing the Irish with doctrinal arguments to counter-act the threat of Protestant proselytism.[124] These Associations were also very proactive in combating anti-Catholicism. When the North Shields organisation received information that a travelling deputation from "one of those societies who wish for the 'conversion of Ireland'" was due to visit the town, it immediately organised a meeting to discuss the best means of preventing this threat to their Catholicism. It was resolved that a hand bill was to be distributed at the door of the meeting, appealing to the people of Shields to "refuse to give their money to the . . . defamers of the Irish people".[125] The Associations were patronised by clergy as a means of diverting the political energies of the Irish Catholics away from secret societies to the defence of their faith.[126] Indeed, at the inauguration of the

---

[120] *Darlington and Stockton Times*, 30 March 1861.

[121] Paz, *Popular Anti-Catholicism,* p. 88.

[122] *Tablet*, 25 October 1845.

[123] Quoted in Scott, 'Comparative Re-examination', p. 108.

[124] *The Tablet*, 29 March, 1 November 1851.

[125] *Tablet*, 19 June 1852, p. 389.

[126] Some local priests also contributed to the national Defence Association in Ireland. The *Sunderland News* noted that the Sunderland priests, Bamber and Kearney, contributed a donation of £1 each. *Sunderland News*, 30 August 1851.

Gateshead branch, Father Betham spoke to a large audience of Irish Catholics about the benefits of the society. It was not, he suggested, a means by which they "could revile their neighbours, members of other churches" but a way in which they could educate themselves as part of a programme of self-improvement.[127] Indeed, in the early 1850s, there were regular toasts were given to the Catholic Defence Association at Roman Catholic Soirées.[128] Although the Catholic Defence Associations were essentially a short-lived phenomenon, disbanding on a national basis after the 1852 general election[129], their activities helped, in turn, to increase anti-Catholicism in the region, particularly as rival Protestant Defence Associations were formed in some towns.[130]

Aside from the more organised Catholic campaigns, the Irish Catholics themselves responded in different ways to the growing evangelical threat. D.M. Lewis suggests that working class attitudes to missionaries in general were shaped by "ignorance, anti-clericalism and class resentment"[131], but the Irish Catholics were undoubtedly a special case given their strong attachment to their religion. Moreover, many Irish Catholics had bitter experience of Protestant missionary efforts in their homeland. Organisations such as the Irish Society and the Irish Church Missions to Roman Catholics were aggressively active in proselytism and it is no surprise that many responded forcefully.[132] Auxiliaries of these societies existed in areas of North East England where Irish immigrants resided in order to raise funds for assisting missionary endeavours in Ireland. The Irish attitude to these societies can be observed in a meeting of the Newcastle auxiliary of the Irish Church Missions to Roman Catholics in October 1850. This meeting had, as its special guest speaker the head of the organisation, Rev. Alexander Dallas. Dallas's aggressive and quasi-militaristic attitude to the conversion of Ireland had made him deeply unpopular among the Irish Catholics back in their homeland and many

---

[127] *Newcastle Guardian*, 29 November 1851.

[128] For example, the *Newcastle Guardian* reports on a toast being given to the organisation at a Soirée in Sunderland in November 1851: *Newcastle Guardian*, 28 November 1851.

[129] Wolffe, *Protestant Crusade*, p. 169.

[130] Bishop Auckland is an example of this.

[131] Lewis, *Lighten their Darkness*, p. 128.

[132] The story of the Irish Church Missions is examined in Desmond Bowen, *The Protestant Crusade in Ireland, 1800-70: A Study of Protestant-Catholic Relations Between the Act of Union and Disestablishment* (Dublin: Queen's University Press, 1978), pp. 208-48, and, in a more recent publication, by Miriam Moffitt, *The Society for Irish Church Missions to the Roman Catholics, 1849-1950* (Manchester: Manchester University Press, 2011).

were, at the very least, aware of his name and the emotions this evoked.[133] Dallas's speech was unlikely to win any converts either. Referring to Ireland as a "great problem" to the English Government, he caused extreme indignation among a considerable portion of Irish Catholics who were present at the meeting by declaring that it "pleased God to visit Ireland with a famine" because "Satan was at work among the Romanists".[134] This was the cue for the Irish, allegedly headed by the respected Matthias Dunn and a priest, to interrupt the meeting with a volley of abuse. Because the Irish did not respond in any physical way, the police were powerless to act and the meeting was brought to an abrupt close.[135] A letter-writer to the *Newcastle Journal* was incensed by the attitude of these Irish Catholic "creatures", and their prevention of what he saw as the English right to freedom of speech:

> "Is it to be borne that in England, the land of liberty, Englishmen can be debarred the exercise of their rights by the miserable slaves of an Italian monk, and denied the protection of law which they are taxed to support? . . . The worthy gentleman and his crew above alluded to may hold as many meetings as they like, to devise measures for convincing the propriety of worshipping an old coat, or for venerating a bit of the Virgin's petticoat . . . None would interfere with their proceedings. Why, then, do they presume to interfere with ours?"[136]

Given the attitude of the Irish Catholics to missionaries in their own country, it is hardly surprising that many often met the local "Ranter" threat head-on with physical violence.[137] Nevertheless, as Lewis argues, violence towards town missionaries appeared to be the exception rather than the rule.[138] Indeed, some Irish Catholics were keen to listen to the vocal exertions of missionaries, a point regularly made in the reports of the Newcastle Town Mission:

> "The difficulty with the Missionaries now is, not how 'to get into a house', but 'how to get out of it'. Their reading of the Scriptures and their exhortations do not fall upon inattentive ears; the people are disposed to

---

[133] Bowen, *Protestant Crusade*, p. 224.
[134] *Newcastle Journal*, 12 October 1850.
[135] Ibid.
[136] Ibid.
[137] See Chapter Six.
[138] Lewis, *Lighten their Darkness*, p. 138.

give a cordial response to their statements, and to enter into conversation with them upon serious subjects".[139]

Similarly, the Sunderland Town Mission reported in 1863 that the Roman Catholics provided the greatest opposition to missionary visits but, in the following year, there was now a "growing disposition to hear the Gospel and to receive the visits of the missionaries".[140] Female missionaries appeared to be particularly welcome in the homes of Irish Catholics, perhaps, as D.M. Lewis suggests, because the majority of the people approached by the agents were women themselves, as they were more likely to be at home during the agent's visiting hours.[141] The Newcastle Ladies Bible Association appeared to be particularly successful, stating the readiness of Roman Catholics to allow "the Scriptures to be read in their houses, even kneeling in prayer with the missionaries".[142] Female missionaries were also sought by the Stockton Mission. In the 1865 annual meeting, one of the secretaries of the organisation, Louis Dodshon, stated that it had become a serious question of appointing a female missionary and it was agreed that "as soon as the funds would allow, they would endeavour to have such an agent".[143]

Indeed, extracts from the journal of the Newcastle missionaries, if they can be trusted as accurate, reveal that there were some notable successes in converting Catholics.[144] The missionary, Mr. Clancy, managed to convert an elderly female Catholic in the workhouse who "was greatly prejudiced against the gospel" but, after hearing his reading of the Bible, her "prejudices gave way" and she began to regularly consult the Bible, exclaiming "Thank God we have the saviour to come to her for our sins".[145] Another missionary in the town, Mr. Willoughby, similarly showed how the power of the Word of God could be harnessed to unlock the prejudice of the Catholic. When he offered a tract to an Irish Catholic one day, the following conversation took place:

---

[139] *Fifteenth Report Scripture Readers Society*, p. 5.

[140] *Sunderland Herald*, 11 December 1863; 9 March 1864.

[141] Lewis, *Lighten their Darkness*, p. 123.

[142] *Newcastle Guardian*, 21 September 1861.

[143] *Durham Advertiser*, 24 February 1865.

[144] These extracts are printed in Newcastle Town Missionary and Scripture Readers Society, *Quarterly Record of the Newcastle-upon-Tyne Town Mission* (Newcastle: [n. pub.] 1857).

[145] Ibid, pp. 2-3.

"**Irish**: 'Och sure now, I want none of that, I don't go in wid the like of those tracts'.
Missionary: 'Why?'
Irish: 'Because they are full of nothing but lies'.
Missionary: – You are wrong informed my friend, there is nothing in the tracts but what is in accordance with the Word of God'.
Irish: – 'Sure the likes of you don't believe in the Word of God?'
Missionary: – 'Yes I do, every word of it'.
Irish: 'Sure, you Protestants don't believe in the holy ointment, and doesn't the Word of the Almighty God make plain enough . . . that without the holy ointment the sinner cannot be saved?'
Missionary: 'No, the Word of God teaches nothing of the sort, it teaches that it is by faith in the sacrifice of the righteousness of the Lord Jesus Christ alone that sinners are saved'".[146]

The Irish Catholic appeared shocked with this explanation and, with his "prejudices yielding to the force of truth", gladly accepted the tracts offered by the missionary.[147]

Nevertheless, conversions to Protestantism were the exception rather than the rule.[148] Missionary efforts were often hampered by the Catholic authorities, who used their influence on their flock to warn against receiving Protestant missionaries.[149] Clancy regularly visited an Irish Catholic, whose wife was a Protestant, but when the priest heard this, he attempted to put a stop to the missionary's efforts:

"When I called this evening he (Irish Catholic) told me what had taken place, saying 'Mr. Clancy, the people told the priest that I had you visiting me, and he has ordered me not to receive you again; I did like to hear you; but you can come to speak to my wife, who is a Protestant, and he has no control over her' . . . I then pointed out to him, from the Word of God, the absurdity of confessing to a priest . . . he listened most attentively".[150]

Clancy was able to visit the Irishman twice more before the pressure of his peers and the priest, who "gave the man no peace", finally persuaded him to close his door to the missionary. It appears that the Catholic was forced to leave the town as a result.[151]

---

[146] Ibid, p. 3.
[147] Ibid, p. 3.
[148] Wolffe, *Protestant Crusade*, p. 191.
[149] R. Samuel, 'The Roman Catholic Church and the Irish Poor', *The Irish in the Victorian City,* p. 281.
[150] *Quarterly Record*, p. 2.
[151] Ibid.

This example reveals the extent of the barriers placed in the way of the missionary in his battle to win over Irish Catholic souls. Even if an Irish Catholic was willing to listen, his peers and authorities did everything in their power to prevent it. A letter in the *Newcastle Journal* complained that a sermon by a town missionary to two hundred people, a large proportion of whom were Irish Catholics, was interrupted by "two decently dressed men" carrying a leather strap:

> "(T)hey flourished (the straps) about their heads, and ordered the audience to disperse and not listen to the preacher, for they said he was preaching 'false doctrine and not the Church of Rome'. The people, however, were not willing to go, and some positively refused. The men then struck several, both men and women, with the straps, and ultimately drove 20 or 30 young men away towards a Roman Catholic chapel at the Wall Knoll".[152]

Moreover, the acceptance of a Protestant Bible by an Irish Catholic was viewed as serious blasphemy by the Catholic authorities. When the police accidentally issued Protestant Bibles to a predominantly Irish Catholic lodging house in Newcastle, a notice was read in St Andrews Church, ordering the Catholics to return them. The penalty for not doing so was denial of the sacraments.[153] In Sunderland in 1851, the local Catholic priest, the Rev. John Bamber was even accused of attempting to burn a Protestant Bible issued to an elderly Catholic, Mr. Drescher. Drescher had called Bamber to his home whilst the latter was on a sick-bed. The priest, having spotted the Bible, told Drescher that he would go to hell if he read it and proceeded towards the fire. Only after much pleading from Drescher did Bamber back down.[154] In Darlington, a more serious controversy ensued when it was alleged at the Protestant Alliance anti-Maynooth meeting in the town that the Bishop of Hexham had been buying up Bibles issued to the Irish Catholics from Protestant missionaries at three times the price they were originally bought for. This aroused Protestant suspicions that Hogarth was effectively "buying out" missionary attempts to convert the Catholics. Hogarth, of course, angrily denied these accusations, telling his own version of events in a letter to the local paper:

---

[152] *Newcastle Journal*, 15 August 1855.
[153] TWAS, 'Church Notice Book of St Andrews, Newcastle', 16 March 1856.
[154] *Sunderland News*, 13 December 1851.

"Some weeks ago a poor girl brought me a Testament which, she said, had been left with her by the *Town Missionary* . . . She said she wished to part with it, and knowing her poverty, I gave her a shilling, and she left me with the Testament. Now, I appeal to any dispassionate man, whether, from the above small act of charity . . . it can fairly be inferred that I am inimical to the *dissemination* of God's Holy Word—that I am *afraid of the Bible, or endeavouring to arrest its progress* . . . (author's italics)" [155]

Hogarth's defence caused an angry response from the anti-Catholics of the town. A letter from the Anglican minister of the town, the Rev. Howell Harris, believed that as "it would not be safe or POLITIC to burn Testaments; they are here taken in exchange for a shilling GIVEN IN CHARITY".[156] The event caused so much anti-Catholic feeling in the town that the Darlington Protestant Alliance organised a public meeting in which Hogarth and the Catholic Church in general were attacked for opposing "the circulation of the Bible". At the end of the meeting, an Irish Catholic was allowed onto the platform and a discussion ensued. The Chairman concluded the meeting by declaring justice to "both parties" and little more was said in the town on the matter.[157]

Some Roman Catholics developed novel ways of preventing missionary efforts. Mr. Swanney, a Roman Catholic in Stockton, accused the local Bible missionary, W.D. Smith, a Wesleyan, of supporting a society which inadequately paid a woman to stitch bibles. Swanney argued that "no lover of liberty" could defend this society, offering to meet Mr. Smith for a discussion in which he would furnish proof of his claim. Swanney conceded that he had not been able to secure the "materials to support his position" but offered Smith another meeting to discuss the matter once he had received the necessary evidence. Smith replied by stating that he had contacted the secretary of the society who had issued a statement refuting Swanney's claim. A vote was then put to the audience as to which claim was to be accepted. In spite of having no evidence, Mr. Swanney received a very large majority.[158]

---

[155] *Darlington and Stockton Times*, 13 March 1852.

[156] *Darlington and Stockton Times*, 20 March 1852.

[157] *Darlington and Stockton Times*, 3 April 1852. This meeting is relatively remarkable as the Protestant Alliance rarely involved itself in local issues, preferring to combat Popery on a national or international level.

[158] *Darlington and Stockton Times*, 17 July 1858.

Religious Instruction and Protestant Proselytism

For both Catholics and Protestants, the fear of proselytism received its greatest expression in the battle for the souls of children. Clashes between rival evangelical Protestant and increasingly militant Catholic groups spilled into this area through religious instruction in educational institutions and the workhouse. Throughout the country, Catholic schools were founded in order to meet the growing problem of the lack of religious education for poor children. London's Brompton Oratory was established by Frederick William Faber who, according to one Protestant evangelical, was "teaching the Irish in London to fathom an abyss of blasphemous worship of the Virgin Mary which they did not do know before".[159] In the North East of England, Protestant evangelicals greatly feared the possibilities of "perversion" of young minds through a Catholic education. In a meeting of the Newcastle Wesleyan Education Movement—an organisation designed to provide Protestant religious teaching to poor children—the Rev. J. Scott urged the establishment of day schools alongside their Sunday schools. "The want of such institutions", he argued, "had driven many of their children to Church schools, and even in some cases Roman Catholic schools".[160]

One of the earliest organisations to offer an educational service to poor children was the Ragged Schools, which, from the late-1840s, were present in many of the large towns in the region. They provided a means by which poor children could receive a basic secular and religious education which would enable them to acquire the skills for self-improvement. It was not the intention of these institutions to be anti-Catholic. Indeed, the *Sunderland Herald* hoped the establishment of a Ragged School might help to solve the problem of how to deal with the growing Irish presence in the town:

> "For a long time back there has certainly been great need of them (Ragged Schools), but now, what with the large influx of Irish labourers and unemployed workmen generally, the destitution of the humbler classes, and their consequent inability to provide instruction for their children . . . it

---

[159] Sheridan Gilley, 'Vulgar piety and the Brompton Oratory, 1850-1860', Swift and Gilley, *The Irish in the Victorian City*, p. 257.

[160] *Newcastle Courant*, 8 October 1852. The fear of Methodists drifting away to other schools reflects Wesleyan concerns nationally in the mid-nineteenth century, evident in the annual Wesleyan Educational Committee Report of 1849. John T. Smith, *Methodism and Education, 1849-1902* (Oxford, Clarendon Press, 1998), p. 17.

is high time that something palpable were done to alleviate the curse of society, that ignorance which is the root of crime in our town".[161]

The Ragged Schools, therefore, did not exclude Catholics from their organisation but, as with the Town Missions, there was a definite Protestant bias in its religious teaching and the fear of the proselytism of Catholic children was ever-present, particularly as many were located in, or near, the Irish slums.[162] Indeed, there is local evidence to suggest that the Catholic authorities were particularly fearful of sending children to these establishments, the *Newcastle Journal* reporting the withdrawal of Catholic children by the local priests.[163]

In Newcastle, the Ragged School that opened in Sandgate in 1847 was one of the earliest in the country[164] but it was forced to compete with the Brotherhood of St. Vincent de Paul. This organisation provided education to poor Catholic children as part of its charitable alms-giving ethos, with auxiliaries existing throughout the region.[165] However, the Newcastle branch found itself in the midst of controversy when it accused the Ragged School of adopting immoral methods to attract Catholic children into their organisation. The 1850-51 report of the Newcastle branch of the Brotherhood was particularly concerned with "rescuing the little ones of Christ from those unholy dens of proselytism, the Ragged Schools, where they are assiduously taught to deny the faith of their fathers". Indeed, one brother accused Ragged School teachers of "souperism" in "seducing" poor children into their schools by "distributing flour and oatmeal weekly".[166] It was a struggle for the Brotherhood to compete, particularly as the Ragged Schools were also adopting increasingly aggressive tactics in their dealings with the Catholic society:

---

[161] *Sunderland Herald*, 22 December 1848.

[162] M.G. Holland, *The British Catholic Press and Educational Controversy, 1847-1865* (New York: Garland Publishing, 1987), p. 133. Moreover, the Earl of Shaftesbury, a notoriously anti-Catholic aristocrat, was the President of the Ragged School Union. Ian Bradley, *The Call to Seriousness: The Evangelical Impact on the Victorians* (Jonathan Cape: London, 1976), p. 47.

[163] *Newcastle Journal*, 3 April 1848.

[164] Shelley O'Rourke, 'Newcastle-upon-Tyne Ragged School, 1847-1859' (unpublished bachelor's dissertation, University of Northumbria, 1998), p. 99.

[165] Morris and Gooch, *Down Your Aisle*, p. 16.

[166] Brotherhood of St. Vincent de Paul, *Report of the Newcastle and Gateshead-on-Tyne Conference of the Brotherhood of St. Vincent de Paul for the Years 1850-51* (Newcastle: [n. pub.] 1852), p. 3.

"(W)e (the Brotherhood) rescued an orphan girl from this perverting
Institute . . . we maintained the girl at the school for about two months
when her father died, and she was taken from us by a person who for a
paltry mess of pottage sent her back again to his school. We found out
where she was, and although threatened with the law, and with being
kicked down stairs, again succeeded in rescuing her from destitution".[167]

This report was greeted with an angry reply by the Rev. Lewis Paige,
Chairman of the Ragged School, and a notable Protestant Alliance
member. In a letter to the *Newcastle Journal*, Paige steadfastly denied
proselytism and coercion. He found it ironic that such an accusation could
arise from the "Romish Party" given she was "not over scrupulous to the
means she adopts in gaining recruits to her communion".[168]
Accusations of proselytism were levelled by both sides and were
reported well into the 1850s. In 1855, the annual report of the Newcastle
SVP again complained of underhand tactics in the methods adopted by the
Ragged Schools:

"The ragged schools, un-Catholic, in the name as in its objects, offers its
free education, its three meals a day, and its periodical outfits of clothing,
to every starving child that will enter it, besides the prospect of assistance
to the wretched parents; but it claims something in turn; the loss . . . of a
Catholic's faith, to say the least, the violation of his conscience".[169]

Equally, however, Protestants accused Catholics of interfering in an
institution that was legally obliged to offer an education to all who entered
it regardless of faith. The *Sunderland Herald* reported the story of four
boys who were sent to the Ragged School for stealing mats from passages.
The father of one of the boys accused the local priest, the Rev. John
Bamber, of entering the school room and ordering the boys out of the
institution.[170] The situation had reached such a crisis point by the mid-
1850s that the *Durham Advertiser* was calling for the complete
reorganisation of the Ragged Schools in order to take into account the
differences of faith:

"Ragged and Industrial Schools, in fact, must be so harmonised as that
ALL SECTS may regard them favourably—or the result will be that

---

[167] Ibid, pp. 3-4.
[168] *Newcastle Journal*, 13 February 1852.
[169] Quoted in *Tablet*, 10 February 1855, p. 86.
[170] *Sunderland Herald*, 17 February 1854.

Sectarian jealousies and prejudices will make them not only very few in number, but very ineffective in working".[171]

One of the solutions to this problem for the Catholics was to provide more denominational schools for the faithful. There was clearly a need for such institutions given that many had little choice but to attend the "Protestant" schools. The *Tablet* commented on the problems this caused for the Catholic children in Felling:

> "The need of a school in the locality of Felling is most urgent and appalling. At present the Catholic children are obliged to attend a Protestant school, where they are subject to the most pernicious and insidious attacks on their faith. On a recent visit of the Anglican Minister to the school, for the inspection of the children, the boys were interrogated in the following manner: 'Who bows down to idols and images?' Answer: —'Roman Catholics!' 'Who worships the Virgin?' Answer:—'Roman Catholics!'"[172]

Even the patronage of local schools by the Catholic gentry was not enough to prevent sectarian squabbles over religious teaching. A controversy arose in 1849 at the Sunderland Bridge School when it was revealed that Catholic parents were withdrawing their children from a school that was patronised by the Salvins, a long-standing and well respected Catholic family. In a letter from Mrs Winifred Salvin to an Anglican master at the school, the Rev. Henry Chayton, she complained that the Catholic children were "not being allowed to read their own Bible".[173] In his defence, Chayton stated that the school had not changed its policy since an agreement with the late John Salvin eighteen years before. The terms of the agreement were "that the Catholic children were to continue to read our authorised version of the Bible and that we, in consideration of that concession on his part, were not to attempt to force the Prayer Book or Catechism of the Church upon them".[174] Mrs Salvin could not believe that her father would consent to this given that he "would have acted contrary to his religion by doing so". She warned that her husband would "withdraw the use of the School House" if an agreement could not be reached between the two parties.[175] The controversy continued into the following year when it was announced by

---

[171] *Durham Advertiser*, 1 February 1856.
[172] *Tablet*, 21 September 1850.
[173] DCRO, Letter from Salvin to Chayton, 18 December 1849, D/SA/C220/1.
[174] Letter from Chayton to Salvin, 18 December 1849, DCRO D/SA/C220/2.
[175] Letter from Salvin to Chayton, 20 December 1849, DCRO D/SA/C220/3.

the Dean and Chapter of Durham that an Anglican school room was to be built on the site of the Sunderland Bridge School—if the Salvins sold it—or, if not, nearby the existing educational room. In a letter to Salvin, Chayton tried to explain the reasons behind this decision:

> "I am truly sorry to perceive from your note received this evening, that you still appear to think we are influenced by a sectarian feeling, and (to use your own words) a desire to proselytise, in wishing to have a School Room in the village . . . but the Dean and Chapter think it is not only desirable, but necessary, that there should be a School Room here, as in every other district Parish, in connection with the Church . . ."[176]

Salvin replied angrily to this explanation:

> "I should certainly regret any deterioration to the elegant appearance of the Church, but equally shall I deplore the fundamental cause, namely that sectarian persecution directed against the Catholic children of the Parish to deprive them of the benefit of education (if) they attend a school the object of which is to proselytise these children".[177]

The heightened religious tension of the 1850s did little to dampen this controversy. Although an Anglican school room had not been built, the situation had caused the Chayton's attitude to harden, particularly as his control over the school room increased. Because Chayton continued to pay his annual subscription for the use of the school room, the Salvins could not legally remove him. A letter from G. Giles to Salvin in 1855 complained of the treatment of Catholic children in the school:

> "You have probably heard that Mr. Chaytor has for some time taken the school at Sunderland Bridge into his own hands, for instance he prohibits Catholic Books being read there, or the Catholic Catechism taught, substitutes the Protestant Bible and moreover has Protestant Clergymen to give sermons against the Catholics in the School Room".[178]

Unfortunately the records do not inform us of the outcome of this issue, but it is likely that the Catholic children experienced discrimination for some time afterwards.

Once a Catholic school was established, and Catholic children were receiving religious education in their faith, the watchful eyes of anti-

---

[176] Letter from Chayton to Salvin, 16 July 1850, DCRO D/SA/C220/17.

[177] Letter from Salvin to Chayton, 20 December 1849, DCRO D/SA/C220/18.

[178] Letter from G. Giles to Salvin, 23 February 1855 DCRO D/SA/C220/20.

Catholics were never far away. The standard of education at these schools was often questioned by the local press, particularly when it was evident in the wider society. *The Sunderland Herald* criticised the Catholic school of St Patrick's in Hartlepool, when it was revealed that two Catholic boys, William Kilbride and John Ranson, could not sign their names to a deposition, after they were called as witnesses to the inquest of the death of a two year-old child. It was alleged that one of the boys could not read either.[179] More serious were the reports of mistreatment of children in these schools. They were often sensationalised by a Protestant media that rarely commented on cases of this nature in Protestant schools and were keen to highlight the sinister and immoral character of Catholic educational institutions. In June 1849, the *Newcastle Journal* reported the story of a child who had suffered at the hands of his Catholic schoolmaster in Sunderland:

> "A judicial investigation took place a few days ago before the magistrates of Sunderland into a charge involving the barbarous treatment of a child about 6 years of age, by the leader of a Popish school in that town. John Dawson was the name of the Popish disciplinarian. The poor child's shoulders and back were in a frightful state from the blow which had been inflicted on them and their appearance caused a shudder throughout the court".[180]

The schoolmaster's fate was sealed when it was revealed that the child involved was the son of Protestant parents. According to the *Journal*, "had that not been so the iniquitousness conduct of the teacher, in all probability, would never have come to light"[181], implying that the Catholic authorities would have successfully covered the matter up if a Catholic child had been involved.

One area of anti-Catholicism which has previously received little attention by historians is the treatment of Catholic children in the workhouse.[182] The problem was particularly acute in many of the

---

[179] *Sunderland Herald*, 7 May 1852.

[180] *Newcastle Journal*, 23 June 1849.

[181] Ibid.

[182] Studies of workhouse life in the nineteenth century refer to anti-Catholicism only in passing, such as M.A. Crowther, *The Workhouse System 1834-1939: The History of an English Social Institution* (London: Batsford Academic and Educational Ltd, 1981) and F. Crompton, *Workhouse Children* (Stroud: Sutton Publishing Ltd, 1997). J. M. Feheney, 'The Poor Law Board August Order, 1859': A Case Study of Protestant-Catholic Conflict', *Recusant History,* 17.1 (1984), 84-91, is the only article-based study but this concentrates on a specific event.

workhouses of the North East for a number of reasons. Firstly, the high levels of Irish children in the workhouses of the major industrial towns ensured that the thorny issue of religious teaching was always likely to be a contentious issue.[183] This was further exacerbated by the attitude of the local Catholic clergy who were willing to do everything in their power to defend the rights of the poor Catholic children against the perceived proselytising tactics of a "Protestant" workhouse. Finally, the religious composition of those in control of the workhouse, the Guardians of the Poor, was overwhelmingly Protestant. In his study of the Sunderland Poor Law Union, Wood has noted that the Guardians were primarily Nonconformists, including a few Quakers.[184] On the face of it, this may have suggested a more tolerant attitude to Catholics but in reality this was far from the case. Nonconformists were just as likely to oppose priestly visitations as Anglicans because they themselves were denied this right for their own denominations. Poor Law officials were also drawn from the ranks of the middle class tradesmen, artisans and small businessmen who had some provincial standing and who wished to join, as Manders suggested of the Gateshead Guardians, the "freemasonry of local influence".[185] The Gateshead Union, for example, contained three farmers[186] which was precisely the class containing the least number of Catholics. It would be unfair to suggest that all Poor Law officials were anti-Catholic, but there was evidently a culture of anti-Catholicism.

The most obvious way in which anti-Catholicism was brought out in the daily running of the workhouse was in the disputes surrounding the rights of Catholic children. Some Unions grudgingly accepted the necessity of affording the Catholics basic rights as part of the general spirit of religious toleration and because the Catholic religion was one of the largest denominations in the workhouse, while others were not so lenient. These rights included allowing Catholics to attend their own church on Sundays, and allowing a Catholic priest to visit them during the week. Some Poor Law officials tried everything in their power to make life difficult for the Catholic inmates, particularly as Clause 19 of the Poor

---

[183] Crowther notes that the level of sectarianism in the workhouse was in direct proportion to the number of Irish Catholic immigrants. Crowther, *The Workhouse System*, pp. 129-30.

[184] P.A. Wood, 'The activities of the Sunderland Poor Law Union, 1834-1930' (unpublished doctoral thesis, Newcastle University, 1975), p. 51.

[185] F.W.D. Manders,'The administration of the Poor Law in the Gateshead Union, 1836-1930' (unpublished master's dissertation, Newcastle University, 1980), p. 34.

[186] Manders 'Gateshead Union', p. 9. Manders also notes that the middle-class tradesmen composition remained virtually unchanged until 1889, p. 33.

Law Amendment Act of 1834, which guarded the rights of different denominations across all Unions, was largely ignored.[187] Different unions appeared to have different levels of toleration in their treatment of Catholics. In the Houghton-Le-Spring Union, R. G. Barker has noted that Catholics were able to attend churches or chapels three times on a Sunday and occasionally during the week.[188] In the Sunderland Union, however, it was not until 1868 that Catholic children were even allowed to attend the Catholic chapel.[189] Thus, applications from priests before this date were flatly refused, such as the rejection of Canon Bamber's application by the Guardians in December 1862 on the basis that it would set a precedent for other religious denominations.[190] Moreover, if the government wished to introduce laws which increased the rights of Catholics then it needed the co-operation of the Guardians to implement them at the local level. If this did not occur, then implementation proved almost impossible.[191]

Religious classification of inmates in the workhouse was a constant bone of contention between local priests and Guardians. Ascertaining the denomination of a pauper child was not always easy and disputes regularly arose between the officials and the priests over their religious identity. Thus, Catholic children were only afforded their rights if they could prove they were Catholic, usually if their parents or godparents were of the same denomination. When this was not possible the child was to be educated as an Anglican.[192] In April 1852, controversy arose over this issue in the Gateshead Union when an application from Father Betham to allow certain children, who did not have any surviving relatives, to attend the Catholic chapel on Sundays. The Gateshead Guardian, Mr. Fawcett, could not agree to the motion, however, because "the law does not sanction it, and that it would be expedient to admit such a precedent as that application involves". He even accused Betham's application as "savouring of the spirit of 'papal aggression'". [193] The following week, a letter from another priest, Rev. Joseph Cullen, complained that in the period since Betham's application, some of the Catholic children had been subject to proselytism by the Protestant ministers.[194] He cited an example of two young Irish

---

[187] A point made by Holland, *The British Catholic Press*, p. 132.

[188] R.G. Barker, 'Houghton-le-Spring Poor Law Union, 1837-1930' (unpublished master's dissertation, Newcastle University, 1974), p. 117.

[189] Wood, 'Sunderland Poor Law Union', p. 179.

[190] *Sunderland Herald*, 26 December 1862.

[191] Feheney, 'August Order', p. 90.

[192] Feheney, 'August Order', p. 84; Crompton, *Workhouse Children*, p. 112.

[193] *Gateshead Observer*, 10 April 1852.

[194] Joseph Cullen, b. 1813, o. 1841, d. 1869. *English and Welsh Priests*, p. 39.

Catholic girls, whose father had left them in the Gateshead Workhouse because he could not afford to keep them but who wished them to be brought up as Catholics. These girls had been Catholics but the elder of the two now declared herself to be Protestant. The younger girl was obliged to follow the religion of her sister.[195] In the Newcastle Union, disputes between the priest and the workhouse authorities over the religious classification of children were just as animated. The Notice Book of St Andrew's Catholic Church was filled with entries requesting those persons who knew the "names of any Catholic children in the workhouse" to notify the priest.[196]

Children who were designated Catholics were usually interrogated thoroughly by the workhouse authorities. In February 1857, an application by the Dominican Father Suffield for the Catholic inmates of the Gateshead Union to attend his church was accepted on condition that the children were interviewed by the Visiting Committee to ascertain their denomination.[197] However, when it was revealed in the interview that four of the fourteen children were not even Catholics his application was rejected.[198] A similar case occurred in the Newcastle Union in the same month. Canon Eyre asked the Guardians for permission to allow John McLaren, James McLaren, Isabella Glennan, Ellen Traior and Margaret Aviey to attend the Catholic chapel on Sundays.[199] The Guardians, however, declined the request:

> "The Committee having interrogated the children named find that their decided wish is to continue to go to the place of worship to which they have been accustomed whilst inmates of the Workhouse and cannot therefore recommend that they should be sent to the Roman Catholic Church against their desire".[200]

Religious services in the workhouse were carried out primarily by an Anglican minister, whose concentration on the Word of God was unlikely to be accepted by the Catholic community. Many Catholics were openly derided for practising their religion. A letter was read to the Gateshead

---

[195] *Gateshead Observer*, 17 April 1852.
[196] See, for example, TWAS, 'Church Notice Book of St Andrews, Newcastle', 19 November 1854.
[197] TWAS, 'Board of Guardians Minutes, Gateshead Union', 3 February 1857. Robert (Rudolph) Suffield, b. 1821 (Cheshire), o.1850, d. 1891. *English and Welsh Priests*, p. 185.
[198] 'Board of Guardians Minutes, Gateshead Union', 17 February 1857.
[199] 'Board of Guardians Minutes, Newcastle Union', 13 February 1857.
[200] 'Board of Guardians Minutes, Newcastle Union', 8 March 1857.

Guardians in April 1866 by Peter Flanagan of the town, complaining of the schoolmaster, George Tennant, "taunting" Catholic boys about their religion.[201] Lord Ravensworth petitioned the House of Lords in 1861, alleging that the Roman Catholics of the Sunderland Workhouse were being discriminated against.[202] In the Gateshead and Darlington Unions, it was alleged that Catholics were denied materials to help them practise their faith, such as Catechisms and Catholic Prayer Books.[203] Accusations of Protestant proselytism were rife. In 1868, a letter from a priest in "a workhouse in the Diocese" argued that "every child who has entered the Workhouse has lost its faith or had it diminished to such an extent, that you can scarce call it a Catholic".[204] This may have been an exaggeration, but there is no doubt that, in an atmosphere where threats were made by the Protestant Alliance to prohibit Catholic services in the workhouse[205], it was essential for the Catholic priest to make regular visits to his flock in order to maintain a vital connection between the Catholic pauper and his religion. Priests were given permission to visit Catholics in the workhouse, but only under strict supervision and within a specified timeframe.

Any attempt by the Catholic clergy to call for a relaxation of the conditions imposed upon them was usually met with a stern rebuke. Thus, in the Newcastle Union in February 1861, Canon Eyre's proposals to increase his curate's visitations in the workhouse to three times a week for those inmates over 16 years of age, and twice a week for those under 16, was rejected immediately by the Poor Law officials.[206] Indeed, even parliamentary efforts to improve the general condition of the priests in the workhouse were not completely welcomed in the local unions. In the South Shields Union, a letter was read out calling on the Poor Law officials to oppose a House of Commons report requesting "certain concessions to Roman Catholic Priests in relation to Workhouse and District Schools".[207]

Nor were priests always treated with courtesy during their visits to the workhouse. Sometimes this could be due to the aggressive stance of the

---

[201] *Newcastle Guardian*, 6 April 1866.

[202] Wood, 'Sunderland Poor Law Union', p. 179.

[203] 'Board of Guardians Minutes, Gateshead Union', 13 February 1857. *Darlington and Stockton Times*, 26 December 1867.

[204] RCHDA, *Catholic Poor Law Schools Circular*, December 1868, RCD, 1/17.

[205] Serious consideration was given to the proposals of the Alliance among the Sunderland Guardians in 1864. See *Newcastle Guardian*, 21 May 1864.

[206] The Board included the Mayor of Newcastle. 'Board of Guardians Minutes, Newcastle Union', 1 February 1861.

[207] *Shields Daily News*, 20 January 1865.

priest himself. Three weeks after Canon Eyre's proposals to increase visitation periods were rejected, two Protestant inmates, John Buchanan and Anthony Hall, complained that the visiting priest, Father Dwyer, had been using "very offensive and very objectionable language, which was calculated to . . . annoy them". The Board's answer was to threaten to impose a ban on the priest.[208] On occasion, it was the Protestant authorities themselves who were to blame. During the controversy surrounding Father Betham and the Gateshead Union in 1852, the priest complained to the Chairman of the Poor Law Board that he had been subject to frosty treatment from the staff at the workhouse, as he "was ushered into the porter's lodge and left, like a person infected with the plague, until the master was sent for to inspect me".[209] The Gateshead Guardians saw little of any substance in this accusation. The Clerk to the Guardians, in writing to the Poor Law Board, argued that they (Guardians) "are aware Mr. Betham has been treated with much courtesy and every facility has been afforded him which the Guardians considered in accordance with the law, or orders of the Commissioners".[210]

In the Hartlepool Union, insults were traded on a regular basis between the Anglican chaplain, the uncompromisingly anti-Catholic, Rev. Lewis Paige, and the French Catholic priest, Father Harival.[211] Harival wrote a letter to the *Hartlepool Free Press*, complaining of Paige's attitude towards him. On visiting the Catholic inmates Harival met Paige who refused to take his hat off. Paige ignored the French priest directly, instead choosing to address the master of the workhouse and, in full-view of Harival, indignantly condemned the priest:

"This man has no right to come here, unless he is especially sent for, and he has no right to see any one but the person who sends for him; I am the chaplain of this house and it is the law of the land".[212]

In his reply, Paige was in no mood to offer any apology, questioning why he should be expected to remove his hat in the presence of the priest:

"What! Submission by a gentleman and a clergyman of England's Church, to a priest of the Church of Rome: a church which contains doctrines more

[208] 'Board of Guardians Minutes, Newcastle Union', 22 February 1861.
[209] *Gateshead Observer*, 10 April 1852.
[210] 'Gateshead Board of Guardians Letter Book', 4 March 1852, pp. 297-8.
[211] Peter Eugene Harivel, b. 1817 (France), o. 1856, d. 1894. *English and Welsh Priests*, p. 41.
[212] *Hartlepool Free Press*, 30 November 1861.

false, more impure, more dangerous, more devilish, than are contained in the Shasters of Hindooism, or in the books of Confucious, or the Koran of Mahomet!"[213]

Given this atmosphere, an attempt to introduce legislation for a permanent Catholic chaplain in all workhouses was never likely to be welcomed by the more zealous anti-Catholic Guardians. Since the mid-1850s, this campaign had been gathering parliamentary momentum in relation to a broader bill concerning Catholic chaplains in prisons and the armed forces. The increase of Catholics in these institutions resulted in the bill being seen as one of urgent necessity rather than religious toleration. Opposition came from the Protestant Alliance, whose rapidly declining influence in the late 1850s led it to concentrate on narrower and more extreme forms of anti-Catholicism. In the Newcastle Union, the question of appointing a chaplain had been an important one since the late 1850s, not least because the workhouse had no permanent minister of any denomination to impart religious instruction. Religious services were generally carried out by the visiting town missionaries whose broad-based scriptural programme was seen as "a fair and ecumenical one, attending to all parties equal rights". Eventually in October 1857, after a series of discussions and public meetings and in spite of much opposition, the Board appointed the Anglican minister, the Rev. R. Shepherd, as chaplain on a salary of £150 per annum.[214] Unsurprisingly, given their reluctance to appoint a chaplain in general, the campaign for a Catholic chaplain was vehemently opposed in the Union. An initial Order from the National Poor Law Board in December 1859 was rejected by the Newcastle Union on the basis that the law would "open the door to religious proselytism and strife".[215] As the parliamentary campaign reached its climax in the early 1860s, the Newcastle Board again reiterated its determination to oppose the issue by sending a petition to Parliament:

"That your petitioners have learnt that the Romish priesthood are seeking for such an alteration of the law as shall sanction the admission of Roman Catholic chaplains and school masters into workhouses. That if such a privilege were granted to Roman Catholics, other religious denominations dissenting from the Church of England could not justly be denied the like privilege".[216]

---

[213] Ibid.
[214] 'Board of Guardians Minutes, Newcastle Union', 26 June, 2 and 16 October 1857.
[215] *Newcastle Guardian*, 24 December 1859.
[216] *Newcastle Daily Journal*, 4 May 1861.

Other Unions were also active in opposing the appointment of Roman Catholic chaplains. The Gateshead Union did so for as much financial as well as a religious reasons, arguing that the bill would "impose additional expense on the ratepayers, and promote religious strife among the inmates of the Workhouse".[217] The Sunderland Union responded directly to the petition of the Protestant Alliance, requesting a copy of the memorial in May 1861 and sending a further petition in response to another Alliance campaign three years later. Of the latter petition, Morgan Wake played a prominent part, expressing his "determination of going through with his opposition to it here at all hazards".[218]

In Sunderland the willingness of the Sisters of Mercy to minister to the Catholic inmates in the local workhouse ensured that they were at constant loggerheads with the local Board of Guardians and, in particular, the Poor Law official, Morgan Wake, who launched a personal campaign to keep them out.[219] The Sisters were initially granted access into the workhouse in 1853; all the more remarkable given the anti-convent mania that was sweeping the country at that time. A motion put forward by Mr. Wake to the effect "that no female clothed in the garb of a certain Romish order commonly known as 'the Sisters of Mercy' shall be allowed to visit the Union Workhouse whatsoever" was rejected by the Guardians and this effectively allowed them access, although only, at this stage, as visitors and not religious teachers. [220] However, five years later, a controversy involving the Sisters that reached the national sectarian press dramatically altered this. Accusations of "souperism" were levelled by the *Bulwark* when it was discovered that Protestant inmates of the workhouse hospital had been receiving presents in order to persuade them to convert to Catholicism. A vivid account of this is described by an inmate, Mary Thompson:

---

[217] 'Board of Guardians Minutes, Gateshead Union', 26 March 1861.

[218] *Sunderland Herald,* 20 May 1864.

[219] The Sisters of Mercy had a long history in the town where a convent had been established as early as 1843. V. Fetherston, 'Irish Catholicism in Sunderland in the 19th Century', *Northern Catholic History,* 43 (2002), pp. 56-7.

[220] 'Board of Guardians Minutes, Sunderland Union', 28 October 1857. Wake was forced to moderate the language of his motion the following week following protests. The revised motion read "That the Sisters of Mercy be refused admission to the Workhouse", 'Board of Guardians Minutes, Sunderland Union', 4 November 1853. A report in the *Sunderland News* reveals that only 2 people supported Wake's motion, one of which was himself. *Sunderland News,* 19 November 1853.

"I frequently saw the Sisters of Mercy; they often brought me spice loaf and candy to become a Catholic. They also brought me some cotton and told me to knit myself some stockings. They gave me a pair of stays, which I am now wearing. They gave me a catechism which I lost, and a hymn book which the children tore up. I got sweetmeats almost every week, and they gave me some glazed calico to make pockets with; they also gave me a night-cap . . . They asked me to become a Catholic, and I did not refuse as they had been so kind to me".[221]

At a Board of Guardians meeting it was decided to ban the Sisters for having "systematically endeavoured to proselytise the inmates professing the Protestant faith to that of Roman Catholicism".[222]

Attempts were made with the help of the Catholic authorities to repeal this ban but to no avail. In January 1863, the Sunderland priest, Canon Bamber, made an application requesting a number of concessions for the Catholics, including the re-admittance of the Sisters of Mercy. Mr. Wake was determined that the "Sisters of Misery" were to be kept out of the workhouse at all costs. For one thing, he argued, they masked their real identities by naming themselves "Saint" and no one could gain admittance to their place of residence other than "priests and people of their persuasion". Thus they did not "come into the house on the same footing as other visitors".[223] For Wake, however, the greatest objection was "their attempts to make the Protestant children Roman Catholics, which they had been proved by evidence to have done when they were allowed admission into the house". On this basis he argued that the application should be refused and the other Guardians agreed.[224] This decision was not universally popular, particularly among the Catholics. A letter from a father of one nun was printed in the *Newcastle Daily Journal*, criticising the Guardians for the "brutal manner in which those ladies were assailed" at the recent meeting. The letter-writer defended the nuns on the basis of their devotion to their cause, something the Guardians, he suggested, could never understand:

"Of course, men of the temper and views of those Guardians who indulged in scoffs and sneers at ladies, who have given up every tie on earth to mitigate human suffering, to devote themselves to works of charity . . .

---

[221] *Bulwark*, October 1858.
[222] Ibid.
[223] *Sunderland Herald*, 23 January 1863.
[224] Ibid.

men like Mr. Wake, of course, cannot conceive the purity of motive which attains such 'heroic charity'".[225]

The Catholic clergy similarly had few kind words for the Sunderland Guardians. At a Soirée in St Patrick's Church in the town, Father Brown described his "bitterness of spirit at the bigotry and intolerance he had recently seen manifested in Sunderland, by some who occupied the position of 'guardians of the poor'".[226] Describing the proselytising accusations of the Sisters as "absurd", he suggested that there was only one remedy for the likes of Wake:

> "Such men as Mr. Morgan Wake should have been sent to France, Spain, and even to the hospitals of the Crimea, to see what was thought of the Sisters of Mercy. While the Turk and the Sepoy respected and spared them, Mr. Wake sneered at and insulted them".[227]

Finally in 1868, ten years after they were initially banned from the workhouse, the Sunderland Guardians repealed the order against the Sisters, albeit with more stringent conditions than was evident in other workhouses where nuns were active. Canon Bamber's application that they should be allowed into the workhouse as visitors and on the understanding that their "ministrations should be confined to Roman Catholics, and that there should be no such irregularities as those which led to the prohibition of such visits in 1858" was agreed to by the Guardians.[228] Many of the Guardians were willing to allow the Sisters back on the basis that it would place them on an equal footing with other Protestant ladies. Unsurprisingly, it was Morgan Wake who most vehemently opposed the motion, indulging in a lengthy tirade against "the body-enslaving and soul-destroying system of the Church of Rome".[229] He argued that the Sisters "could not do other than proselytise", given that they were "entirely under the jurisdiction of the priests of Rome". In spite of his best efforts, however, the original motion was passed by a large majority.[230]

Given this atmosphere of overt anti-Catholicism, the Catholic community tried various ways to influence proceedings in the regional

---

[225] *Newcastle Daily Journal*, 23 January 1863.
[226] Joseph Brown, b. 1794 (Durham), o. 1820, d. 1877. *English and Welsh Priests*, p. 38.
[227] *Newcastle Guardian*, 14 February 1863.
[228] *Newcastle Weekly Chronicle*, 25 July 1868.
[229] Ibid.
[230] Ibid.

workhouses. One option was to try to place Catholics in positions of influence as Poor Law officials. The *Tablet* saw this as a matter of urgency in 1854, calling on the Catholics of Newcastle to "take measures to return at least one or two guardians to the board who may be present to defend the rights and privileges of the Catholic ratepayers".[231] By the 1860s, the situation had not changed a great deal, although the *Tablet* reported with some satisfaction in 1865 that two respectable Catholics, Councillor Turnbull and David Donkin, were on the Tynemouth and Newcastle Boards respectively.[232] Another option was for individuals to foster workhouse Catholics and thus remove them from that environment. The Gateshead priest, Father Betham, successfully managed to remove the Catholic pauper, Margaret Whitton, from the workhouse in the town so that she could be raised as a domestic servant. Betham admitted to the Guardians that his real purpose was to "preserve the girl from the Protestant faith", but the Board still accepted Betham's application. Other individuals were not quite as successful. In the Newcastle Union, a similar application, with similar reasoning, was submitted by Mr. and Mrs Young, for a Catholic orphan child to be placed under their care. The application was rejected, an outcome which the *Tablet* believed was yet another "remarkable instance of the fanatical bigotry of the Protestant administrators of the poor law".[233] In any case, this method was never likely to be a large-scale rescue plan for all the Catholics in the Workhouse.

It was with this in mind that plans were drawn up by the Catholic community to introduce a system whereby Catholic children could be removed from the workhouse and receive their education in an alternative Catholic educational establishment. An idea of this nature had been envisaged on a national scale when a bill was introduced into Parliament for this purpose in 1862. The bill was passed but it effectively placed the decision to remove the Catholic children on the heads of Guardian officials, and many of these officials were unwilling to remove them anyway.[234] Indeed, when the Darlington priest, the Rev. Henry Coll, submitted an application on the basis of this law in 1867, it was rejected by the Darlington Guardians. The following motion was submitted by the Guardian, J. H. Bowan:

---

[231] *Tablet*, 13 May 1854.

[232] *Tablet*, 29 April 1865.

[233] *Tablet*, 13 May 1854.

[234] Crowther, *The Workhouse System*, p. 70. The Sunderland Poor Law officials memorialised against this proposal on the basis that it would remove Roman Catholic children "from the care of the Guardians", see *Sunderland Herald*, 9 May 1862.

"That inasmuch as the guardians of the poor are *in loco parentis*, it is their imperative duty to have the workhouse children taught the Word of God as the basis of all religious instruction, and no claim, priestly or otherwise, can be allowed to interfere with an obligation so clearly paramount".[235]

The same problem was encountered by the recently consecrated Bishop of Hexham, James Chadwick, when he attempted an ambitious plan to open a Catholic Poor Law School in 1871. The plan was first initiated in April 1868, when a meeting was organised for this purpose. Chadwick, who spoke at this meeting, argued that the Catholic children were "at imminent risk of losing their faith" in the Protestant workhouses of the region. The plan was to raise enough money to purchase a plot of land to build the school and it was hoped that Catholics of all classes would contribute to this "noble and pressing charity".[236] By December, the project had raised £400.[237] It was finally completed in November 1871, when the building was formerly opened in Tudhoe. However, the plan was effectively ruined when "none of the Board of Guardians seem(ed) willing to give up Roman Catholic children under their charge".[238]

The response of the Protestant community to the Catholic "invasion" in the North East of England was arguably little different from elsewhere in the country. It was not generally one of outright hostility but neither was the Catholic revival welcomed with open arms. With the exception of the institutionalised anti-Catholicism of the Board of Guardians, who appeared reluctant to allow even the slightest concession of religious instruction to Catholics in their care, Catholics were allowed to worship as they pleased so long as this in no way interfered with their Protestant neighbours. When this did happen, however, the façade of Protestant toleration became all too apparent. The influx of poor and largely non-practising Irish Catholic immigrants had also posed substantial problems for the Catholic authorities, particularly when faced with the increasingly militant anti-Catholic missionary, who was more than aware of the possibilities of conversion in the battle for the souls of their adversaries.

[235] *DC*, 18 May 1867. Coll's original motion was voted for by only six Guardian members. 26 voted for Brown's amendment.
[236] RCHNDA, 'Meeting of the Catholic Fraternity to Erect a Catholic Poor Law School', April 1868, RCD 1/17.
[237] RCHNDA, *Catholic Poor Law Schools Circular*, 23 December 1868, RCD 1/17.
[238] RCHNDA, *Catholic Poor Law Schools Circular*, 16 November 1871, RCD 1/17. There are no further references to the school following this date which suggests that it ceased to operate.

The lack of success of the missionaries, however, reveals the ultimately impossible nature of their task. Moreover, the inability of the Catholic Church to cope with the Irish influx was to the detriment of many Irish Catholic children in the region, whose want of religious instruction could not be met by either the overworked priest or the local Union, and often anti-Catholic, official. Given this atmosphere, it is not surprising that many Irish Catholics chose to respond with physical violence to the increased anti-Catholic threat. The next chapter will therefore examine the nature of Irish immigration and Protestant-Catholic religious violence in the North East. It will highlight the way in which violence was generally initiated by the Irish themselves as a reaction to the attacks on their faith by the Protestant community, but that this reaction was dependent on time and place.

CHAPTER SIX

IRISH IMMIGRATION
AND SECTARIAN VIOLENCE

The expression of religious feeling through religious violence had been a common trait of Catholics and Protestants for centuries. Events such as the Civil War and the Gordon Riots had engendered an inflammatory response to religious issues that had certainly not declined in the comparatively ordered society of Victorian Britain. Indeed, Irish immigration from the 1840s had arguably regenerated this form of popular expression as a means by which religious animosity could be commonly demonstrated. While disturbances were often due to a variety of economic, political and cultural reasons, the negative perception of the religious practices of the "Other" would undoubtedly have played its part. Irish immigrants became resident in many English towns and cities but the response they received from the host community was not always hostile.

Indeed, outbreaks of ethnic and religious violence were dependent on a number of factors, including not only the extent and character of immigration, but also local cultural conditions. Religious rioting was almost institutionalised in Liverpool, where both Irish Protestant and Catholic immigration were high, and political factions developed along sectarian lines. However, other towns and cities responded in different ways. From those studies carried out, it is apparent that disorder and conflict were more evident in Bradford, Leeds, Manchester and Wolverhampton, than in Hull and Bristol.[1] Even in towns with large-scale immigration, violence was ostensibly rare, and only frequent at times of heightened tension. Phillips has noted that even in the heartlands of Lancashire, violence was sporadic. Bolton did not experience any major riots involving the Irish until 1868. Perhaps the most bloody anti-Irish/anti-Catholic riot of the Victorian era, the Stockport riot of 1852, was

---

[1] G. Davis, 'Little Irelands', *The Irish in Britain, 1815-1939*, ed. by Roger Swift and Sheridan Gilley (London: Pinter, 1989), pp. 116-9.

the only outbreak of working class violence in the town before 1870.[2] Durey has suggested that the bulk of the English working class were "apathetic and dogmatic in their own religious beliefs" and "failed to use religious differences as an excuse for attacking the Irish" outside of periods of extreme tension.[3] Indeed, much of the violence, as Swift has noted generally, was "between and among rather than against Irish people".[4]

It is the intention of this chapter to demonstrate that violence associated with Protestant-Catholic tensions in the North East of England was not dissimilar to the same phenomenon in other areas of the country. It will highlight how this violence was attributable to a variety of causes that were just as likely to be initiated by the local Irish Catholics in response to anti-Catholicism, rather than simply an expression of the anti-Irish prejudice of the English working class in which the Irish Catholics were merely passive victims. Moreover, religious violence was not purely a product of English-Irish tensions. English-Irish violence often combined with intra-Irish party factions, into which, as D.M. MacRaild has shown, the "Famine-sharpened political culture"[5] of Irish sectarianism was effectively transplanted to an English setting. All these disturbances however, whether English-Irish or intra-Irish, were dictated by the place, time, and context of the battleground on which they were fought.

Early English-Irish Disturbances

The origins of English-Irish tensions during the mid-nineteenth century undoubtedly lay in the Irish Famine and subsequent mass emigration of the late 1840s. In these early years, religion did not appear to be a divisive factor in ethnic relations. The immediate concerns were naturally socio-economic. In September 1847, the *Sunderland Herald* complained of recently arrived immigrants "becoming troublesome to the parochial authorities" in the town. Similar sentiments were expressed by the *Newcastle Journal,* which was concerned that the presence of "a number of lawless strangers" may cause "much alarm to the inhabitants of

---

[2] P. T. Phillips, *The Sectarian Spirit: Sectarianism, Society and Politics in Victorian Cotton Towns* (Toronto: University of Toronto Press, 1982), pp. 26, 90.
[3] Michael Durey, 'The Survival of an Irish Culture in Britain 1800-1845', *Historical Studies,* 20 (1982), p. 24.
[4] Roger Swift, 'Anti-Irish Violence in Victorian England: Some Perspectives', *Criminal Justice History,* 15 (1994), p. 129.
[5] MacRaild, *Faith, Fraternity and Fighting,* p. 182.

Sunderland".[6] The arrival of the Irish in Newcastle also angered the Conservative newspaper. In spite of many commentators suggesting that Irish immigrants were not a burden on poor relief, the contemporary view of the *Journal,* that the newly arrived immigrants had effectively doubled the expenditure[7], was likely to be believed by a population that would have had little idea of the true reality of the situation. The negative perception of an "infestation" was reflected in other places. The *Durham Advertiser* believed Darlington had "swarmed" with Irish reapers in the summer of 1848. The paper feared that a "great portion of them must of necessity either remain unemployed, or entirely supersede our own labouring poor". These economic issues are reflected in the nature of Anglo-Irish violence in the North East during the late 1840s. Certainly, there was a genuine belief among English workers that their Irish compatriots would work for less and, as a result, depress wages. This cannot be underestimated in the forging of ethnic hostility. Frank Neal has shown that "rows" between English and Irish navvies were commonplace occurrences during the construction of the Newcastle-Berwick line and at the Consett Iron Works near Shotley Bridge.[8]

The economic issues of poor relief and competition for jobs were still very much prevalent but it was the heightened religious tension of the early 1850s that ultimately drove a wedge between the two communities. Historians have noted that the Irish problem had been further exacerbated by the Papal Aggression and the "anti-popery mania" surrounding it which, although not directly aimed at the Irish themselves, would have done little to improve English perceptions of the Irish and vice versa.[9] Riots between English and Irish broke out sporadically throughout the country as a result. Some of these were directly related to the Papal Aggression and the religious nature of the conflict was notably evident in Liverpool, Birkenhead and Cheltenham.[10] After a serious riot in Stockport in June 1852[11], violence receded gradually, although there were still

---

[6] *Sunderland Herald*, 8 September 1847; *Newcastle Journal*, 27 March 1847.
[7] *Newcastle Journal*, 1 May 1847.
[8] Neal, *English-Irish Conflict*, p. 22.
[9] Neville Kirk has noted the increase in ethnic violence in the late 1840s and early 1850s as a result of famine immigration and Papal Aggression in Lancashire. N. Kirk, 'Ethnicity, Class and Popular Toryism, 1850-1870', *Hosts, Immigrants and Minorities: Historical Responses to Newcomers in British Society, 1870-1914*, ed. by K. Lunn (Folkestone: Dawson, 1980), p. 66.
[10] Paz, *Popular Anti-Catholicism*, pp. 248-252, 254.
[11] For an account of this riot, see Millward, 'Stockport Riots, pp. 207-24.

disturbances at Oldham, Preston, Blackburn and Wigan[12] and serious violence in Ashton, where a crowd of three hundred English operatives attacked the Irish quarter of the town.[13]

In the North East, the atmosphere was no less charged. In many towns in the region, where the Irish presence was large enough to be noticeable, Anglo-Irish relations were at breaking point. The latent anti-Catholicism of the period led to a renewed defence of their faith at the very hint of attack by the Irish Catholics. On New Year's Eve, 1850, a crowd of three hundred Irish navvies stood guard in front of the Catholic chapel of St Cuthbert's in Durham, having heard a rumour that their chapel was to be burnt to the ground by Protestants.[14] In South Shields in June 1852, religious tensions between Protestants and Catholics came to a head when fighting broke out in the streets near the Ragged School in the town in which a Bethel service was being held for seamen by local Protestant evangelicals. It was common practice to hang a Bethel flag outside the place of worship, but this flag was becoming increasingly "obnoxious to the Roman Catholics", who started hooting and yelling at the congregation as they entered the building. Stones were thrown into the room and a minor skirmish occurred although there appear to have been no serious injuries.[15]

Anti-Missionary Violence

It was in the Sandgate area of Newcastle where the sectarian tensions of the early 1850s, combined with the increasingly anti-Catholic militancy of the town missionaries, caused the most serious violence. [16] As shown in the last chapter, the Irish in Sandgate experienced unenviable social conditions. They were, however, not isolated in their chosen living quarters. They made up only 28.8% of all the inhabitants of Sandgate, effectively living side-by-side with the English.[17] In spite of Colin Pooley's assertion that the poor Irish must have had more in common living amongst the equally poverty—stricken English working class than

---

[12] Paz, *Popular Anti-Catholicism*, p. 256.

[13] N. Kirk, *The Growth of Working Class Reformism*, p. 318-9.

[14] *Durham Chronicle*, 3 January 1851.

[15] *Shields Gazette*, 18 June 1852.

[16] This riot was so well known to contemporaries that the local musician J.P. Robson wrote a popular song about it (*The Horrid War I' Sangeyt*) *Allan's Tyneside Songs* (Menston, Yorkshire: The Scholar Press, 1862), pp. 381-4.

[17] Scott, 'Comparative Re-examination', p. 263.

the middle-class Irish families living in the suburbs[18], poverty was also just as likely to be the source of friction between the two groups in an area, as the *Newcastle Courant* was quick to point out, where "the public house brawl along with other disorderly proceedings" were facts of life in this "sink of profligacy and vice".[19] However, in spite of the possibility for trouble, nothing had ever occurred on the scale of the events of 11 May 1851.

It was the appearance of a street preacher by the name of "Ranter Dick" on 11 May 1851 who helped to provide the catalyst in an already volatile mix of inter-communal tension.[20] The Ranter began preaching to a crowd of Irishmen who were certainly in no mood to listen, responding with a barrage of stones. It is difficult to say what exactly the Ranter was preaching about at this stage. Both the *Newcastle Guardian* and the *Newcastle Chronicle* report the testimony of a policeman who believed that he was preaching a teetotal lecture.[21] However, the *Newcastle Journal* argued that his lectures made "allusions to the Pope" and the *Tablet* reported he was carrying out an "ignorant tirade against the Pope and Popery".[22] No doubt the latter two papers, for contrasting reasons, wished to exaggerate the amount of sectarian tension in the locality, but it is difficult to believe that Ranter Dick would have chosen to ignore topics relating to anti-Catholicism given the tenor of the times. Whatever his choice of subject, he surely could not have predicted the effect of his preaching on the Irish crowd. They launched an attack on English property, smashing windows and breaking doors. Many men carried weapons including "huge sticks, iron rods, pokers, tongs (and) coal rakes" and were accompanied by "women and lads" carrying brick bats and missiles. One of the rioters, who was said to be the ringleader, was heard to exclaim "Och by Jasus, we'll take Sandgate tonight and be revenged on every English b____d in it!"[23] No resistance was offered initially, as the two policemen called to the scene were clearly inadequate to deal with the rioters and, after being attacked, fled the scene to obtain reinforcements. When these reinforcements eventually did arrive many of the Irish were apprehended but the English residents—who up until this time had

---

[18] C. Pooley, 'Segregation or Integration? The Residential Experience of the Irish in Mid-Victorian Britain', *The Irish in Britain, 1815-1939*, p. 81.

[19] *Newcastle Courant*, 17 May 1851.

[20] Little is known of Ranter Dick. He was referred to in the court proceedings as a "Methodist preacher".

[21] *Newcastle Guardian*, 17 May 1851; *Newcastle Chronicle*, 17 May 1851.

[22] *Newcastle Journal*, 17 May 1851; *Tablet*, 24 May 1851.

[23] *Newcastle Journal*, 17 May 1851.

remained well-hidden in consequence of the ferocity of the Irish attack—chose to exact physical revenge. After a great deal of effort, the police were eventually able to restore order and bring the rioters into custody. The next morning, forty of them were brought before the magistrates and twenty-three were charged with a variety of offences committed during the previous evening's events.[24]

Anti-Catholicism played its part in providing both the contextual and immediate cause of the riot but the behaviour of the rioters during the event itself conforms to a more ethnic rather than a purely religious motivation. The slogans shouted by the Irish were clearly of an anti-English rather than a specifically anti-Protestant nature. The above "Och by Jasus" phrase, as well as phrases such as "Blood for blood!" and "Sandgate shall flow with the blood of the English!"[25] certainly conforms to an ethnic rather than a religious contest. The choice of rioters' "targets"—English property and English windows—is further evidence of this. One Irishman, Peter Maloney exclaimed, "There's another English window, let's break it!"[26] It appears that the Irish were fairly comprehensive in their destruction of property. Two English publicans, George Dixon and Mr. Moore, each had 30 and 21 panes of glass broken respectively.[27] The English retribution saw them directly target those Irishmen who had caused destruction to their property. Indeed, even the progress of the riot seemed to develop along ethnic lines—the Irish attacking the English and vice versa. It is important to point out also that there is no evidence of any religious antipathy during the riot itself, such as cries of "No Popery" from the English or similar contrary sentiments from the Irish. Furthermore, unlike the Stockport Riots, where two Catholic chapels were ransacked,[28] there was no destruction of church property in this instance. It is clear that religious hostility in this heightened period of anti-Catholic sentiment would have played its part in moulding ethnic perceptions and prejudice—the Irish in particular had a strongly "nationalist" Catholicism—but it was certainly not the only cause of ethnic division.

The behaviour of the Irish rioters in particular also points to another dimension at play. Swift has argued that "popular disturbances involving the Irish sometimes contained an anti-police element, although on the

---

[24] Ibid.
[25] *Newcastle Chronicle*, 17 May 1851.
[26] Ibid.
[27] Ibid.
[28] Millward, 'Stockport Riots', p. 209.

surface they were attributable to other causes".[29] This is clearly evident in
this riot. The Irishman Patrick Devlin struck P.C. Thompson with a poker
while a similar fate befell P.C. Graham. The Irishman John McGuinness
also threw a brick at P.C. Short.[30] Irish violence against the police was
commonplace in Ireland and migrants attempted to transfer these values to
an English setting.[31] However, it could be possible that more localised
factors were to blame in Newcastle. In March, the Watch Committee had
dismissed P.C. Nicholson and P.C. Pike from the force for mistreatment of
an Irishman. In spite of their dismissal, the Newcastle Irish undoubtedly
retained grievances against the police for this, so much so that the two
policemen who were dismissed were not replaced for fear of revenge
attacks. [32] This grudge against the police is evident in the behaviour of the
Irishman Patrick Devlin. After chasing P.C. Thompson who had given him
the slip, Devlin was heard to exclaim— "I can't get my revenge on the
b____d . . . I would take his life if I could get him".[33] Perhaps Devlin had
wrongfully assumed this policeman was one of those involved in the
original incident in March as it is probable he, like many of the other Irish,
would not have known of the outcome of the Committee's internal
investigation.

If mistreatment of an Irishman was one of the main motivations for the
riot, did the police fare any better in dealing impartially with the Irish in
this instance? Their initial response to the riot cannot be questioned. In the
Stockport Riots of 1852, it has been suggested that the police were
deliberately slow in arriving on the scene in order to allow time for the
English—who originally started the riot—to wreak as much havoc as
possible on the Irish.[34] If this were the case then a swift response would be
expected from the Newcastle police in this instance, as the Irish were the
original perpetrators. This, however, was not apparent, and a substantial
police presence was only evident once the Irish had caused considerable
damage. This tends to suggest a lack of efficiency and manpower rather
than a deliberate prejudicial policy.

The behaviour of the police during the riot was undoubtedly more
questionable. Reports in the press point to the police heroically protecting
the Irish in the second stage of the riot but the very fact that only the Irish

---

[29] Swift, R 'Another Stafford Street Row: Law, Order and the Irish Presence in
Mid-Victorian Wolverhampton', *Irish in the Victorian City*, p. 184.
[30] *Newcastle Guardian*, 17 May 1851.
[31] Paz, *Popular Anti-Catholicism*, p. 260.
[32] TWAS, Watch Committee Report, 13 March 1851.
[33] *Newcastle Journal*, 17 May 1851.
[34] Millward, 'Stockport Riots', p. 212.

suffered "broken hands and torn faces" tends to suggest that, as Caroline L. Scott believes, the police "assisted" the English in their attack.[35] Indeed, the police treatment of the Irish became the subject of several subsequent Watch Committee meetings in which two Irishmen, John McLean and Bernard McGrath, lodged formal complaints to the Committee claiming that the police exercised unlawful authority "in the discharge of their duty". The Watch Committee dismissed both accusations. In responding to McLean, it claimed that this was decided "after hearing all parties and considering all the circumstances of the case".[36] McLean, however, was not satisfied. In July 1851 he called on the Mayor to assist him. The Mayor dutifully wrote a letter to the Committee asking for the matter to be fully re-investigated. Again, however, McLean was unsuccessful—the Committee dismissed his case again and the Mayor appeared satisfied with the decision.[37] In October, McLean again tried to reopen the case—this time issuing a summons of £10 for damages to the policeman he deemed to be responsible for his mistreatment, P.C. John Parker. The Committee requested that the "necessary steps be taken to defend him (Parker)".[38]

The response of the judicial authorities to the Irish Catholic rioters also suggests a similar bias against them. First, it is apparent that the defence lawyer for the Irish, G. W. Hodge, was completely unprepared, having been brought in as a last-minute replacement for Mr. Stoker who was unable to attend. Mr. Hodge, in the light of this substitution, asked the Mayor to adjourn the case. The Mayor's response, however, was to claim dismissively that it was better to proceed as "an adjournment would only keep up the excitement".[39] Because of this, Mr. Hodge was not able to offer an adequate defence of the Irish, speaking out only once to ask the court to take into account "the excited state of their (Irish) blood".[40] It also became clear that the magistrates were not planning to deal leniently with the Irish. Indeed, in wanting to give Patrick Devlin the highest punishment possible, they exceeded their legal jurisdiction by committing Devlin to pay £5, on default of which he would be imprisoned for two months. However, it was found that the magistrates only had the power to commit to one month's imprisonment and they were thus forced to overturn the

---

[35] Scott, 'Comparative Re-examination', p. 104.

[36] Watch Committee Report, 6 June 1851.

[37] Ibid, 4 July 1851.

[38] Ibid, 24 October 1851. The Watch Committee Reports are only available until the end of October so the outcome of this case is unknown.

[39] *Newcastle Guardian*, 17 May 1851.

[40] Ibid.

decision.[41] In the end, all the rioters who were charged were Irish, ignoring the clear involvement of the English in the second stage of the riot.[42]

John Wolffe's assertion, that violence against Protestant missionaries "did not lead to large-scale riots",[43] is therefore questionable. Moreover, this riot was not the only occurrence in which Scripture readers bore the brunt of Irish violence, particularly in the major towns where both the presence of missionaries and the increase in popularity of open-air preaching inflamed sectarian tensions. In 1860, an Irish labourer, Patrick Brennan, was charged at the Sunderland Police Court with assaulting the town missionary, John Routledge. Routledge, an elderly man, was dragged down a stairwell by two men, including Brennan, as he preached anti-Catholic sermons. Similarly, in May 1863, a popular preacher was attacked by Irishmen in Darlington. The preacher began his sermon next to a fountain at the top of Tubwell Row, handing out texts entitled 'A Little City' to the crowd which was steadily congregating. There was nothing controversial in his sermon but, as the preacher began, he was met with shouts, hisses and "other signs of disapprobation" from a group of Irish Catholics. The Catholics, it was noted, had felt aggrieved by anti-Catholic comments the lecturer had made the week before. After making their presence felt vocally, the Irishmen made a rush towards the preacher, jostling him and knocking his hat into the fountain. Nevertheless, the preacher was still allowed to continue his sermon and, at the conclusion, walked away unscathed.[44] A parallel incident occurred in Newcastle in 1864, when the Quayside preacher, David Davies, was attacked by Patrick McCabe, an Irish Catholic. Davies was a controversial preacher whose "eccentricities had made him notorious".[45] He deliberately incited other religious groups and was known for regularly disturbing Quaker meetings.[46] His favourite targets, however, were Roman Catholics. On this occasion, McCabe came up and struck Davies on the head after it was alleged the preacher had begun calling the Pope a "devil" and all the priests his "imps".[47] The following year, Davies made the local headlines again after being dragged through the streets of Newcastle by a group of

---

[41] Ibid.

[42] Neal, *English-Irish Conflict*, p. 31.

[43] Wolffe, *Protestant Crusade*, pp. 191-2.

[44] *Durham Advertiser,* 8 May 1863.

[45] *Newcastle Weekly Chronicle*, 19 February 1870.

[46] *Durham Chronicle*, 5 February 1869.

[47] *Shields Gazette*, 4 June 1864.

"roughs". According to the *Sunderland Herald*, this procession was followed and abetted by several thousand people.[48]

Missionaries could be attacked by a disgruntled adversary even when they were not on duty. Patrick Donolly, whom the *Durham Advertiser* described as a "savage-looking young Irishman", was charged with assaulting the missionary John Shiells in Durham.[49] Unlike his compatriot in Darlington, Shiells was engaged in missionary work to the Roman Catholics of the city, which suggests that he may have been an employee of the anti-Catholic organisation, the British Reformation Society. Shiells had gained notoriety in the immediate neighbourhood following a series of anti-Catholic lectures at the end of 1862.[50] On 30 May of the following year, Shiells claimed he was tripped up by Donolly and another man whilst walking near St. Nicholas's Church. He then shouted at Shiells, "You are the ____ that lectured at Framwellgate Moor last winter; I will not be satisfied until I draw the blood of every ____ Protestant in this country". Shiells threat to call for the assistance of the police was met with "tremendous" blows on his face and other parts of his body, his hat was crushed and his clothes torn. The attack was only ended when a witness called for the police and Donolly fled the scene. In the trial which followed, Shiells claimed that the surgeon, Mr. Shaw, had told him that his nose was broken. He was finding it difficult to breathe and was in constant pain. After consultation with the bench, the Recorder stated that the incident was "a most unprovoked assault on an individual who had never done him any harm or gave him any provocation". Donolly and other Roman Catholics, the Recorder argued, "had the fullest liberty of conscience allowed them" but the defendant had abused this right. Because of the serious nature of the assault and in order to set a precedent for others, Donolly was sentenced to imprisonment in the house of correction for six weeks and ordered to pay the costs of the trial.[51]

A more serious incident occurred to an off-duty missionary in Deptford, near Sunderland, in September 1869. A preacher and tract-seller named John Lewins, who was described by the *Sunderland News* as a "quiet and inoffensive man, somewhat simple in appearance", was so seriously assaulted by the Irish Catholic, Edward McGravery, that at one

---

[48] *Sunderland Herald*, 12 May 1865.

[49] *Durham Advertiser,* 12 June 1863.

[50] For example, Sheills lectured to crowded audiences of both Protestants and Catholics in Newcastle on 'The Prophecies Relating to the Apostacy', in which he described the Church of Rome as one of the beasts of the Apocalypse. *Durham Chronicle*, 31 October 1862.

[51] *Durham Advertiser,* 12 June 1863.

stage "his life . . . (was) almost despaired of". Unlike previous cases, there is no evidence that Lewins at any time preached against Catholicism, but the *Sunderland News* suggested that McGravery had a "grudge against the poor fellow" because of his religion. With the encouragement of two other Irishmen, McGravery knocked Lewins to the ground and attacked him as he lay. Lewins, who received serious injuries to the chest, was taken to the workhouse in a dangerous condition, although he eventually recovered.[52]

No Popery Demagogues

These incidents described above may have been localised and sporadic, but they do highlight the readiness of Irish Catholics to resort to violence in order to defend their religion from attacks by anti-Catholic evangelicals. This form of anti-Catholic incitement to religious violence, however, received its greatest expression in the reaction to the controversial "No Popery demagogues". These men toured the country and charged fees for lectures which employed vulgarised and pornographic anti-Catholic ideas, often with the deliberate intention of encouraging sectarian violence.[53] Allport has suggested that demagogues in general were successful only by inviting the "externalisation of hatred and anxiety",[54] and No Popery demagogues were certainly able to tap into the lucrative market of Anglo-Irish and Protestant-Catholic animosity. The Murphy Riots of the late 1860s were perhaps the most famous, but there were others and the North East was visited by many during the late 1850s and 1860s. Some were more effective in stirring up trouble than others and it is the intention of this section to examine three—Andre Massena (the "Baron de Camin"), William Murphy and Patrick Flynn—in order to highlight the way in which large-scale sectarian riots were just as possible in the North East as they were in other areas of the country, although their success was largely dependent on the context of time and place.

The origins of Andre Massena are generally unknown. Sketchy details in the press describe him as a French "ex-inquisitor" who styled himself the "Baron de Camin" and quickly developed a reputation for encouraging Anglo-Irish disorder in the mid-nineteenth century, most notably in Yorkshire, Lancashire and the Midlands.[55] Thus, the Baron's lecture tour of the North East during 1859-60 certainly had the potential for disorder.

---

[52] *Sunderland News,* 11 September 1869.
[53] Paz, *Popular Anti-Catholicism,* p. 26.
[54] Allport, *The Nature of Prejudice,* p. 419.
[55] Swift, 'Stafford Street Row', pp. 189-90; Paz, *Popular Anti-Catholicism,* p. 252.

This was clearly the expectation of the local press when he began his tour in Newcastle in July 1859. The *Newcastle Chronicle* was horrified at the prospect of Massena's visit and launched a personal crusade against him. For the *Chronicle*, the Baron's real intentions were obvious:

> "The mission of this person is . . . not only absurd, but it is also wicked. He appeals to one of the worst forms of irrational and cruel bigotry, and by imposture and misrepresentation does all in his power to unite those angry feelings which stand in the way of the intercommunion of persons differing in opinion".

Indeed, the paper asked why the authorities were not trying to suppress his lecture tour, "the uniform result of which has been a row or a riot".[56] In the interests of free speech, and much to the disgust of the local Catholics, he was not prevented from lecturing and secured the Music Hall as his chosen oratory. A strong police presence both in the Hall and the neighbouring streets were on call but, as it transpired, they were not to be needed.

On the opening night (Monday), a small crowd gathered around the Hall at the appointed time of 7pm. The *Newcastle Guardian* suggested that this crowd was not there to see Massena, but to listen to an Irishman who was delivering an alternative lecture that mingled expletives with references to the Catholic religion. When Massena arrived in a pair-horse cab, the Irishman warned the crowd "The Emperors's coming, and he'll teach you what it is to meddle with us". The Baron, dressed in flamboyant attire, certainly could not have ignored the crowd of Irishmen gathered at the door, greeting "his comical cut with a hearty laugh". This is a particularly revealing response given the Baron's reception elsewhere in the country and suggests that the Newcastle Irish pitied rather than despised him.

The Baron's fortunes did not improve as he entered the Music Hall and was received by an audience of only 60 people. His offer of postponing the lecture was met with an angry response from many of the spectators who demanded their money back, so he was forced to proceed. As well as attacking the local press for its lack of support, the Baron's lecture concentrated principally on the ever-popular topic of convents. He did not hold back on his denunciations:

> "Nuns were deluded women, who no sooner had they become fully alive to the character of the nunnery then they wished themselves out. Nunneries

---

[56] *Newcastle Daily Chronicle*, 23 July 1859.

were no better than brothels; and Sisters of Mercy were but priests disguised, five or six, out of every ten, as women".[57]

Shortly after the commencement of his lecture, Massena was met with opposition from "a champion of the anti-Baron cause" who proceeded to scream continuously and without intermission "Judas, Judas!". The police stationed in the Hall refused to remove the offender in spite of the Baron's request, causing a large percentage of the already slim audience to leave the building. The lecture was ended shortly afterwards.[58]

If the intention of Massena's lectures was to foment Protestant-Catholic tensions in Newcastle, while simultaneously lining his pockets, the plan on both counts failed dismally. Indeed the only violence occurred to the Baron himself. On the day of his second lecture in the town he was assaulted by four Catholics, one of whom was a bookseller on Mosley Street. The particulars of the case were brought out in the subsequent trial at Manors Police Court where there was an "immense concourse" of people. The Catholics, Messrs Lynch, Fenton, Pattinson and Leadbitter, entered Bell's Temperance Hall and, on seeing the Baron, questioned him on the subject of his previous night's lecture. When the Baron attempted to leave the room, he was set upon by Lynch who struck him and pulled his garment off, with the others assisting him. The other three men managed to escape punishment, although Lynch was fined 10s.[59]

Massena continued his lecturing tour in the south of County Durham where he fared slightly better. In October he lectured at Stockton, the inhabitants being favoured with "specimens of mutilated English, in the shape of lectures on Popery". He was fortunate to obtain good audiences on the two nights he lectured. On the second night, ladies were not admitted, implying the lurid nature of his discourse.[60] In Darlington, where notions of religious Liberalism were stronger than elsewhere owing to the Quaker dominance of the town, the Baron was only able to lecture one night out of the two advertised. The strength of the Catholic community in the town was influential enough to limit his appearances but this did not reduce the potential for trouble. The reporter of the *Darlington and Stockton Times* found his entrance to the Central Hall, where the Baron was lecturing, barred by Irish labourers who occupied the passages and stairs. His lecture was continually interrupted by a "continued fire of discordance, shouting, and other noises" and at the end of his lecture the

---

[57] *Newcastle Guardian*, 30 July 1859.
[58] Ibid.
[59] *Newcastle Weekly Chronicle*, 30 July 1859.
[60] *Hartlepool Free Press*, 8 October 1859.

Baron found his exit blocked. He was "held in a state of siege till 11 o'clock", although no actual violence broke out.[61]

The Baron de Camin's lecture tour of the North East did not generate the same level of violent rioting as it did elsewhere. Nevertheless his mixed reception in different towns highlights the way in which local factors played their part. In Newcastle, the vulgar stereotypes of Massena's rhetoric did not entice the crowds, but, perhaps more surprisingly, it did not cause Irish retaliation. In the southern areas of County Durham, the Irish reaction was not only stronger, but the Baron received good audiences in both places. Given the propensity of the Newcastle Irish to respond to attacks on their religion on previous occasions this calls for an explanation. One reason could be the lack of militant organisation amongst the Irish Catholics. As will be shown, the late-1850s was a period in which the local Catholic authorities were attempting to eradicate secret societies in Newcastle and, given the link between these societies and violence, the lack of disorder suggests that the Irish Catholics were responding to the bidding of their priests. Although there was also a notable absence of violence in Massena's Stockton lectures, the relative size of the crowds suggested an appetite for this form of vulgarised anti-Catholicism that appeared to be absent further north.

If the Baron's relative failure in the North East was largely dependent on the timing of his visit, two further "firebrands", who lectured in the area in the late-1860s, were more successful. Both the tours of William Murphy and Patrick Flynn must be seen within the broader context of an increase in Anglo-Irish tension during the mid-to late-1860s. The main reason for this was the substantial panic generated by the Irish independence movement, the Fenian Brotherhood. Originally a moderate movement, it gained notoriety during 1867 following a series of high-profile incidents that culminated in a bungled Fenian bombing at Clerkenwell gaol which killed twenty people.[62] Donald MacRaild has suggested that this event generated a tense and hysterical atmosphere towards the Irish throughout the localities of England. This was certainly apparent in the North East of England. In January 1868, the *Durham Chronicle* observed that a rumour of "several suspicious characters lurking about" the city was being circulated. From this rumour it was inferred that their ultimate design was to blow up Durham Cathedral, although there was no evidence to suggest anything of the sort.[63] In Newcastle, at the dinner of the Newcastle Farmer's Club, the Vicar of St Nicholas's Church

[61] *Darlington and Stockton Times*, 14 April 1860.
[62] MacRaild, *Irish Migrants*, pp. 138-42.
[63] *Durham Chronicle*, 24 January 1868.

claimed he had received a letter from a Fenian shortly before Christmas. In this letter, the Fenian warned the Vicar to "take care of yourself on Christmas Day for there may be an explosion under your church". The Vicar suggested that on another day he would have destroyed the letter but "no one knew in the present day when those invisible beings would strike", and was met with a round of applause from the audience when he confirmed that the Mayor had made the necessary precautions to "render any unpleasantness impossible".[64] In Durham, the Mayor of the city commissioned 24 Special Constables to assist the Mayor of Gateshead, who believed that a Fenian rising was imminent in the town.[65] In this atmosphere, it appeared that every Irish Catholic was a Fenian. Many Catholics were therefore determined to distance themselves from the activities of the Brotherhood. A meeting of the Catholics in Crook, consisting of 800 Irish, expressed their "disapproval and abhorrence of the outrageous acts of violence which have been lately perpetrated by the Fenian brotherhood in London and the provinces".[66]

Into this tense situation of seemingly nationwide anti-Irish paranoia and distrust came that "notorious demagogue" William Murphy.[67] A converted Protestant from County Limerick, Murphy first came to prominence in England after a series of disturbances in Plymouth in June 1866 and Wolverhampton in February 1867 were caused by his inflammatory lectures. It was, however, in Birmingham in June 1867 where he became a household name. His lectures on the 'Errors of Roman Catholicism' resulted in street rioting for several days, with crowds estimated to be between 50,000 and 100,000.[68] The following year saw a trail of destruction wherever Murphy chose to lecture, with small-scale riots occurring in the Lancashire towns of Rochdale, Bacup and Bolton, with more serious outbreaks at Stalybridge, Ashton and Oldham. In these places Irish Catholics and English Protestants were "whipped into a frenzy", as Irish districts became the main target for English operatives who invaded Catholic chapels, pulling down confessional booths, smashing altars and destroying images.[69] Arnstein has suggested that Murphy's lecture tour caused "a Victorian dilemma" for the local authorities: how to maintain the liberty of free speech that was so beloved

---

[64] *Newcastle Weekly Chronicle*, 18 January 1868.

[65] *Durham Advertiser*, 10 January 1868.

[66] *Durham Chronicle*, 3 January 1868.

[67] Murphy's lecture tours and the violence that followed are thoroughly examined in Arnstein, 'The Murphy Riots', pp. 51-73.

[68] Arnstein, 'The Murphy Riots', p. 57.

[69] Arnstein, *Protestant Versus Catholic*, pp. 95-9.

of John Stuart Mill and Liberal Victorians, while at the same time maintaining the public peace.[70] By mid-1868, the balance was beginning to turn in favour of suppressing Murphy. He was barred from entering Liverpool and was arrested and prevented from speaking in Manchester, where he even offered to stand as a candidate in the forthcoming election.[71] By the time Murphy reached the North East early in 1869, this dilemma was far from resolved; indeed, his tour in the region merely accentuated the problem.[72]

Murphy's North East lecturing tour began in North Shields in March 1869. He managed to obtain the use of the Oddfellows Hall in Saville Street and here he was as successful as anywhere else in causing a riot. His lectures on the 15th and 16th passed off peacefully but when it was anticipated that a riot would take place on St Patrick's Day, Murphy, at the request of the authorities, surprisingly postponed his lecture to the 19th. The final evening's lecture, the 'Confessional Unmasked', was perhaps the most eagerly anticipated of the three. When Murphy lectured in Wolverhampton, 6,000 tickets were sold for a venue holding only 3,000 to listen to lurid tales of priestly seduction.[73] In North Shields, the appetite for this "pornography of the Puritans" was no less keenly felt. The charge for admission was three times that of the previous nights but the hall was crowded and when Murphy made his appearance on the platform he was loudly cheered. For the *Chronicle*, Murphy was clearly guilty of hypocrisy in lambasting the confessional:

> "Murphy makes it a high crime against the Catholic priest that in confessional they put questions to men and women of an indelicate and beastly character, such as no-one should put to man and woman; yet he pours the whole mass of filth before his audiences, and charges 1s and 6d each admission to hear it".[74]

He had only managed about half of his lecture when he was interrupted by the sound of breaking glass as stones and pistol shots flew through the window. The entrance hall was forced open and a great number of

---

[70] Arnstein, 'The Murphy Riots', p. 51.

[71] Ibid, pp. 64-5.

[72] In spite of the notoriety of Murphy, his lecturing tour of the North East has never been examined in any detail, although narrative accounts have been supplied by both Neal, *English-Irish Conflict*; and MacRaild, *Faith, Fraternity and Fighting*, pp. 189-90.

[73] Arnstein, 'The Murphy Riots', p. 59.

[74] *Newcastle Daily Chronicle*, 22 March 1869.

Irishmen rushed through the passage towards the lecture theatre. Those inside the hall prepared themselves by breaking the legs off chairs.

There appears to have been a great deal of quasi-militarism on the part of the Irish Catholics in their attack on the Oddfellows Hall, which suggests a high level of organisation that is also evident in other towns where Murphy lectured.[75] It had become increasingly clear that something was about to happen when bands of Irish from the outlying areas were seen entering the town and heading for Saville Street. They assembled as a collective at the west end of Saville Street and, on the announcement of a Irishman shouting "Now form!", they rushed along the street towards the hall. Shouts of "We'll kill Murphy, suppose we are hung for it!" were heard as the Irishmen descended on the Hall, splitting into two groups, with one portion breaking open the entrance while the other concentrated on throwing stones through the window.[76]

In their defence, the local authorities had, as is evident in other towns, clearly anticipated that a riot was about to occur and tried to prevent Murphy from lecturing. The Mayor of the town, Edward Shotton, as well as other magistrates, had been in communication with government officials initially to apprehend Murphy on the premise that he would incite a riot but the Home Secretary refused this request on the grounds that it would be illegal to do so.[77] As a precaution, the Mayor and the magistrates were offered the use of the 40th Regiment, stationed at Tynemouth Castle. Four policemen were also positioned at the entrance to the Oddfellows Hall, while the rest waited in reserve at the police station. When the riot broke out, information was immediately sent to the police station and, within a few minutes, the reserve force was charging the Irishmen. A number of Irishmen received bloody injuries from truncheon blows but managed to retreat along the back streets of the neighbourhood. The Mayor despatched a messenger to Tynemouth Castle and, in thirty minutes, a detachment of the 40th Regiment arrived in the town, although by this stage the trouble had passed. As a further precaution, a number of police were sent to the Catholic chapel and the newly-built convent in case of a reprisal.[78] The following day, Murphy gave a lecture solely to a crowded audience of women on the topic of the confessional and it was

---

[75] This militarism is evident in the Murphy riot in Wolverhampton. Swift has noted that there were rumours of a meeting of Irish Catholics in which it was decided to send missionaries to other parts of the Black County to encourage opposition to Murphy. Swift, 'Stafford Street Row', p. 191.

[76] *Newcastle Courant*, 20 March 1869.

[77] *Newcastle Weekly Chronicle*, 27 March 1869.

[78] *Shields Gazette,* 20 March 1869.

expected that a second attack on the hall was to take place. The authorities therefore deployed one hundred Special Constables to patrol the streets and keep the peace, although no further disorder occurred.[79]

The authorities won praise for their preparations and the prompt response of the police forces, but this was not the end of the matter. In the conclusion of his lecture on the 19th March, Murphy had promised to return. He was denied the future use of Oddfellows Hall so he threatened to transport a wooden "tabernacle" capable of holding 2,000 people to the town. "If the Roman Catholics pulled that building down", he warned, "the Protestants would pull the Roman Catholics down".[80] The simple answer, therefore, was not to offer him any place to lecture. This was the course adopted by the towns of Sunderland and Newcastle, where Murphy failed to secure a platform.[81] He was more fortunate, however, in Durham where the proprietor of the Assembly Rooms was duped into giving Murphy permission to lecture in that building. However, in this city, Murphy's lectures were a disaster to rival Massena's in Newcastle a decade before. On the four nights he was due to lecture, Murphy's largest audience was the opening night of Monday when only 60 people turned. Given this state of affairs it is hard to disagree with the *Durham Advertiser's* concluding on Murphy's lack of success: "People fight and riot about his (Murphy's) lectures in other parts of the country, but in Durham he is treated with contemptuous indifference".[82]

Murphy may have failed to antagonise the people of Durham but he knew he could always rely on the simmering Anglo-Irish tensions in the industrial heartlands of Tyneside. Indeed, the urgency of the authorities to prevent the "proved enemy of public order" was made more apparent when Murphy's original threat to return to North Shields became a reality in early April. He had somehow managed to obtain access to the Circus in the Borough Road with placards announcing that he would preach twice on Sunday 3 April, and lecture in the same place on Monday, Tuesday and

---

[79] *Newcastle Daily Chronicle*, 22 March 1869. The riot did not reach the level of the Wolverhampton disturbances where, unlike the North Shields episode, many Irishmen had managed to obtain seats inside the hall and thus the Wolverhampton police found difficulty in controlling the riot. Swift, 'Stafford Street Row', p. 191.

[80] *Newcastle Journal*, 20 March 1869. This wooden "tabernacle", holding 3,000 people, had been assembled in Birmingham in response to the Mayor of Birmingham's refusal to grant the Town Hall to Murphy. Arnstein, 'The Murphy Riots', p. 56.

[81] *Sunderland Times*, 8 March 1869; *Newcastle Weekly Chronicle*, 27 March 1869.

[82] *Durham Advertiser*, 26 March 1869.

Wednesday. The Mayor was forced to resort to drastic measures, enforcing a law dating back to the French Revolution in issuing the following notice:

> "'Notice is hereby given, that every person who may attend, all or any of the lectures given by Mr. Murphy . . . is liable to a penalty of twenty pounds, under the provision of the Act 30th, George 3rd, chapter 79, section 15'".

Murphy's reply was to issue a counter bill that increased the excitement in the town "tenfold":

> "'Protestants! Be not deceived by the bills you see posted on the walls. I, William Murphy demand my rights at the Circus tomorrow (Sunday) . . . Come in thousands to hear the gospel, and 'no surrender'!'"

Following all this publicity, Murphy was virtually guaranteed a good crowd for the opening Sunday "sermon". However, on his arrival at 2pm, he was faced with a barricade of police who refused to allow the lecturer to enter the Circus. Not to be outdone, Murphy then announced that he had received permission from the Duke of Northumberland himself to preach on the North Quay and proceeded towards his destination. He took his stand upon a cask, and commenced with his service. 8000 people were assembled on the streets and the windows of nearby houses and the rigs of vessels were thronged with those eager to see the performance. It was not long before disturbances broke out. A number of the Irish began to throw stones before the Protestants turned upon them and "a riot of the most disgraceful description took place" that involved both men and women.[83] One Irishman had his hand "lamed" while others had serious facial injuries.[84] Trouble continued throughout the day, although his lecture in the evening on Long Sands Beach in Tynemouth passed off peacefully as a considerable police presence ensured that the crowd remained subdued. Tension remained in the town for several days even after Murphy had left to seek legal advice in London about his exclusion from the Circus.[85] On the Monday evening, two men were attacked in the street by a gang of Irishmen under the mistaken belief that one of the men was Murphy himself.[86]

---

[83] *Durham Chronicle*, 9 April 1869.

[84] *Shields Gazette*, 5 April 1869.

[85] *Shields Gazette*, 5 April 1869.

[86] *Shields Gazette*, 6 April 1869.

Opinion was divided as to whether the Mayor's conduct was right. The *Newcastle Journal* praised Shotton for his firm stance against Murphy, suggesting that more trouble would have occurred if his lecture had taken place in a building, "from which the audience would have been unable to escape readily in the event of a 'free fight'". The paper hoped that the Mayor's example would be followed in all places where Murphy "tried to throw his firebrand".[87] Not everyone was satisfied, however, and even the Catholics were incensed at the decision to close the Catholic chapel as a precaution. In a letter to Lord Grey, Councillor Turnbull complained that this had caused much consternation among the Catholic community who had been prevented from "the opportunities of attending Divine worship".[88]

The issue also brought about a wider debate, as it had in other towns, concerning the constitution of free speech.[89] A letter to the *Shields Gazette* was highly critical of the Mayor for not allowing Murphy the liberty to speak, an ideology which "had cost too much to be easily let slip" and one which was "so precious to every true born Briton".[90] However, a reply the following day accused Murphy of defending not the ideology of liberty of speech but the "liberty of insult, liberty of debauching the minds of the young, and outraging the feelings of a large body of Christians, who have a right to be protected by their civil and religious freedom . . ."[91] Shotton's decision to re-enact an archaic law received nationwide attention because it had wider legal implications. The matter was brought up in Parliament by Sinclair Ayton, the member for the Kirkcaldy Burghs, who gave notice that he would ask the Home Secretary personally if Shotton had exceeded his authority by issuing the proclamation.[92] After a brief inquiry, it was found that Shotton had been acting in accordance with statute law and was therefore perfectly entitled to prevent Murphy's oration. The irony of the authorities finding a way to prevent the lecturing tour of the "self-styled champion of Protestantism" with recourse to the "Protestant Constitution" would not have been lost on Murphy. Authorities in other towns and cities used this method to bar Murphy from lecturing, most notably in Birmingham in July 1869. The one exception was in Whitehaven in April 1871 when the magistrates allowed him to speak in the town's Oddfellow's

---

[87] *Newcastle Journal*, 5 April 1869.
[88] DUASC, Letter of Ralph Turnbull to Earl Grey, 8 April 1869, GRE/B/45/1.
[89] This is apparent in Wolverhampton. Swift, 'Stafford Street Row', pp. 192-3.
[90] *Shields Gazette*, 12 April 1869.
[91] *Shields Gazette*, 13 April 1869.
[92] *Shields Gazette*, 14 April 1869.

Hall. He was attacked by 300 miners from the nearby-mining village of
Cleator Moor, eventually dying of his injuries in March 1872.[93]

The Murphy Riots in general, and the associated violence and
destruction that followed them, are well-known. Less well documented is
the No Popery tour of Patrick Flynn, who toured the southern area of
County Durham at the end of 1868.[94] Patrick Flynn was very much in the
mould of William Murphy. A Protestant Irishman who adopted vulgar
anti-Catholic stereotypes in order to foment Protestant-Catholic tensions in
the town he visited, Flynn was also the spokesperson of a religious
organisation, the Protestant Evangelical Society. The local press even
described him as a "Murphyite" and an "imitator of Murphy" and there is
evidence to suggest that two shared a close working relationship.[95]
Although Flynn never appeared to gain the same level of notoriety as his
more famous Irish contemporary, his visits to Hartlepool and Stockton
during September and October 1868 were at least as destructive, and
revealed the extent to which anti-Catholicism and anti-Irishness appeared
culturally embedded in these areas.

In comparison to other areas of the North East, South Durham
appeared to have a strong tradition of popular and rabid sectarianism
which closely mirrored the industrial towns of Lancashire. In order to
understand why, it is necessary to examine the recent history of English-
Irish/Protestant-Catholic relations in this area. Certainly the first major
English-Irish riot in Hartlepool had definite religious causes. In July 1851,
the "champion of Catholicism", Charles Larkin, lectured in the Town Hall.
Here he employed controversial language in describing Protestants as
"poor, creeping, benighted creatures, crawling in the dark through that
book they call the *bible*". The *Sunderland News* was clearly not impressed
by Larkin's performance, describing the lecturer's statements as "daring
and reckless assumptions without any kind of proofs—illogical
declarations and false conclusions mixed up with an amazing amount of
palpable absurdities". Many of the Protestants present at the lecture
undoubtedly agreed with the view of the *Sunderland News* as a general
rush towards the lecturer was made. Larkin, and the Catholic priest of the

---

[93] MacRaild, *Irish Migrants*, p. 178.

[94] While the local newspapers devoted numerous column spaces to the 'Flynn
Riots', there appears to be no secondary account of his activities in existence.
Indeed, this author has not come across a single reference to him in any secondary
work.

[95] For example, along with Messrs Houston and Mackay, both Flynn and Murphy
were honoured at a grand presentation event in Blackburn for their lectures against
Popery. *The Blackburn Standard*, 8 January 1868.

town, the Rev. William Knight, managed to escape the melee, although the latter's coat was ripped to shreds.[96]

In consequence, a Protestant lecturer, H.A. Lamb, was invited to the town to lecture and defend the Protestant religion.[97] Lamb planned to deliver two lectures in the open air which infuriated the Catholics in Hartlepool. They promised that, if Lamb were to do so, "*a riot would be the consequence*". Lamb's first lecture took place on the 12th July, a day evidently chosen to cause the greatest amount of trouble and, although large crowds attended, the lecture passed off peacefully. However, that evening a riot ensued in the largely Irish Catholic Northgate area of the town. It began after a discussion between Catholics and Protestant navvies, evidently influenced by the recent lecture tours, and resulting "in one of the former adopting a physical force argument, viz, his fist on the head of his opponent". A general melee took place in which rioters suffered "broken heads" and windows were smashed. Eventually the police intervened and successfully managed to restore order.[98] Although Lamb's second lecture on the Town Moor during the following month resulted in no further trouble,[99] it was clear that the police were not prepared to take any chances. On the 20th August, the local Watch Committee reported that it had received a letter from Sir George Grey, MP for South Durham, who had entered into correspondence with the Mayor concerning possible "disturbances on the occasion of the opening of the new Catholic Church" in the town. The Chief Constable assured a Watch Committee meeting that the army would be prepared to "render any assistance" if necessary.[100]

The 1860s saw no easing of tension between the English and Irish communities; a problem compounded by local economic factors. Iron was the major industry of the Cleveland and Teesside areas. The Cleveland Hills were exploited for their iron by the local magnate, Ralph Ward Jackson in the 1850s and 1860s.[101] Chase has noted that the majority of the Irish in this area were employed in local ironworks. The "rapidly deteriorating industrial relations" of this industry in the 1860s brought with it greater tensions between the English and Irish, as the latter were under-represented in organised trade union activity and were therefore

---

[96] *Sunderland News*, 12, 19 July 1851.

[97] See previous chapter, p. 78

[98] *Durham Chronicle*, 18 July 1851.

[99] *Durham Chronicle*, 8 August 1851.

[100] Teesside Archives, Hartlepool Watch Committee Constables' Book', 20 August 1851.

[101] Wood, *West Hartlepool*, p. 52.

susceptible to unemployment unlike their English rivals.[102] This may also help to explain sectarian tensions in other places where iron was the main industry, such as Consett and the surrounding villages.[103] Furthermore, the shipbuilding industry in West Hartlepool, which similarly employed English and Irish workers, was in disarray in the late 1860s. In 1866 Pile, Spence and Co., the main shipbuilders in the town, declared themselves bankrupt, causing severe economic depression as hundreds faced unemployment. It was not until 1869, when the new shipbuilding company Denton Gray formed and became one of the largest shipbuilding yards in the country, that unemployment rates dropped.[104] The intervening years must have seen an increase in English-Irish tension in the area, as both communities competed for scarce employment.

Aside from its Irish dimension, popular sectarianism in South Durham was also encouraged by other means throughout the 1850s and 1860s. Anti-sacerdotalism (hatred of priests) was common throughout this period as the previous chapter has shown. This included major court cases involving priests that received international attention; the production of popular tracts with anti-sacerdotal themes; and the often violent victimisation of local priests. In addition to this, popular anti-Catholicism was also evident in the observance of Guy Fawkes Day which appeared to be celebrated more rigorously in South Durham than elsewhere in the region. Robert Storch has argued that the celebration of the 5th November was largely confined to southern towns which were "never great Chartist or union strongholds . . . remaining locked into older repertories of collective expression long after they shrivelled elsewhere".[105] While it is true that the North East in general did not participate in this anniversary, some localities of the region still maintained the popular celebration. For example, the local press regularly reported on illegal Guy Fawkes celebrations in the towns of Darlington, Stockton and Hartlepool but rarely

---

[102] M. Chase, 'The Teesside Irish in the Nineteenth-Century', *The Irish in British Labour History*, ed. by John Belchem and Patrick Buckland (Liverpool: Liverpool University Press, 1993), pp. 51-2. In spite of this assertion, Chase makes no reference to the lecturing tours of Patrick Flynn in causing inter-communal tension.

[103] It can also be noted in other places in England, such as Cleator Moor in Cumbria, where the miners who beat William Murphy to death were employed in the local ironworks.

[104] N. McCord, and D. J. Rowe, 'Industrialisation and Urban Growth in North East England', *International Review of Social History*, 22.1 (1977), p. 36.

[105] Robert D. Storch, '"Please to Remember the Fifth of November": Conflict, Solidarity and Public Order in Southern England, 1815-1900', *Popular Culture and Custom in Nineteenth Century England*, ed. by Robert D. Storch (London: Croom Helm, 1982), p. 80.

on celebrations further north. Most reports centred on the activities of large groups of juveniles rolling flaming tar barrels and setting off fireworks, although there was no evidence of explicit anti-Catholicism other than the symbolic burning of the Guy.[106]

When Patrick Flynn arrived on the scene in 1868, he therefore found a ready-made audience for his vulgar denunciations of the priesthood and the Catholic religion generally.[107] His first steps in the region were initially unsuccessful, although he did receive notoriety following a proposed lecture in Darlington at the end of August 1868. He announced that he would lecture in the Mechanics Hall but, on his arrival, he found the building blocked by an Irish mob "headed by a priest". Flynn sent a letter to a Liberal newspaper, the *South Durham and Cleveland Mercury*, claiming that the priest, Father Coll, was the leader of the mob whose purpose was to cause as much trouble as possible. The lecturer claimed that he was always anxious to avoid anything that could lead to a breach of the peace and was therefore keen to leave as soon as he could.[108] The notion that a priest was inciting violence became the main topic of dispute in the town for days afterwards until it was finally confirmed that Father Coll's presence there was one of peacemaker. The previous Sunday, he had forbid anyone to attend Flynn's lectures and he was among the crowd on the night of the lecture to try to "exhort the people to disperse and return peaceably to their homes".[109]

Flynn's growing reputation was firmly cemented during a series of lectures in Stockton in early September. His first two lectures at the Temperance Hall, in early September 1868, were poorly attended so, for his third lecture, Flynn decided to employ more provocative language in his placards. They caused so much "offence to the Irish Catholic community" that the trustees of the Hall were forced to prevent him from lecturing there in fear of causing a breach of the peace. Flynn, unlike Murphy in North Shields, seemed happy to comply, presumably because the trustees of the Hall stated they would hold him personally accountable if any damage occurred.[110] However, the announcement that he would conduct an open-air sermon at the Market Cross, High Street, on Sunday was clear evidence that Flynn did not wish to let the matter rest. When he

---

[106] *The Hartlepool Free Press*, particularly during the late 1850s and 1860s, regularly reported disturbances associated with this celebration.
[107] *Birmingham Daily Post*, 11 April 1868.
[108] *South Durham and Cleveland Mercury,* 26 August 1868.
[109] *Darlington and Stockton Times,* 5 September 1868.
[110] *Darlington and Stockton Times*, 12 September 1868; *Stockton Herald,* 11 September 1868.

arrived at the Market Cross, he found a crowd of Irishmen blocking the steps surrounding the Cross. Instead of keeping his distance, Flynn walked up as near as he could, about ten or fifteen yards, and began preaching "in strongly condemnatory language against the Roman Catholics".

Several of the 1,000-strong crowd "invited" Flynn up to a field in Yarm Lane. While he was lecturing a number of young Englishmen "spotted several men who they took to be Irish" and launched an attack on them, knocking the Irishmen to the ground and kicking them. *The Stockton Herald* believed that these men, who were respectably dressed, were in fact local Orangemen.[111] Although a large body of police were present, they stood by and did not interfere.[112] One Englishman, John Pearson, was eventually brought to trial and fined five shillings plus costs for attacking an Irish Catholic, Philip Gilroy. In his defence, Pearson stated that Gilroy was "causing a disturbance in the crowd, and had to be forcibly expelled, in order to preserve the peace of the community". A law suit was also issued against Flynn himself by Cornelius O'Donnell, the beerhouse-keeper of the Shoulder of Mutton pub, who accused Flynn of causing a breach of the peace. The magistrates refused the warrant against him, hoping that "if possible, Flynn should be kept away from the town". [113]

This rather lax attitude enabled Flynn to lecture again in the town three weeks later. Tension was reaching boiling point as a result of the previous disturbances and the attitude of the authorities who appeared to be demonstrating an overtly sectarian policy. According to the *Stockton Herald*, one hundred Special Constables had recently been sworn in to preserve the peace "in consequence of the frequent disposition to riot shown by the lower classes of the Irish population in this town".[114] If the magistrates could not prevent Flynn then it became the responsibility of the Catholic Church to steer away their flock from attending his lectures and in this they were partially successful as the lecturer was surprisingly ineffective in whipping up disorder when he lectured again at the Market Cross. This was the result, according to the *Durham Chronicle*, of the efforts of the officiating priests who had warned in the Sunday morning services that there would be consequences for anyone attending the "Murphyite lectures".[115] The *Stockton Herald*, however, took a rather different view:

---

[111] *Stockton Herald*, 25 September 1868.
[112] *Newcastle Weekly Chronicle*, 26 September 1868.
[113] *Darlington and Stockton Times*, 26 September 1868.
[114] *Stockton Herald*, 9 October 1868.
[115] *Durham Chronicle*, 16 October 1868.

"The riotous spirit of the Irish has been quelled. They do not appear on the scene of action, knowing that thousands of Englishmen and Welshmen were in attendance . . . to defend the rights of Englishmen to fair play and freedom of speech".[116]

If Flynn had only modest success in Stockton it was in the neighbouring town of West Hartlepool where the most serious disorder was to occur. Flynn arrived in the town the day after the Stockton disturbances, announcing that he would lecture the next two nights in the Oxford Music Hall. In spite of the best efforts of the local Catholic priest, the Rev. John O'Dwyer, the magistrates allowed the first lecture on the topic of 'Romanism' to take place that night.[117] The lecture, however, passed off relatively peacefully notwithstanding a large number of "Irish roughs" hooting and whistling throughout Flynn's performance. The second night saw an even larger Irish presence including Irishmen from the neighbouring towns of Hartlepool, Stockton and Middlesbrough who were clearly intent on causing trouble. Anticipating this, the proprietor of the hall forbid Flynn from lecturing and called for the police. A strong body arrived and quickly dispersed the crowd. The Irish retreated as a body along Church Street, raising their caps and cheering "lustily" at St Joseph's Catholic Church, but the considerable police presence ensured that no serious trouble occurred.[118]

It was Flynn's decision to preach "under the broad canopy of heaven" in the Market Place the following weekend that finally "set the people by the ears". Flynn's open-air preaching at Stockton had brought notable disturbances, but this dangerous tactic at West Hartlepool led to a full-scale riot. Saturday's sermon was greatly anticipated by a crowd of about 1,200 people which, according to the *South Durham & Cleveland Mercury*, was evidence of Flynn's "unenviable notoriety which he had gained for himself in this neighbourhood during the week previous". All sections of the community were present:

"Some were highly respectable residents of the town, who had been drawn, thither, probably out of curiosity. Others were half-grown men, chiefly of the artisan class, who seemed bent on mischief; and others, by far the most numerous, were men and women of all trades and professions, and of no profession at all".[119]

---

[116] *Stockton Herald,* 16 October 1868.
[117] John O'Dwyer, b. 1834 (Waterford, Ireland), o. 1859, d. 1925. *English and Welsh Priests*, p. 44.
[118] *Newcastle Weekly Chronicle*, 26 September 1868.
[119] *South Durham and Cleveland Mercury*, 30 September 1868.

Flynn's orations were similar in nature to those of William Murphy's. The Catholic Church and the priesthood were typically lambasted as Flynn accused Roman Catholic priests of being "debauchers of women, and Catholic women as corrupted by priests" as well as describing Queen Isabella of Spain as "the kept mistress of the Pope". The lecturer used alleged Catholic works in order to "prove" his allegations, many of which he claimed to have read whilst in the process of seminary training himself. Flynn also read extracts from the *Confessional Unmasked*, a favourite work of extreme anti-Catholics and used the platform to defend his right to freedom of speech and to attack the local press for calling on his lectures to be banned. Unfortunately, while Flynn was happy to defend the doctrine of free speech for his own purposes, those members of the crowd who exercised their right to criticise his performance were soundly prevented, in some cases by physical violence that was encouraged by the lecturer himself. An eyewitness was particularly horrified at the following incident:

> "After dwelling on this subject (the Pope) for some time, a person . . . shouted out 'Come to the Bible; we have heard plenty about the Pope'. 'What do you say?' replied Flynn; 'young man, if you don't keep quiet there are persons here who will make you'. And thereupon some dozen young fellows pressed towards the interrupter, got into an angry colloquy with him, Flynn stopping the lecture and looking on, apparently enjoying the mischief; and, as the numbers of his supporters surrounding the unfortunate increased in their pressure, the interrupter, shouting 'It's unfair, do you call that freedom of discussion?' was buffeted, hustled, kicked, and jostled right out of the crowd . . ."[120]

Flynn continued to antagonise the Irish portion of the crowd relentlessly. When a group of Irishmen and women pushed their way to the front of the crowd, Flynn pulled from his pocket a number of scapulars "tied up with blue, red and white ribbons" and shook them at the advancing crowd. This drew cries of "Shame!", from which Flynn responded in "angry and provoking terms". This led to a number of isolated fights between the Irish and English portions of the crowd.

The response of the police to Flynn's provocation and the related incidents suggests that the lecturer clearly had a number of supporters within the local constabulary. The police reaction to the physical attack on the initial heckler was not only one of indifference, but seemingly active support for Flynn's henchmen. As the dissident was thrown out of the

---

[120] Ibid.

crowd, policemen were spotted laughing and cheering along with others and two were even observed clapping their hands at the incident. They continued to remain passive throughout and only once interfered when an Irishman was carried far from the crowd and attacked, suffering serious facial injuries. Even as a larger contingent arrived on the scene, "they also appeared to be mere spectators, and served the purpose rather of a bodyguard to Flynn than of protectors of the peace or preservers of public order". Even the magistrates joined in, with the occupants of the house of Mr. Miller, a local magistrate, cheering Flynn on from windows overlooking the scene.[121]

Worse was to follow the next day (Sunday) when Flynn again preached in the Market Place. Matters finally came to a head when an Irishwoman was attacked near Lynn Street Methodist Chapel. Blood was pouring from her mouth when a knot of Irishmen came to her defence and dashed forward to assault a group of Englishmen. One of the English group flourished a heavy bar of iron over his head, gesticulating to his English friends to come to his defence. An immense crowd then pushed the Irish back into John Street where they took refuge in their homes. Here they were effectively under siege as stones and bricks smashed through their windows, leading one Irishman to threaten the assailants with a gun. A heavy shower of rain brought the lecture to an abrupt close, sending many home, but it failed to wash away the excitement and ill-feeling between Flynn's "Orange abettors" and the Hartlepool Irish. Riots broke out near Messrs Walker's Saw Mill, as "stones and brickbats flew in all directions; pokers and shillelaghs were freely banded about; and many persons were more or less injured". The Irish were victimised wherever they were spotted and a number of them suffered considerable injuries. One Irishman was chased on board a Prussian vessel where both he and the owner of the vessel were badly assaulted by an English mob. The police were finally forced into action and, notwithstanding serious injuries, eventually managed to restore order after five hours of sustained rioting.[122]

The reaction of the judicial authorities in the ensuing trial again brings up the question of State impartiality towards the Irish Catholics. Most of the men who were charged were Irish Catholics, ignoring the fact that much of the crowd were, as one witness put it, "hunting the Irish". The *Hartlepool Free Press*, in its report of the riot, had placed great emphasis on the three policemen who were injured in the violence and the sentences handed out to those accused of the assaults, reflecting the prejudices of the

---

[121] Ibid.
[122] Ibid.

middle classes towards the "disorderly Irish Catholics".[123] Patrick Cairns, a labourer, was charged with attempting to assault P.C. Hudspith with a poker aimed at his head. He was fined £5 or two months labour. Similarly, Peter McGlynn received an identical punishment for his role as ringleader in a group of thirty Irishmen who assaulted P.C. Monkhouse.[124] The only exception was an Englishman, Richard Nodding, who, with a group of friends, assaulted an Irishman named Isaac Spooner, although he appeared to receive a lighter sentence of ten shillings or fourteen days hard labour.[125]

In certain parts of Lancashire, it has been suggested that William Murphy's lecturing tours led to an increase in anti-Catholicism and anti-Irishness amongst the newly-enfranchised working classes. Conservative parties in these areas exploited this increase in sectarian tension for their own benefit and encouraged the working classes to oppose the Liberalism of their mill-owning employees. It's possible that Flynn's visit to West Hartlepool may have helped to generate a similar outcome. Murphy came too late to the North East to influence the election, but his "Murphyite" contemporary had the power to influence the proceedings in the newly enfranchised towns of South Durham, particularly as the Tory MP of West Hartlepool, Ralph Ward Jackson, was victorious in the election. How far Flynn actually affected the election is difficult to ascertain, but it is clear that Ward Jackson himself did not appreciate an alleged association with the "No Popery demagogue". In a letter to the *South Durham & Cleveland Mercury*, the Conservative MP denied that he, or any of his agents, had "anything whatever to do with this person's presence in the town".[126] Stockton, where Flynn first came to local prominence, at first glance seemed to have been unaffected by his appearance and the Liberal candidate, Vane, won the seat quite comfortably. The Conservative *Stockton Herald*, however, made frequent reference in its report of the Flynn disturbances to the use of Liberal agitators amongst the lecturer's

---

[123] *Hartlepool Free Press*, 3 October 1868. The headline of the report in this paper read: 'Murphyite Riot at West Hartlepool: Three Policemen Injured' thereby directing the blame away from the provocation of Flynn and his abetters towards the Irish Catholics. Most of the report blamed the Irish for commencing the affrays, praising the police unquestionably for their conduct.
[124] One of the leading Irish Catholics of the town, a respectable trader named Mr. Magorie, was later accused by Flynn of paying the fines of these two Irishmen and urging Irish Catholics to attack the lecturer, although Magorie denied these allegations. *South Durham and Cleveland Mercury*, 3 October 1868.
[125] *South Durham and Cleveland Mercury*, 30 September, 3 October 1868.
[126] *South Durham and Cleveland Mercury*, 3 October 1868.

supporters and therefore accused the Liberal Party, rather than the
Conservatives, of fomenting sectarian tension. In its report of the
abandoned lecture in the town in early September, the paper alleged that
there was an obvious political undertone to the proceedings:

> "A small audience was gathered in the hall before the time appointed for
> the lecture, among whom were several Liberals. Outside the hall, and
> among the Irishmen, were several active Liberals, who used their
> endeavours to excite them to acts of violence. One of them, who is well-
> known, offered half a crown to anyone who would go into the hall and
> begin a row".[127]

The paper suggested that the Liberals opposed Flynn because he was a
defender of the Anglican Church and, with Irish disestablishment on the
political agenda, it was in their interests to "get up a row and drown the
voice of truth".[128] Neither Flynn nor Murphy ever declared a specific
allegiance to any political party, but it is clear that the sectarian tension
generated by their appearances could be exploited by both parties for their
own ends.

Throughout the latter months of 1868, Flynn continued his campaign
in South Durham and disorder seemed to follow him wherever he went. A
crowd of over a thousand people watched him lecture on the Town Moor
at Hartlepool in mid-October, as words and stones were thrown towards
the orator. As in West Hartlepool three weeks before, those who expressed
an opinion contrary to Flynn's were roughly handled by his supporters
although more serious trouble was averted by the presence of a strong
police force who, at least in this case, appeared to be mindful of their role
in preserving public order.[129] Flynn returned to West Hartlepool in mid-
December, announcing a lecture on the 'Life and Times of William III, the
Orange King'. Here, an unfortunate puddler who had strayed into the hall
unexpectedly during the lecture and took issue with Flynn was attacked
and badly beaten by the "Flynnites".[130] Flynn did attempt to lecture further
north although with comparatively little success. At Gateshead, he was
denied the use of the Temperance Hall and although he was successful in
obtaining a similar venue at North Shields, surprisingly his lecture passed
off peacefully given what was to occur when William Murphy visited the

---

[127] *Stockton Herald*, 11 September 1868.
[128] Ibid.
[129] *Durham Chronicle*, 23 October 1868.
[130] *Newcastle Weekly Chronicle*, 12 December 1868.

town three months later.[131] Nevertheless, he had still left his mark on the south of the region where English-Irish hostility remained for some time. The following August, a serious riot took place between the Stockton Irish and English in which the latter, as the *Sunderland News* tactfully put it, "took the Irish in hand and thrashed every gem of the Emerald Isle they could lay their hands on".[132] Furthermore, Chase has noted that a serious riot, albeit political in origin, occurred two years later in Stockton during a rally in support of the amnesty for Fenian prisoners, in which 2,000 Irishmen were routed by 10,000 English and Welshmen.[133]

Orange and Green

The appearance of Orangemen among the contingent of Patrick Flynn's supporters points to the way in which both English-Irish and intra-Irish religious violence were encouraged by the transplantation of the Orange Order into the heartlands of the industrial North East. The Order began its existence in Ireland in 1795, developing out of the atmosphere of religious hatred and sectarian violence that characterised Irish society at the end of the eighteenth century. It functioned as an ultra-Protestant secret society, largely as a response to the perceived threat of growing Catholic power and persecution. Its ideology emphasised a militant Protestant outlook and an anti-Catholic stance that not only helped it spread rapidly in size and importance throughout Ireland but also to other parts of the world through the activities of British militia groups and Irish immigrants. Orangeism took root in Britain as elsewhere in the Irish Diaspora and consequently became a way of life not only for the newly-arrived Irish Protestants, but also as a vehicle by which English Protestants could express their indignation at the growing Irish Catholic population. As MacRaild has argued, it very quickly "internalised a wider, more mainstream and politically conservative ideology, avowedly defending the principles of the Established Church and the Tory Party".[134]

While it is true that the Orange Order in England acted primarily as a friendly society, offering sickness and burial benefits to Irish and English members alike, it is perhaps more famous for its annual 12 July parading tradition, where members of the Order protested their "right to walk" through the Irish Catholic areas of cities. The threat of violence was never

---

[131] *Newcastle Weekly Chronicle,* 5 December 1868; 19 December 1868.

[132] *Sunderland News,* 21 August 1869.

[133] Chase, 'Teesside Irish', p. 54.

[134] MacRaild, *Irish Migrants,* p. 110.

far from the forefront, particularly in the larger urban cities, such as Manchester and Liverpool, where the organisation became firmly ensconced. Elsewhere in the country, Orange lodges were formed in almost every northern town and in some places further south.[135] In the North East, Orangeism took root as it had elsewhere, although not to the same extent as in other areas. Frank Neal has suggested the main reason for this lies in the lack of local aristocratic support in the formative years of the Order's arrival in England[136], while Cooter argues the reason is more cultural: the Order did not have a strong Tory-Anglican base to court support as in other counties.

While it cannot be denied that Orangeism was weaker in the North East than in some areas, the assertion of Cooter—that there is a distinct lack of reference in the local newspapers to the organisation in the North East—ignores numerous press reports of Orange meetings and affrays. Donald MacRaild's recent study of the Orange Order in Northern England is also keen to play down the role of the organisation as a vehicle for sectarian violence in the North East, arguing that the organisation remained effectively "hidden from view".[137] While there can be no doubt that large-scale Orange-Green rioting was rare in comparison to Liverpool, isolated incidents and small-scale brawls were more the norm. The Orange Order in the North East was never as visible as in Liverpool but neither was it anywhere else in the country during this period. Lowe has suggested that even in certain parts of Lancashire noted for their ethnic disturbances, such as Manchester and Oldham, references to Orangeism before 1870 were sketchy.[138] In comparison, the North East attracted far more attention than has previously been acknowledged. Orange parades and violence during the late-1860s were regularly reported in the press, where a combination of the Fenian threat, Irish Protestant immigration and No Popery demagogues brought about a wave of Orange-Green clashes which, on occasions, bore more resemblance to Ulster than Tyneside.

The organisation of the Irish Catholics in the North East of England in responding to threats to their religion ensured that they were not simply a passive instrument of Orange hostility. Many formed secret societies of

---

[135] The geographical span of Orangeism seems to be concentrated in the north, although a recent essay by Shirley Matthews has pointed to the existence of lodges on the south coast in Portsmouth and Southampton. Matthews, "'Second Spring'", p. 95.

[136] Neal, 'English-Irish Conflict', p. 13.

[137] MacRaild, *Faith, Fraternity and Fighting*, p. 199.

[138] W.J. Lowe, *The Irish in Mid-Victorian Lancashire: The Shaping of a Working-Class Community* (New York: Peter Lang, 1989), pp. 163-4.

their own, the most famous being the Ribbon and Hibernian Societies. Like the Orange Order, these organisations initially appeared to play an integral role for the Irish migrant, particularly in the famine years where they provided a social outlet for immigrants.[139] Certainly, as John Belchem has suggested, Ribbonism allowed traditionally disparate groups of Irish Catholics to band together "against the hereditary enemy, the Orangemen".[140] Indeed, numerous references in the press to the involvement of these societies in intra-Irish and, occasionally anti-English, disturbances were commonplace. Even when the reference was not direct, it can be observed in the way the Irish were organised during disturbances that there must have been some element of leadership. On the other hand, references in the press to Ribbonmen were often based on generalisation. Irish Catholics were seen as Irish Catholics but Irish Catholics involved in affrays, disorder, rioting etc. were automatically tagged with whatever particular society was receiving press attention at that time (Ribbonmen, Hibernians, Repealers, Fenians etc.). Nevertheless, Cooter's assertion that cells of secret societies were a fabrication of the press seems a little naïve given the abundance of both the public and clerical attention these groups received.[141]

Perhaps the most serious incidence of Orange-Green rioting in the region, involving English Orangemen and Irish Catholics, occurred in Felling in 1856.[142] There was certainly nothing exceptional about the year in which the riot took place; indeed, it was during a period of relative quietude in Anglo-Irish and Protestant-Catholic relations. This suggests the existence of a local sectarian culture, apparent by the historic lack of cordiality in Anglo-Irish relations in the area that was not necessarily dictated by the national scene. Tension had clearly been growing between the local English and Irish since the Famine years. Workplace animosity had boiled over in 1846 when the English and Irish employees of Messrs Lee and Allen's chemical factories came to blows over a wage dispute.[143]

---

[139] This has been noted amongst Ribbon groups in Lancashire. Ibid, p. 181.

[140] J. Belchem, 'The Liverpool-Irish Enclave', *The Great Famine and Beyond: Irish Migrants in Britain in the Nineteenth and Twentieth Centuries*, ed. by D. M. MacRaild (Dublin: Irish Academic Press, 2000), p. 138.

[141] Cooter, *Paddy*, p. 34.

[142] There are various narrative accounts of this riot, see Neal, *English-Irish Conflict*, pp. 16-17; Godfrey Duffy, 'Sectarian Conflict in Felling', *The Journal of the Northumberland and Durham Family History Society* (Summer 2002), pp. 48-50; and MacRaild, *Faith, Fraternity and Fighting*, p. 174. Duffy's account also includes a social profile of the Irish Catholics involved.

[143] *Durham Chronicle*, 12 June 1846.

Fighting was resumed again in July 1853 when a pleasure cruise along the Felling Shore ended in a drunken riot between English and Irishmen in which one man was nearly drowned.[144] Moreover, there is evidence of a growing culture of sectarian tension in the immediate neighbourhood of Newcastle. On St Patrick's Day in 1854, local Orangemen decided they were not to be outdone by the usual parade of Hibernians marching through the streets of the town and produced a counter meeting in the Nelson Street Reading Room.[145] The riot on the 12 July 1856, therefore, must be seen in the context of a wider culture of Anglo-Irish hostility in the area.

The Felling riot of July 1856 began after two local Orange societies, one from the house of T. Dixon, proprietor of the Black Swan pub in Clayton Street, Newcastle, and the other from Mr. Lawrence's Wheat Sheaf Inn in Gateshead, formed a joint procession with the intention of marching to Felling on Saturday 12 July. The procession, consisting of only fifty people, clashed with a large group of Irish Catholics, referred to by the press as "Ribbonmen", some of whom were brandishing guns and numbering between 200 and 400, just outside the village of Felling. The Catholics clearly outnumbered the Orangemen and many of the latter were severely wounded—two having to be removed to Newcastle Infirmary with one man receiving a shot in the thigh, while the other had "five or six shots in different parts of the body, and also had his teeth knocked out".[146] The Orange fraternity beat a hasty retreat to Gateshead, eventually outrunning the Catholic contingent a quarter of a mile down the road. For the rest of the day, great crowds thronged the streets of both Gateshead and Felling where some shops closed in the anticipation of further trouble, although peace was restored by the evening.

In the aftermath of this riot, the Ribbonmen, and secret societies involving the Irish Catholics generally faced a stern rebuke from their Church. Attempts to suppress secret societies were one way of ensuring that tribal loyalties did not degenerate into disorder. According to Mary Hickman, the Catholic Church attempted to restrict the political involvement of Irish migrants in an attempt to "render the Irish more culturally acceptable to the indigenous population".[147] They were, however, frowned upon by the Church as the cause of sectarian and ethnic

---

[144] *Gateshead Observer*, 23 July 1853.

[145] T. McDermott, 'The Irish Workers on Tyneside', *Essays on Tyneside Labour History*, ed. by N. McCord (Newcastle-upon-Tyne: Newcastle-upon-Tyne Polytechnic, 1977), p. 168.

[146] *Newcastle Guardian*, 19 July 1856.

[147] Hickman, *Religion, Class and Identity*, p. 120.

bitterness at the popular level. For the Catholic Church in particular, the threat from secret societies was very real and numerous attempts were made to suppress them. The first Bishop of Hexham, William Hogarth, had an intense dislike of secret societies long before the Felling Riot. As early as April 1852, he had lamented the existence of these groups in his diocese:

> "We know that many of the worst crimes which disgrace human nature have been the offering of SECRET SOCIETIES, to which many misguided men have associated themselves as members, and to which they obstinately adhere, in spite of every effort of their pastors to withdraw them from such wicked combinations".[148]

However, it was the Orange-Green riot at Felling that persuaded Bishop Hogarth and the local clergy to launch a personal crusade against the societies. This problem became all the more immediate as the threat of violence on St Patrick's Day the following year increased in reaction to the news that Irish Catholics were to hold their annual parade through the streets of Newcastle and Gateshead. It was feared that there would be an Orange reprisal after the previous year's fracas on 12 July. The Mayor of both towns, perhaps in consultation with the local clergy, gave notice to the effect that the processions were to be prohibited.[149] Although these notices were respected and the day passed off peacefully, the Catholic bishop and his clergy did not rest on their laurels.[150] The following month Hogarth drew up a declaration for all members of secret societies to sign before they were able to take the sacraments.[151] In February 1858, he complained in a pastoral letter that the "Hibernian Society is too widely spread among the industrious poor of our Diocese".[152] In the same year, a street fight involving Ribbonmen in Sunderland culminated in a major interrogation of supposed Ribbon members by the bishop's secretary.[153]

---

[148] *Gateshead Observer*, 16 April 1852.

[149] *Newcastle Guardian*, 21 March 1857.

[150] Joan Allen has noted that St. Patrick's Day in the North East "generally proceeded without incident" owing to the role of the local Catholic clergy, Allen, "'High Days and Holy Days'", p. 143.

[151] RCHNDA, 'Declaration to be Made by the Members of the Hibernian and Other Secret Societies Before They Are Admitted to the Sacraments', August 1856, RCD 1/15.

[152] RCHNDA, William Hogarth, Pastoral Letter, 9 February 1858, RCD 1/14.

[153] This incident has been described in D.M. MacRaild, "'Abandon Hibernicisation": Priests, Ribbonmen and an Irish street fight in the north-east of England in 1858', *Historical Research*, 76.194 (1993), pp. 557-73.

By the end of the decade, there were signs that this campaign was working. In February 1859, the Bishop was confidently able to state that there had been a "gradual decrease . . . of unlawful and secret societies effected . . . by the zeal and preserving energies of our Clergy".[154] Many were becoming fearful of declaring themselves a member of these societies. Walter Raske, a landlord of a notorious "Ribbon" public house renounced his membership to the Ribbon Society in February, banning meetings from taking place there.[155] Furthermore, the muted response of the Irish to the Baron de Camin's visit in July of that year is evidence of a lack of an organisational structure compared with the violence connected with the "No Popery" lecturers of the late-1860s. This suggests that the local secret societies were in disarray in this period and that the Catholic Church, at least in the short-term, had been successful in stamping out this threat.

Outside of the major urban areas of Newcastle and Gateshead, however, the reality was far different. The Felling riot was by far the most serious Orange-Green affray but it was not the only example. Throughout the 1850s and first half of the 1860s, Orangeism began to build up a head of steam, largely as a response to increasing English-Irish tensions in the industrial villages of County Durham. A quick glance at the newspapers during this period reveals that Anglo-Irish tensions in the pit villages and surrounding ironworks were far from harmonious. The large-scale riots in Consett (1847) and Blackhill (1858) are well-documented but there were others on a smaller scale: Witton Park (1850); Willington (1854); Seaton Colliery (1855); Coundon (1861); Spennymoor (1861, 1862); and Brandon Colliery (1865)[156] among others. Most of the newspapers commented on the regularity of English-Irish disturbances in the respective villages. Indeed, the *Durham Chronicle* was acutely aware of the general situation in its report of the first Spennymoor riot in October 1861:

> "In nearly all the pit districts, where any considerable number of Irish are employed there are perpetual feuds between the Hibernians and the English, and fights and brutal outrages are of constant occurrence, when either one party or other are inflamed with drink".

---

[154] Pastoral Letter, 23 February 1859.

[155] TWAS, 'Church Notice Book of St. Andrew's, Newcastle, 1852-59', 27 February 1859.

[156] *Durham Advertiser*, 19 November 1847, 4 October 1850, 29 December 1854, 15 December 1865; *Durham Chronicle*, 16 February 1855, 25 October and 15 November 1861, and 23 May 1862.

This was not simply an exaggerated comment designed to encourage anti-Hibernian opinion, as the paper was notorious for its relatively fair treatment of the Irish. Indeed, the report argued that, in all cases, "both parties are equally to blame, and ignorance and drink are at the bottom of all these disturbances".[157]

At the heart of these communal riots, there can be no doubt that workplace tensions were their main cause but, in some instances at least, it is quite clear that the Orange Order could sometimes be used by English and Irish Protestants as a vehicle to express their difference from their Irish Catholic adversaries. In the Willington disturbances, the Orange Order played a relatively key part as the victims. When a group of Irish Catholics attacked a number of Orangemen in a pub in Willington on Christmas Eve 1854, the English came to their aid in the subsequent riot which followed.[158] Similarly it is also clear that English-Irish rioting often had the result of helping to form local sectarian societies. Thus in the aftermath of the Blackhill riot, the *Durham Chronicle* noted that "several affiliated societies, connected with the secret societies of the Orangemen and Ribbonmen in Ireland, have been established in Shotley Bridge" and, although it never actually occurred, it was anticipated that a serious sectarian riot was about to take place in the village.[159]

Outside the Durham industrial villages, Orangeism was strongest in the shipbuilding towns on the banks of the Tyne, growing in prominence throughout the 1860s.[160] In part, this increase can be explained by patterns of migration from Ireland including a substantial number of Irish Protestants from Ulster. At a meeting of Orangemen in North Shields in April 1865, the district master Mr. Hopper noted with some satisfaction that the association in North and South Shields had increased markedly since its formation in 1859. In that year, only one lodge existed with 5 members; by 1865, however, this had increased to five lodges with over 800 members.[161] The national trend was a rapid rise in Orange lodges

---

[157] *Durham Chronicle*, 25 October 1861.

[158] *Durham Advertiser*, 29 December 1854.

[159] *Durham Chronicle*, 16 July 1858.

[160] This resurgence appears to have been evident in other localities. MacRaild has noted that Cumbrian Orangeism experienced a revival in the 1860s owing to similar circumstances. D.M. MacRaild, "'The Bunkum of Ulsteria": the Orange Marching Tradition in Late Victorian Cumbria', *The Irish Parading Tradition: Following the Drum*, ed. by T. G. Fraser (Basingstoke: Macmillan, 2000), p. 46.

[161] *Shields Daily News*, 19 April 1865. It is worth noting that a number of Protestant ministers spoke at this meeting, suggesting a strong level of clerical

during the 1860s[162] and North and South Shields were fast becoming the very heartlands of Orange influence in the region as the decade progressed. In 1868, Orangemen celebrated the "Twelfth" by parading through both towns. Shortly after William Murphy's visit in March 1869, a grand demonstration was held in the town, comprising of between 30 and 40 lodges from the surrounding area, including South Shields, Jarrow, Gateshead as well as North Shields.[163] The North Shields Orangemen were again a visible presence in the town a few months later, parading through the streets on 12 July.

The leaders of the local lodges hoped to promote what they considered to be the essential ethos of Orangeism: "peace on earth and goodwill to all men".[164] The reality on the streets was far different, however. Although the 12 July parades passed off peacefully, the underlying tensions between Orangemen and Irish Catholic groups were plain to see during the late 1860s as the tenor of the times helped to initiate a wave of Orange-Green disturbances in a number of Tyneside towns. It must be stressed that these disturbances were primarily intra-Irish affrays, rather than English-Irish, but they do illustrate how the heightened sense of tension allowed the importation of anti-Catholicism and sectarian violence into the English small-town setting. A number of isolated incidents took place in the towns of North and South Shields associated with the two factions of Irishmen. After a fracas in North Shields between a party of Irishmen in September 1867, the *Durham Chronicle* noted that fights amongst "the sons of Erin are now of frequent occurrence in Shields".[165] Two years later, a Protestant Irishman named John Bush was stabbed by the Irish Catholic Joseph Sexton.[166] In South Shields, a number of men in Orange sashes were attacked in the streets on the evening of the 12 July 1868.[167] In July 1870, an Irish Protestant, John Davidson, was attacked in the street for admitting he was an Orangeman to a group of Irish Catholics.[168]

---

support which is in stark contrast to the Catholic Church's views on secret societies among their brethren.

[162] O'Day, 'Varieties of Anti-Irish Behaviour', p. 33.

[163] *Shields Daily Telegraph,* 30 March 1869. It is possible that Murphy may have contributed to an even greater upsurge in Orange support, as this occurred in Cumbria after 1871. MacRaild has noted crowds of 5000-6000 watched an Orange parade in Askam in 1877. MacRaild, "'Bunkum of Ulsteria'", pp. 47-8.

[164] *Shields Daily News*, 19 April 1865.

[165] *Durham Advertiser*, 20 September 1867.

[166] *Sunderland News*, 19 October 1869.

[167] *Durham Advertiser*, 17 July 1868.

[168] *Shields Gazette*, 3 July 1870.

During the 1860s, by far the most troubled areas in this sense were the neighbouring towns of Jarrow and Hebburn. Both towns were little more than hamlets in the 1840s, but industrial expansion had increased their population substantially. This increase was in no small part due to Irish immigrants who comprised one in three of Jarrow's inhabitants by 1872.[169] That not all these incoming Irish were Catholics can best be observed by the increase in sectarian tension throughout the 1860s. Assaults between different Irish groups were becoming more and more frequent as the decade progressed. The *Shields Gazette* noted as early as January 1864 that "the number of cases of assaults at Jarrow has been very large recently" among the Irish portion of the population.[170] In May 1866, the *Newcastle Guardian* reported on "one of those disgraceful 'Irish rows'" which so frequently disturb the peace of Jarrow and its neighbourhood", that resulted in an Irishman inflicting a serious facial injury to a woman with a poker. In Hebburn, in the same month, a man was stabbed in the thigh after an argument in a pub.[171] Two months later, the same paper reported on a series of separate "outrages" over one weekend in Jarrow. It is perhaps no coincidence that these "outrages" happened to coincide with the aftermath of the "Twelfth" celebrations.[172]

Indeed, by the late 1860s, these "rows" were evidently becoming more and more sectarian in character as groups became more partisan in the face of the Fenian threat. The Catholic Church may have claimed victory in its battle against Ribbonism but, by the late 1860s, many Irish Catholics were joining the far more militant Fenian Brotherhood. The official stance of the Church on Fenianism mirrored its opinion of all Irish secret societies with the famously outspoken Cardinal Cullen proclaiming it as the biggest threat to "the rights and liberties of the Catholic Church in Ireland".[173] Nor were the Catholic clergy slow to act in the localities where the North East was allegedly "honeycombed with Fenians". As early as November 1865, the Bishop of Hexham issued a pastoral letter, ordering the clergy to treat "the Fenian society as they would any other organisation" by denying communion to its members.[174] Other more passive methods were attempted. In January 1866, the Sunderland Irish Catholic Association was organised to try to improve the minds of "the humbler classes of Roman

---

[169] 'Irish in England', *Nation*, Letter 15, 19 October 1872, p. 662.

[170] *Shields* Gazette, 23 January 1864.

[171] *Newcastle Guardian*, 26 May 1866.

[172] *Newcastle Guardian,* 21 July 1866.

[173] Quoted in J. Newsinger, *Fenianism in Mid-Victorian Britain* (London: Pluto Press, 1994), p. 38.

[174] *Shields Gazette*, 13 November 1865.

Catholics" with the added intention of diverting them from the Fenian society.[175]

The response of the Church and, indeed, the local press to the alleged activities of the supposed Fenians only appeared to make the Fenians and the Irish Catholics in general more defensive as faction fights began to dominate the local headlines. The *Newcastle Weekly Chronicle*, commenting on an Irish faction fight in Jarrow, in which an Irishman was "almost kicked to death", saw these party affrays as deplorable:

> "Seldom does a week pass without some row that would disgrace a pack of Siberian wolves in a polar famine. Fenians and Orangemen are all very well in their way but they should keep out of each others' way and everybody else's way. If they are willing to die on the altar of their country or faith, by all means let them take the Japanese method of 'happy dispatch', and let the sacrifice be performed privately and not in decent houses of resort and to the disgust of the respectable working man".[176]

In Hebburn, the situation was even less peaceful. In May 1869, an Irish Catholic, Stephen Sweeney, was accused of assaulting an Irish Protestant, William Patterson. Sweeney had allegedly knocked Patterson to the ground, claiming that he would "kick his Orange soul out of him" before repeatedly kicking him in the head. Sweeney, in contrast, argued that it was Patterson who was the main perpetrator, with the former claiming that the latter had provoked him by shouting that he would knock "seven Popes out of him". It was also said by Sweeney that Patterson was drunk and had been involved in several rows throughout the day. The result was that the Irish Catholic received one month's hard labour.[177] Another incident two months later centred on the Orange Day celebrations. On a Sunday morning in July, a crowd of between 400 and 500 people watched a prize fight between two Irishwomen "over their respective religions". One was wearing an orange apron and the other a green apron. A row among the men in the afternoon was prevented by Superintendent Waugh, who managed to confiscate an 18-inch Morgan Rattler. These men were then forced to pay £5 in sureties that their wives would not breach the peace for two months.[178]

The following year, the violence had not abated. In June, a group of Jarrow Irishmen fired a number of shots into a beer house at Bill Quay,

---

[175] *Durham Chronicle*, 5 January 1866.
[176] *Newcastle Weekly Chronicle*, 19 June 1869.
[177] *Newcastle Weekly Chronicle*, 15 May 1869.
[178] *Newcastle Weekly Chronicle*, 24 July 1869.

near Hebburn, with the intention of "engaging in a party fight" with other Irishmen. A riot ensued and the local police were forced to despatch a telegram to Gateshead to call for more support. When this support did arrive the riot was eventually quelled and surprisingly no-one was taken into custody.[179] The 12 July celebrations were again marred by isolated assaults and the gossip column of the *Chronicle* found itself commenting again on the Irish relationship to violence:

> "The warm weather appears to have a remarkably exhilarating effect on Celtic blood. As a rule, it is thin, and apt to chase away through the veins in a helter-skelter fashion; but when the thermometer stands above seventy in the shade, Paddy cannot prevent his blood from boiling . . . I suppose I must congratulate them on the magnificent rows which occasionally enliven the weary routine of life down the river".[180]

Elsewhere in the region, Orange-Green confrontation was rare but still prone to the occasional outburst. Further west along the river in the normally peaceful village of Ryton, a group of Irishmen from Allhusen's factory began fighting amongst themselves on what was supposed to be a day's holiday in the Willows in July 1868. The two parties made "Protestant and Catholic rallying cries, and a thorough and most determined riot took place". The police eventually managed to control the affray but not without serious injuries. One policeman was attacked, having "the flesh almost entirely removed from his cheek".[181] In the south of the region, both Stockton and Darlington saw riots involving Protestant and Catholic Irishmen.[182] The pit villages too saw an increase in sectarian violence, particularly in the vicinity of Consett, where the "Twelfth" became a source of much consternation in the late 1860s and early 1870s.[183]

This chapter has highlighted the extent to which religious violence in the region appeared little different from elsewhere, with anti-Catholicism in particular playing a primary role in fomenting English-Irish and intra-Irish tension. This was largely due to the propensity of the local Irish Catholic community to defend their faith at all costs and the attempts to institutionalise religious differences into structured organisations. Religious violence was, however, sporadic and prone to local circumstances for its

---

[179] *Newcastle Weekly Chronicle*, 18 June 1870.
[180] *Newcastle Weekly Chronicle*, 16 July 1870. It is noteworthy that, in this instance, both Protestant and Catholic Irishmen are implicated in this stereotype of 'Paddy'.
[181] *Shields Gazette*, 27 July 1868.
[182] *Newcastle Weekly Chronicle*, 2 April 1870; 11 December 1869.
[183] *Neal, English-Irish Conflict*, p. 47.

ignition, with hostility never matching the scale of either Liverpool or Glasgow. Nevertheless sectarian relations in the North East were certainly far from the celebrated *bonhomie* that some historians suggest.[184] How far religion as a source of consternation in violent affrays actually mattered after 1870, however, is debatable. In recent years there has been a tendency to reject the notion that sectarian violence declined in the years after 1870[185], but it cannot be denied that, at least in its relation to religion, English-Irish and intra-Irish disturbances became ostensibly rarer. The Home Rule crisis diverted local attention away from religious differences to a more secular focus on nationalist aspirations and so any further Orange-Green affrays in the 1870s and 1880s must be seen within this context.

---

[184] Most notably Cooter, *Paddy*.
[185] See MacRaild, *Irish Migrants*, pp. 178-84.

CONCLUSION

This study has shown that the cultures of anti-Catholicism in the North East of England mirrored many of the prejudicial excesses inherent in other areas of the country. It therefore questions the received notion of an exceptionally tolerant attitude towards the Catholic religion, and Irish Catholics in particular, which has underpinned the regional identity of North East England. It would be incorrect, however, to posit a definitive anti-Catholic culture in the North East, as different areas influenced, and were influenced by, different forms of anti-Catholicism.

The heightened religious tension during the mid-nineteenth century provided an impetus for anti-Catholic ideological expression which was prevalent throughout the region. All the major tenets of anti-Catholic ideology were present, conforming to traditional and stereotypical perceptions of Catholic theology that were often moulded by key elements of Victorian philosophy. There was no single, unifying anti-Catholicism, however, as anti-Catholic ideology was composed of a number of disparate strands that could, on occasion, conflict with each other.

The political culture of the North East did not, as has previously been suggested, act as a barrier to the expression of anti-Catholic feeling. Liberalism was the dominant ideology in the region but it was not exclusively so. This study has revealed the extent to which the pockets of Conservative support for the anti-Maynooth campaign and the campaign against Irish disestablishment, were very influential and could often garner impressive support. Moreover, Liberalism and anti-Catholicism were not mutually exclusive with many Liberal political campaigns playing on anti-Catholic ideology, including the campaign for Italian independence and the anti-convent movement. Nor did the lack of support for the Church of England in the region stifle anti-Catholic campaigning and organisation. The strongly politicised Dissenting communities could be as equally opposed to the Catholic religion as their Anglican adversaries with the largest anti-Catholic organisation in the North East, the Protestant Alliance, largely staffed and supported by Nonconformists. The Papal Aggression agitation was particularly evident in the North East because it encouraged the active co-operation of all Protestant denominations to combat the twin threats of Popery and Puseyism. These chapters also highlight the role of the Catholic communities in defending the faith at the political level. Catholics saw little distinction between these events and were equally opposed to every campaign.

Regional cultures of anti-Catholicism should not be viewed simply as a reaction to national political events but also in the way in which they responded to the perceived threat posed by the growth of Catholic communities at the local level. The Roman Catholic Relief Acts had given Catholics the legal right to practise their religion and local Catholics were determined to exercise this. Opposition to Catholic worship was rare, although not uncommon and, in many places in the North East of England, Catholics were generally tolerated if not accepted. Some groups, however, faced this threat head on. Protestant missionaries embraced the anti-Catholic tenor of the times and took their fight to the Irish Catholic poor in the battle to win souls. Those Catholics who were forced to enter the workhouse did not find a spirit of toleration among the Boards of Guardians where anti-Catholicism was almost institutionalised.

This book has also shown that the role of sectarian violence amongst both the English and Irish communities, and within Irish communities, in the villages, towns, and cities of North East England, has been greatly underestimated by historians. However, small and large-scale violence was more or less dependent not only on time and place, but also the nature of Irish settlements and their attachment to their religion. The different varieties of anti-Catholicism also generated their own forms of religious violence in different places. These included Orange-Green disturbances on the banks of the Tyne or popular anti-Catholic violence associated with No Popery demagogues evident more in the south of the region. Some areas remained clear of any noticeable culture of violence associated with anti-Catholicism, although this did not mean that serious disturbances were not possible, only that the conditions were not present to stimulate it.

It was not the intention of this study to suggest that the North East of England experienced anti-Catholic cultures on a comparable *scale* to Liverpool and Glasgow. Indeed, this study has challenged the traditionally held viewpoint that anti-Catholicism is only worth studying in major areas with exceptional circumstances. Viewed broadly, anti-Catholicism was more or less prevalent throughout the region, with a variety of different anti-Catholic cultures existing in different areas that were as equally offensive to local Catholic communities. How far these cultures continued to matter after 1870, however, is a question that can only be answered by further research.

BIBLIOGRAPHY

Primary Sources

Tracts and Pamphlets

Anon., *Protestant Aggression. Remarks on the Bishop of Durham's Letter to the Archdeacon of Lindisfarne by a Catholic Clergyman Resident within the Diocese of Durham* (Newcastle: G.B. Richardson, 1851)

[B.C.]., *The Confessional Unmasked Showing the Depravity of the Priesthood, Questions Put to Females in Confession, Perjury and Stealing Commanded and Encouraged etc. Being Extracts from the Theological Works of Saint Alphonso M. De. Liguori, Peter Dens, Bailly, Delahogue, and Cabassutius* (London: Johnston, 1851)

Blunt, J.H., *The Real Presence: A Sermon by John Henry Blunt, Curate of Tynemouth, in the Diocese of Durham* (Durham: Andrews, 1853)

Central Anti-Maynooth Committee, *Proceedings of the Anti-Maynooth Conference* (London: Blackburn and Pardon, 1845)

Cooke, W., *The Inspiration and Divine Authority of the Holy Scriptures* (London: John Bakewell, 1846)

Coxe, R.C., *Thoughts on Important Church Subjects, Seven Lectures* (Newcastle: St. Nicholas, 1851)

Crozer, J., *A Glimpse of all the Denominations of the Priesthood...* (Newcastle: W.B. Leighton, 1845)

Dunn, Samuel, *An Exposure of the Mummeries, Absurdities and Idolatries of Popery* (Newcastle: Blackwell & Co., 1846)

Fox, G.T., *The Bible the Sole Rule of Faith: A Sermon Preached in St. Hilda's Church, South Shields on Sunday Morning, December 8th 1850* (Durham: Andrews, 1850)

—. *A Few Words about Popery and Tractarianism: A Sermon Preached in Trinity Church, South Shields on Sunday Evening, December 8th 1850* (Durham: Andrews, 1850)

—. *Priestly Celibacy Exposed: A Lecture, Delivered in the Borough Hall, Stockton-upon-Tees. . .* (Stockton-on-Tees: Jennett & Co., 1854)

—. 'The Doctrines of the Bible Contrasted With Those of Rome', *Sermons Preached in St. Nicholas Church, Durham* (London: James Nisbett & Co., 1866)

Grey, John, *Letter to the Churchwardens and Other Parishioners of Houghton-Le-Spring*, (Durham: R. Robinson, 1853)

Harper, S., *Do Not Be Duped! A Letter of Counsel to the Labouring Classes on the No Popery Movement by the Writer of 'A Voice from the North'* (Newcastle: Kaye, 1850)

Harries, H., *'The Holy Catholic Church, Out of Which None can be Saved'. A Sermon Preached at Trinity Church, Darlington, on Sunday September 19, 1852* (Darlington: Harrison Penney, 1852)

Lamb, A.H., *Popery Opposed to the Laws of Nature and Revelation* (London: [n. pub.] 1854)

Maltby, E., *'Salutary Cautions Against the Errors Contained in the Oxford Tracts': A Charge to His Clergy, Delivered at St Nicholas' Church, Newcastle-upon-Tyne on Mon. August 9th 1841, by the Lord Bishop of Durham* (Newcastle: Blackwell & Co, 1841)

Newcastle Chronicle, *Inquiry into the Condition of the Poor of Newcastle-upon-Tyne* (Newcastle: M & M.W. Lambert, 1850)

Newcastle Journal, *Blasphemy, Idolatry and Superstition of the Roman Catholic Church* (Newcastle: Bell, 1847)

Newcastle Town Missionary and Scripture Readers Society, *Report of the Town Missionary and Scripture Readers Society* (Newcastle: [n. pub.] 1848)

Newcastle Town Missionary and Scripture Readers Society, *Fifteenth Annual Report of the Town Missionary and Scripture Readers Society* (Newcastle: [n. pub.] 1861)

Newcastle Town Missionary and Scripture Readers Society, *Quarterly Record of the Newcastle-upon-Tyne Town Mission* (Newcastle: [n/ pub.] 1857)

Newcastle Town Missionary and Scripture Readers Society, *Sixteenth Report of the Town Missionary and Scripture Readers Society* (Newcastle: [n. pub.] 1862)

[Ord, B.T.] *The Beginning of the End, or the Destruction of Babylon and the Fall of the Beast* (Hartlepool: Hartlepool Free Press, 1864)

—. *A blue book: or, an exposition of the manner in which the priesthood plunder and devour their flocks* (Hartlepool: Hartlepool Free Press, 1865)

Plummer, Matthew, *Letter to the Lord Bishop of Durham In Reference to the Late Proceedings of the Parish of Heworth* (Newcastle: Robert Robinson, 1852)

Pottinger, T., *The Bible is the Glory of Our Land: The Substance of a Sermon Delivered in Tulhill Stairs Chapel, Newcastle on November 15th 1849* (Newcastle: [n. pub.] 1849)

Brotherhood of St. Vincent de Paul, *Report of the Newcastle and Gateshead-on-Tyne Conference of the Brotherhood of St. Vincent de Paul for the Years 1850-51* (Newcastle: [n. pub.] 1852)

Ronge, J., *Autobiography of Johannes Ronge* (Newcastle: [n. pub.] 1850)

Protestant Alliance, *Second Annual Report of the Protestant Alliance* (London [n. pub.] 1853)

Street, James, C., *The Night-Side of Newcastle...A Lecture Delivered in the Church of Divine Unity* (Newcastle: Joseph Barlow, 1865)

Official Publications

'Return of the Number of Addresses which have been presented to Her Majesty on the Subject of the Recent Measures taken by the Pope for the Establishment of a Roman Catholic Hierarchy in this Country', *Parliamentary Papers*, 1851, 59 (84), pp. 649-739

Newspapers and Journals

Political/religious stance where known:

British Protestant (Anglican Evangelical/Anti-Catholic)
Bulwark (Scottish Anti-Catholic)
Catholic Standard (Catholic)
Darlington and Stockton Times (Liberal/Dissenting)
Durham Advertiser (Conservative/High Church Anglican)
Durham Chronicle (Liberal/Dissenting)
Hartlepool Free Press (Conservative/Anglican Evangelical)
Newcastle Courant (Conservative/Anglican)
Newcastle Journal (Conservative/High Church Anglican)
Newcastle Chronicle (Liberal/Dissenting)
Newcastle Guardian (Liberal/Dissenting/Evangelical)
Shields Gazette (Liberal/Anglican)
Sunderland Herald (Liberal/Dissenting)
Sunderland News (Liberal/Dissenting?)
South Durham and Cleveland Mercury (Liberal/Dissenting)
Tablet (Catholic/Ultramontane)

Archives and Manuscripts

TYNE AND WEAR ARCHIVES SERVICE
Diary of Thomas Davidson, 1845-6, DX55/1/2-3
Gateshead Board of Guardians Letter Book, 1837-91, T371
Gateshead Board of Guardians Minute Books, 1836-90, T371
Newcastle Board of Guardians Minute Books, 1836-1930, PU.NC
Newcastle United Presbytery, Minute Book, 1847-55, PB.NCU/1/3
Newcastle Watch Committee Minute Book, 1836-51, MD.NC/274/1
Sunderland Board of Guardians Minute Books, 1836-1930, PU.SU
St Andrews Roman Catholic Church, Church Notice Book, 1852-59,
    C.NC76/8/1

DURHAM COUNTY RECORD OFFICE
Letter from Mary Raine (Mrs William Raine) to Crozier Surtees Raine, 12
    December 1850, D/X 332/171
Letter from G.T. Fox to [unknown], 17 March 1855, , D/X 487/10/16
Salvin Family of Croxdale, Correspondence (Part 1), D/SA/C220

DURHAM UNIVERSITY LIBRARY SPECIAL COLLECTIONS
Letter from General Charles Grey to Caroline Grey, 4 March 1847,
    GRE/D/V/2/1-15
Letter from Ralph Turnbull to Earl Grey, 8 April 1869. GRE/B/45/1
Letter from the Rev. Temple Chevallier to the Rev. George Corrie, 11
    May 1850, Add. MSS.837/109

TEESSIDE ARCHIVES
Watch Committee Letter Book, 1851-80, DC/H 2/11

ROMAN CATHOLIC HEXHAM AND NEWCASTLE DIOCESAN
    ARCHIVES
Address of the Clergy and Laity of the Northern District, 1 March 1849,
    RCD 1/11/28
Address to the Holy Father from Catholics in Newcastle and Gateshead,
    28 January 1860, RCD 1/16
Catholic Poor Law Schools Circular, 23 December, December 1868, 16
    November 1871, RCD, 1/17
Declaration of the Catholic Bishops of England, 1850, RCD 1/11/89
Petition Against the Convent Bill, RCD 1/12
William Betham, *Appeal for the funding of a new church in Gateshead*,
    October 1850, RCD 1/11/86

William Hogarth, *Declaration to be Made by the Members of the Hibernian and Other Secret Societies Before They Are Admitted to the Sacraments*, August 1856, RCD 1/15
—. *Pastoral Letter*, 9 February 1858, RCD 1/14
—. *Lenten Pastoral*, February 1860, RCD 1/16
—. *Pastoral Letter*, 1 May 1860, RCD 1/16

USHAW COLLEGE LIBRARY
Wilkinson Papers, UC/P16
Casartelli Papers, UC/P4

Secondary Sources

Adams, Max, *The Prometheans: John Martin and the Generation that Stole the Future* (London: Quercus, 2010).
Addison, W.G., *Religious Equality in Modern England* (London: SPCK, 1944).
Allen, Joan, *Joseph Cowen and Popular Radicalism on Tyneside* (Monmouth: Merlin Press, 2007).
—. "'High Days and Holy Days' St. Patrick's Day in the North East of England, c.1850-1900", *Faith of our Fathers: Popular Culture and Belief in Post Reformation England, Ireland and Wales*, ed. by Joan Allen and Richard C. Allen (Newcastle: Cambridge Scholars, 2009), pp. 137-56.
Allen, Louis, 'Tract 90 and Durham University', *Notes and Queries*, 212 (1967), pp. 43-7.
Allport, G.W., *The Nature of Prejudice* (Cambridge, Massachusetts: The Beacon Press, 1954).
Altholz, J.L., *The Liberal Catholic Movement in England: The Rambler and its Contributors, 1848-1864* (London: The Ditchling Press, 1962).
—. Altholz, J.L., 'The Political Behaviour of the English Catholics, 1850-67'. *Journal of British Studies*, 4.1 (1964), pp. 89-103.
Arnstein, Walter L., 'The Murphy Riots: A Victorian Dilemma', *Victorian Studies*, 19.1 (1975), pp. 51-73.
Arnstein, Walter L., *Protestant Versus Catholic in Mid-Victorian England: Mr. Newdegate and the Nuns* (Columbia: University of Missouri Press, 1982).
Aspinwall, B., 'Rev. Alessandro Gavazzi and Scottish Identity: A Chapter in Nineteenth Century Anti-Catholicism', *Recusant History*, 28.1 (2006), pp. 129-52.

Atkin, Nicholas and Tallet, Frank (eds), *Priests, Prelates and People: A History of European Catholicism since 1750* (London: I.B. Taurus, 2003).

Barker, R.G., 'Houghton-le-Spring Poor Law Union, 1837-1930' (unpublished master's thesis, Newcastle University, 1974).

Battersby, W.J., 'Educational Work of the Religious Orders of Women: 1850-1950', *The English Catholics 1850-1950*, ed. by George A. Beck (London: Burns Oates, 1950), pp. 337-64.

Beales, D.E.D., 'Garibaldi in England: The Politics of Italian Enthusiasm', *Society and Politics in the Age of the Risorgimento. Essays in Honour of Denis Mack Smith*, ed. by J. Davis and P. Ginsborg (Cambridge: Cambridge University Press, 1991), pp. 184-216.

Bebbington, David W., *The Nonconformist Conscience: Chapel and Politics, 1870-1914* (London: George Allen and Unwin, 1982).

—. *Evangelicalism in Modern Britain: A History from the 1730s to the 1980s* (Cambridge: Cambridge University Press, 1989).

—. 'The Life of Baptist Noel', *Baptist Quarterly*, 24 (1972), pp. 390-401.

Belchem, J., 'The Liverpool-Irish Enclave', *The Great Famine and Beyond: Irish Migrants in Britain in the Nineteenth and Twentieth Centuries*, ed. by D. M. MacRaild (Dublin: Irish Academic Press, 2000), pp. 128-46.

Bell, P.M.H., *Disestablishment in Ireland and Wales* (London: SPCK, 1969).

Bellenger, Dom Aidan, 'France and England: The English Female Religious from Reformation to World War' in *Catholicism in Britain and France since 1789*, ed. by Nicholas Atkin and Frank Tallett (London: The Hambledon Press, 1996), pp. 3-11.

Bentley, J. *Ritualism and Politics in Victorian Britain* (Oxford: Oxford University Press, 1978).

Best, G.F.A., 'Evangelicalism and the Victorians', *The Victorian Crisis of Faith*, ed. by A. Symondson (London: SPCK, 1967), pp. 37-56.

—. 'Popular Protestantism in Victorian Britain' *Ideas and Institutions in Victorian Britain: Essays in Honour of George Kitson Clark*, ed. by R. Robson (London: Bell and Sons, 1967), pp. 115-42.

—. 'The Protestant Constitution and its Supporters, 1820-29', *Transactions of the Royal Historical Society*, 8 (1958), pp. 105-27.

—. 'The Religious Difficulties of National Education in England, 1800-70', *Cambridge Historical Journal*, 27 (1984), pp. 155-73.

Biagini, Eugenio F., *Liberty, Retrenchment and Reform: Popular Liberalism in the Age of Gladstone, 1860-1880* (Cambridge: Cambridge University Press, 1992).

Billington, Ray Allen, *The Protestant Crusade 1800-1860: A Study of the Origins of American Nativism* (Chicago: Quadrangle, 1964).

Binns, L.E., *The Evangelical Movement in the English Church* (London: Methuen and Co, 1932).

Bossy, John, *The English Catholic Community, 1570-1850* (London: Darton, Longman and Todd, 1975).

Bowen, Desmond, *The Idea of the Victorian Church: A Study of the Church of England, 1833-1889* (Montreal: McGill University Press, 1968).

—. *The Protestant Crusade in Ireland, 1800-70: A Study of Protestant-Catholic Relations Between the Act of Union and Disestablishment* (Dublin: Queen's University Press, 1978).

Bradley, Ian, *The Call to Seriousness: The Evangelical Impact on the Victorians* (London: Jonathan Cape, 1976).

—. *The Optimists. Themes and Personalities in Victorian Liberalism* (London: Faber and Faber, 1980).

Briggs A., *Victorian Cities* (London: Penguin, 1963).

Briggs, J.H.Y., *The English Baptists in the Nineteenth Century* (London: Baptist Historical Society, 1994).

Brown, K.D., *A Social History of the Nonconformist Ministry in England and Wales, 1800-1930* (Oxford: Clarendon Press, 1988).

Bruce, Garistord, *The Life and Letters of John Collingwood Bruce* (Edinburgh and London: William Blackwood, 1905).

Bruce, Steve, *No Pope of Rome: Militant Protestantism in Modern Scotland* (Edinburgh: Mainstream, 1985).

Burstein, M.E., 'Anti-Catholic Sermons in Victorian Britain', *A New History of the Sermon in the Nineteenth Century* ed. by R. H. Ellison (Boston: Brill Academic, 2010), pp. 233-67.

Busteed, M., 'Little Islands of Erin: Irish Settlement and Identity in Mid-Nineteenth-Century Manchester', *The Great Famine and Beyond: Irish Migrants in Britain in the Nineteenth and Twentieth Centuries*, ed. by D. M. MacRaild (Dublin: Irish Academic Press, 2000), pp. 94-127.

Butterfield, Herbert, *The Whig Interpretation of History* (London: G. Bell and Sons, 1931).

Cahill, G.A., 'Irish Catholicism and English Toryism', *Review of Politics*, 19 (1957), pp. 62-76.

—. 'The Protestant Association and the Anti-Maynooth Agitation of 1845', *Catholic Historical Review*, 43.3 (1957), pp. 273-308.

Callcott, M., 'The Challenge of Cholera: The Last Epidemic of Newcastle-upon-Tyne', *Northern History*, 10 (1984), pp. 167-84.

Carrick, J., *Evangelicals and the Oxford Movement* (Bridgend: Evangelical Press of Wales, 1984).

Casteras, S.P., 'Virgin Vows: The Early Victorian Portrayal of Nuns and Novices', *Religion in the Lives of English Women, 1760-1930*, ed. by Gail Malmgreen (Indianapolis: Indiana University Press, 1986), pp. 129-60.

Chadwick, Owen, *The Victorian Church*, 2 vols (Adam and Charles Black, 1971-2).

Chase, M., 'The Teesside Irish in the Nineteenth-Century', *The Irish in British Labour History*, ed. by John Belchem and Patrick Buckland (Liverpool: Liverpool University Press, 1993), pp. 47-59.

Clark, Kitson G., *The Making of Victorian England* (London: Methuen and Co, 1962).

—. *Churchmen and the Condition of England, 1832-1885* (London: Methuen and Co, 1973).

Clayes, G., 'Mazzini, Kossuth and British Radicalism 1848-1854', *Journal of British Studies*, 28.3 (1989), pp. 225-62.

Clifton, R., 'The Popular Fear of Catholics during the English Revolution', *Past and Present*, 52 (1971), pp. 168-87.

Coleman, B.I., *The Church of England in the Mid-Nineteenth Century: A Social Geography* (London: Historical Association, 1978).

Colley, L., *Britons: Forging the Nation 1707-1837* (London: Pimlico, 1994).

Conacher, J.B., 'The Politics of the "Papal Aggression" Crisis, 1850-51', *Canadian Catholic Historical Association Report*, 26 (1959), pp. 13-27.

Connolly, G., '"Little Brother Be At Peace": The Priest as Holy Man in the Nineteenth Century Ghetto', *Studies in Church History: The Churches and Healing*, ed. by W. J. Shiels (Oxford: Blackwell, 1982), pp. 191-205.

Connolly, Gerald, 'The Transubstantiation of Myth: Towards a New Popular History of Nineteenth-Century Catholicism in England', *Journal of Ecclesiastical History*, 35.1 (1984), pp. 78-104.

Cooter, R.J., *When Paddy Met Geordie: The Irish in County Durham and Northumberland 1840-80* (Sunderland: University of Sunderland Press, 2005).

—. 'Hibernians and Geordies in the Nineteenth Century', *Northern Catholic History*, 4 (1976), pp. 20-30.

—. 'Lady Londonderry and the Irish Catholics of Seaham Harbour: "No Popery" Out of Context'. *Recusant History*, 13.4 (1976), pp. 288-98.

Cowherd, Raymond C., *The Politics of English Dissent: The Religious Aspects of Liberal and Humanitarian Reform Movements from 1815 to 1848* (London: Epwith, 1956).

Cox, Jeffrey, 'The Missionary Movement', *Nineteenth Century English Religious Traditions: Retrospect and Prospect*, ed. by Denis G. Paz (London: Greenwood Press, 1996), pp. 197-220.

Crangle, L.P., 'The Roman Catholic Community in Sunderland from the 16th Century', *Antiquities of Sunderland*, 24 (1969), pp. 63-78.

Crompton, F., *Workhouse Children* (Stroud: Sutton Publishing Ltd, 1997)

Crowther, M.A., *The Workhouse System 1834-1939: The History of an English Social Institution* (London: Batsford Academic and Educational Ltd, 1981).

Cunningham, H., 'The Language of Patriotism', *History Workshop Journal*, 12 (1981), pp. 8-33.

Currer, B., 'Catholic Participation in the National System of Education, 1833-1860, in the North East', *Northern Catholic History*, 37 (1996), pp. 26-35.

Curtis, L.P., *Anglo-Saxons and Celts: A Study of Anti-Irish Prejudice in Victorian England* (Bridgeport: University of Bridgeport, 1968).

Davies, G.C.B., *Henry Phillpotts: Bishop of Exeter, 1778-1869* (London: SPCK, 1954).

Davies, Horton, *Worship and Theology in England*, IV, *From Newman to Martineau, 1850-1900* (Princeton: Princeton University Press, 1962).

Davies, John A., 'Garibaldi and England', *History Today*, 32.12 (1982), pp. 21-6.

Davis, G., *The Irish in Britain* (Dublin: Gill and Macmillan, 1991).

—. 'Little Irelands', *The Irish in Britain 1815-1939*, ed. by Roger Swift and Sheridan Gilley (London: Pinter, 1989), pp. 104-34.

Dickey, Brian, '"Going about and doing good": Evangelicals and Poverty c.1815-1870', *Evangelical Faith and Public Zeal: Evangelicals and Society in Britain 1780-1980*, ed. by John Wolffe (London: SPCK, 1995), pp. 38-59.

Dillow, James, *Memoirs of an Old Stager* (Newcastle: A. Reid, 1928).

Dodds, Glen Lynton, *A History of Sunderland* (Sunderland: Albion Press, 1995).

Doherty, S., 'English and Irish Catholics in Northumberland, 1745-1860' (unpublished doctoral thesis, Queen's University, Belfast, 1987).

Donovan, R.K., 'The Denominational Character of English Catholic Charitable Effort, 1800-1865', *Catholic Historical Review*, 42 (1976), pp. 200-23.

Drummond, A.L., 'Father Ignatius, 1837-1908'. *Church Quarterly Review*, 151.301 (1950), pp. 63-86.

Drury, Marjule Anne, 'Anti-Catholicism in Germany, Britain, and the United States: A Review and Critique of Recent Scholarship', *Church History*, 70.1 (2001), pp. 98-131.

Duffy, Godfrey, 'Sectarian Conflict in Felling', *Journal of the Northumberland and Durham Family History Society*, Summer (2002), pp. 48-50.

Durey, Michael, 'The Survival of an Irish Culture in Britain 1800-1845'. *Historical Studies,* 20 (1982), pp. 14-35.

Durkheim, E., *The Elementary Forms of the Religious Life* (London: George Allen and Unwin Ltd, 1976).

Edwards, T.C., 'Papal Aggression: 1851', *History Today*, 1.12 (1951), pp. 42-9.

Elbourn, Elizabeth, 'The Foundation of the Church Missionary Society: the Anglican Missionary Impulse' *The Church of England c. 1689-1833: From Toleration to Tractarianism*, ed. by John Walsh, Colin Haydon and Stephen Taylor (Cambridge: Cambridge University Press, 1995), pp. 247-64.

Ellens, J.P., *Religious Routes to Gladstonian Liberalism: The Church Rate Conflict in England and Wales* (Pennsylvania, Pennsylvania State Press, 1994).

Ellison, R.H. and Engelhardt, C.M., 'Prophecy and Anti-Popery in Victorian London: John Cumming Reconsidered', *Victorian Literature and Culture*, 31.1 (2003), pp. 373-89.

Emes, Marion, 'Anti-Catholicism in York from the General Election of 1826 to the Opening of the New St. Wilfrid's Church in 1864' (unpublished master's thesis, York University, 1996).

Engelhardt, Carol M., 'The Paradigmatic Angel in the House: The Virgin Mary and Victorian Anglicans', *Women of Faith in Victorian Culture: Reassessing the 'Angel in the House'*, ed. by Anne Hogan and Andrew Bradstock (Basingstoke: Macmillan, 1998), pp. 159-71.

Englander, D., 'The Word and the World: Evangelicalism in the Victorian City', *Religion in Victorian Britain*, ed. by Parsons, G., 4 vols (Manchester, 1988), II, pp. 14-38.

Epstein, J., '"Our Real Constitution": Trial Defence and Radical Memory in the Age of Revolution', *Re-Reading the Constitution: New Narratives in the Political History of the Long Nineteenth Century*, ed. by J. Vernon (Cambridge: Cambridge University Press, 1996), pp. 22-51.

Feheney, J.M., 'The Poor Law Board August Order, 1859': A Case Study of Protestant-Catholic Conflict', *Recusant History,* 17.1 (1984), pp. 84-91.

Fenton, E., *Religious Liberties: Anti-Catholicism and Liberal Democracy in Nineteenth-Century U.S. Literature and Culture* (New York: Oxford University Press, 2011).

Fetherston, V., 'Irish Catholicism in Sunderland in the 19th Century', *Northern Catholic History,* 43 (2002), pp. 47-59.

—. 'Irish Social Catholicism and Religious Tensions in Sunderland, 1829-1870' (unpublished master's thesis, University of Sunderland, 2002).

Finnigan, F., 'The Irish in York', *The Irish in the Victorian City,* ed. by Roger Swift and Sheridan Gilley (London: Croom Helm Ltd, 1985), pp. 59-84.

Fitzgerald-Lombard, Charles, *English and Welsh Priests, 1801-1914: a working list* (Bath: Downside Abbey Trustees, 1993).

Flindall, R.P., 'Anglican and Roman Attitudes, 1825-75'. *Church Quarterly Review,* 169.371 (1968), pp. 206-211.

Ford, C.S., 'Pastors and Polemicists: The Character of Popular Anglicanism in South East Lancashire 1847-1914' (unpublished doctoral thesis, Leeds University, 1991).

Foster, R.F., *Paddy and Mr. Punch: Connections in Irish and English History* (London: Penguin, 1993).

Fowler, H.C., 'Edward Maltby: His Episcopal Superintendence and Views as Bishop of Durham, 1836-1856' (unpublished master's thesis, University of Durham, 1989).

Fowler, J.T., *Life and Letters of John Bacchus Dykes* (London: John Murray, 1897).

Franchot, Jenny, *Roads to Rome* (Berkeley: University of California Press, 1994).

Franklin R.W., 'Pusey and Worship in Industrial Society' *Worship,* 57 (1953), pp. 386-412.

Fraser, D., *Urban Politics in Victorian England: The Structure of Politics in Victorian Cities* (Leicester: Leicester University Press, 1976).

Gay, J.D., *The Geography of Religion in England* (London: Gerald Duckworth and Co, 1971).

Gilbert, A.D., *Religion and Society in Industrial England: Church, Chapel and Social Change* (London: Longman, 1976).

Gilley, Sheridan. 'English Attitudes to the Irish in England, 1780-1900', *Immigrants and Minorities in British Society,* ed. by C. Holmes (London: Allen and Unwin, 1978), pp. 81-110.

—. 'Vulgar Piety and the Brompton Oratory, 1850-1860', *The Irish in the Victorian City*, ed. by Roger Swift and Sheridan Gilley (London: Croom Helm Ltd, 1985), pp. 255-66.

—. 'The Church of England in the Nineteenth Century', *A History of Religion in Britain: Practice and Belief from Pre-Roman Times to the Present*, ed. by Sheridan Gilley and W. J. Sheils (Oxford: Blackwell, 1994), pp. 291-305.

—. 'The Roman Catholic Church in England, 1780-1940', *A History of Religion in Britain: Practice and Belief from Pre-Roman Times to the Present*, Sheridan Gilley and W. J. Sheils (Oxford: Blackwell, 1994), pp. 346-62.

—. 'Roman Catholicism and the Irish in England', *The Great Famine and Beyond: Irish Migrants in Britain in the Nineteenth and Twentieth Centuries*, ed. by D. M. MacRaild (Dublin: Irish Academic Press, 2000), pp. 346-62.

—. 'Protestant London, No Popery and the Irish Poor, 1830-1860: Part I', *Recusant History*, 10 (1970), pp. 210-23.

—. 'Protestant London, No Popery and the Irish Poor, 1850-1860: Part II', *Recusant History*, 11 (1971), pp. 27-40.

—. 'The Garibaldi Riots of 1862', *Historical Journal,* 16.4 (1973), pp. 697-732.

—. 'The Legacy of William Hogarth, 1786-1866', *Recusant History*, 25.2 (2000), pp. 249-62.

Gooch, Leo, 'Thomas Wilkinson 1825-1909, Bishop of Hexham and Newcastle 1889-1909', *Northern Catholic History*, 13 (1981), pp. 26-31.

—. 'Papists and Profits: The Catholics (Silvertop, Brandling and Salvin Familes) of Durham and Industrial Development', *Durham County Local History Society Bulletin*, 42 (1989).

—. 'Lingard v. Barrington, et al: Ecclesiastical Politics in Durham 1805-29'. *Durham University Journal*, 85.1 (1993), pp. 7-26.

Gooch, Leo, 'The Durham Catholics and Industrial Development, 1560-1850', (unpublished master's thesis, University of York, 1984).

—. 'From Jacobite to Radical: the Catholics of North East England, 1688-1850' (unpublished doctoral thesis, University of Durham, 1989).

Gray, R., 'The Platform and the Pulpit: Cultural Identities and Civic Networks in Industrial Towns, c. 1850-1870', *The Making of the British Middle Class? Studies of Regional and Cultural Diversity since the Eighteenth Century*, ed. by A. Kidd and D. Nicholls (Sutton: Stroud, 1998), pp. 130-47.

Green, Adrian and Pollard, A.J., 'Introduction: Identifying Regions',
    Regional Identities in North East England, 1300-2000, ed. by Adrian
Green and A.J. Pollard (Woodbridge: Boydell Press, 2007), pp. 1-25.

Griffin, J.R., 'Dr. Pusey and the Oxford Movement', *Historical Magazine
    of the Protestant Episcopal Church*, 42 (1973), pp. 137-53.

Griffin, Susan M., *Anti-Catholicism and Nineteenth-Century Fiction*
    (Cambridge: Cambridge University Press, 2004).

Gunn, Simon, *The Public Culture of the Victorian Middle Class: Ritual
    and Authority and the English Industrial City* (Manchester: Manchester
    University Press, 2000).

—. 'The "Failure" of the Victorian Middle Class: A Critique', *The Culture
    of Capital: Art, Power and the Nineteenth-Century Middle Class*, ed.
    by J. Seed and John Wolffe (Manchester: Manchester University Press,
    1988), pp. 17-44.

Guttsman, W.L., 'The General Election of 1859 in the Cities of
    Yorkshire', *International Review of Social History,* 2 (1957), pp. 231-
    58.

Gwynn, D.R., *The Second Spring, 1818-52: A Study of the Catholic
    Revival in England* (London: Burns Oates, 1942).

Hackett, Sarah, 'The Asian of the North: Immigrant Experiences and the
    Importance of Regional Identity in Newcastle upon Tyne During the
    1980s', *Northern History*, 46.2 (2009), pp. 293-311.

Haile, Martin and Bonney, Edward, *Life and Letters of John Lingard,
    1771-1851* (London: Herbert and Daniel, 1911).

Hall, B., 'Alessandro Gavazzi: A Barnabite Friar and the Risorgimento',
    Studies in Church History, 12 (1975), pp. 303-56.

Hammond, Peter C., *The Parson and the Victorian Parish* (London:
    Hodder and Stoughton, 1977).

Hanham, H.J., *Elections and Party Management: Politics in the Time of
    Gladstone and Disraeli* (London: Harvester Press 1959).

Harrison, Brian, 'Philanthropy and the Victorians', *Victorian Studies*, 9.4
    (1966), pp. 353-74.

Harrison, J.F.C., *The Second Coming: Popular Millenarianism 1780-1850*
    (London: Routledge and Kegan Paul, 1979).

Haydon, C., *Anti-Catholicism in Eighteenth Century England, c. 1714-80*
    (Manchester: Manchester University Press, 1993).

Hayes, J.F., 'Roman Catholic Education in County Durham, 1580-1870'
    (unpublished master's thesis, University of Durham, 1968).

Heasman, K., *Evangelicals in Action: An Appraisal of their Social Work in
    the Victorian Era* (London: Geoffrey Bles, 1962).

Heimann, Mary, *Catholic Devotion in Victorian England* (Oxford: Clarendon Press, 1995).

Helmstadter, Richard J., 'Orthodox Nonconformity', *Nineteenth Century English Religious Traditions: Retrospect and Prospect*, ed. by Denis G. Paz (London: Greenwood Press, 1996), pp. 57-83.

Hempton, D., *Methodism and Politics in British Society 1750-1850* (London: Hutchinson Publishing Group, 1984).

—. *Religion and Political Culture in Britain and Ireland: From the Glorious Revolution to the Decline of Empire* (Cambridge: Cambridge University Press, 1996).

—. 'Bickersteth, Bishop of Ripon: The Episcopate of a Mid-Victorian Evangelical', *Religion in Victorian Britain,* ed. by G. Parsons, 4 vols (Manchester: Manchester University Press, 1988), IV, pp. 41-60.

—. 'Religious Life in Industrial Britain, 1830-1914', *A History of Religion in Britain: Practice and Belief from Pre-Roman Times to the Present*, ed. by Sheridan Gilley and W. J. Sheils (Oxford: Blackwell, 1994), pp, 306-21.

—. 'Evangelicalism and Eschatology', *Journal of Ecclesiastical History*, 31.2 (1980), pp. 179-90.

Henriques, Ursala, *Religious Toleration in England, 1787-1833* (London: Routledge and Kegan Paul, 1961).

Hexter, J.H., 'The Protestant Revival and the Catholic Question in England 1778-1829', *Journal of Modern History*, 8 (1936), pp. 297-319.

Hickey, J., *Urban Catholics* (London: Geoffrey Chapman, 1967).

Hickman, Mary J., *Religion, Class and Identity: The State, the Catholic Church and the Education of the Irish in Britain* (Aldershot: Avebury, 1995).

Hill, A.G., 'The Tractarian Challenge', *Theology*, 66 (1963), pp. 280-7.

Hilton, Boyd, *The Age of Atonement: The Influence of Evangelicalism on Social and Economic Thought, 1785-1865* (Oxford: Oxford University Press, 1992).

Holladay, J.D., '19th Century Evangelical Activism From Private Charity to State Intervention, 1830-50', *Historical Magazine of the Protestant Episcopal Church,* 51 (1982), pp. 53-79.

Holland, M.G., *The British Catholic Press and Educational Controversy, 1847-1865* (New York: Garland Publishing, 1987).

Holmes, J.D., *More Roman than Rome: English Catholicism in the Nineteenth Century* (London: Burns and Oates, 1978).

Hoppen, K.T., *Elections, Politics, and Society in Ireland, 1832-1885* (Oxford: Clarendon Press, 1984).

—. 'Tories, Catholics and the General Election of 1859', *The Historical Journal*, 13 (1970), pp. 48-67.

Howsam, Leslie, *Cheap Bibles: Nineteenth Century Publishing and the British and Foreign Bible Society* (Cambridge: Cambridge University Press, 1991).

Hughes, Philip, 'The English Catholics in 1850', *The English Catholics 1850-1950*, ed. by George A. Beck (London: Burns Oates, 1950), pp. 42-85.

Hughes, T.O., 'When Was Anti-Catholicism? A Response' *Journal of Ecclesiastical History*, 56.2 (2005), pp. 326-33.

Hunter-Blair, C.H., *The Mayors and Lord Mayors of Newcastle. 1216-1940* (Newcastle: Northumberland Press, 1940).

Hurt, John, *Education in Evolution: Church, State, Society and Popular Education, 1800-1870* (London: Rupert Hart-Davis, 1971).

Hylson-Smith, Kenneth. *Evangelicals in the Church of England, 1734-1984* (Edinburgh: T. and T. Clark, 1988).

—. *High Churchmanship in the Church of England From the Sixteenth Century to the Late Twentieth Century* (Edinburgh: T. and T. Clark, 1993).

Inglis, K.S., *Churches and the Working Classes in Victorian England* (Toronto: University of Toronto Press, 1963).

—. 'Patterns of Religious Worship in 1851', *Journal of Ecclesiastical History*, 11 (1960), pp. 74-86.

Ingram, Philip, ''Protestant Patriarchy and the Catholic Priesthood in Nineteenth-Century England', *Journal of Social History*, 24:4 (1991), pp. 783-97.

Jackson J.A., *The Irish in Britain* (London: Routledge and Kegan Paul, 1963).

Jackson, D.M., '"Garibaldi or the Pope!"': Newcastle's Irish Riot, 1866', *North East History*, 35 (2001), pp. 49-76.

Jenkins, Philip, *The New Anti-Catholicism: The Last Acceptable Prejudice* (Oxford: Oxford University Press, 2003).

Johnson, Dale A., *The Changing Shape of English Nonconformity, 1825-1925* (Oxford: Oxford University Press, 1999).

Joyce, M.B. 'The Education of the Roman Catholics of Northumberland, 1558-1870' (unpublished master's thesis, University of Newcastle, 1975).

Kerr, D.A., *Peel, Priests and Politics: Sir Robert Peel's Administration and the Roman Catholic Church in Ireland, 1841-1846* (Oxford: Clarendon Press, 1982).

Kirk, N., 'Ethnicity, Class and Popular Toryism, 1850-1870', *Hosts, Immigrants and Minorities: Historical Responses to Newcomers in British Society, 1870-1914*, ed. by K. Lunn (Folkestone: Dawson, 1980), pp. 64-106.

—. *The Growth of Working Class Reformism in Mid-Victorian England* (London: Croom Helm, 1985).

Klaus, R.J., *The Pope, the Protestants, and the Irish: Papal Aggression and Anti-Catholicism in Mid-Nineteenth Century England.* (New York and London: Garland Publishing, 1987).

Knight, Frances, *The Nineteenth-Century Church and English Society* (Cambridge: Cambridge University Press, 1995).

—. 'The Influence of the Oxford Movement in the Parishes: a Reassessment', *From Oxford to the People: Reconsidering Newman and the Oxford Movement*, ed. by P. Vaiss (Leominster: Gracewing, 1996), pp. 127-40.

Knox, R.B., 'Dr. John Cumming and Crown Court Church, London', *Records of the Scottish Church History Society,* 22 (1984), pp. 57-84.

Kollar, Rene, 'Foreign and Catholic: A Plea to Protestant Parents on the Dangers of Convent Education in Victorian England'. *History of Education*, 31.4 (2002), pp. 335-350.

———. 'Allegations of Convent Violence, the Campaign Against Sisterhoods in Victorian England, and the Response of Parliament', *Studia Monastica*, 50.2 (2008), pp. 255-73.

Kumar, K., *The Making of English National Identity* (Cambridge: Cambridge University Press, 1993).

Larkin, Emmet, 'The Devotional Revolution in Ireland, 1850-1875', *American Historical Review*, 77 (1972), pp. 625-52.

Larsen, Timothy, *Friends of Religious Equality: Nonconformist Politics in Mid-Victorian England* (Woodbridge: The Boydell Press, 1999).

Lee, R., 'Class, Industrialization and the Church of England: The Case of the Durham Diocese in the Nineteenth Century', *Past and Present*, 191.1 (2006), pp. 165-88.

Lees, L.H., *Exiles of Erin: Irish Migrants in Victorian London* (Manchester: Manchester University Press, 1979).

Lewis, D.M., ed., *The Blackwell Dictionary of Evangelical Biography: 1730-1860* (Oxford: Blackwell Publishing, 1995).

———. *Lighten Their Darkness: The Evangelical Mission to Working-Class London, 1828-1860* (Connecticut: Greenwood Press, 2001).

Linker, R.W., 'The English Roman Catholics and Emancipation: The Politics of Persuasion', *Journal of Ecclesiastical History*, 27 (1976), pp. 151-80.

Loades, David Michael, 'The Origins of English Protestant Nationalism', *Studies in Church History*, 18 (1982), pp. 297-307.

Lohrli, Anne, 'The Madiai: A Forgotten Chapter of Church History'. *Victorian Studies*, 33.1 (1989), pp. 28-50.

Lowe, J.C., 'The Tory Triumph of 1868 in Blackburn and Lancashire', *Historical Journal*, 16 (1973), pp. 733-48.

Lowe W.J., *The Irish in Mid-Victorian Lancashire: The Shaping of a Working-Class Community* (New York: Peter Lang, 1989).

Machin, G.I.T., *The Catholic Question in English Politics 1820 to 1830* (Oxford: Oxford University Press, 1964).

—. *Politics and the Churches in Great Britain, 1832-68* (Oxford: Clarendon Press, 1977).

—. *Politics and the Churches in Great Britain, 1869-1921* (Oxford: Clarendon Press, 1987).

—. 'The Maynooth Grant, the Dissenters and Disestablishment, 1845-7' *English Historical Review*, 82 (1967), pp. 61-85.

—. 'Lord John Russell and the Prelude to the Ecclesiastical Titles Bill, 1846-51', *Journal of Ecclesiastical History*, 25.3 (1974), pp. 277-95.

Machin, Ian, 'Disestablishment and Democracy, c.1840-1930', *Citizenship and Community: Liberals, Radicals and Collective Identities in the British Isles, 1865-1931*, ed. by Eugenio F. Biagini (Cambridge: Cambridge University Press, 1996), pp. 120-47.

MacRaild, D.M., *Culture, Conflict, Migration: The Irish in Victorian Cumbria* (Liverpool: Liverpool University Press, 1998).

—. *Irish Migrants in Modern Britain, 1750-1922* (Basingstoke: Macmillan 1999).

—. *Faith, Fraternity and Fighting: The Orange Order and Irish Migrants in Northern England, c.1850-1920* (Liverpool: Liverpool University Press, 2006).

—. '"The Bunkum of Ulseria": the Orange Marching Tradition in Late Victorian Cumbria', *The Irish Parading Tradition: Following the Drum*, ed. by T. G. Fraser (MacMillan Press: Basingstoke, 2000), pp. 44-59.

—. '"Abandon Hibernicisation": Priests, Ribbonmen and an Irish Street Fight in the North East of England in 1858', *Historical Research*, 76.194 (2003), pp. 557-573.

Manders, F.W.D., 'The Administration of the Poor Law in the Gateshead Union, 1836-1930' (unpublished master's thesis, Newcastle University, 1980).

Mangion, C.M., *Contested Identities: Catholic Women Religious in Nineteenth Century England and Wales* (Manchester: Manchester University Press, 2008).

Mansergh, Nicholas, *The Irish Question, 1840-1921* (London: George Allen and Unwin, 1965).

Matthews, Shirley, '"Second Spring" and "Precious Prejudices": Catholicism and Anti-Catholicism in Hampshire in the Era of Emancipation', *Evangelicals and Catholics in Nineteenth-Century Ireland*, ed. by James H. Murphy (Dublin: Four Courts Press, 2005), pp. 85-96.

Matthews. W.F., 'The Sunderland Election of 1852', *Northern History*, 68.2 (2011), pp. 315-36.

Maynard, W.B., 'Pluralism and Non-Residence in the Archdeaconry of Durham, 1774-1856: The Bishop and Chapter as Patrons', *Northern History*, 26 (1990), pp. 103-30.

Maynard, W.B., 'The Ecclesiastical Administration of the Archdeaconry of Durham, 1774-1856' (unpublished doctoral thesis, University of Durham, 1973).

McAllister, A., *John Bull's Italian Snakes and Ladders: English Attitudes to Italy in the Mid-Nineteenth Century* (Newcastle: Cambridge Scholars Publishing, 2007).

McConnell, F., 'The Irish in Durham City, 1841-61', *Durham County Local History Society Bulletin*, 47 (1991), pp. 68-82.

McCord, N., and Rowe, D.J., 'Industrialisation and Urban Growth in North East England', *International Review of Social History*, 22.1 (1977), pp. 30-64.

—. 'The Regional Identity of North East England in the 19th and Early 20th Centuries', *Issue of Regional Identity*, ed. by Edward Royle (Manchester: Manchester University Press, 1998), pp. 102-17.

McDermott, T., 'The Irish Workers on Tyneside', *Essays on Tyneside Labour History*, ed. by N. McCord (1977), pp. 154-77.

McDermott, T.P., 'Charles Larkin, Radical Reformer, 1800-1879, *Northern Catholic History,* 28 (1988), pp. 13-17.

McDonnell, K., 'Roman Catholics in London, 1850-1865', *Studies in London History – Presented to Philip Edmund Jones*, ed. by A. E. J. Hollaender (London: Hodder and Stoughton, 1969), pp. 429-43.

McElrath, D., *The Syllabus of Pius IX: Some Reactions in England* (Louvain: Bibliothèque de l'université, Bureau de la Revue, 1964).

McFarland, E., *The Orange Order in Scotland* (Edinburgh: Edinburgh University Press, 1990).

McIntire, C.T., *England against the Papacy 1838-1861* (Cambridge: Cambridge University Press, 1983).

McLeod, Hugh, *Religion and Society in England, 1850-1914* (Basingstoke: Macmillan, 1996).

—. 'Protestantism and British National Identity, 1815-1945', *Nation and Religion: Perspectives on Europe and Asia*, Peter Van der Veer and Hartmut Lehmann (Princeton: Princeton University Press, 1997), pp. 44-70.

McManus, Michael, 'Folk Devils and Moral Panics?: Irish Stereotyping in Mid-Victorian Durham' in *Durham County Local History Bulletin*, 53 (1994), pp. 27-42.

McManus, Michael, 'From Townland to Township: The Complex Evolution of a Dissipative Famine Irish Community in County Durham', *North East History*, 35 (2004), pp. 7-53.

Meacham, Standish, 'The Church in the Victorian City' *Victorian Studies*, 11 (1968), pp. 359-78.

Middlebrook, S., *Newcastle Upon Tyne: Its Growth and Achievement* (Newcastle: Andrew Reid and Company, 1950).

Milburn, G.E., 'Catholicism in Mid-Nineteenth Century Northumberland', *Tyne n' Tweed*, 32 (1978), pp. 16-22.

—. *Church and Chapel in Sunderland, 1780-1914* (Sunderland: Sunderland Polytechnic, 1988).

Mill, J.S., *Utilitarianism, On Liberty, and Considerations on Representative Government* (London: J. M. Dent and Sons Ltd, 1972).

Miller, J.R., 'Anti-Catholic Thought in Victorian Canada', *Canadian Historical Review*, 66 (1985), pp. 474-94.

Millward, P., 'The Stockport Riots of 1852: A Study of Anti-Catholic and Anti-Irish Sentiment', *The Irish in the Victorian City* ed. by Roger Swift and Sheridan Gilley (London: Croom Helm Ltd, 1985), pp. 207-24.

Moffitt, Miriam, *The Society for Irish Church Missions to the Roman Catholics, 1849-1950* (Manchester: Manchester University Press, 2011).

Morden, Barbara C., *John Martin and Apocalypse Now!* (Northumbria Press: Newcastle, 2010).

Morris, J., 'The Regional Growth of Tractarianism: Some Reflections', *From Oxford to the People: Reconsidering Newman and the Oxford Movement*, ed. by P. Veiss (Leominster: Gracewing, 1996), pp. 141-59.

Morris, Michael and Gooch, Leo, *Down Your Aisles: The Diocese of Hexham and Newcastle* (Hartlepool: Northern Cross, 2000).

Morris, R.J., 'Voluntary Societies and British Urban Elites, 1780-1850: An Analysis', *Historical Journal*, 26 (1983), pp. 95-118.

Mumm, Susan, *Stolen Daughters, Virgin Mothers: Anglican Sisterhoods in Victorian Britain* (London and New York: Leicester University Press, 1999).

Munden, A.F., 'The Origin of Evangelical Anglicanism in Newcastle-upon-Tyne', *Archaeologia Aeliana*, 11 (1983), pp. 301-7.

Mundler, Peter, '"Race" and "Nation" in Mid-Victorian Thought', *History, Religion and Culture: British Intellectual History 1750-1950*, ed. by Stefan Collini, Richard Whatmore and Brian Young (Cambridge: Cambridge University Press, 2000), pp. 224-40.

Neal, Frank, *English-Irish Conflict in the North East of England* (Salford: University of Salford, 1992).

—. *Sectarian Violence: The Liverpool Experience 1819-1914* (Manchester: Manchester University Press, 1988).

—. *Black 47: Britain and the Famine Irish* (Basingstoke: Macmillan, 1998).

—. 'Irish Settlement in the North East and North-West of England in the Mid-Nineteenth Century', *The Irish in Victorian Britain: The Local Dimension*, ed. by Roger Swift and Sheridan Gilley (Dublin: Four Courts Press, 1999), pp. 75-100.

—. 'The Foundation of the Irish Settlement in Newcastle upon Tyne: The Evidence in the 1851 Census', *The Great Famine and Beyond: Irish Migrants in Britain in the Nineteenth and Twentieth Centuries*, ed. by D. M. MacRaild (Dublin: Irish Academic Press, 2000), pp. 71-93.

—. 'The Birkenhead Garibaldi Riots of 1862', *Transactions of the Historic Society of Lancashire and Chesire*, 131 (1982), pp. 87-111.

—. 'A Statistical Profile of the Irish Community in Gateshead – The Evidence of the 1851 Census', *Immigrants and Minorities*, 27.1 (2009), pp. 50-81.

Newman, Gerald, *The Rise of English Nationalism: A Cultural History, 1740-1830* (London: Weidenfeld and Nicholson, 1987).

Newsinger, J., *Fenianism in Mid-Victorian Britain* (London: Pluto Press, 1994).

Nicholson, T.C., *The Catholic Churches of Newcastle-upon-Tyne* (Newcastle: [n. pub.] 1871).

Nikol, J., 'The Oxford Movement in Decline: Lord John Russell and the Tractarians, 1846-1852', *Historical Magazine of the Protestant Episcopal Church*, 63 (1974), pp. 341-58.

Nockles, P., *The Oxford Movement in Context: Anglican High Churchmanship* (Cambridge: Cambridge University Press, 1994).

—. 'Church Parties in the Pre-Tractarian Church of England 1750-1833: the 'Orthodox' – some problems of definition and   identity',   *The Church of England c. 1689-1833: From Toleration to Tractarianism*, ed. by John Walsh, Colin Haydon and Stephen Taylor (Cambridge: Cambridge University Press, 1995), pp. 334-59.

Norman, Edward R., *Anti-Catholicism in Victorian England* (London: Allen and Unwin, 1968).

—. *Church and Society on England, 1770-1970* (Oxford: Clarendon Press, 1976).

—. *The English Catholic Church in the Nineteenth Century* (Oxford: Clarendon Press, 1984).

—. *Roman Catholicism in England from the Elizabethan Settlement to the Second Vatican Council* (Oxford: Oxford University Press, 1985).

—. 'Church and State since 1800', Gilley, S and Sheils, W J *A History of Religion in Britain: Practice and Belief from Pre-Roman Times to the Present* (Oxford: Blackwell, 1994), pp. 277-91.

Norris, P., 'The Irish in Tow Law, County Durham, 1851-71', *Durham County Local History Society Bulletin*, 33 (1984), pp. 41-70.

Nossiter, T.J., *Influence, Opinion and Political Idioms in Reformed England: Case Studies from the* North East *1832-74* (Hassocks, Sussex: Harvester Press, 1975).

Nowlan, K.B., *The Politics of Repeal, 1841-50* (London: Routledge and Kegan Paul, 1965).

O'Brien S., 'Terra Incognita: The Nuns in Nineteenth Century England', *Past and Present*, 121 (1988), pp. 110-40.

O'Connor, K., *The Irish in Britain* (Dublin: Torc, 1972).

O'Day, Alan. 'Ireland's Catholics in the British State, 1850-1922', *The Formation of National Elites: Comparative Studies on Governments and Non-Dominant Ethnic Groups in Europe, 1850-1940*, ed. by Andreas Kappeler, Fikret Adanir and Alan O'Day, 6 vols (Aldershot: Aldershot Publishing for the European Science Foundation, 1992), VI, pp. 41-75.

—. 'The Political Representation of the Irish in Great Britain', *Governments, Ethnic Groups and Political Representation: Comparative Studies on Governments and Non-Dominant Ethnic Groups in Europe, 1850-1940,* ed. by G. Alderman, 4 vols (New York University Press: Dartmouth, 1993), IV, pp. 31-84.

—. 'Varieties of Anti-Irish Behaviour in Britain', *Racial Violence in Britain in the Nineteenth and Twentieth Centuries*, ed. by P. Panayi (Leicester: Leicester University Press, 1996), pp. 127-40.

O'Farrell, Patrick *The Catholic Church and Community in Australia. A History* (Kensington, New South Wales: New South Wales University Press, 1992).

O'Leary, P., 'When was Anti-Catholicism? The Case of Nineteenth- and Twentieth-Century Wales', *Journal of Ecclesiastical History*, 56.2 (2005), pp. 308-25.

O'Rourke, Shelley, 'Newcastle-upon-Tyne Ragged School, 1847-1859' (unpublished bachelor's dissertation, University of Northumbria, 1998)

O'Sullivan, P., ed., *The Irish World Wide,* vol.5, *Religion and Identity* (London: Leicester University Press, 1996).

O'Tuathaigh, M.A.G., 'The Irish in Nineteenth Century Britain: Problems of Integration', *The Irish in the Victorian City*, ed. by Roger Swift and Sheridan Gilley (London: Croom Helm Ltd, 1985), pp. 13-36.

Oliver, W.H., *Prophets and Millineriaists: The Use of Biblical Prophecy in England from the 1790s to the 1840s* (Auckland: Auckland University Press, 1978).

Ollard, S.L., *A Short History of the Oxford Movement* (London: A.R. Mowbray and Co., 1915).

Orde, Anne, *Religion, Business and Society in North East England: The Pease Family of Darlington in the 19th Century* (Stamford: Shannon Tyas, 2000).

Orr, Edwin, *The Second Evangelical Awakening in Great Britain* (London: Marshall, Morgan and Scott, 1949).

Owen, David, *English Philanthropy, 1660-1960* (Cambridge, Massachusetts: Harvard University Press, 1965).

Oxford Dictionary of National Biography (Oxford: Oxford University Press, 2004).

Parry, J.P., 'Religion and the Collapse of Gladstone's First Government, 1870-1874', *Historical Journal*, 25 (1982), pp. 71-101.

Parsons, Gerald, 'A Question of Meaning: Religion and Working-Class Life', *Religion in Victorian Britain,* 4 vols, ed. by G. Parsons (Manchester: Manchester University Press, 1988), II, pp. 63-87.

—. 'Victorian Roman Catholicism: Emancipation, Expansion and Achievement', *Religion in Victorian Britain,* 4 vols, ed. by G. Parsons (Manchester: Manchester University Press, 1988), I, pp. 146-68.

—. 'Reform, Revival and Realignment: the Experience of Victorian Anglicanism', *Religion in Victorian Britain,* 4 vols, ed. by G. Parsons, I (Manchester: Manchester University Press, 1988), pp. 14-66.

Paz, Denis G., *The Politics of Working Class Education in Britain, 1830-50* (Manchester: Manchester University Press, 1980).

—. *Popular Anti-Catholicism in Mid-Victorian England* (Stanford: Stanford University Press, 1992).

—. 'Popular Anti-Catholicism in England, 1850-51', *Albion*, 11   (1979), pp. 331-59.

—. 'Another Look at Lord John Russell and the Papal Aggression, 1850', *The Historian*, 45.1 (1982), pp. 47-64.

Pease, Alfred E., *The Diaries of Edward Pease: The Father of English Railways* (London: Herdley Brothers, 1907).

Phillips, P.T., *The Sectarian Spirit: Sectarianism, Society and Politics in Victorian Cotton Towns* (Toronto: University of Toronto Press, 1982).

Pickering, W.S.F., *Anglo-Catholicism: A Study in Religious Ambiguity* (London: Routledge, 1989).

Pinnington, J.E., 'Bishop Blomfield and St. Barnabas, Pimlico: The Limits of Ecclesiastical Authority', *Church Quarterly Review*, 168 (1967), pp. 289-96.

Pooley, C., 'Segregation or Integration? The Residential Experience of the Irish in Mid-Victorian Britain', *The Irish in Britain 1815-1939* ed. by Roger Swift and Sheridan Gilley (London: Pinter, 1989), pp. 60-103.

Porter, Andrew, *Religion Versus Empire: British Protestant Missionaries and Overseas Expansion, 1700-1914* (Manchester: Manchester University Press, 2004).

Prochaska, F.K., *Women and Philanthropy in Nineteenth Century England* (Oxford: Clarendon Press, 1980).

Proud, Keith, *Durham City: A History* (Chichester: Phillimore and Co., 1992).

Purdue, A.W., 'The History of the North East in the Modern Period: Themes, Concerns, and Debates Since the 1960s', *Northern History*, 62 (2005), pp. 107-17.

Quinn, D., *Patronage and Piety: The Politics of English Roman Catholics, 1850-1900* (Basingstoke: Macmillan, 1993).

Ralls, W.G., 'The Papal Aggression of 1850: A Study in Victorian anti-Catholicism', *Religion in Victorian Britain*, ed. by G. Parsons, 4 vols (Manchester: Manchester University Press, 1988), IV, pp. 115-32.

Raponi, D. 'Religious Reformation and National Unity: British Protestants and Italy, 1860-1870', ed. by R. Crone, D. Gange and K. Jones, *New Perspectives in British Cultural History* (Newcastle: Cambridge Scholars Publishing, 2007), pp. 78-89.

Reed, J.S., '"Ritualism Rampant in East London": Anglo-Catholicism and the Urban Poor', *Victorian Studies*, 31 (1988), pp. 375-403.

—. *Glorious Battle: The Cultural Politics of Victorian Anglo-Catholicism* (Nashville: Vanderbilt University Press, 1996).

Renton, D., *Colour Blind?: Race and Migration in North East England Since 1945* (Sunderland: University of Sunderland Press, 2007).

Richardson, W., *History of the Parish of Wallsend* (Newcastle: Northumberland Press, 1923).

Richter, Donald C., *Riotous Victorians.* (Ohio: Ohio University Press, 1981).

Roberts, M.J.D., *Making English Morals: Voluntary Association and Moral Reform in England, 1787-1886* (Sydney: Macquarie University, 2004).

Robertson, W.B., *St. John's Presbyterian Church, South Shields Tercentenary Year Book, 1662-1962* (South Shields: [n. pub.] 1962).

Robinson, J., 'The Coming of the Irish to Jarrow and Hebburn', *Journal of the Northumberland and Durham Family History Society*, 6.3 (1981), pp. 70-1.

Rogers, J.G., *An Autobiography* (London: James Clarke and Co, 1901).

Romani, Roberto, 'British Views of the Irish National Character, 1800-1846: An Intellectual History', *History of European Ideas*, 23 (1997), pp. 193-219.

Rosman, D., *Evangelicals and Culture* (Beckenham: Croom Helm, 1984)

Ross, J.W., *1852-1969: North Shields Town Missionary Society* (North Shields: [n. pub.] 1969).

Rowell, Geoffrey, *The Glorious Vision: Themes and Personalities of the Catholic Revival in Anglicanism* (Oxford: Oxford University Press, 1983).

Rudé, G., *Paris and London in the 18th Century* (London: Collins, 1970).

Russell, B., 'Toleration', *Ideas and Beliefs of the Victorians: An Historic Revaluation of the Victorian Age*, compiled by the British Broadcasting Corporation (London: Sylvan Press, 1949), pp. 268-76.

Samuel, R., 'The Roman Catholic Church and the Irish Poor', *The Irish in the Victorian City* ed. by Roger Swift and Sheridan Gilley (London: Croom Helm Ltd, 1985), pp. 267-300.

Samuel, R., 'An Irish Religion', *Patriotism: The Making and Unmaking of British National Identity*, ed. by R. Samuel, II (London: Routledge 1989), pp. 94-120.

Schupf, H.W., 'Education for the Neglected: Ragged Schools in Nineteenth Century England', *History of Education Quarterly,* 12 (1972), pp. 162-83.

Scott, C.L., 'A Comparative Re-examination of Anglo-Irish relations in nineteenth century Liverpool, Manchester and Newcastle-upon-Tyne' (unpublished doctoral thesis, University of Durham, 1998).

Selén, M., *The Oxford Movement and Wesleyan Methodism in England, 1833-1882: A Study in Religious Conflict* (Lund, Sweden: Lund University Press, 1992).

Sellers, Ian, *Nineteenth Century Nonconformity* (London: Edward Arnold, 1977).

Senior, H., *Orangeism in Ireland and Britain 1795-1836* (London: Routledge and Keegan Paul, 1966).

Shearman, Hugh, *Privatising a Church: The Disestablishment and Disendowment of the Church of Ireland* (Lurgan: Ulster Society, 1995).

Sidenvall, E., *After Anti-Catholicism: John Henry Newman and Protestant Britain, c.1845-1890* (London: T. and T. Clark, 2005) .

Singleton, John, 'The Virgin Mary and Religious Conflict in Victorian Britain', *Journal of Ecclesiastical History*, 43.1 (1992), pp. 16-34.

Smith, H.J. et al. *Crook and Billy Row in 1851: An Analysis of Census Returns* (Durham: University of Durham, 1975).

Smith, Jeff, 'The Making of a Diocese, 1851-1882', *Newcastle upon Tyne: A Modern History*, ed. by Robert Colls and Bill Lancaster (Chichester: Phillimore, 2001), pp. 93-112.

Smith, John T., *Methodism and Education, 1849-1902* (Oxford: Clarendon Press, 1998).

Smyth, Jim, 'The Men of No Popery: the Origins of the Orange Order'. *History Ireland*, 3.3 (1995), pp. 48-53.

Stack, J.A., 'The Catholics, the Irish Delinquent and the Origins of the Reformatory Schools in Nineteenth-Century England and Scotland', *Recusant History,* 23.3 (1997), pp. 372-88.

Stanley, Brian, 'British Evangelicals and Overseas Concerns, 1833-1970', *Evangelical Faith and Public Zeal: Evangelicals and Society in Britain 1780-1980*, ed. by John Wolffe (London: SPCK, 1995), pp. 81-97.

Stapleton, Julia, 'Political Thought and National Identity, 1850-1950', *History, Religion and Culture: British Intellectual History 1750-1950,* ed. by Stefan Collini, Richard Whatmore and Brian Young (Cambridge: Cambridge University Press, 2000), pp. 245-69.

Steele, E.D., 'The Irish Presence in the North East of England, 1850-1914', *Northern History*, 12 (1976), pp. 220-42.

Stevenson, J., *Popular Disturbances in England 1700-1870* (London: Longman, 1979).

Storch, Robert D., '"Please to Remember the Fifth of November": Conflict, Solidarity and Public Order in Southern England, 1815-1900', *Popular Culture and Custom in Nineteenth Century England*, ed. by Robert D Storch (London: Croom Helm, 1982), pp. 71-99.

—. 'The Plague of the Blue Locusts: Police Reform and Popular Resistance in Northern England, 1840-57' *International Review of Social History*, 20 (1975), pp. 60-90.

Storey, L.A.G., *Flying Angel: The Story of the Missions to Seamen* (London: Metheum and Co, 1956).

Sunderland, N., *A History of Darlington* (Manchester: E.J. Morten, 1972).

Supple, Jennifer F., 'Ultramontanism in Yorkshire, 1850-1900', *Religion in Victorian Britain,* 4 vols, ed. by G. Parsons (Manchester: Manchester University Press, 1988), IV, pp. 135-49.

Sutcliffe, M.P., 'Negotiating the "Garibaldi Moment" in Newcastle upon Tyne (1854-1861)', *Modern Italy*, 15.2 (2010), pp. 129-48.

Sutherland, Gillian, *Elementary Education in the Nineteenth Century* (London: The Historical Association, 1971).

Swift, Roger, 'Another Stafford Street Row: Law, Order and the Irish Presence in Mid-Victorian Wolverhampton', *Irish in the Victorian City*, ed. by Roger Swift and Sheridan Gilley (London: Croom Helm, 1985), pp. 179-206.

Swift, Roger, 'Anti-Irish Violence in Victorian England: Some Perspectives', *Criminal Justice History*, 15 (1994), pp. 127-39

—. 'Identifying the Irish in Victorian Britain', *Irish Identities in Victorian Britain*, ed. by Roger Swift and Sheridan Gilley (Abingdon: Routledge, 2011), pp. 6-23.

Thompson, D.M., 'The Liberation Society, 1844-1868', *Pressure From Without in Early Victorian England*, ed. by P. Hollis (London: Edward Arnold, 1874), pp. 210-38.

Todd, N., *The Militant Democracy* (Whitley Bay: Bewick Press, 1991).

Toon, P., *Evangelical Theology, 1833-1856: A Response to Tractarianism* (London: Marshall, Morgan and Scott, 1979).

Treble, J.H., 'Irish Navvies in the North of England 1830-50', *Transport History*, 6 (1973), pp. 227-47.

Turton, Jacqueline, 'Mayhew's Irish: the Irish Poor in Mid Nineteenth-Century London', *The Irish in Victorian Britain: The Local Dimension*, ed. by Roger Swift and Sheridan Gilley (Dublin: Four Courts Press, 1999), pp. 122-55.

Tweedy, J.M., *Popish Elvet: The History of St. Cuthbert's, Durham: Part I* (Durham: [St. Cuthbert's Church], 1981).

—. *Popish Elvet: The History of St. Cuthbert's, Durham: Part II* (Durham: [St. Cuthbert's Church], 1984).

Usherwood, S., '"No Popery" Under Queen Victoria', *History Today*, 23.4 (1973), pp. 274-9.

Vincent, John, *The Formation of the Liberal Party, 1857-1868* (London: Constable, 1966).

Waller, P.J., *Democracy and Sectarianism: A Political and Social History of Liverpool, 1868-1939* (Liverpool: Liverpool University Press, 1981).

Wallis, F.H., *Popular Anti-Catholicism in Mid-Victorian Britain* (Lewiston: Edwin Mellen Press, 1993).

—. 'The Revival of the Anti-Maynooth Campaign in Britain, 1850-52' *Albion*, 19 (1987), pp. 527-48.

Walsh, B., *Roman Catholic Nuns in England and Wales, 1800-1937: A Social History* (Dublin: Irish Academic Press, 2002).

Ward, William Reginald, 'Oxford and the Origins of Liberal Catholicism in the Church of England', *Studies in Church History*, 1 (1964), pp. 233-52.

Watts, Michael R., *The Dissenters. Vol II: The Expansion of Evangelical Nonconformity* (Oxford: Oxford University Press, 1995).

Webb, R.K., 'Quakers and Unitarians', *Nineteenth Century English Religious Traditions: Retrospect and Prospect*, ed. by Denis G. Paz (Greenwood Press: London/Westport, Connecticut, 1996), pp. 85-115.

Weber, M., *The Protestant Ethic and the Spirit of Capitalism* (London: Unwin, 1930).

Welch, P.J., 'Bishop Blomfield and the Development of Tractarianism in London', *Church Quarterly Review*, 155.317 (1954), pp. 332-44.

Welford, R., *Men of Mark 'Twixt Tees n' Tweed*, 3 vols (London: Walter Scott, 1895).

Wheeler, Michael, *The Old Enemies: Catholic and Protestant in Nineteenth-Century English Culture* (Cambridge: Cambridge University Press, 2006).

Whyte, J.H., *The Independent Irish Party, 1850-59* (Oxford: Oxford University Press, 1958)

Wiener, C.Z., 'The Beleaguered Isle: A Study of Elizabethan and Early Jacobean Anticatholicism', *Past and Present*, 51 (1971), pp. 27-62.

Wild, G., *The Darlington Catholics* (Darlington: Darlington Camel, 1983).

Williams, N.P. and Harris, C., eds., *Northern Catholicism: Centenary Studies in the Oxford and Parallel Movements* (London: SPCK, 1933).

Wolffe, John, *The Protestant Crusade in Great Britain, 1829-1860* (Oxford: Clarendon Press, 1991).

—. *God and Greater Britain* (London: Routledge, 1994).

—. 'Anti-Catholicism and Evangelical Identity in Britain and the United States, 1830-1860', *Evangelicalism: Comparative Studies of Popular Protestantism in North America, the British Isles, and Beyond 1700-*

1990, ed. by Mark A. Noll, David W. Bebbington and George A. Rawlyk (New York: Oxford University Press, 1994), pp. 179-97.

—. 'Change and Continuity in British Anti-Catholicism, 1829-1982', *Catholicism in Britain and France since 1789*, ed. by Nicholas Atkin and Frank Tallett (London: The Hambledon Press, 1996), pp. 67-83.

—. 'Anglicanism', *Nineteenth Century English Religious Traditions: Retrospect and Prospect*, ed. by Denis G. Paz (London: Greenwood Press, 1996), pp. 1-31.

—. 'A Transatlantic Perspective: Protestantism and National Identities in Mid-Nineteenth-Century Britain and the United States', *Protestantism and National Identity: Britain and Ireland, c. 1650-c. 1850*, ed. by Tony Claydon and Ian McBride (Cambridge: Cambridge University Press, 1998), pp. 291-309.

—. 'British Protestants and Europe, 1820-1860: Some Perceptions and Influences', *The Development of Pluralism in Modern Britain and France*, ed. by R. Bonney and D. J. B. Trim (Bern: Peter Lang Ltd., 2007), pp. 207-25.

—. 'The Evangelical Alliance in the 1840s: An Attempt to Institutionalise Christian Unity', *Studies in Church History*, 23 (1986), pp. 333-46.

Wood, P.A., 'The Activities of the Sunderland Poor Law Union, 1834-1930' (unpublished doctoral thesis, Newcastle University, 1975).

Wood, Robert, *West Hartlepool: The Rise and Development of a Victorian New Town* (Hartlepool: West Hartlepool Corporation, 1967).

Yates, Nigel, *The Oxford Movement and Parish Life: St Saviour's, Leeds, 1839-1929* (York: Borthwick Papers, 1975).

—. *Anglican Ritualism in Victorian Britain, 1830-1910* (Oxford: Oxford University Press, 1999).

Young, Michael J., *Catholic Jarrow, St Bede's: 1860-1940* (Jarrow: [n. pub.] 1940).

INDEX

Page numbers which include an "n" refer to footnotes.